FISH, LAW, AND COLONIALISM
The Legal Capture of Salmon in British Columbia

D1548515

Pacific salmon fisheries, owned and managed by Aboriginal peoples, were transformed in the late nineteenth and early twentieth centuries by commercial and sport fisheries backed by the Canadian state and its law. Through detailed case studies of the conflicts over fish weirs on the Cowichan and Babine rivers, Douglas Harris describes the evolving legal apparatus that dispossessed Aboriginal peoples of their fisheries. Building upon themes developed in literatures on state law and local custom, and on law and colonialism, he examines the controversial nature of the colonial encounter at the local level. In doing so, Harris reveals the many divisions both within and among government departments, local settler societies, and Aboriginal communities.

Drawing on government records, statute books, case reports, newspapers, missionary papers, and secondary anthropological literature to explore the roots of the continuing conflict over the salmon fishery, Harris has produced a timely legal and historical study of law as contested terrain in the legal capture of Aboriginal salmon fisheries in British Columbia.

DOUGLAS HARRIS is an assistant professor in the Faculty of Law, University of British Columbia.

Fish, Law, and Colonialism

The Legal Capture of Salmon
in British Columbia

DOUGLAS C. HARRIS

UNIVERSITY OF TORONTO PRESS
Toronto Buffalo London

© University of Toronto Press Incorporated 2001
Toronto Buffalo London
Printed in Canada

ISBN 0-8020-3598-1 (cloth)
ISBN 0-8020-8453-2 (paper)

Printed on acid-free paper

National Library of Canada Cataloguing in Publication Data

Harris, Douglas C. (Douglas Colebrook)
Fish, law, and colonialism : the legal capture of salmon in British
Columbia

Includes bibliographical references and index.
ISBN 0-8020-3598-1 (bound)   ISBN 0-8020-8453-2 (pbk.)

1. Salmon fisheries – Law and legislation – British Columbia –
History.   2. Indians of North America – Fishing – Law and legislation –
British Columbia – History.   I. Title.

KEB529.5.H8H37 2001   343.711'07692756   C2001-901513-5

University of Toronto Press acknowledges the financial assistance to its
publishing program of the Canada Council for the Arts and the Ontario
Arts Council.

This book has been published with the help of a grant from the Humanities
and Social Sciences Federation of Canada, using funds provided by the
Social Sciences and Humanities Research Council of Canada.

University of Toronto Press acknowledges the financial support for its
publishing activities of the Government of Canada through the Book
Publishing Industry Development Program (BPIDP).

Contents

Acknowledgments

It is with great pleasure that I thank the many people who contributed to this book.

The project originated in my graduate work at the Faculty of Law at the University of British Columbia and I owe a great debt to my supervisor, Wes Pue, who guided my theoretical explorations, provided constant support, was enthusiastic about my writing, and who as Director of the Graduate Program at the Faculty of Law, built an extraordinary environment of camaraderie and shared intellectual enquiry. Hamar Foster, although at the University of Victoria, agreed to be my secondary reader. He offered extensive comments at various stages and shared his obvious delight in the legal history of British Columbia. His knowledge of that legal history was invaluable. The students who gathered around the graduate program at UBC provided the invaluable support that comes from others embarked on the same journey. From this group, I owe particular thanks to Lyndsay Campbell, Karen Pearlston, Sara Ramshaw, Annie Rochette, and Alex Semple.

The erosion of disciplinary boundaries at the university creates its perils, but it also produces wonderful possibilities. One such is my continuing collaboration with Michael Thoms, a doctoral candidate in UBC's history department, who has shared and, truth be told, often inspired my continuing interest in the fishery. We have talked, read, and commented on each other's work so extensively that it is difficult sometimes to untangle in whose head an idea first arose.

In its later stages, this project has also benefited greatly from my involvement in the graduate program at Osgoode Hall Law School, York University, under the direction of Eric Tucker. Doug Hay, my supervisor, whose work as a legal historian is itself an inspiration, patiently allowed me to complete this project while the clock was ticking on my doctorial dissertation. In the end, he will have provided numerous comments and insight on what amounts to two book-length manuscripts. He and Paul Craven provided invaluable guidance for my discussion of master and servant law. Brian Slattery and Kent McNeil helped me to frame issues of Aboriginal law.

Numerous librarians contributed their expertise to help me find useful material, including those at the Department of Fisheries and Oceans libraries in Ottawa and Vancouver, the Koerner and Law libraries at the University of British Columbia, the Osgoode Hall Law School library at York University, Robarts Library at the University of Toronto, the Pacific Salmon Commission library, and the Union of British Columbia Indian Chiefs Resource Centre in Vancouver. A similar number of archivists helped direct my search at the British Columbia Archives, the National Archives of Canada, Special Collections at the University of British Columbia, and the United Church Archives at Victoria University, University of Toronto. Particular thanks are owed to Jana Buhlman at the Pacific Region Archives and Record Centre of the National Archives of Canada, Priscilla Davis, curator and manager of the Cowichan Valley Museum, Luc Soucy at the Archives Deschâtelet in Ottawa, and Doreen Stephens at the Anglican Archives in the Vancouver School of Theology, UBC.

Linda Vandenberg of Vandenberg & Associates opened her extensive collection of Department of Indian Affairs documents to me. Independent historian and researcher Anne Seymour helped me navigate the extensive records of the Indian Reserve Commissions and provided useful additional material. Bob Galois provided some timely archival direction and Dan Clayton steered me towards useful bodies of social theory. Eric Leinberger, the cartographer at the Department of Geography at UBC, drew the maps.

Several people read and commented on the entire manuscript at various stages including Jo-Anne Fiske, Peter Fitzpatrick, Richard Mackie, Michael Thoms, and Jean Wilson. Tina Loo and an anonymous reviewer unselfishly provided pages of detailed and helpful critique. Rebecca Brown and Alan Grove read and commented on the first chapter. Matthew Evenden and June McCue provided their thoughts on the Lake Babine chapter. Eamon Gaunt, Andrew MacDougall, Dan Marshall, and Abner Thorne read and commented on the Cowichan chapter. Renisa Mawani provided her thoughts on the introduction and final chapter.

Jim Phillips, who organizes the Legal History Group at the University of Toronto, provided me with opportunities to present several portions of the book, including the discussion of master and servant law and an extract from the chapter on the Cowichan fishery. Similarly, Brian Slattery, who organizes the Aboriginal Law Discussion group at Osgoode Hall Law School, provided me with an opportunity to present my theoretical explorations in the final chapter, with valuable comments from John Borrows, Doug Hay, Patrick Macklem, Peter Russell, and Bill Wickham. All the chapters were presented in some form to meetings of the Canadian Law and Society Association.

The British Columbia Heritage Trust, the Law Foundation of British Columbia, the Osgoode Society for Canadian Legal History, and the Social Science and Humanities Research Council provided financial assistance.

Several families opened their homes to me while I was researching away from home, including Norman and Heather Keevil in Victoria, and Anne Lawson and John Hannaford, and Colin Harris and Janet Chow in Ottawa.

Finally, my parents and Candy Thomson have contributed to this project in so many more ways than I can adequately recognize.

FISH, LAW, AND COLONIALISM
The Legal Capture of Salmon in British Columbia

Introduction

People who have law make and debate claims about what law permits and forbids that would be impossible – because senseless – without law and a good part of what their law reveals about them cannot be discovered except by noticing how they ground and defend these claims.[1]

This is a study of human conflict over fish in late-nineteenth and early-twentieth-century British Columbia, and of how that conflict was shaped by law. Put another way, it is a study of competing legal cultures in a shared time and place, and of how they produced a conflict over fish. People caught fish, creating a fishery, and defined that fishery with a collection of rights of use and exclusion – with law. Whether the emphasis is placed on fish or on law matters little. Law gathered around a fishery that it, in part, created. When one fishery sought to replace another, its laws had to replace the other's.[2]

This is also a study of colonialism, of a distant imperial power and a local settler society displacing existing systems of control with their own, for their own benefit. The Dominion of Canada entered what it thought was an open-access fishery on the Pacific coast in the late nineteenth century. A commons perhaps, the fisheries were not unregulated.[3] A web of entitlements, prohibitions, and sanctions governed the Native fisheries, allowing certain activities, proscribing others, permitting one group to catch fish at certain times in particular locations with particular technology, prohibiting others. Native fishers were not operating outside law, as Dominion officials frequently claimed; rather, they were fishing within alternative legal frameworks that preceded non-Native settlement. The Canadian state insistently denied the legitimacy and even the existence of these systems of Native management and resource allocation, taking the resource as its own, refusing to negotiate. Dominion officials justified imposing state law on the Native fisheries by finding an absence of law.

Initially, the Dominion did not expect that the details of its fisheries law, designed for a Great Lakes and Atlantic coast fishery, would apply to British Columbia. And even after specific regulations for the province were in force, the law was unevenly applied. In some places fisheries officers could not enforce the law as written; in other places they did not try. Whether or not they applied the law as written, however, Dominion fisheries officers assumed that Natives were subjects of the Crown and subject to Dominion law. Crown sovereignty in the late nineteenth century was generally recognized by nation states to extend three miles beyond the tidal foreshore and thus to fish within those waters as well. The displacement of the Native fisheries that followed from the assumption of Crown sovereignty did not go unchallenged, but neither was it stopped. Some Native people worked within the new fishery, accommodating their patterns of life to take advantage of the changing legal and economic order. Others resisted, choosing instead to defend their fisheries from the encroaching state and to justify their resistance on the basis of their own legal traditions. Many combined accommodation and resistance, alternately working within the imposed legal framework and rejecting it. That the system was imposed, however, is not in doubt. Through myriad colonial strategies designed to induce fear, foster division, create truths, and assimilate the other, the Canadian state replaced indigenous fisheries law with its own. Only in the last few years, more than a century after the processes of colonialism began, are Natives and non-Natives beginning to untangle the colonial nets and release indigenous legal forms. While the emerging laws may bear only a faint resemblance to earlier forms of Native resource allocation, they share the defining characteristic of legitimacy in the eyes of many Native peoples.[4]

The history of the conflict over fish in late-nineteenth and early-twentieth-century British Columbia is the history of conflicting legal cultures. Rights-based claims enveloped the conflict, justifying both intervention and resistance. Law was the 'rhetoric of legitimation' used by Native peoples to defend their fisheries and by the Dominion to capture control.[5] Of course these appeals to law and legal tradition did not stand alone. On the one hand, they were backed by the information-generating power of the state and capital, and reflected in such diverse disciplines as cartography, anthropology, political economy, and the natural sciences that were refashioning a territory and a people within the imperial orbit.[6] On the other hand, Native peoples accommodated and countered the colonial penetration, such as they could, with their own claims of traditional management, ownership, and communal resource allocation.[7] As a settler society established itself in Native territory in the late nineteenth century, however, the conflict crystallized around competing claims of sovereignty, legal authority, and right that defined power to control particular fisheries. Law, both state and indigenous, became a principal vehicle of oppression and resistance.

Using old statute books, case reports, government records, missionary reports, private correspondence, and newspapers, I have pieced together the fisheries legislation and regulation, the enforcement policy, and the court decisions that constituted the fisheries law of the Dominion government. These records, most of them generated by the state, catalogue its effort to colonize a resource. They reveal, however, that the process was neither settled nor determined, but rather was much contested, even among government departments. The term 'Canadian state' is useful shorthand for the collection of institutions and bureaucracies whose authority is constructed or maintained by parliament, but it masks as much as it reveals. The state was not a single unified presence, although it might have appeared as such to Native peoples defending their fishing grounds. Instead, it was the locus of the conflicting claims and interests within settler society, each vying to assert a particular order over much-contested fisheries. The records also reveal fragmentary yet vivid glimpses of Native strategies of resistance and accommodation through Native voices that appear repeatedly, sometimes using, sometimes rejecting the Canadian legal system to defend their claims. What emerges is the story of struggle within the many layers of Canadian legal space.

The danger lies in seeing the struggle only through the prism of the Canadian legal system. Native legal spaces are difficult to reconstruct. To attempt to do so is to rely on the reports of anthropologists and other observers (including fur traders and government officials), and on oral histories that are dimmed by more than a century of colonial interference. No court or newspaper reporters were at the potlatches and feasts where, through the giving of gifts, titles were recognized and resource entitlements confirmed. The potlatch and feast, repositories of legal authority in many Native societies, provided the forum where hereditary status and the rights associated with that status were confirmed or validated.[8] Anthropologist Philip Drucker compared the effect of the procedure 'to that of notarizing a document or of registering a deed.'[9] Later, he and Robert F. Heizer would argue of the potlatch that '[i]n a broad sense, it was simply a process at civil law.'[10]

The Canadian state refused to recognize these legal spaces, eventually prohibiting the potlatch in an effort to eradicate what it thought a wasteful and destructive practice that retarded the transition of Native peoples to civilized, productive society. The law against the potlatch, first enacted in 1884, was intended to hasten the assimilation of Native peoples, pushing them into a market economy and wage labour.[11] By outlawing and thereby weakening important Native legal spaces, settler access to land and resources once governed by Native laws increased. This was part of the process by which the state established its legal hegemony. The authority of the potlatch diminished and Native peoples' ability to govern resource allocation declined, creating or accentuating divisions within Native society. This effect becomes apparent in the following chapters in the disputes within Native communities between those who controlled the weir fisheries, and thus sought to keep them, and those who did not and might have preferred to use nets. There were many competing claims for resources within Native societies, sometimes muted in response to the challenges posed by an intrusive state, sometimes emphasized and exploited by the state as it asserted its order. Reconstructing the legal spaces of the rapidly changing Native societies on the Northwest Coast in the late nineteenth and early twentieth centuries is no easy task. Painstaking current ethnographies might reveal them, but there are few such legal studies.[12] I use the salvage or 'total' ethnographers of the late nineteenth and early twentieth centuries, and other more current anthropological and ethnographic writing,[13] but my main sources are those of a historian, particularly a legal historian. These archival records allow me to provide a detailed account of the state's legal forms but only a cursory and much more abstracted account of their Native counterparts. I am not equipped, either with sources or training, to go further. Nonetheless, the sources I have collected can be read attentively for the Native voices they do contain, voices that are strong and frequent enough to support the study of the rights-based argument that collected around disputes over control of and access to the West Coast fisheries.

Legal anthropologists are interested in law and legal processes as cultural phenomena in particular historical settings, and in how 'legal systems encode asymmetrical power relations.'[14] They pay varying attention to the particular rules or laws that are the focus of study for traditional Western legal scholars. These legal scholars are inclined to limit their study of law to formal instruments such as statutes and judicial decisions, or to the judicial process, and to understand law as originating from a sovereign command, whether through parliament or state-appointed courts, or in the judicial process itself. In this study I intend to take both approaches seriously: to understand the particular legal rules as would a legal scholar, but to situate those rules in a particular colonial context riven by asymmetrical power relations. This approach requires that I use the term 'law' broadly to describe both state regulation and patterns of indigenous governance. In doing so I am not denying the important differences between systems of social control in different societies. Perhaps most significantly for the purposes of my discussion in this book, Native societies prospered without a state and the fixed points of power in its administrative structure.[15] Definitions of law or of the rule of law that require a bureaucracy that independently administers the application of rules or principles do not include Native forms of social ordering. Nonetheless, indigenous societies had rules and a variety of mechanisms, including coercion, to enforce compliance. The important point is that Native peoples controlled their fisheries through rights of use and exclusion that predated non-Native interference. The fishery may have been a commons, but it was not unregulated. Native peoples owned and managed their fisheries.[16] The justifications for ownership varied, but at their core were spiritual, developed from centuries of coexistence of Native people and fish. The Natives' claim was a moral and ultimately a legal claim, based not only on efficient management or material need but also on a sense of right that originated within their cultures.

Although the legal regimes that surrounded the fisheries were very different, both Native and European legal systems responded to the life cycles of the fish. If law defined the fisheries, fish, and principally the anadromous Pacific salmon (*Oncorhynchus*), created the possibility of a fishery. *Anadromous*, derived from Greek and meaning running upwards, describes the migration of salmon from the ocean to their spawning grounds in the freshwater lakes and rivers of northwestern North America. It is this regular, predictable migration of salmon, concentrating vast amounts of protein in relatively accessible rivers and lakes that supported indigenous peoples for thousands of years and, much later, attracted the attention of the industrial commercial canneries. In his remarkable little book on the Columbia River, Richard White describes the importance of salmon in mythic terms: 'In the beginning it had been salmon that had drawn humans to the river. The places where the river's energy was greatest ... had concentrated the salmon when they returned to spawn, and at these places fishermen, too, concentrated. The energy harvested and stored by salmon for their journey had become calories that supported human life along the river. Salmon had knit together the energy of land and sea; they had knit together human and nonhuman labour; salmon had defined the river for millennia.'[17] They continue to define the major rivers in British Columbia, particularly the Fraser and Skeena, much more than they now define the heavily dammed and diverted Columbia.

Five species of Pacific salmon reproduce on the North American continent: sockeye (*Oncorhynchus nerka*), pink (*Oncorhynchus gorbuscha*), chum (*Oncorhynchus keta*), chinook (*Oncorhynchus tshawytscha*), and coho (*Oncorhynchus kisutch*).[18] The life histories of each are different, but there are basic similarities. Pacific salmon deposit their eggs in the gravel beds of rivers or lakes. Once hatched, the young fish spend up to two years in freshwater before migrating to the ocean, where they disperse over much of the North Pacific Ocean and Bering Sea for up to four years. They then return in most cases to their home rivers and natal breeding grounds between late summer and early winter to spawn. Before re-entering the freshwater, salmon cease feeding, thereafter relying on their energy reserves to carry them inland, in some cases hundreds of kilometres, to spawn, to defend their redd (nest), and then, exhausted and emaciated, to die. Stores of protein and fat diminish, creating a leaner fish that, with indigenous technologies and interior climates, could be preserved more easily. The combination of rivers, fish, climate, and indigenous cultures produced focal points of human activity – at the entrance to the Fraser canyon[19] and near the confluence of the Bridge and Fraser rivers.[20] Thousands of people would descend on these places in late summer and early autumn to catch and preserve salmon. There were many other locally important sites, some of which I explore in the following chapters on the Cowichan and Lake Babine fisheries. It was around these sites that Native peoples defined rights of access to a resource that provided subsistence and generated wealth. And it was the technology used to catch fish at these sites that was outlawed when a different culture with different technology captured control of the fishery.

Chapter 1 surveys the pre-existing Native regulation of the West Coast fisheries, early non-Native involvement in those fisheries, and the Canadian state's appropriation of the Native fisheries through Anglo-Canadian law. It is a province-wide study, intended to survey the early conflict over the salmon fishery and the legal forms that informed it.

When British Columbia joined the Dominion of Canada in 1871, the non-Native fishery was inconsequential. The Hudson's Bay Company (HBC) had purchased fish from Native people for food and, for a time, had exported barrels of salted, Native-caught salmon to destinations around the Pacific, but there were few non-Natives catching fish.[21] Unlike the Atlantic cod fishery that had been the focus of European interest from the early sixteenth century, the Pacific salmon fishery was too far removed from European markets for fish to be transported profitably until canning technology was introduced. Once this technology arrived on the Fraser, a West Coast industry based on the export of canned sockeye salmon developed rapidly.[22] In the 1870s and 1880s an industrial commercial fishery in British Columbia expanded to dominate the fishery and, with sawmilling and mining, the provincial economy. In many regions of the province, particularly in the north on the Skeena and Nass rivers, Native fishers and cannery workers provided essential labour for the canning industry. However, as Dominion regulation spread across the province, Native peoples lost control of their fisheries. Earlier treaty promises that guaranteed the right to continue fishing as formerly were ignored. The *Fisheries Act* and *Regulations*, enforced by a hierarchy of Department of Marine and Fisheries ('Fisheries') officials, increasingly determined how fish were caught and by whom. With other legal forms, notably the common law doctrine of the public right to fish and the law of master and servant, fish were re-made as an industrial resource and Native peoples as an industrial labour force.

Chapter 1 ends in 1894 for several reasons. First, in 1894 the Dominion formally removed any independent Native control by requiring Indians to seek permission from Fisheries to fish for food. Previously, the government regulated the commercial fishery, but left the Indian food fishery to operate largely unfettered. After 1894, no part of the Native fishery was exempt under Canadian law from state regulation; in this sense the legal capture of the resource was complete. Second, in 1894 Fisheries officials charged a Cowichan man for fishing with a net in the Cowichan River, contrary to the *Fisheries Act*, the beginning of the state's direct legal intervention in the Cowichan fishery. The survey approach of chapter 1 becomes the detailed case study, in chapters 2 and 3, of the Lake Babine and Cowichan fisheries. Although the conflict begins earlier on the Cowichan River, it continues much longer and involves many competing uses of the fishery and the river. The shorter, blunter intrusion in the Lake Babine fishery is, perhaps, a more typical colonial encounter, at least more representative of the late-nineteenth and early-twentieth-century conflict over fish on Canada's Pacific coast.

Chapter 2, the struggle for control of the Lake Babine fishery, is a detailed study of law and the processes of colonialism. Every August and September, until 1905, the Lake Babine people fished with weirs, catching salmon returning to spawn in the Babine River and the tributaries of Babine Lake. The late-summer catch, smoked and stored, supplied the bulk of their food for the ensuing winter and spring and a valuable trade good; it had supported them for longer than any could remember. In September 1904, towards the end of the Babine's fishing season, a Fisheries officer told the Babine that fishing with weirs (he called them barricades) was illegal. He informed them that the *law* prohibited barricades and, threatening imprisonment, insisted that they dismantle them. This marked the beginning of a short, but intense, conflict for control of a large sockeye salmon run. The canning industry located near the mouth of the Skeena River co-opted the state to secure a fishery for its use, and in this was largely successful; state law reproduced a particular order and justified that order. Similarly, the Babine used their law to resist the state's intrusion and to justify that resistance. Two years after the initial confrontation the Babine conceded their weirs, but only after meetings with Dominion officials in Ottawa where they secured certain concessions in what became known as the 'Barricades Treaty,' the details of which have been in dispute ever since.

Chapter 3 is the story of the late-nineteenth and early-twentieth-century struggle to allocate, or re-allocate fish in the Cowichan River. More generally, it illustrates how the forces of colonialism and resistance unfolded on one particular river that was increasingly surrounded by a settler society. By 1894 the key elements of the Dominion's fisheries laws were in place in British Columbia, but the struggle over fish had just been engaged. The disputes over conflicting uses of the Cowichan River emerged as a struggle over appropriate fishing technology, and they became most visible in the local courts. In this forum the weirs were challenged and defended, vilified and supported, condemned and justified. Reports of the trials, combined with the records of the departments of Fisheries and Indians Affairs, provide many details of the state's attempt to impose its law and of Cowichan resistance. These documents also illustrate how state law, constructed and imposed from a distance, was modified both by Cowichan resistance and by the presence of local settlers who were committed to the British Crown and its law, but also neighbours of the Cowichan. All involved, whether Cowichan, missionary, state official, settler, lumber-mill owner, or angler, invoked law to support their claims, and the language of rights, customs, entitlements, and privileges pervaded the conflict that enveloped the weirs.

In chapter 4 I step back to consider law and colonialism more generally, and then to reconsider the historical and legal detail of the earlier chapters in this light. A much more theoretical chapter that draws on studies of law and colonialism in other places, it is intended as an overview and conclusion, and to make explicit some of the theoretical work that underlies the detail of the earlier chapters. One approach particularly inspired my own and warrants mention here. E.P. Thompson's studies of law, custom, and rural practice in eighteenth-century England reveal the local struggles for control of resources. He argues that law became a site of conflict between rulers and peasants where differing conceptions of right were advanced and contested, and control of resources determined.[23] Law mediated class relations for the benefit of the ruling class, while at the same time offering space for resistance. Peasant foresters and farmers filled this space with claims based on customary use. Thompson insists on taking the claims of plebeian England seriously: to look for the legal in local custom, the moral in food riots, the ritual in marriage breakdown, and the community norms in public disapprobation.[24] He writes of enforcement and resistance, of law on the ground, among the people. Without ignoring the role of the state, he captures what a study of legal doctrine or of political history misses – the local struggles framed in legal forms, broadly construed, to dominate and resist. Thompson, of course, is not the only scholar to approach law as a site of conflict, and some of the related work is considered in chapter 4. Nonetheless, his analysis is particularly evocative because eighteenth-century England was in transition from a society where reciprocal rights and obligations, generated and understood locally, regulated access to resources, to one based on private property and market exchange, protected and supervised by a central state. Although there are important differences (addressed in chapter 4), these transitions from local to central control, from communal to private property, from reciprocal rights and obligations to market exchange, also describe the forces at work in late-nineteenth-century British Columbia as Native peoples confronted settler society and its governments.

Law, understood broadly, ordered both the colonial project and resistance to that project in British Columbia. This, I hope, is illustrated in the following chapters about contested fisheries. Laws, legal cultures, and legal discourses ordered the colonial encounter, but that lopsided cultural meeting also formed the laws. In the language of social theory, law constituted and was constituted by the society of which it was a part. In Thompson's somewhat less formal terms, 'I found that law did not keep politely to a "level" but was at *every* bloody level.'[25] This tension – between law as constituted and law as constitutive – lies below the surface in the chapters on the Cowichan and Babine fisheries; the explicit discussion is left to chapter 4. The question that lingers in the background is whether law is a useful category of historical inquiry. How is one to extricate law, so deeply 'imbricated'[26] in the economic and cultural fabric, as a distinct form?[27] The prominent American legal historian J. Willard Hurst, best known for his *Law and Economic Growth: The Legal History of the Lumber Industry in Wisconsin, 1836–1915*, wrote in the introduction of that book: 'The particular story of law and lumber in Wisconsin is a matter only of secondary interest in this book; of prime concern is to learn, from trying to tell a particular story, how better to tell the story of the distinctive parts which law has played in the general course of social experience.'[28] I would not make the same claim for the study that follows. The particular story of law and salmon in British Columbia is a matter of primary importance, and of continuing consequence to an indigenous population and a settler society struggling with the terms of their relationship. Our understanding of the historical detail matters in the present, and for this reason I have chosen to emphasize that detail in the first three chapters, leaving the theoretical discussion to the concluding chapter. But to the extent that law was, and remains central to, an unfolding relationship, I am also interested, as Hurst was, in understanding its distinctive role. At this stage, perhaps it is enough to observe that the people involved, both Native and non-Native, those supported by the state and those at odds with it, thought they were defending legal rights to access particular fisheries. That there was no consensus over the sources of legal authority does not diminish Ronald Dworkin's observation that people who have law make and debate legal claims that would be senseless without law. Native and non-Native British Columbians made legal claims to support their access to the fisheries. The resulting story is one of legal capture. The slow, sometimes disruptive, but continuing release of indigenous legal forms in the late twentieth century is a subject for another book. That which is released may only faintly resemble that which was caught, but such is the transformative power of colonialism.

CHAPTER ONE

Legal Capture

There is no law governing fish in British Columbia. Fishing is carried on throughout the year without any restrictions. This state of things is well suited to a new and thinly populated country. The restrictions of a close season would be very injurious to the Province at present, and for many years to come.[1]

These comments in 1872 from H.L. Langevin, the Minister of Public Works for the Dominion of Canada, were part of the first report to the Parliament of Canada on the state of British Columbia's fisheries. Canning operations had just appeared on the Fraser River, and Langevin was an enthusiastic promoter of the industry. Salmon, herring, sturgeon, oolican, and other species were plentiful, the resource was underdeveloped, and if only a few more fishing-minded immigrants would arrive on the coast, he argued, the wealth of the province could begin to be realized.[2] That wealth lay not in the gold that had attracted so much attention, but in the relatively under-appreciated fishery. Langevin believed the fishing industry needed encouragement – but not government regulation – to realize its promise.

When British Columbia joined the Canadian confederation in 1871, it ceded control of the fisheries to the Dominion government; under the *Constitution Act, 1867*, 'Seacoast and Inland Fisheries' were a Dominion responsibility, supervised by the Fisheries Branch of the Department of Marine and Fisheries ('Fisheries').[3] The Canadian parliament had passed a *Fisheries Act* in 1868,[4] but according to the Terms of Union with British Columbia, it was not immediately law in the western province and would not be adopted until 1877. The Dominion had not yet intervened, and that, argued Langevin, was as it should be. The government must maintain a discreet distance while the fledging industry established itself on the Pacific coast.

Langevin was correct that the Dominion had not yet turned its legislative or regulatory attention to the West Coast fishery. He was mistaken, however, to claim an absence of law. Coastal and freshwater fisheries, the principal source of subsistence and wealth for Native peoples in British Columbia, were neither unregulated nor un-owned. They were, instead, surrounded, even constructed, by a multitude of rules governing their access and use. The opening section of this chapter provides an outline of the patterns of ownership and management that characterized Native fisheries, paying particular attention to the regulation surrounding weirs. Later in the chapter I return to the Native fisheries to gather the evidence of the Native legal forms that survived and responded to the imposition of Canadian fisheries legislation. Legal pluralism characterized the late-nineteenth-century fishery, even as the state sought to assert its dominance.

Anglo-Canadian law was also a presence in the West Coast fisheries even if fisheries legislation was not yet in force. The common law doctrine of the public right to fish opened the fisheries to all British subjects in the colony and constrained the Crown's ability to allocate exclusive fisheries. It constructed fish as an open-access resource. This open access did not, however, reflect some pre-social state of nature, as Garrett Hardin and others have suggested.[5] It was, instead, a legal construct, drawn from centuries-old English law and moulded by the laissez-faire liberalism of the mid-nineteenth century. Unrecognized by Langevin, and ignored in the existing literature on British Columbia's fisheries, the public right to fish formed the foundation for subsequent fisheries legislation. It receives a section in this chapter.

Between these two legal regimes sit the fourteen treaties negotiated between the HBC (on behalf of the Crown) and Native peoples on Vancouver Island in the early 1850s. These treaties, covering a small fraction of Vancouver Island, were exceptions to the general practice in British Columbia, where colonial and later Dominion and provincial governments allowed settlement without first securing the land from Native peoples through treaty. The brief text of these treaties describes the lands surrendered by the Native signatories, and the terms of that surrender. These included a guarantee that Native fisheries would not be disturbed: the signing groups could continue their fisheries 'as formerly.' These treaties, their interpretation and enforcement, are the focus of another section in this chapter.

Other English laws, which were not specific to fishing, defined particular roles for the participants in the emerging industrial fisheries before specific legislation was in force. Under the law of master and servant, Native fishers were transformed into employees subject to imprisonment for breach of employment contract. A remarkable series of cases in the New Westminster Police Court in 1877 illustrate the law's impact. These legal forms – the public right to fish and the law of master and servant – enforced by the Dominion and its courts, shaped the fisheries before laws specifically designed to regulate the fishery were in place. The law defined access to fish (open access for British subjects) and structured particular relationships (master and servant), but these legal forms had so permeated Anglo-Canadian culture that they were invisible to a minister of the Dominion government.

The remainder and bulk of the chapter describes the application and enforcement of Canadian fisheries legislation and regulation, and the changing treatment and characterization of the Native fishery within it. Several important studies have examined aspects of this process. Reuben Ware's *Five Issues, Five Battlegrounds: An Introduction to the History of Indian Fishing in British Columbia, 1850–1930,* charts the creation of an 'Indian food fishery' in Anglo-Canadian law, paying particular attention to the Stó:lō fishery in the lower Fraser River.[6] In this 1983 study, full of quotations and extended appendices from the primary sources, Ware claims, correctly, that the distinction between Indian food fishing and commercial fishing that developed in the 1880s was an artifice imposed on the Native fishery by the Dominion government to limit the Native catch. Ware marks the 1880s as the beginning of Dominion efforts to regulate the Native fishery on the Fraser, and suggests that in the following two decades regulation spread throughout the province, confining the Native fishery.

Geoff Meggs, in *Salmon: The Decline of the British Columbia Fishery,* provides a more general survey of a century of conflict between Natives and non-Natives, workers and managers, fishers and government, over the spoils of a once valuable resource that, he argues, has been greatly reduced by over-harvesting and mismanagement.[7] Meggs also collaborated with Duncan Stacey to produce a wonderful array of photographs and a useful accompanying text, *Cork Line and Canning Lines: The Glory Years of Fishing on the West Coast,* to chronicle the rise of the canning industry with particular attention to the lives of working people, including Native workers who, for the industry's first twenty years, formed the majority of fishers and shore workers.[8]

Dianne Newell's 1993 book, *Tangled Webs of History: Indians and the Law in Canada's Pacific Coast Fishery*, is the only comprehensive study of Native fisheries on the Pacific and of federal fisheries legislation.[9] Newell surveys what she labels 'the politics of resource regulation' from Confederation to the 1990s, and argues that the responsibility to conserve salmon stocks became a burden that consistently fell most heavily on the Native fishery. Conservation claims became the means by which Fisheries justified taking control of the resource on behalf of the industrial canneries. Newell does not dispute the importance of conservation, but suggests that such claims need to be followed by the question; For whom are fish conserved? The answer, she concludes, is that Native people, despite their long history of effective resource management, bore the brunt of conservation for the sport and industrial fisheries. Fish, particularly salmon, were *conserved* by the state for the canneries.[10] Newell is right to focus on federal fisheries legislation, but in covering more than a century she is unable to devote enough attention to the details of enforcement in the late nineteenth century. The law on the books was not the law on the ground, at least not initially, and this is revealed only through closer study. To explore the numerous instances of enforcement and resistance, and the conflicts between the departments of the Dominion, one must delve further into the departmental correspondence. Furthermore, Newell and the other authors underemphasize the non-statutory Anglo-Canadian legal forms that surrounded the fishery, particularly the common law doctrine of the public right to fish that, when invoked in British Columbia by a settler society and its state, created an open-access fishery, erasing any pre-existing claims of Native ownership. These omissions notwithstanding, Newell's is an important contribution both in its scope and in the attention it pays to the effects of technological change; the following study complements rather than rejects her principal conclusions.

On a somewhat different track, *Cheap Wage Labour: Race and Gender in the Fisheries of British Columbia* is Alicja Muszynski's attempt to 'develop a general theoretical framework that can help us understand how salmon canners engaged their shore plant labour forces according to criteria of race and gender.'[11] She focuses on the shore workers – those who worked in the canneries rather than on the fish boats – and on the patriarchal, racial, and colonial assumptions that, in addition to the modes of production, set conditions of work and wage rates of working women and men. Her book, a jumble of history and theory, is an intriguing if not entirely successful attempt to chart the *making* of shore workers in the industrialization of the British Columbia fishery. The Aboriginal fishery was captured by the state, she argues, in the process turning Natives, particularly Native women, into 'cheap wage labour.' Drawing from the work of numerous Marxist scholars, Muszynski employs the idea of *relative autonomy* to suggest that although manipulated by the canneries, the state was not entirely subservient in its regulation of the fishery.[12] It acted generally in the interests of the canneries, she argues, but not always and not entirely. Nowhere, however, does she provide a sustained analysis of the state's principal device for re-allocating the fishery – the law – and how that institution mediated state power. The role of law in the efforts to both dominate and resist is revealed in local settings, closely studied, something that is developed in this chapter, but perhaps even more so in the chapters on the Babine and Cowichan fisheries.

Other scholars have written about the exclusion of Native peoples from their traditional fisheries in Atlantic Canada,[13] Ontario,[14] and Manitoba.[15] A great deal has been written about the Indian fisheries in Washington State, particularly in the aftermath of Justice Boldt's decisions in the 1970s that the resident tribes were entitled, under treaty, to 50 per cent of the commercial fishery.[16] Further south, Joseph E. Taylor III has produced a remarkably well-documented history of the relationship between fish and humans in the Oregon country, focusing on the demise of the Columbia River fisheries.[17] Arthur McEvoy has considered the American Indian experience on the Pacific coast in several chapters of *The Fisherman's Problem: Ecology and Law in the California Fisheries, 1850–1980*.[18] Despite these useful contributions, both in British Columbia and beyond, the role of law in appropriating local fisheries and resisting is underplayed. By probing these details, I attempt to provide what is not yet in the literature – a thorough study of the colonization, through law, of British Columbia's salmon fisheries.

Native Fisheries

The abundant resources of the temperate Northwest Coast supported one of the world's densest non-agrarian populations. The region, argues Wayne Suttles, 'refutes many seemingly easy generalizations about people without horticulture or herds. Here were people with permanent houses in villages of more than a thousand; social stratification, including a hereditary caste of slaves and ranked nobility; specialization in several kinds of hunting and fishing, crafts, and curing; social units larger than villages; elaborate ceremonies; and one of the world's great art styles.'[19] Along the West Coast and inland to the Western Cordillera, fish, predominantly salmon, were the principal sources of Native sustenance and wealth. According to anthropologist Philip Drucker, '[e]xploitation of fisheries was the foundation of native economy. This fact was reflected in more than just the daily food-quest routine and diet. It gave the areal culture an orientation toward the sea and river that regulated settlement patterns and was reflected in social organization and religion.'[20] The coastal and interior fisheries were central to Native lives – to some they were the Salmon People[21] – and access to the fisheries was regulated, not by the common law or the *Fisheries Act*, but by the Native peoples themselves.

The social structures and patterns of Native resource ownership varied greatly in what is now British Columbia but some generalization is possible.[22] The principal unit of social organization on the Northwest Coast was the local group, usually a collection of related kin groups that lived together in a village for much of the year, coordinating activities such as the gathering or harvesting of resources and defence of territory. 'The localized groups of kin,' wrote Drucker, 'defined who lived together, worked together, and who jointly considered themselves exclusive owners of the tracts from which food and other prime materials were obtained.'[23] These local groups were socially stratified, usually consisting of 'a wealthy elite (the "chiefs" or "nobles"), their followers (the "commoners"), and their slaves.'[24] Status and privilege were inherited, either from the male or female line, or in some combination thereof. The degree of social distinction varied, being most pronounced on the north coast, and least important among the peoples of the interior.

Given the importance of fish to most local groups, the sites for their capture and harvest were prized, and thus closely surrounded with regulation. In some areas the important fishing sites, like other important food-gathering sites, were owned by high-ranking individuals or families. In other areas, similarly high-ranking members of a local group would own a resource area that included an entire salmon stream.[25] Ownership of these sites or resource areas was inherited, indivisible, and was confirmed or validated by a feast. Title was vested in an individual who had the authority to exclude members of the local group, but ownership more commonly implied the right to manage a fishery by allocating the resource among the local group and those who through kinship connections had claims of access. The owner assumed the role of steward, ensuring that all members of the group were provided for and that the fishery remained healthy for future genera-tions. Those outside the local or family group were excluded, but those within, although needing to ask permission from the person who owned the resource, had access. Drucker describes the concept of ownership for peoples along the Pacific coast, and provides a specific illustration from the Nuu'Chah'Nulth (Nootka) on the west coast of Vancouver Island:

> Nootkan custom illustrated the nature of such rights very clearly. Almost every inch of Nootkan territory, the rarely visited mountainous back-country, the rich long-shore fishing and hunting grounds, and the sea as far out as the eye could reach, was 'owned' by someone or other. An owner's right consisted in the right to the first yield of his place each season – the first catch or two of salmon, the first picking of salmon-berries, etc. When the season came the owner called his group to aid him in building the weir or picking the berries, then he used the yield of the first harvest for a feast given to his group, at which he stated his hereditary right (of custodianship) to the place, then bade the people to avail themselves of its products. Any and all of them might do so. (Outsiders were prohibited from exploiting these owned places, except where they could claim kinship to the owner, i.e., for the time identify themselves with his local group.) The essence of individual 'ownership,' was thus simply a recognition of the custodian's right.[26]

In this way, ownership of the fisheries blurred with management. Gil-bert Malcolm Sproat, a young Englishman who operated a lumber mill in Nuu'Chah'Nulth territory in the 1860s, knew of a Nuu'Chah'Nulth of some standing who would not allow others to enter a lake without his permission. Sproat speculated that this gatekeeping was not for personal gain, but rather that the individual was acting on behalf of his people 'to prevent the salmon from being disturbed in their ascent up the river.'[27]

Interior groups owned their fisheries as well. Some fishing sites in Stl'átl'imx territory along the Fraser near Lillooet were individually owned, other sections of the river were associated with residence-groups, and still other sites were public, open to all Stl'átl'imx and some outsiders.[28] The individually owned rocks provided the owner with prime access to the spring (chinook) salmon, the preferred species, but did not create an exclusive property right. The following account re-flects a characteristic balance between ownership and stewardship:

A fishing rock can't be sold from way back. It can be handed down to relations like son, nephew, or anybody else, whoever the old guy that owns the rock, that fixes the platform, whoever he thinks will be capable to keep doing it, keep fixing it. But it doesn't mean for just himself. When he fixes that platform or that rock where he fishes, it's not only him that fishes. Everybody. When he sees anybody come and set, they wait for him, and he just calls them over. He tells them, 'Come on and fish.' They don't hog one rock. If he gets what he needs, the other fellow gets a share, and everybody else gets a share.[29]

The residence-group sites were most often associated with the proximate village whose members had defined access to sites along the adjacent stretch of river. The most productive sites – at Six Mile and the mouth of the Bridge River – were public in the sense that they were open to all Stl'átl'imx and many neighbouring people, particularly those with whom the Stl'átl'imx had reciprocal access to their lake fisheries.[30] However, Aubrey Cannon argues that shared access appears to have been 'a localized phenomena, based on kin and other immediate ties.'[31] Her study of the correlation between conflict and salmon on the interior plateau of British Columbia suggests that relative scarcity and abundance of salmon produced trade and, in some cases, conflict between local groups, and she refutes generalizations that emphasize communitarian principles and open-access resources. Resources or their procurement sites were owned by local groups, and access was traded for or fought over.[32]

The myths and stories of many Native societies suggest the density of regulation that surrounded the Native fisheries. In his introduction to James Teit's annotated collection of the myths of the Nlha7kápmx (Thompson), whose winter villages were located along the middle Fraser and lower Thompson rivers in south-central British Columbia, anthropologist Franz Boas recounted one of the Coyote myths of the Chinook people who lived near the mouth of the Columbia River. Both the Nlha7kápmx and Chinook, like many of the peoples in western North America, shared Coyote as the trickster, transformer, and cultural hero. The following synopsis of the Chinook story begins with a hungry Coyote:

He [Coyote] made a little man of dirt, who he asked about the method of obtaining salmon. This artificial adviser told him how to make a net, and informed him regarding all the numerous regulations referring to the capture of salmon. He obeyed only partially, and consequently was not as successful as he hoped to be. He became angry, and said: 'Future generations of man shall always regard many regulations, and shall make their nets with great labour, because even I had to work, even I had to observe numerous regulations.'[33]

The regulations included rules on the preparation, cooking, and eating of the first salmon caught every year, the making and deployment of nets, the use and movement of canoes while fishing, and the limits on consumption.[34]

Other myths suggest not only knowledge of salmon life cycles, but also management of human behaviour that might affect stocks that supported numerous peoples. A recurring story told by peoples along the Columbia River and its tributaries describes Coyote destroying a downstream weir to allow migrating salmon through to people upstream. The following version, 'Coyote Introduces Salmon,' collected by Teit from the people who lived along the Similkameen in south-central British Columbia, includes many of the common elements.

Coyote came to Similkameen from the Thompson country. He had already introduced salmon in the Columbia, and many of these fish were at that time running up the Similkameen River. They could not get to its head waters, however, as the two *wi'lawil* sisters had a weir across the river at Zu'tsamEn (Princeton). Coyote stopped when he came to the weir, and said, 'Here I find you!' The sisters answered, 'Yes, we are settled here.' He looked over the weir, and said to them, 'You have plenty of food. I will stay a while.' The elder sister disliked him, while the younger sister liked him. The former said to her sister, 'Have nothing to do with him. He is Coyote, and he will play tricks. Perhaps he intends to destroy the weir that we have erected with so much labour.' Coyote was angry because the elder sister disliked him: so one day when they were away digging bitter-roots on the flats near by, he covered his head with a spoon of sheep-horn, and broke the weir. The elder sister felt that something bad was happening, therefore the sisters hastened home. When they arrived, Coyote had almost broken down the weir. They attacked him with clubs, and beat him over the head to kill him or make him stop; but he continued to demolish the weir, the pieces of which soon floated downstream.[35]

Similar stories were told by people in many parts of the Fraser River system.[36] To recount them as evidence of comprehensive Native management of river systems as vast as the Columbia and the Fraser is almost certainly to distort their meaning. Myths and stories served many functions in Native societies: to confirm rights of ownership or access to a resource; to impart lessons of human behaviour; and to describe particular relations between humans and the environment of which they were a part. They were also told to entertain, to mock, to esteem, to provoke laughter and tears. Perhaps most importantly, they were spoken (not written) in Native languages and accompanied by expressions, gestures, and varying intonation. Interpretation requires a close contextual analysis. Nonetheless, these stories about animals and humans in the mythical age provide evidence that the fisheries, far from being unregulated, were in fact constructed by the regulations that surrounded them.[37]

Anthropologists T.T. Waterman and A.L. Kroeber describe the plethora of rules and rituals that marked the construction, use, and dismantling of the Kepel Fish Dam, a weir built by the Yoruk people on the Klamath River in northern California. The Yoruk took exactly ten days to build their weir, caught vast quantities of fish for ten more days, and then dismantled the weir. The dismantling of the weir before the end of the salmon run perplexed the observers; it appeared an unnecessary step given that the river's current during the winter rains would have destroyed the structure. Waterman and Kroeber suggest that the weir was dismantled to prevent the intervention of people upstream who depended on the salmon runs as well.[38] Others have suggested that weirs were removed out of an 'ethic of reciprocity' that extended not only to human neighbours, but also to the salmon who had given their lives to humans as a gift.[39] 'We cannot be sure,' wrote anthropologists Michael J. Kew and Julian Griggs of a weir that the Shuswap people removed each evening from a small tributary in the Fraser system, 'that the dam was broken for the sake of "conserving" the fish, but that is beside the point when the removal of the dam is an act called for by the protocol of proper relationships with the fish who are gift-bearing visitors, and the rules of access that underpinned a system of communal property rights.'[40] An ethnographic manuscript by Alexander Caufield Anderson, a trader with the HBC from 1832 to 1858 and later the first Dominion Inspector of Fisheries in British Columbia, supports this view. Anderson described some of the Native fishing technology on the Fraser, including a variety of fish weirs. He noted their efficiency and the 'understanding' that existed between the different peoples on the river system to ensure adequate food supplies and reproduction. 'The fence, however, is rarely so secure but that the main portion of the shoal contrives to force a passage; and even admitting it were perfectly close, *the natives have a conventional understanding that the fish shall be allowed to pass towards their neighbours further inland, who in turn do not seek to intercept the main body from their spawning grounds.*'[41] This statement reveals the depth of understanding about life cycles, spawning habits, fishing practices, and the human impact on a resource that characterized the Native fishery. Social structures, patterns of ownership, and conventions varied around the region, but the general point – that Natives owned and managed their fisheries closely, reflecting the importance of fish in their material and spiritual lives – holds for the coast and for rivers and lakes in the interior.[42]

Joseph Taylor's extensive survey of the anthropological literature in the Oregon country reveals that Native peoples, specialists who relied on salmon as their principal staple of food and trade, had developed technology for catching and preserving salmon that, if fully deployed, could threaten the continued existence of salmon stocks. The healthy stocks, however, were a testament to Native understandings of salmon and to the effective, if unintentional, moderation of harvest.[43] 'Dependence on salmon,' he suggests, 'created complicated forms of respect. Indians feared the disappearance of salmon, and episodes of scarcity underscored the need to treat fish carefully. These themes pervaded cultural forms of celebration and deference.'[44] Taylor describes the mutually constitutive or circular relationship between cultures and salmon that was remarkably stable and enduring, although not to be confused with static or unchanging. Technological change, for example, by altering the methods of harvest, could create value where it had not existed and diminish what had once been valuable. Kew has suggested that pre-contact Native fishing technology evolved, the new technology allowing earlier access to salmon and creating new resource procurement sites around which new rights of access would develop.[45] Storage techniques were fundamentally important as well, argues Randall Schalk, particularly in the middle latitudes of the Northwest Coast (45–60° north), where anadromous fish migrations were highly seasonal. Before a population could specialize in anadromous fish, they needed the capacity to store their harvest through the winter; until that point was reached the dependence on salmon would be minimal. Once achieved, however, the shift to a specialized economy dependent on salmon 'would be quite abrupt and systemic.'[46]

It seems likely, however, that Native consumption of fish, particularly salmon, was at low ebb in the second half of the nineteenth century. Native peoples along the Pacific had been decimated by their contact with Europeans. Warfare had taken its toll, but the biggest killers were exotic diseases – smallpox, measles, influenza, and others. In some areas disease moved more quickly than Europeans, arriving through adjoining Native populations before the Europeans themselves. Each epidemic brought horrendous suffering, and the cumulative effect was massive depopulation, perhaps by as much as 90 per cent in British Columbia in the contact century, as elsewhere in the Western Hemisphere.[47] When the canning industry appeared on British Columbia's Pacific coast in the 1870s, the Native population was a fragment of its former size and its use of salmon was greatly reduced. Some have projected a 'conservational effect' from the declining Native population that produced an unusual abundance of salmon. Others reject this hypothesis, arguing that competition among an increased number of spawning salmon can actually destroy more spawn than the additional salmon create. Whichever hypothesis one prefers, a much reduced Native harvest coincided with technological advances in transportation and canning that enabled the fishing industry to catch and preserve fish and ship the product to distant markets.[48]

Although reduced, the Native fishery had by no means disappeared. In 1879, Fisheries began to keep track of the 'Home Consumption of Fish by the Indians of British Columbia, exclusive of European supply.' In what was admittedly the most rudimentary of guesses, 'and probably a good deal short of the truth,' A.C. Anderson, in his capacity as the Dominion's Inspector of Fisheries in British Columbia, valued the Native catch of 17,000,000 salmon, 3,000,000 pounds of halibut, as well as sturgeon, trout, herring, oolichan and other fish at $4,885,000.[49] A retired officer of the HBC, he recognized the potential for a lucrative commercial fishery in British Columbia, but was also aware that the fishery supported the Native population. Nevertheless, within a decade this separate category, 'Home Consumption of Fish by the Indians,' which accounted for a Native food fishery distinct from commercial fisheries, would be formalized in law as an Indian food fishery. It would become the remnant within Canadian fisheries legislation of an earlier regime of locally controlled Native fisheries.

How the massive depopulation along the Pacific in the century after European contact affected the Native regulation of the resource is difficult to estimate and perhaps impossible to recover. It is equally difficult to ascertain how Native legal forms responded to the opportunities presented by the European- and American-based trading companies, particularly the HBC, which in 1821 received from Britain an exclusive licence to trade with Native peoples west of the Western Cordillera. Native peoples, however, did not concede ownership of the fisheries, and traders did not demand it. In the 1840s, salmon purchased from Native traders became the principal HBC export from Fort Langley on the lower Fraser River. Although it traded extensively for fish with Native peoples, the HBC was not interested in regulating the fishery except to defend its trading monopoly against other British subjects and Americans. As with fur-bearing animals, it made little or no effort to catch fish itself, or to regulate or interfere with the Native fishery. Rather than devote scarce resources and limited knowledge to catching fish, the company found it more efficient to purchase fish supplied by Natives. As HBC's chief trader at Fort Langley, Archibald McDonald, reported in 1831, '[W]e made several attempts ourselves last Summer with the Seine & hand scoop net but our success by no means proved that we could do without Indian Trade, nor does even this appear to me a source of great disappointment as in years of scarcity the best regulated fishery of our own would miscarry, while in years of plenty such as the last the expense in trade would hardly exceed the very cost of Lines and Twine.'[50] McDonald had considerably more faith in the Native ability to catch fish and, importantly, to manage the fishery than he did in his own. The HBC offered Native fishers a new market for their fish – one that they took advantage of – but the fishery remained within the Native domain.

Even when the HBC monopoly ended, in 1849 on Vancouver Island and 1858 on the mainland, there was little non-Native activity in the fishery. Most settlers came to farm or to prospect, and the loosened trade rules did not immediately create a rush to exploit the fisheries. Hugh McKay established a fishery at Beecher Bay on Vancouver Island in 1852, barrelling Native-caught fish for export, but few other settlers followed his lead.[51] On the mainland of British Columbia the HBC defended its trading monopoly, which it held until 1858, to prevent competition for the valuable Fraser River sockeye. James Cooper, who in 1873 would become the Dominion's first fisheries appointee in British Columbia, sought to establish a competing saltery on the Fraser in 1852, packing and shipping fish that he purchased from Natives. The HBC refused to sell him barrels, and enforced its exclusive right to trade with Natives to prevent Cooper from opening a competing business. It also employed various strategies to prevent American traders from purchasing Native-caught fish at what it considered inflated prices.[52] This activity, however minimal in the 1850s, did not operate in a legal vacuum. Native fisheries laws remained in place, but the common law also informed earlier settler activity.

The Common Law of Fisheries

Langevin's sweeping statement in 1872 about the absence of law ignored the common law, but the common law had not ignored fisheries. Although legislation became the focus of fisheries law in British Columbia, the common law doctrine of the public right to fish underlay the development of the fishery. It has not received any attention in the existing literature on the British Columbia fisheries, but it is the focus of a lively debate over the rights of Native peoples in Ontario to the Great Lakes fisheries,[53] and it figures prominently in several recent Supreme Court of Canada decisions.[54] To ignore the common law doctrine is to create the impression that Anglo-Canadian law was absent in the Pacific fishery before the introduction of the *Fisheries Act* in 1877. Newell, for example, begins her third chapter of *Tangled Webs* with the following statement: 'In the colonial era, the BC fisheries were not regulated to any extent.'[55] She is right, as was Langevin, to the extent that the colonial government legislated few restrictions on the fisheries, but the statement is misleading in that it suggests an absence of law. Anglo-Canadian law, and the doctrine of the public right to fish in particular, created the conditions under which a non-Native fishery could insert itself into the existing Native fishery. Understanding how the doctrine was interpreted and applied in British Columbia in the mid- to late nineteenth century is crucial, not only to make sense of the fisheries legislation that followed, but also to recognize how the law was used to reallocate the fisheries. Put simply, the public right to fish, as interpreted by Fisheries officials, established a principle of open access to a resource that had been a closely and locally regulated commons. Based on this principle of open access, the Canadian state built a legislative framework, primarily through a system of licences and leases, that confined and excluded the pre-existing Native fishery, at the same time opening it to industrial capital.[56]

English common law, the vast body of uncodified judicial decisions, followed British settlers to their colonies. Except where it was inappropriate given local circumstances, English law, including statutes and the common law, applied in British settler colonies as it existed on the date of reception, a date determined by the colony. The mainland colony of British Columbia received English law in 1858 when it became a colony, the colony of Vancouver Island when it joined the mainland in 1866.[57] English law would continue to apply in the colony as it was on the date of reception until modified by colonial judges or until the local assembly legislated otherwise. The mid-nineteenth-century English common law of fisheries, therefore, applied to settlers in British Columbia and, many assumed, to Native peoples as well.

The common law did not recognize property in fish until they were caught, but it did establish who had the right to fish.[58] The presumption was that the right to fish in riparian waters belonged to the owner of the underlying soil – the *solum*. This right could be severed from ownership of the soil or divided, but neither was presumed. Moreover, ownership of land included ownership of the *solum*, and therefore the fishery, to mid-stream – *ad medium filum aquae*. In the sea and tidal waters, the right of fishing belonged to the Crown, but the public right to fish was a burden on the Crown's ownership. In the late eighteenth century, the English Lord Chief Justice Mathew Hale described this relationship in the following terms:

> The right of fishing in this sea and the creeks and armes thereof is originally lodged in the crown ... But though the king is the owner ... and as a consequent of his propriety hath the primary right of fishing in the sea and the creekes and armes thereof; yet the common people of England have regularly a liberty of fishing in the sea or creekes or armes thereof, as a publick common of piscary, and may not without injury to their right be restrained of it, unless in such places creeks or navigable rivers, where either the king or some particular subject hath gained a propriety exclusive of that common liberty.[59]

According to Hale, the Crown could grant exclusive fisheries in the sea or tidal waters, or such fisheries could be recognized as customary rights, but the common law presumed a public right to fish for the Crown's subjects. The right was also said to exist in navigable waters, but in England tidal and navigable were virtually synonymous.

Although confirming the public right to fish, Hale did not suggest that the Crown's prerogative to grant exclusive fisheries was limited. By the early nineteenth century, however, it appears that courts would only recognize Crown grants for exclusive fisheries in tidal or navigable waters that predated the thirteenth century reign of Henry II. Joseph Chitty's 1812 treatise on game laws, for example, suggests that the Magna Carta (1215) precluded the medieval king and his heirs from granting exclusive fisheries where the public right existed: 'Hence it seems that a private right of fishery in the sea or a navigable river, cannot be expressly claimed under an existing *grant* from the crown, as a grant to support it must be as old as the reign of Hen. 2d, and therefore beyond time of legal memory.'[60] Authority to encroach on the public right had to come from parliament. Beyond the territorial waters of nation states (which extended three miles from the low-water mark in the mid-nineteenth century), the high seas were an open-access fishery.[61]

In England, tidal and navigable waters were virtually synonymous; the vast inland waterways and Great Lakes in North America were geographical features that the common law had not encountered. Did the public right to fish apply to these navigable, but non-tidal waters? The weight of contemporary Canadian authority suggests that the public right only applies to tidal waters,[62] but before the 1914 decision of the Judicial Committee Privy Council in *Attorney General for British Columbia v. Attorney General for Canada*,[63] Canadian courts tended towards the navigable rule. Mid-nineteenth-century Fisheries officials in the Province of Canada West (Upper Canada) certainly believed that the public right applied to the Great Lakes, and its enforcement produced extended conflict with various Native peoples, including the Saugeen Ojibway and Mississauga, who believed that their long defended rights to exclusive fisheries were in some cases unceded, and in others protected by treaty.

Roland Wright, in something of a revisionist history of fisheries legislation in Upper Canada, argued that the public right of fishing 'is the necessary starting point for any study of government fishing policy and Indian fishing rights in pre- and post-Confederation Canada.'[64] He suggested that the public right to fish prevented the Crown from ceding Native fisheries to non-Natives, but it also prevented the Crown from protecting Native fisheries. Lakeshore or riverside reserve allotments in Upper Canada were insufficient to protect a Native fishery, if the body of water were navigable, he argued, because the Crown's ability to grant exclusive fisheries was limited by the public right to fish. Wright suggested, somewhat controversially, that post-1857 amendments to the Province of Canada's *Fisheries Act* 'can only be viewed as beneficial to the Indians' because they established 'administrative (instead of legislative) control of the resource through a broadly based lease and licence system.'[65] By this he meant that it was only after 1857 that the legislature gave the fledging Fisheries Department the authority to recognize exclusive fisheries, and thereby the means to protect Native fisheries from the public right to fish. To support his argument, Wright cited a variety of mid-nineteenth-century opinion, beginning with an 1845 letter from the attorney general of the Province of Canada and culminating with an 1866 memorandum prepared by W.F. Whitcher, head of the Fisheries Branch in the province, and supported by an opinion from the solicitor general, arguing that whatever rights Natives held to their fisheries, they could not infringe the public right to fish:

> ... at Common Law, piscarial rights are public and general. That fisheries cannot belong exclusively to Indians, whether as pertaining to navigable waters about ceded Reserves, or belonging to water impinging upon conceded islands or tracts of Indian lands. Members of Indian bands can exercise only individual or tribal rights in common with all other Communities or persons as integral parts of the public. Exclusive fishing rights & special privileges of occupation of beaches, barren Islands and shores, and other locations suitable for carrying on fisheries are granted by the Crown only under authority of Act of Parliament in derogation to the Common Law.[66]

Wright concludes that from this point forward there was no doubt among senior government officials that the public right to fish precluded exclusive Native fisheries, except where recognized by Crown grant authorized by legislation.

Wright's argument is vulnerable in several places. Mark Walters, in a meticulous exploration of the public right to fish, argues that its applicability to the Great Lakes was far from certain in the mid-nineteenth century, Whitcher's opinions notwithstanding.[67] Moreover, Peggy Blair and Michael Thoms provide many examples of exclusive Native fisheries that were recognized and in some cases protected by treaty in the late eighteenth and early nineteenth century.[68] More importantly, however, these authors argue that Native fishing rights did not arise, as Wright assumes, from Crown grant. Rather, they arose from long use of the fishery that preceded the assertion of British sovereignty and that was protected in the Great Lakes region, until ceded by treaty, by the

Royal Proclamation of 1763. The rights to exclusive fisheries, recognized as they were in English law, could only be reduced through negotiation and treaty.

Wright is not alone, however, in mistaking the origins of Native fishing rights. In his discussion of the public right to fish, Gerard La Forest contends that with the exception of a few grants by the French crown that preceded English sovereignty, there could be no other limits on the public right to fish, protected as it was in the Magna Carta, because Canada 'was not settled before then.'[69] This was (and is) the central assumption that inhibited the recognition of Native fisheries in Anglo-Canadian law. Canada *was* settled before Europeans arrived, its fisheries managed and used by Native peoples, but these fisheries were not granted by the Crown, and therefore not thought to be protected from public access. At least this is what Fisheries officials believed.[70]

Wright is correct, nonetheless, to emphasize the importance of the public right. It was the legal instrument that was used to appropriate and to justify the appropriation of traditional Native fisheries, not only in the Great Lakes but also in British Columbia. After Confederation, Whitcher became the Commissioner of Fisheries for the Dominion, and his approach in central Canada became Fisheries' policy across the country. In 1875, six months before the Dominion *Fisheries Act* would come into force in British Columbia, Whitcher sent a circular to all the Fisheries overseers (local Fisheries officials) and Indian Affairs forwarded it to its Indian agents. There were no Fisheries overseers in British Columbia yet, and it is not clear whether Israel Wood Powell, British Columbia's first Indian Superintendent, received a copy, but Whitcher's approach to the question of Indian fishing rights across the country was clear:

Fisheries in all the public navigable waters of Canada belong *prima facie* to the public, and are administered by the Crown under Act of Parliament, which Statute imposes various restrictions on the public exercise of the right of fishing, and subjects the privilege to further regulation and control necessary to protect, to preserve, and to increase the fish which inhabit our waters.

Indians enjoy no special liberty as regards either the places, times or methods of fishing. They are entitled only to the same freedom as White men, and are subject to precisely the same laws and regulations. They are forbidden to fish at unlawful seasons and by illegal means or without leases or licenses. But regarding the obtainment of leases or licenses the Government acts towards them in the same generous and paternal spirit with which the Indian tribes have ever been treated under British rule.[71]

All fishing privileges, in Whitcher's estimation, would flow from the Crown to whites and Indians alike, through the Department of Fisheries acting under the authority of the 1868 *Fisheries Act*.

In 1881, Whitcher addressed the public right to fish in British Columbia. Peter O'Reilly, the Indian Reserve Commissioner who was travelling the province allocating land for reserves, began allocating exclusive Native fisheries in the interior, along the middle Fraser River between Quesnel and Lytton, and then in the waters of the lower Nass River.[72] Indian Affairs forwarded these decisions to Fisheries, and Whitcher demanded to know on what authority O'Reilly was acting when he allocated exclusive fisheries.[73] Sir John A. Macdonald, Prime Minister and Superintendent of Indian Affairs, responded that 'in view of the complications which have been caused by the conflict between Indians and Whitemen's claims to Fisheries in the older Provinces of the Dominion,' he had 'considered it expedient and proper to instruct him, while engaged in assigning these lands, to mark off the fishing grounds which should be kept for the exclusive use of the Indians.'[74] The Minister of Marine and Fisheries, with reference to the earlier opinions produced for the Province of Canada, responded that Indians could only use the fishery on the same terms as whites, and that Indian agents or the Reserve Commissioner had no authority to exclude the public from particular fisheries.[75] Indian Affairs would respond with a request that none of the fisheries set apart by the Reserve Commission for Indians be disposed of without its consent.[76] Whitcher replied that

as the common law and statutes, now in force in those Provinces [British Columbia, Manitoba, Keewatin and the North West Territories], entitle 'every subject of Her Majesty' to use these fishing privileges, this Department cannot undertake to debar the public fishermen from exercising their legal rights in the premises, especially in view of the fact that the *ex parte* reservations in question obviously exceed the reason and justness of any arrangement found in due regard for the relative rights of public fishermen and the necessitous claims of Indians.[77]

The common law doctrine of the public right to fish, which had effectively turned a closely regulated and managed fishery into an open-access fishery in the Great Lakes and provided the foundation on which a new fisheries management and regulatory scheme could be built, was firmly entrenched in British Columbia. Believing it to have erased any prior claim that Native peoples might have to their fisheries, the state erected its own regulatory structure.

Treaty Rights

The treaties between the HBC, on behalf of the Crown, and fourteen Native groups on Vancouver Island in the early 1850s mark the first formal attempts to define a relationship between the varied legal regimes, Native and non-Native, that now constructed the fisheries: the closely held, locally controlled Native fisheries on the one hand, and the public right to fish on the other. By mid-century, some boundary between the two was required.

In 1849, Vancouver Island became a proprietary colony open for settlement under the direction of the HBC. The prospectus announced that the tidal fishery should be accessible to all British subjects: 'every freeholder will enjoy the right of fishing all sorts of fish on the seas, bays, and inlets of, or surrounding, the said Island.'[78] The public, at least those holding property, would enjoy their right to fish. James Douglas, the HBC's chief trader and future governor of Vancouver Island and British Columbia, remarked on 'valuable fisheries which will become a source of boundless wealth,'[79] but he also recognized the need to protect Native fisheries. 'I would strongly recommend,' he wrote the HBC, 'equally as a measure of justice, and from a regard to the future peace of the colony, that the Indians Fishere's, [sic] Village Sitis [sic] and Fields, should be reserved for their benifit [sic] and fully secured to them by law.'[80] The following year Douglas purchased land from Native peoples on southern Vancouver Island. These fourteen purchases, negotiated between 1850 and 1854 and formally recognized as treaties by the courts in 1964,[81] were the only land cessions that the Crown or its representatives negotiated with Native peoples in British Columbia during the colonial era. Based on New Zealand precedents, the written text of the purchases was minimal and, as anthropologist Wilson Duff argued, '[t]o read a treaty is to understand the white man's conception (or at least his rationalization) of the situation as it was and of the transaction that took place.'[82] The first paragraph of each treaty described in general terms the lands ceded. Later surveys would confirm the exact boundaries. The second paragraph (reproduced below) described the terms of the sale, including the transfer of lands to whites and the guarantee that Natives could continue fishing as before:

> The condition of or understanding of this sale is this, that our [Indian] village sites and enclosed fields are to be kept for our own use, for the use of our children, and for those who may follow after us; and the land shall be properly surveyed, hereafter. It is understood, however, that the land itself, with these small exceptions, becomes the entire property of the white people for ever; it is also understood that we are at liberty to hunt over the unoccupied lands, and to carry on our fisheries as formerly.[83]

The Native fisheries were now, as Douglas thought they should be, 'fully secured to them by law.'

This clause did not *create* a right to the fishery; it simply recognized what already existed: Native-owned fisheries. But why was it included? Newell suggests that the lack of HBC and settler interest in the fishery in the 1850s 'partly accounts for inclusion of guarantees for traditional Indian fishing practices.'[84] This is likely correct, but perhaps more importantly, Governor Douglas had heard the strong and consistent Native representations of ownership of their fisheries, repeated since Europeans arrived on the coast, that would have made any other arrangement impossible without armed intervention. Natives would only agree to treaties, such as they understood them, if their fisheries were guaranteed and protected. Those who wanted access would have to negotiate. Gilbert Malcolm Sproat, in 1876 a member of the Joint Indian Reserve Commission (JIRC) that was established by the provincial and Dominion governments to allocate Indian reserves and to resolve the pressing land question without treaties, observed that 'if the Crown had ever met the Indians of this provinces in council with a view to obtain the surrender of their lands for purposes of settlement, the Indians would, in the first place, have made stipulations about their right to get salmon to supply their particular requirements, and ... land and water for irrigating it would have been, in their mind, secondary considerations.'[85] Later that year, after struggling through the interior in an increasingly difficult attempt to find reasonable land for Indian reserves amid the settler pre-emptions and purchases, Sproat would write again: 'They have had no treaties made with them, and we are trying to compromise all matters without treaty making. Had treaties been made, stipulations as to salmon would have been in the front. It is, with absence of treaties, all the more necessary to recognize the actual requirements of the people.'[86]

Native fisheries were undeniably important. Sproat understood that the JIRC and the succeeding Indian Reserve Commission (of which he and then O'Reilly were the sole commissioners) were attempts to allocate reserve land without addressing the question of Native title or the need for treaties. He argued, however, that Native rights, such as those to their fisheries, did not disappear simply because there were no treaties. A dispute over the location of a sawmill on part of the Cowichan Reserve (discussed in chapter 3) became a fisheries issue when the owners proposed to float logs down the Cowichan River to the mill, ruining the Cowichan weir fishery. Sproat wrote to Indian Superintendent Powell that the Cowichan, although not signatories of a treaty, had a right to continue fishing as formerly and therefore it would be necessary to receive their consent before floating logs down the river, something that probably could not be acquired without compensation.[87]

Inspector of Fisheries and member of the JIRC, A.C. Anderson agreed. In response to complaints about the Native fishery from cannery owners, and to support his position that the *Fisheries Act* should not apply to Native fisheries, Anderson referred the minister to the fourteen treaties on Vancouver Island that, he pointed out, guaranteed the Native fisheries. This right, he argued, attached not just to the fourteen signing groups, but was recognition that Native people across the province had a right to continue practising their fisheries.

It seems clear, then, that the brief clause, 'to carry on our fisheries as formerly' was intended to protect Native fisheries.[88] But what was the scope of those fisheries? Perceptions probably differed between the two sides, although perhaps not so much as may be assumed. Fish were their principal source of sustenance and wealth for most Native people along the coast, access to those fish was closely and locally controlled, and it was the rights of access and use that Native groups believed they had secured in the treaties. Governor Douglas, on the other hand, probably sought to balance the public right to fish with Native rights of access. The vagueness of the clause 'to carry on our fisheries as formerly' gave him discretion to recognize one or the other, depending on the circumstances. Douglas certainly intended that non-Natives would participate in the fishery; it was one of the principal attractions of the colony to settlers and, Douglas thought, a source of future wealth. He also intended to protect Native fisheries, that they

should be 'fully secured to them by law.' Just as certain areas of land –
village sites and enclosed fields – should be reserved exclusively for
Natives, so should their fisheries.[89] In a letter to the HBC reporting on
the first nine treaties, Douglas paraphrased the language used in the
treaties, expanding somewhat on what he had promised with regard to
the fishery: 'I informed the natives that they would not be disturbed in
the possession of their Village sites and enclosed fields, which are of
small extent, and that they were at liberty to hunt over the unoccupied
lands, and to carry on their fisheries with the same freedom as when
they were the sole occupants of the country.'[90] Moreover, Douglas
would not have understood the protected fisheries to be limited to food
fishing; the Native sale of fish was too common and too important to
the fur trade in the Western Cordillera to be so confined. Many HBC
posts relied on Native-caught salmon as a source of food and often as a
product to export. Protecting the Native fishery, therefore, would include the exclusive right, in certain locations, to catch fish for food and
trade. At very least, a non-Native fishery could not interfere with Native fishing.

What, then, is one to make of the colonial legislation that appeared to
infringe these treaty rights? In 1859, Vancouver Island's House of Assembly passed a *Preservation of Game Act* that closed the commercial
hunting of deer and certain birds in the colony for six months from
January 1. The preamble suggests contradictory motives, but it appears
that the intent of the act was to protect enumerated species for those
who hunted for food, commerce, and sport: 'Whereas, Birds and Beasts
of Game constitute an important source of food, and the pursuit thereof
affords occupation and the means of subsistence to many persons in
this Colony, as well as a healthy and manly recreation; And Whereas
Game is unwholesome and unfit for food, and it is expedient to prohibit the destruction and use thereof in the breeding season ...'[91] Governor Douglas does not appear to have given the act his assent and
therefore it never became law, but in 1862 he did assent to an amendment of the act that appeared to incorporate the earlier version. The
amendment extended the hunting restriction to other birds and also
restricted fishing: 'That from and after the passage of this Act, no
person shall use or employ any net, seine, drag net, or other engine of a
like description for the purpose of taking or capturing Fish in Victoria
Arm above Point Ellice, or in any Lake, Pond, or standing water in this
Colony, under a penalty not exceeding fifty pounds (£50), to be recov-
ered as aforesaid.'[92] The amendment followed a Colonial Office dis-

patch that included a memorandum on protecting the salmon fishery and copies of fisheries legislation from the United Provinces of Canada.[93] Douglas acknowledged receipt of the documents, 'which afford so much useful information on the methods of preserving and regulating Fisheries.'[94] This dispatch was probably the immediate catalyst for the amendment to restrict fisheries, but how is one to reconcile the *Preservation of Game Act* with the earlier treaty protection? Natives in the colony were considered British subjects, the law applied to them, and it appeared to restrict Native and non-Native net fisheries indiscriminately. Historian John Lutz argues that the legislation was intended to preserve the fishery for anglers and to conserve game for the white 'sportsman.'[95] Certainly by the late 1880s, provincial enforcement of the game acts near settled areas had drastically reduced Native hunting to the point of hardship.[96] There is no record of enforcement in the 1860s, however, and legislated restrictions were not a priority for the colonial governor or the House of Assembly. Local abundance was presumed, and elected officials seemed more interested in promoting rather than restricting the fishery.[97]

Occasionally colonial officials did interfere with Native fishing, but only in the pursuit of other objectives. Lieutenant Edmund Hope Verney, commander of the HMS *Grappler*, a small gunboat that patrolled the coast between 1862 and 1865, reported an expedition from Bute Inlet to Harper's Ferry, fifty kilometres up the Homathco River, 'to prevent the Chillicoaten Indians from coming here to fish.'[98] This expedition, mounted in the immediate aftermath of the killing of eighteen workmen on the Bute Inlet railway, was a strategic move to limit the movements of the Chilcotin and to force them to surrender the wanted men;[99] it had nothing to do with regulating the fishery. Apart from vigorous boosterism, or the tangential effects of the effort to assert control of the territory, the colonial government did not regulate fishing.

This lack of colonial interest in regulating the fishery reflected developments in Britain. Two commissions on the British fisheries – an 1863 royal commission on the Scottish herring fishery[100] and an 1866 commission on sea fisheries of the United Kingdom[101] – concluded that state regulation of the fishery was unnecessary; it did not preserve fish stocks and succeeded only in favouring one class of fishers over another. Both commissions recommended that the British government deregulate the fishery – a vivid reflection of the dominant liberal paradigm. State interference, it was held, simply reallocated the resource to those who lobbied most effectively, damaging fishing communities and the national economy. The commissioners believed the ocean fishery to be inexhaustible; if heavy fishing reduced fish stocks in one area, low returns would force fishers from that area, allowing the fish population to recover.[102] The invisible hand of the market and the common law would provide the necessary regulation.

But did the House of Assembly intend to restrict the Native fishery in the 1862 amendment to the *Preservation of Game Act*? It seems likely that the Native fisheries were exempt, and possibly that the act was intended to protect rather than infringe treaty rights.[103] Both before and after signing the treaties, Douglas had explicitly recognized a moral and legal obligation to protect the Native fisheries; he had promised that Natives could continue fishing as they had before European settlement. The House of Assembly may have been less committed to the protection of treaty rights, but Douglas as governor had to give his assent before the act became law, something that he was unlikely to do if it infringed those rights. Fifteen years later, in 1877, Fisheries would informally exempt Native peoples in British Columbia from the *Fisheries Act* and *Regulations* after strong representations from its local officials. This sentiment was not new in 1877. HBC officials and even many settlers not connected with the fur trade recognized the importance of fish to the Native economy. It is unlikely, therefore, that the 1862 fisheries regulations, minimal as they were, were intended to apply to the Native fishery. And even if the legislation did apply generally, its focus on a particular technology – nets – and its geographical restriction suggests that it was directed at the settler population and not at Native fishing. The Songhees, whose territory included Victoria harbour, relied primarily on a reef net fishery (gill nets anchored to land and extending perpendicular from the coast to trap migrating salmon) conducted from a few select points on the southwest coast of Vancouver Island and on the San Juan Islands.[104] The ban on nets in Victoria's inner harbour did not affect their fishery. Moreover, had the colonial legislature wanted to minimize a Native freshwater fishery, it would have prohibited weirs and nets in rivers and streams. Although Natives did fish with nets in 'standing water,' the river-based weirs were of far greater concern to the angling community, as the dispute on the Cowichan River (discussed in chapter 3) amply illustrates. Finally, there is no record of enforcement against Native or non-Native fishers, so that even if the amendment to the *Preservation of Game Act* applied generally and was intended to restrict the Native fishery, its effect was minimal. That would change, but only after the canning industry became a dominant force in the provincial economy. The treaties would become the touchstone for both Native and non-Native who sought to defend the Native fishery.

The *Fisheries Act*, 1877

The industrial commercial fishery on the West Coast depended on canning, a preserving technique first used for fish in Great Britain and Ireland in the early nineteenth century. In the mid-1860s canning technology reached San Francisco Bay on the West Coast. From there it moved north to the Columbia River, and to the mouth of the Fraser River in the late 1860s. It was not until the early 1870s, probably 1871,[105] that the canning industry established a permanent presence, and by 1873, when Fisheries began keeping records of British Columbia's fishing industry, the firm of Findlay, Durham & Brodie canned 115 tons of Fraser sockeye. Several other smaller operations together canned another 80 tons. That year Fisheries hired James Cooper to act as its agent on the Pacific coast. Cooper agreed with Langevin's assessment that to extend the 1868 *Fisheries Act* to British Columbia would not benefit the nascent industrial commercial fishery, and the cannery operators themselves gave no indication that they wanted regulation. Cooper was also concerned that enforcing the *Fisheries Act* that would 'probably lead to complications with the Aborigines,'[106] an early observation about the disjuncture between Native fishing practices and the *Fisheries Act* that would prove entirely accurate.

The reticence of Dominion officials and of the fishing industry in British Columbia towards the *Fisheries Act* was short-lived. As the industrial commercial fishery grew, so did cannery-owner concerns about their competitors' fishing practices and about competing uses of the rivers. Alexander Ewen, initially a partner in the New Westminster canning operation of Loggie & Co., wrote to Cooper in 1875, complaining that gold miners were destroying the spawning beds and Indians were destroying the spawn. He asked that the government intervene to stop the 'wholesale destruction by Indians,' and that it consider establishing fish hatcheries as the Americans had done on the Columbia and Sacramento rivers.[107] Cooper forwarded this and other material to Fisheries as part of his yearly report, in the process making it clear that the industry was ready for government regulation, at least of Indians and gold miners. By the time industry complaints reached Ottawa, the

Dominion had already begun the process to implement the *Fisheries Act*. In May 1874 it passed an act to extend the *Fisheries Act* to British Columbia,[108] and after proclaimed by the governor general in 1876,[109] the law came into effect on 1 July 1877. Six years after British Columbia joined the Canadian confederation, its fisheries were subject to Dominion law.

A.C. Anderson, who had been appointed the Inspector of Fisheries the year before, was well aware that in 1877 British Columbia received a *Fisheries Act* based on the first comprehensive fisheries legislation of the United Provinces of Canada from 1857, and modified for the Maritime provinces in 1868.[110] None of the sections had been drafted with the West Coast fishery in mind, and much of it was irrelevant. Anderson wrote repeatedly to Ottawa, in an increasingly frustrated manner, that the Pacific salmon, unlike the Atlantic salmon, only spawned once and therefore the regulations for the province would need to be different. Officials in Ottawa, although ignorant of the details, were well aware that the *Fisheries Act* needed revision before it could be enforced in British Columbia.[111] Nonetheless, parts of the act were general enough to apply to either coast and the commercial industry was soon clamouring for Anderson to enforce those parts against the Native fishery.

The 1868 *Fisheries Act* contained many provisions that, although generally applicable, were intended to restrict Native fisheries. Indians, however, were only mentioned in order to exempt them, when they were fishing for their own use under licence from the minister, from a section that prohibited particular (predominantly Native) fishing technology:

> 13(8) It shall be unlawful to fish for, catch or kill salmon, trout (or 'lunge') of any kind, maskinongé, winnoniche, bass, barfish, pickerel, white-fish, herring, or shad, by means of spear, grapnel hooks, negog, or nishagans; provided, the Minister may appropriate and licence or lease certain waters in which certain Indians shall be allowed to catch fish for their own use in and at whatever manner and time are specified in the licence or lease, and may permit spearing in certain localities.[112]

This subsection, similar to one first enacted in 1857, was intended to place all Native fisheries under control of Fisheries through a system of licences and leases. It was not, however, enforced in British Columbia.

In response to the obvious legislative shortcomings, Anderson took what he believed to be the pragmatic approach: he would apply those parts of the *Fisheries Act* that were appropriate to British Columbia's fishery, adapt other sections as needed, and would generally manage the fishery in what he thought were the best interests of all fishers. In his annual report for 1876, he wrote:

> With regard to the provisions of the Fishery Act, at large, there are many portions which, under the showing I have made, are necessarily inapplicable to this Province. Their application, indeed, would in some cases neutralize all fishing operations: for instance, of the salmon, at present the most lucrative. I have therefore assumed that such portions, only, of the Act, as are obviously of general application, with such other portions as, on more minute enquiry, may be found to be of particular application, shall be locally adopted. Without, therefore, interfering, and injuriously as I conceive, with existing practice, I shall continue, as hitherto, to exercise a captiously watchful *surveillance* for the common benefit; reporting from time to time, the result of my observations, and under your sanction, extending such further protective portions of the law, as may be found necessary or expedient.[113]

In essence, Anderson undertook to manage and police the fishery as he saw fit. The *Fisheries Act* was a point of reference, some of its general provisions were applicable, but otherwise it was largely irrelevant to British Columbia. Anderson, with the blessing of Fisheries, adopted a highly discretionary approach to applying and enforcing the act. The industry would soon question the wisdom and fairness of vesting so much discretion in one man, but in the early days of fisheries regulation Anderson took little direction from either parliament or the government. In fact, in the first years of his appointment Anderson's discretionary policy amounted to general non-enforcement. He spent the 1877 fishing season travelling in the interior as the Dominion representative on the JIRC and was not a presence on the fishing grounds near the mouth of the Fraser or at New Westminster, site of the emerging canning industry. An editorial in the *Daily British Colonist* remarked on the inspector's absence, suggesting that in future he 'personally supervise the fisheries during the season.'[114]

With heightened activity on the fishing grounds and increasing competition for fish among the five canning operations on the Fraser, disputes flared and, in the absence of state regulation, competitors turned to the local courts. Ewen and Wise, owners of a cannery at New Westminster, charged John Deas, owner of a cannery on the South Arm, with 'having, on 9th July, at South Arm, Fraser River, used violent and threatening language towards certain fishermen in their employment, thereby intimidating said men and preventing them from working.'[115] Deas, according to historian H.K. Ralston, was protecting a drift that he had cleared of net-damaging snags,[116] and for which Anderson had refused to grant an exclusive lease. He appeared unrepresented by legal counsel in Police Court before two justices of the peace, W.D. Ferris and W. J. Armstrong, who sentenced him to three weeks' imprisonment. The conviction was overturned on appeal, but valuable fishing time had been lost and enough damage had been done that Deas left the industry at the end of the season.[117] Later that summer the courts heard two cases involving Samuel Herring, owner of a salmon salting business at New Westminster, and Henry Holbrook, a cannery owner, involving an altercation over the setting of a drift net. An agreement to share a stretch of river had gone awry, a net had been damaged, and Herring was awarded $5.[118]

These cases highlight the lack of intervention by Fisheries, and a rather disgusted editorial in the *Mainland Guardian* suggested that the altercation between Deas and Buck could have been avoided if all the cannery owners had met before the fishing season to establish rules for the fishery.[119] This had not happened, but the suggestion itself indicates the lack of direct government regulation in these early years. Notwithstanding Anderson's appointment and the extension of the *Fisheries Act* to British Columbia, fishers on the Fraser had to make their own rules. Although there had not been a formal pre-season meeting, it is clear from these cases that the fishery was governed by a series of informal arrangements. Drifts were shared with some, and defended against others. The vast majority of these arrangements between fishers and between canneries went unrecorded, but when the sharing went awry or the defence became too heated, the parties turned to the courts. The Dominion was beginning to put a regulatory structure in place by passing legislation and appointing officers, but in 1877 it was not yet a presence on the fishing grounds. It spent a paltry $635 that year on the British Columbia fishery, including Anderson's salary.[120] When serious disputes arose in this regulatory vacuum, the protagonists resorted to threats and then to the local courts to resolve their differences. End-of-season editorials in the New Westminster papers demanded that the Dominion take more action and spend more money to regulate the fishery.[121] The cannery operators expressed similar sentiments. At a meeting chaired by Anderson they proposed a $20 boat licence and taxes of $.08 per case of canned salmon and $.25 per salted barrel to cover the cost of a hatchery.[122]

Provincial officials blamed the Native fisheries for the perceived crisis. In 1878, the legislature requested that the Dominion take 'immediate steps' to stop the 'highly pernicious practice now pursued by Indians, in annually taking and using for food the spawn' of salmon and herring.[123] Anderson, however, recommended that Fisheries exempt Native people from the *Fisheries Act*. To enforce the law that, among other things, prohibited nets in non-tidal waters would eliminate much of the Native fishery. He suggested to the minister that, 'as a rule, the provisions of the Fishery Act, as modified to suit the exigencies of this Province, shall not be deemed to apply to the Indians, working to supply their own wants in their accustomed way.'[124]

Except in cases of gross violation of the *Act*, Anderson argued against any interference in the Native fishery. A few days after his appointment, he wrote to the minister to refute allegations from cannery owners that the Native fishery in the interior was destroying salmon spawn and fry.[125] That fishery, Anderson stated in his annual report for 1876, was not the cause of any perceived reduction in the salmon stock. The sockeye runs were cyclical, explained Anderson, with a large run (1873) followed by three successively weaker years. The big runs would return, and Native fishing was not responsible for diminishing catches in the commercial fishery. Anderson considered 'the native modes of fishing to be altogether unobjectionable, and economical, and that any interference with their proceedings, under these modes, would be unadvisable, save when, through bad example, they infringe a general protective law – as in the case of the occasional use of explosive compounds.'[126] With regard to fish weirs, which were to become the source of much conflict on the Cowichan and Babine rivers, Anderson thought them 'quite innocuous.'[127] He would not hold their builders accountable, even though weirs were now prohibited by law. The Minister of Fisheries apparently agreed: '[T]he Minister also directs that your Department [DIA] be informed that the position and wants of the Indians of British Columbia will be scrupulously regarded. It was on account of the danger of interfering with them, that the Minister refrained from putting into force the fisheries laws in this Province until such time as all the circumstances would be considered, and effects weighed.'[128] Anderson had been instructed to use his discretion when applying the *Fisheries Act* generally, and not to apply the act to Native fishers.

Salmon Fishery Regulations, 1878

The demand for more government intervention was apparently heard in Ottawa, for the following year, 1878, British Columbia had its first set of regulations that, although minimal, dealt specifically with the Pacific coast fishery. The two sections of the *Salmon Fishery Regulations for the Province of British Columbia* banned nets in non-tidal and fresh waters, restricted the obstruction of rivers, and closed the fishery on weekends:

> 1. Drifting with salmon nets shall be confined to tidal waters; and no Salmon net of any kind shall be used for Salmon in fresh waters.
> 2. Drift nets for Salmon shall not be so fished as to obstruct more than one-third of the width of any river.
> Fishing for salmon shall be discontinued from eight o'clock A.M. on Saturdays to midnight on Sundays.[129]

The regulations reflected the lack of knowledge in Ottawa about Pacific salmon and the fishing industry. Most fish were caught by net in the tidal, but fresh waters of the lower Fraser, and the first section of the regulations prohibited such a freshwater fishery.[130] Despite this potentially devastating restriction, the regulations were not changed, but nor were they enforced. Nets were allowed in tidal waters, whether fresh or salt water. The minister also instructed Anderson to reduce the weekend closures, which the industry thought too long, from 40 to 36 hours.[131] In fact, the weekend closures appear not to have been enforced during the peak salmon run in July and August 1881, and it is unlikely that canneries were held to even the reduced closure in previous years.[132] Fisheries, however, did not alter the regulations. Anderson had complete discretion, and he took an entirely detached approach to managing the fishery on the West Coast anyway. Even after the *Regulations*, there remained little enforcement of any kind.

The new rules did, however, prompt a reaction from Gilbert Malcolm Sproat who, by 1878, was the sole commissioner on what had become the Indian Reserve Commission.[133] Enforcing them, he argued, 'would simply deprive the numerous Indian population on the Fraser and in the interior of the country of an essential and much prized article of diet which in fact constitutes their staple food during the whole year. The Government of England, 25 years ago, might as well have prohibited the cultivation of potatoes by the Irish.'[134] Sproat was at a loss. When he was appointed to the JIRC in 1876, the Dominion and provincial governments had instructed him when allocating reserves not to disturb Native fisheries and, where possible, to secure their fishing stations.[135] The other reserve commissioners had received similar instructions.[136] In fact, reserve land was allocated by the JIRC and later by Sproat and his successor, Peter O'Reilly, on the basis that the fishery would provide Native people with their enduring sustenance. To the extent that Native peoples were prepared to accept the reserves allotted by the commission, they did so on grounds that they would retain access to their fisheries. To the extent that the Dominion and provincial governments could justify these reserves, they did so, in part, on the grounds that Native peoples of the province were fishers and did not need a large agricultural land base. The provincial attorney general, G.A. Walkem, in the provincial government's report on Indian reserves, recommended that fisheries, not just fishing stations, should be set aside for Natives: 'No good reason exists why "Fisheries," such as those established by our merchants on Fraser River for curing and exporting salmon, and other merchantable fish, should not be erected in suitable places for the benefit of the Indians, and be in time profitably controlled and conducted by themselves.'[137] Before such time as the Natives could control their fisheries, however, the provincial government assumed they would work as wage labourers, providing essential labour for the canneries and logging operations.[138]

Both Native resignation with and government justification for the small reserves were undermined by the 1878 *Regulations*. Without an exemption for Indians they removed the foundation on which Sproat and the other commissioners had built their painstaking efforts to settle the land question in the absence of treaties. Natives in British Columbia were well aware that in other parts of the country the Crown was signing treaties, allotting larger reserves, and paying compensation in the form of annuities for Native land. They were incensed that the Crown was not affording them the same respect and the commissioners attempted to meet Native concerns by guaranteeing them undisturbed access to their fisheries, and in some cases exclusive access.[139]

Eventually conceding that the Native fishery needed special consideration, in August 1878 the Minister of Fisheries, by letter, authorized Anderson 'to suspend the application in regard to the Indians, of the fishery enactments.'[140] Unsatisfied with this informal recognition, Anderson requested that the government formally exempt the Indians of the province by order-in-council. Officials in Indian Affairs made similar requests. Powell, the Indian Superintendent for British

Columbia, argued that the 1878 regulations, if enforced, 'would act disastorously [sic] upon the Indians,' and asked that they be modified.[141] Chief Justice Sir Matthew Begbie thought that a Native food fishery should be protected. The regulations should not apply, he argued, 'to Indians fishing by their accustomed methods for the support of themselves or their tribes and not for exportation.'[142] David Mills, Minister of the Interior, wrote to Sir Albert Smith, Minister of Marine and Fisheries, citing the protection of Indian fishing rights under treaty and requesting 'important modifications' to the regulations, 'insofar as Indians are affected.'[143] None of these requests, however, was granted. Whitcher, the Commissioner of Fisheries, informed Indian Affairs that 'the Inspector of Fisheries for British Columbia has been instructed practically to exempt Indians from the operation of the Fishery Regulations of 30th May last, affecting the salmon fishery, in all instances where the fishing is not carried on amongst white people and does not injuriously affect other fishermen.'[144] Earlier that year, in response to a request from Sproat that the Cowichan weirs should be exempt from the weir prohibition in the Fisheries Act, Whitcher had provided a somewhat contradictory answer: '[I]t should be clearly understood that Indians and whitemen are all alike subject to the fishery laws. There is, however, no present intention to apply the Fisheries Act to the Indians of British Columbia.'[145] Indians were subject to Dominion law, at least when fishing in competition with whites, but it would not apply to Indians, at present.

Both Anderson and Sproat argued the Native fishery should be left alone, not only on compassionate grounds or because it was an effective and efficient fishery, but also because Native people were *legally* entitled to continue their fisheries. 'I have so far sought to place this subject before the Department,' Anderson wrote, 'on grounds solely of humanity, of justice, and of prudential consideration. I have now to add that, in my opinion, the exercise of the aboriginal fishing rights cannot be legally interfered with.'[146] Later in the same report he added unequivocally: 'I am quite prepared to advocate and to sustain the legitimate and hereditary rights which I conceive to be inalienably secured to the Indians, both on grounds of abstract justice, and of formal concession by the Crown.'[147] Anderson was referring to the treaties and to the work of the JIRC, both of which, so he thought, had secured their fisheries.

Not everyone in the provincial government agreed with Anderson's assessment of a legal right.[148] According to provincial officials, any concession to a Native fishery was made on compassionate grounds and not because the Crown had a legal obligation. But fisheries were a Dominion responsibility, and Anderson was the Inspector of Fisheries, the most senior fisheries official in the province. Unlike most government officials in British Columbia in the 1870s, Anderson's roots in the province lay in the fur trade. He had arrived at Fort Vancouver near the mouth of the Columbia River in 1832, while still a boy, and had remained in the active service of the HBC until he retired in 1854. As reflected by his cultural prejudices, Anderson thought the interior hunting tribes superior to those who, with little exertion, fished on the coast,[149] but he also took the Native sale of fish for granted and even necessary for the continued viability of the fur trade. If Natives fished in their 'accustomed way' and 'to supply their own wants,' then their fishery should be undisturbed and they should be allowed to sell fish freely.[150] The phrase 'to supply their own wants' included more than a food fishery. Anderson expected that Native people would sell fish as a means of supporting themselves. In his 1878 report, he described the salting operation of a Mr Huson near the mouth of the Nimpkish River on Vancouver Island. According to Anderson, 'Mr. Huson procures his supply of fish chiefly from the Indians of the Nim-Kish River, at a very economical rate.'[151] Similarly, Anderson noted that the HBC at Fort Babine relied on fish purchased from the Babine. That post, wrote Anderson, 'has always been a staple mart where large supplies of dried fish were procurable, for the supply of other posts, less fortunately situated on the head waters of the Fraser, not far distant. Twenty or thirty thousand salmon, or more if required, have thus been annually procured by the Company for many years, bought from the Indians out of their enormous superfluity.'[152] Anderson knew that the Babine fishery was a commercial weir-based fishery, conducted contrary to the *Fisheries Act* and *Regulations*, but did not consider that it was a problem or suggest that it stop. Both the Nimpkish and Babine fisheries fit nicely within an ex–fur trader's paradigm: Native people supplying a staple product, fish in this case, to a commercial company for food or export. A long-established 'intertribal traffic,' such as that reported by Sproat 'between the net-using Indians on the banks of the muddy Fraser and the spear-using Indians who live on the smaller clearwater rivers and streams,'[153] would also have fit within Anderson's fur trader's model.

In the fur trade, cordial relations with Natives were a business imperative, and Anderson believed that conflicts over fishing sites could be avoided if whites behaved honourably. He commented at length on the diligent, prudent efforts of a Mr Robertson to build a small sawmill and fishing station on the Nass in 1878. According to Anderson, Robertson's relations with the people of the Nass were exemplary; commercial enterprise need not jeopardize relations with Natives. He did, however, report conflict between Native fishers and cannery owners over access to fishing grounds at the mouth of the Skeena, and Anderson blamed the latter.[154] Indian Superintendent I.W. Powell made a pointed reference to the growing conflict on the north coast in his annual report, stating that canners needed to act prudently, but also that the government must recognize and protect *hereditary rights* as the canning industry expanded north:

> There are some instances of dispute and consequent dissatisfaction between North-West Coast Indians and the Whites engaged in canning and salting fish, in regard to alleged fishery encroachments, which I greatly trust will be disposed of and settled during the ensuing year.
>
> Coast Indians attach as much value and importance to their customary fishing grounds as interior Tribes do to their grazing and agricultural lands, and look with much jealousy upon the approach of white settlers to these places so necessary to their prosperity and existence.
>
> On the Northern coast there are certain salmon streams to which for ages their rights have never been questioned, and I have no doubt that extreme care will have to be taken in considering their claims and adjusting their differences if a friendly feeling is to be perpetuated.
>
> I do not think the difficulties of arranging these matters are by any means insuperable, but I feel quite certain that the *hereditary rights* to which they are so devotedly attached ought not to be longer left in abeyance.[155]

Conflicts developed elsewhere as well. Sproat reported that settler pre-emptions and water rights along the Thompson River were creating disturbances on small streams where Natives caught fish for food and for trade.[156] Native and non-Native interests were increasingly in conflict, but Anderson believed diplomacy would resolve most concerns. Diplomacy would delay confrontations, not eliminate them.

At least for the moment, Fisheries was prepared to leave the enforcement of its fisheries laws, with respect to Native people, to the discretion of local officials, but it was not prepared to recognize this policy officially or publicly. Whitcher, however, could not understand the fuss over the regulations. Natives might *perceive* that canning and logging operations were encroaching on their fishing rights – he would not concede that this was so – but this was a function of increased settlement, he argued, not fisheries law.[157] What he omitted in his report was that canners and loggers used the fisheries law, which prohibited certain Native fishing practices, to justify their encroachment on the Native fishery and to demand government action when Native fishers competed with or hindered their operations. As Newell observes, Natives were to be helpers in the industrial fishery, not competitors.[158] This was apparent in 1877, when local courts in New Westminster sentenced Native fishers to jail for breach of contract under the law of master and servant.

Master and Servant Law in the Fisheries, 1877

The law of master and servant has received little attention in the existing literature on British Columbia,[159] but it was the law that surrounded employment contracts in Britain and its empire through most of the nineteenth century, requiring employees to perform their duties faithfully, and employers to pay wages when due.[160] The law's fundamental inequality and its eventual undoing lay in the different remedies for breach of contract. Employees could sue their employers in a civil action for non-payment of wages or for inadequate notice before termination. Employers, by contrast, had recourse to criminal sanctions. Employees could be arrested and imprisoned if they failed to begin or complete a contract, or if they were guilty of misconduct or misdemeanour in carrying out their duties. The criminal sanctions, moreover, did not end an employee's obligation; the employer could still enforce the remainder of the contract. In sum, an employer could be sued for damages, but an employee could be compelled on threat or use of criminal punishment to work. Repealed in Westminster in 1875,[161] in New Westminster, British Columbia, the law of master and servant provided employers with penal sanctions as late as 1877.[162] That year the New Westminster Police Court heard several breach of employment contract disputes originating in the fishery.

In 1877 there were many sockeye salmon to be caught and, with the growing capacity to process fish, fishers were in short supply. Salmon-saltery owner Samuel Herring took some of his former employees to court in mid-season for breach of contract. The fishers, all Native, had started the season working for him, but appear to have left after a cannery offered better terms. Herring prosecuted his employees under an 1823 English statute, *An Act to enlarge the Powers of Justices in determining Complaints between Masters and Servants*.[163] This act, which consolidated earlier statute and common law, gave justices of the peace the authority, on a complaint from an employer, to issue a warrant for the arrest of variously named tradespeople, hear the particulars of the complaint, and sentence an employee found in breach of the employment contract to up to three months hard labour or order that the employee return to work.

In the first case, *Samuel Herring v. David Bailey*, Herring claimed before Justices of the Peace W.D. Ferris and J. Cunningham that Bailey, identified in the newspaper report as a 'half-breed,' broke a written employment contract for three months' labour at $45 per month.[164] Bailey, he deposed, had received $1.50 in cash and $7 in goods, but then had left after working only ten days to work for another fish-processing operation. Both men were represented: H.V. Edmonds[165] for Herring and W. Norman Bole[166] for Bailey. It appears that cannery operator Henry Holbrook had offered Bailey better terms and it seems likely that Holbrook had hired Bole as Bailey's counsel. Herring conceded under Bole's cross-examination that he had never given a copy of the contract to Bailey and, more generally, that he had many legal disputes with his men. In his submissions, Bole argued that the 1823 statute did not apply because 'fishermen' were not included in the enumerated trades. The justices, however, ruled that the statute applied and that the parties had entered the three-month employment contract described by Herring. They denied his claim, nonetheless, because the defendant was a minor and, they reasoned, not competent to make such a contract.

The next case, *Samuel Herring v. John Browne* was considerably more involved.[167] Justice of the Peace Ferris presided over three days of hearings in mid-July at the height of the fishing season, when everyone involved was losing valuable fishing time. Edmonds represented Herring again, and Bole represented the respondent, Browne. The basis of Herring's complaint was that Browne, 'an Indian,' left his employment as a fisher after working seven and a half days of a three-month contract and collecting $7 in cash and $7.50 in goods. Herring alleged that Browne had gone to work for Holbrook's cannery, and he charged Browne with obtaining money under false pretences and for leaving his employment while under contract. Edmonds elected to proceed on the first charge, obtaining money under false pretences, but it was reserved for a hearing in the Supreme Court. Herring withdrew the second charge, breach of contract, when it became apparent that the court would not allow two offences to be joined in one information or summons. Browne, who had been in custody, was released on bail, but Herring immediately swore another information, alleging that Browne had left his employment while under contract. Browne was arrested again and held in custody overnight.

The following day Bole argued that the court had no jurisdiction to hear the second charge (leaving employment) because it was really the same as the first (obtaining money under false pretences), and the first charge was set for trial at the Supreme Court. Ferris determined that he had jurisdiction to hear the matter, and Browne would remain in custody until court reconvened the following morning.

On the third day, Bole repeated his argument that the act under which the complaint had been brought did not include fishermen. Ferris ruled that 'fishermen' fell within the 'other Person' category and, as he had done with Bailey, proceeded to hear evidence on the nature of the contract, whether its terms had been sufficiently explained to Browne in Chinook (the pidgin language of the fur trade and the workplace), and whether Browne understood when he entered the contract that he might be punished for a breach of its terms. Herring claimed to have explained the contract in Chinook, but when Bole wrote a few sentences in Chinook and asked Herring to read them, Herring replied that he did not know Latin. He also admitted that it was the 'custom of the country' not to have written contracts with Indians, but stood by his testimony that he had provided Browne with a copy of the contract. Mr Howison, apparently the manager of Herring's operation, testified that he only remembered giving an Indian, perhaps it was Browne, $7 worth of goods and did not record any cash advance in his ledger. One witness testified that he had seen Browne sign a contract, but two others swore that no agreement had been read or explained.

Ferris retired for an hour to consider and returned to announce: 'I have given the matter my best attention and I think the man ought to be punished, but I have my doubts upon the point as to whether he is a labourer within the meaning of the act.' He proposed postponing the case until the provincial attorney-general's opinion could be sought. Bole agreed, but Edmonds wanted a decision so that Herring could return to the fishery with his labour force intact. 'I object,' Edmonds argued, 'as the present Government are notoriously slow in all their movements, and we may not have a decision for six weeks, when the fishing season will be over and the good effect of an example lost.' He asked Ferris 'to give the prisoner and the other Indians a caution.' Ferris addressed the defendant, informing him that the courts would enforce contracts: 'If the other Indians who have made agreements with Herring break them they will be punished.' Bole intervened, asking Ferris to limit his comments to the case at hand: '[I]f it goes out that any man going from Herring to any other fishery will be sent to gaol, a serious injury will be inflicted upon Mr. Holbrook and others, as the Indians will think Sam Herring has privileges in court that no one else has.' Unhappy with defence counsel's intervention, and anticipating an appeal whatever the sentence, Ferris sentenced Browne to one month's imprisonment for breach of contract. He was released pending appeal and there is no further record of the case.

The last two fisheries cases of the summer involved Herring as well. In *Samuel Herring v. Harrison River Charlie*, he deposed that the defendant, who was also held in custody before trial, left his employment before the three-month contract had expired, and that he had induced other Indians to breach their contracts. This time Bole acted for Herring and argued, against Charlie's counsel Mr Morrison, that the 1823 statute did indeed apply to fishermen. Ferris concurred and heard the now familiar evidence. Herring testified that Charlie had left his employment before the end of the three-month contract and that he had induced other Indians to do so as well. He admitted to owing Charlie wages, but insisted they would have been paid had Charlie completed the contract. Ferris refused to hear Charlie's testimony on the peculiar grounds that he had legal counsel and therefore could not speak for himself. On the question of remedies, Bole argued that punishing Indians for breach of contract was the only option; it was 'a perfect absurdity' and a waste of time and money to bring Indians to civil court, he suggested, presumably because collection would be very difficult. Ferris convicted the prisoner and sentenced him to three weeks' imprisonment. There is no record that Charlie was released pending appeal. In a case heard the next day, *Samuel Herring v. Paul*, reported to be similar to the previous case, Ferris order the defendant, identified as an Indian, to return to work for Herring.[168]

What conclusions can be drawn from these four master and servant law cases at New Westminster in 1877? The evidence is slim, but nonetheless suggestive, and it coincides with some of the general conclusions about the law of master and servant in other contexts. Douglas Hay's conclusion, for example, that 'the taint of criminality' permeated the entire proceedings in England by the mid-nineteenth century, from arrest to the labelling of the defendant employee as 'the prisoner,' certainly applies.[169] Newspaper accounts describe Herring as the prosecutor and the Native defendants were treated and sentenced as criminals. Their punishment was intended as an example and deterrent; damages for breach of contract were raised, only to be dismissed as a useless remedy. The cases also coincide with Paul Craven and Hay's general finding that in the British Empire, '[t]wo salient characteristics of master and servant law were a liberal use of penal sanctions for breach by the worker and summary enforcement before lay magistrates and cognate officials.'[170] The justices had no legal training and newspaper editorials repeatedly decried the quality of justice dispensed in the police courts that year.[171]

More generally, these cases reinforce the work of labour historians who, arguing against representations of Natives as largely irrelevant after the fur trade, have suggested that Native labour was an integral component of the early canning industry in British Columbia.[172] These cases appear to be as much about competition between fish processors for labour as they were disputes between employers and employees.

The *Mainland Guardian* ran a series on the New Westminster canneries that summer and the reports reveal an extensive and segregated workforce. Natives and whites fished; Natives and Chinese men cleaned fish, although not together; and Chinese men worked in the canneries under white supervisors. English & Co., for example, the largest cannery on the Fraser in 1877, employed fifty men and women, 'mostly Indians,' to clean and trim the salmon in sheds near the landing dock; 250 Chinese men worked inside the cannery, supervised by fifty white men.[173] The operation relied on ninety fishers to supply the salmon.[174] At Finlayson & Lane, 100 Chinese men, 'aided and superintended by about fifty white men,' worked in the cannery; 'about seventy-five white men and Indians engaged especially in fishing.'[175]

It is possible, furthermore, that a few key prosecutions might, over the short term, keep a Native labour force intact. Anthropologist Philip Drucker suggests that canners hired 'Indian bosses,' prominent Natives, often young chiefs, who spoke English or Chinook and had influence among their people, to act as recruiters for the cannery.[176] Through these Indian bosses the canners would try to secure the services of the skilled and knowledgeable Native fishers who, even in the 1870s, were in short supply. Herring may have been trying to compel one such boss and the fishers he recruited to remain working for the saltery when he prosecuted Harrison River Charlie for breach of contract and for inducing other Native fishers to breach their contracts.

These cases also reveal that Herring was a litigious fellow, at odds with both his employees and with the other fish processors. A letter to the *Mainland Guardian* in September 1877 suggests some of the local feeling about Herring's attempts to secure Native labour. 'An American citizen,' the author wrote of Herring, 'is fishing on our river; he has got several Indians to put their mark to a printed paper, which he purports to be an agreement for them to work for him at wages, generally under the current rate, for three months, at so much per month. The Indians finding no money forthcoming to pay their wages or make settlement with them, refuse to work; they are then, on this party's complaint, brought up as prisoners under warrant, and on Monday last one was committed to jail for three weeks.' Would the government act to prevent such abuse of Indians by foreigners, the author asked, before there was bloodshed?[177] The author of the letter is not identified, but it may well have been Henry Holbrook, Herring's principal adversary in these cases. Holbrook appears to have been somewhat unusual among cannery operators and the settler society in general for his concern about the Native population in British Columbia. During the confederation debates he had argued in the Legislative Council for a clause in the terms of union with Canada to protect the Native population. He was cautioned and then reprimanded by fellow council members for raising a motion that could foment unrest among Indians, and his motion was defeated twenty votes to one.[178] Although Herring was the American, it appears that Holbrook's sentiments were the more unusual, for it was Canadian courts that were imprisoning Natives for breach of contract or requiring that they complete their contracts. The blame for this could not fall on a maverick American for whom the law was a willing accomplice.

Perhaps most importantly, these cases reveal an imposed legal system beginning to delimit a role for Natives in the fishery even if the specific legislation designed to regulate the industry was not yet enforced. The exchange between Native fisher and non-Native processor, once described as trade, now more closely resembled an employment relationship. Although the state was not regulating the fishery through its fisheries law, the law of master and servant applied and could be enforced by individuals through the courts and jails. Natives were welcome participants in the industrial commercial fishery – their labour in these early years was essential – but on terms that were enforceable in the Canadian criminal courts. This is a significant change, and one insufficiently noted by labour historians studying the role of Native people in the wage economy. Although the cases are few, the participants believed they were establishing important precedents, defining the role of labour, particularly Native labour, in relation to capital. The cases are insufficient to sustain a claim that the law of master and servant was an important element in the dispossession of the Native fishery. Even the symbolic effects of these cases likely dissipated within a season. Nonetheless, these few cases mark a fundamental shift in the control of the fisheries from Natives to Anglo-Canadian and American-based capital. Those who had been owners, or who had defined access to a fisheries commons, became employees subject to the statutes and common law that defined a relationship between master and servant. When labour historian John Lutz, building on the influential work of Rolf Knight, argues that '[t]wenty-five years after the gold rush, aboriginal people had not been marginalized – rather they remained at the centre of a transformed, capitalist, economic activity,' he underemphasizes this fundamental change.[179] Natives did provide essential labour, and in that sense were at the centre of a transforming economy, but increasingly their labour was all they owned. Their connection to the fishery had been transformed from ownership to a right to 'lucrative employment' in the industrial fishery, as Minister of Fisheries L.P. Brodeur would describe it in the aftermath of the dispute over fish weirs on the Babine River in 1906 (see the discussion in the following chapter). The resources that Natives once controlled, including fish, were confiscated by the state for capital, and the law of master and servant was one of the means by which this was achieved before fisheries regulations were in place.

Increasing Surveillance, 1878–1887

Fisheries had agreed that the *Fisheries Act* and *Regulations* would not apply to Native fishers, at least when they were not fishing for the canneries in competition with whites. Nonetheless, the department did intend to gain control over the fishing industry. It directed Anderson to appoint an officer, and he hired George Pittendrigh in 1878 to patrol the Fraser and all its tributaries below Yale, as well as Burrard Inlet and all its tributaries.[180] Pittendrigh was responsible for the lower 150 kilometres of the Fraser drainage basin and for the extensive watershed of Burrard Inlet, a huge territory for one man to patrol in a rowboat, but not as impossible a task as it now sounds. Although one cannery at New Westminster (King & Co.) had a steamer to haul its fish boats to the fishing grounds, in 1878 fish were caught from boats powered by paddle, oar, and sail. Furthermore, the salmon-processing operations were relatively concentrated; Pittendrigh was responsible for six canneries and three salting operations at New Westminster and two canneries near the mouth of the Fraser on the south arm.[181] Such concentration eased the job of managing the industrial fishery, but enforcement was light. Pittendrigh levied several moderate fines for violations, hardly a clampdown, but enough of a presence to prevent a repeat of the ruckus in 1877.

In 1879 Fisheries took a large step, at least on paper, towards controlling the salmon fishery. The Dominion adopted a nation-wide regulation that prohibited fishing for salmon, except under the authority of a lease or licence from the Department of Marine and Fisheries.[182] The regulation did not specify a licence fee, and initially the licensing provision appears to have been ignored in British Columbia. However, in 1881 Anderson wrote to the minister, recommending that Fisheries establish a licensing scheme to control the fishing practices of the twelve operating canneries. By 1882 there were twenty canneries in British Columbia, thirteen on the Fraser alone, and Anderson reported that the licensing scheme he had been authorized to implement 'worked very effectively.'[183] It also provided Fisheries with its first revenue from the BC fishery – $672.50.[184] The following year Pittendrigh posted a 'Notice to Fishermen!' in New Westminster's *Mainland Guardian*, reminding them that they must renew their licences before the start of the 1883 season.[185]

Cannery owners wanted state involvement to protect their interests. At least one cannery owner, John Deas, had applied to Fisheries for an exclusive lease on salmon drifts near his operation in 1877, but Anderson had refused the request '[i]n view of the complications connected with existing Indian rights.'[186] The provincial legislature also passed a resolution requesting that the Dominion 'not grant exclusive rights to fish for salmon in the waters of British Columbia.'[187] It was not concerned with the Native fishery, but rather with 'preventing a great injustice to the fishing interests,' meaning the canneries. If concern about Native rights or cannery access ruled out exclusive leases, the established cannery owners suggested that the Dominion limit competition by restricting the number of licences. Concerned that Anderson was issuing licences too freely, the British Columbia Board of Trade produced a report in 1882 that warned of the dangers of over-fishing.[188] The following year it passed a resolution questioning the inspector's discretionary power to issue licences.[189] The cannery owners wanted to restrict the number of licences to protect the fish stocks, and also their fishing grounds from new competitors. The board proposed that a committee of three – the Inspector of Fisheries, the 'Indian Commissioner' (probably the senior Indian Affairs official in the province, the Indian Superintendent), and a third person selected by the Board of Trade – 'should have the power of determining the fishery limits of each river or other fishing place in this province and of regulating the number of licenses to be issued.'[190] The canneries were attempting, through a state-controlled licensing scheme that was ostensibly meant to conserve salmon stocks, to monopolize commercial fishing on the Fraser. Aware of Native interests, the canners proposed that a Dominion official represent those interests; they were, in 1883, prepared to include a Native food and inter-tribal fishery in their effort to exclude others.[191] Anderson, however, was opposed, and limited licences would not be introduced on the Fraser until 1889.

Although generally unregulated during Anderson's tenure, the Native fishery did receive some attention. When Natives were using modern technology and selling to the canneries in competition with non-Native fishers, Anderson enforced the *Fisheries Act* and instructed his officers to do likewise: '[W]here fishing with white men and with modern appliances, the Indians so fishing should be considered as coming in all respects under the general law.'[192]

In 1881, in one of the earliest if not the first instance of direct action against a Native fishery, Anderson investigated a report from Guardian Pittendrigh that Natives, fishing above the tidal water on a tributary of the Fraser, were selling their catch to a cannery on the coast. The fishery was illegal, but it would almost certainly have been left alone were it not that Native people were selling to a cannery that was in competition with other canneries that were purchasing fish from non-Native fishers who were prohibited from fishing in non-tidal waters. To allow a commercial Native fishery in non-tidal waters, and prohibit a similar non-Native fishery, seemed to Anderson an abuse of 'Indian privilege.' He was also concerned that the fish were unfit for canning and that if they reached market they would impugn the reputation of Fraser sockeye, but that seems the secondary concern. The relevant passage of Anderson's report is reproduced below, and it marks an important turning point in fisheries policy:

Indian fishermen, fishing above tide-water with their own appliances, had been encouraged by several of the canneries to bring salmon down for sale, for canning purposes. On the report of Mr. Pittendreigh [*sic*], I went to New Westminster, early in October, and after enquiry the practice was interdicted. A wide field for abuse was being opened, both in regard to the Indian privilege and the maintenance of the character of the River brands; since the fish thus procured in a stale condition were not fit for canning.[193]

In closing the Native fishery, Anderson referred not to a *right*, but to a *privilege*, to describe the Native entitlement to a fishery. In an earlier letter, Anderson had used 'hereditary right' and 'hereditary privilege' interchangeably, suggesting that he was not fully aware of the distinction.[194] This time, however, his intention was clear: the Native fishery had to be curtailed because the Indians were abusing their *privilege* by selling fish.

The distinction between a right and a privilege is important. Privileges have a long constitutional history in Britain, particularly in reference to the privileges of Parliament, and in certain contexts they can amount to a claim as strong as a rights claim. However, English dictionaries of the late nineteenth and early twentieth centuries suggest a fundamental distinction between the two words. A right is a 'just claim'[195] or a 'justifiable claim, on legal or moral grounds, to have or obtain something, or to act in a certain way.'[196] A privilege, by one definition, is 'a right, advantage, or immunity *granted* to or enjoyed by a person, or a body or class of persons, beyond the common advantages of others.'[197] A privilege, therefore, is granted or invested by something or somebody else; it is not rooted, as a right, in a moral or legal claim. Although it has value and may, in some cases, be rigorously upheld or defended, a privilege suggests a discretionary benefit that may be removed by the one who has conferred it. By using the word privilege, Anderson suggested that any special claim Native people had to the fishery came to them by virtue of a Crown grant. Native fishing entitlements could be traced to the Crown, and not to any moral or legal foundation inherent to Native peoples. Thus, despite his stated belief that Native people were entitled to legal recognition of their fishery, in this case Anderson thought he was curtailing a privilege, something he could do at his discretion and without compensation, and not interfering with a right.[198] It represented a marked change in his policy towards the Native fishery. Both Anderson's actions and choice of words suggest that regulating the Native sale of fish to the canneries was an important first step towards confining it, eventually, to a food fishery.

Historian Ruben Ware has described the early enforcement of fisheries laws against Native fishers as 'arbitrary,'[199] and it is difficult, given Anderson's unfettered discretion, to describe the early regime as subject to the rule of law, understood as a set of rules based on broadly known principles and enforced predictably. However, there was method to Anderson's regulation of the Native fishery. An old fur trader, Anderson was cut from the same cloth as James Douglas, and his changing approach to the Native fishery, followed by the change in Fisheries' policy after his death in 1884, paralleled a change in Douglas's land policy and then in the approach adopted by his successors.

Much has been written about the colonial land policy under Governor Douglas, and of the change that occurred when Joseph Trutch assumed responsibility for land as Provincial Commissioner of Lands.[200] Douglas had formally recognized a burden on Crown sovereignty in the 1850s by purchasing land from Native peoples on southern Vancouver Island. The Crown made no further purchases to extinguish title thereafter, and a recognition of Native title disappeared as colonial policy in British Columbia. Nonetheless, Douglas adopted a relatively generous although entirely discretionary policy of reserve grants: Native peoples were to have their villages, burial grounds, important resource procurement sites, and other lands they deemed necessary. Reserve allocations, however generous under Douglas, were based on perceptions of need, not on negotiated settlements to extinguish Native title. Furthermore, few of these reserve grants were officially recorded, and the discretionary nature of the policy made it relatively easy to change when Douglas left. When Trutch became Commissioner of Lands in 1864 he ignored the issue of Native title, and exercised his discretion to ignore or in some cases reduce existing reserves, and to minimize future grants. Anderson's discretionary approach towards the Native fishery, increasingly based on Native *privileges* rather than *rights*, continued for a few years after his death, but on terms less favourable to Natives. Confining the Native fishery to a food fishery, a process that had begun under Anderson, gathered speed.

When Anderson died in 1884 (after a short illness precipitated by exposure during an unexpected night on a patrol ship) he was replaced as Inspector of Fisheries by Pittendrigh, the guardian for the lower Fraser. Both the yield and market price for salmon were relatively poor that year and even worse in 1885, especially for what should have been a dominant year for Fraser sockeye. Only six canneries operated on the south coast that year, only nine on the entire coast, down from twenty-four in 1883 and seventeen in 1884. While Anderson had defended the Native fishery from charges of waste, Pittendrigh attacked it, blaming declining stock on Native consumption of young salmon: '[E]ven when spared from these perils [natural hazards for salmon spawn such as floods, dry spawning beds, and predators] the instant it is hatched, the fish is exposed to new dangers, more especially in the fry state, becoming easy prey of the Indians who, if not closely watched, capture them in buckets full, and make them, with vegetables added, into soup.'[201] While Native people were undoubtedly catching salmon fry, the charge that they were damaging the salmon stock by using fry to make soup is incredible given the enormous number of mature fish that had been caught in preceding years by the cannery boats.

Pittendrigh's tenure as Inspector of Fisheries lasted only until 1886, but it marked a distinct change in fisheries policy towards Native people. Anderson had shielded the Native fishery from direct attack by the cannery owners, intervening only when Natives were fishing in direct competition with whites. Pittendrigh and the inspectors who followed were openly hostile to any Native fishery, and pushed it to the margins of the industry, first by confining it to a food fishery and then by restricting the food fishery. Pittendrigh, for example, wanted to place local fisheries officers on the Cowichan and Nanaimo rivers on Vancouver Island to remove the Native fish weirs that Anderson had considered innocuous. Nonetheless, state regulation in these early years was sporadic at best. When he assumed the responsibilities of fisheries inspector for the province, Pittendrigh was also a justice of the peace in the New Westminster Police Court and spent much of his time, even during the fishing season, conducting trials unrelated to the fishery. Before 1885, state regulation on the Fraser was minimal, and almost non-existent elsewhere. Anderson had made several trips up the north coast, accompanying Indian Superintendent Powell to inspect fishing stations and canneries in 1879 and 1881, but Fisheries was not a regular presence on the fishing grounds.

This would soon change, and the subsequent expansion of Fisheries surveillance was driven, in large part, by the desire to control and restrict Native freshwater fisheries. In 1885, Fisheries hired a 'fisheries guardian' to patrol the Skeena River from Port Essington. The following year Thomas Mowat, previously the manager of the Bon Accord fish hatchery at New Westminster, replaced Pittendrigh as the Inspector of Fisheries, and he hired guardians for the Cowichan, Nanaimo, Comox, Alberni, and Sooke rivers and at Shawnigan and Sooke lakes, all on Vancouver Island. The ostensible purpose of these appointments was to manage the Native weir fisheries, and at the end of the season the guardians on the first four rivers reported that the weirs had been opened to allow fish through during the weekly close times of the commercial fishery. On the mainland, Mowat divided the lower Fraser between two guardians – one responsible for the lower reaches near its mouth, the other for the river below Yale. To justify these appointments, Mowat weighed various explanations for the continuing salmon shortfall, including fluctuating water levels in spawning beds and the cyclical nature of the salmon, and concluded that to stop the excessive catch in the estuaries by the cannery boats and Native fishing in the headwaters was 'the most plausible solution to the difficulty.'[202] Nonnative fishing was 'excessive' and needed to be regulated, but the Native weir and other inland fisheries, whether for food or sale, needed to be stopped.

Native Fisheries Law

Although Canadian fisheries law was descending around the Native fisheries, the historical record is replete with examples of the Native regulation that had managed the resource and that was transforming to meet new opportunities and to contest the imposition of state law. The Native sense of ownership did not diminish with the arrival of a settler society, and on some parts of the coast Natives demanded recognition and payment for the use of prominent resource sites. Methodist Missionary A.E. Green, who arrived at Port Simpson at the mouth of the Nass in 1877, remarked on the Coast Tsimpsean claims to the land and sea, and on the arrangements made with white immigrants: 'Every mountain, every valley, every stream was named, and every piece belong to some particular family. This claim was recognized by all the white men, viz. Harvey Snow, James Grey, J.J. Robinson, who rented small sites from the Indians for fishing purposes, and paid the Indians regular rent for the same.'[203] This arrangement appears to have ended when the immigrants applied for and received land grants from the province in 1880. It only marked the beginning, however, of the struggle between Natives and a settler society for control of the fishery.

In 1887, John McNab, guardian on the Skeena and Nass rivers, reported that the existing licensing scheme was not working in the northern region. Cannery salmon were caught 'almost exclusively' by Natives, he reported, and although some of their boats were licensed, a good portion of the catch was transferred to these boats from unlicensed boats, and then delivered to the canneries as though caught under licence.[204] Inspector of Fisheries Mowat believed that some of the canneries wilfully ignored this practice, and suggested that this fostered discontent among Natives when the guardians attempted to enforce the law. By circumventing the law, he argued, the canneries encouraged Natives to think they had a right to sell fish without a licence. Although the 1879 regulation requiring a licence to fish for salmon had been adopted by Anderson on the Fraser in 1882, there had been little enforcement on the Northwest Coast. When the guardians attempted to enforce the licence requirement in 1888, they met strong resistance from Native fishers. Informed that the Tsimpsean and Gitksan on the Skeena were refusing to purchase licences, Mowat went to investigate at the end of the 1888 fishing season.

The Gitksan at Hazelton questioned him about the fisheries laws, about licences and, about who received the licence money. They stated emphatically that they would not purchase licences and, further, that they would continue to fish as they were accustomed. Gitksan laws divided land, including hunting and fishing grounds, between clans. Other people might be allowed to use those lands, but only with the permission of the clan chief and in the company of members of the clan who owned the lands. Ownership, furthermore, was not divisible:

> One of the strictest laws is that no hunting-ground can ever be cut in half and given to anyone. No one is allowed to make any such hunting-ground smaller or larger, even if they own or have power over it. This also applies to all fishing-grounds and all natural resources in and under the ground. This law is so severe and powerful that no one from another clan or without clan rights can come to hunt, fish, mine, cut timber, or do any other thing on these lands without the consent of the head chief and his council.
>
> These laws go back thousands of years and have been handed down from one generation to another, and they must be held and protected at all costs by the people owning these lands. These laws are the constitutional laws, going back many thousands of years and are in full force to-day and forever.[205]

Unable to compel Native fishers to buy licences, Mowat attempted to enforce the licensing scheme through the canneries. He informed the cannery operators that if they purchased fish from unlicensed Native fishers, then they must purchase the necessary licences. Fish had to be caught under licence, even if canneries purchased the licences when Native fishers refused. However, as Mowat told the minister, the only way to enforce the regulations and stop the illegal fishery was to send a 'sufficient force of guardians or a small armed cruiser to seize all nets, boats and canoes which do not comply with the regulations.'[206]

McNab encountered similar difficulties on the Nass. In the middle of the 1888 season he met with the Nisga'a at Kincolith, at their request. They asserted ownership of the river in their territory, and rejected any attempt by the Dominion to assert its jurisdiction, particularly the efforts of Fisheries to collect licence fees. Furthermore, they refused to buy licences and insisted that any licence fees collected from non-Native fishers belonged to them. In fact, by sending its officers to collect licence fees, the Dominion had violated hereditary laws. The Nass was not an open-access fishery; it was owned by powerful families who rejected the Dominion's competing claim. McNab reported:

> They asked me many questions about the law in regard to catching salmon of the Naas River; wanted to know exactly how much money I had collected this year, and what I had done with it. After being satisfied on these points, the chief very gravely informed me that I had done very wrong in collecting money for fishing on the Naas, without having asked permission from him, that the river belonged to him and to his people, that it was right that white men should buy licenses, but that he and his people should receive the money, that they were entitled to it all; but that as I had been sent to collect it, they were willing that I should retain half for my trouble. After consultation amongst themselves, I was told that they had intended to demand half the money collected this year, but would let it pass until next year, and charge me to inform the Government to that effect.[207]

This is as powerful a Native voice asserting ownership of the fisheries as one finds in the historical record. As far as the Nisga'a were concerned, human use of the Nass River was subject to their laws, not Dominion law. The fishery was theirs to allocate; the Dominion had no authority to issue licences. The decision to allow McNab to keep half of the licence fees he had collected was, perhaps, less recognition of Dominion sovereignty than a reflection of the practice that allowed Fisheries officers to keep half of the fines levied for *Fisheries Act* offences. The Dominion, on the other hand, assumed sovereignty, dismissing the need to negotiate access or jurisdiction.[208]

These strong declarations of ownership were accompanied by continuing attempts to manage the fishery. In 1857, one year before a gold rush lured twenty thousand American miners north from San Francisco to the Fraser, Douglas noted the Native claims to own gold and other precious metals and that they had 'a well-founded impression that the shoals of salmon which annually ascend those rivers and furnish the principal food of the inhabitants will be driven off and prevented from making their annual migration from the sea.'[209] Twenty years later, to counteract the increasingly strident complaints from the canneries about the Native fishery, Anderson sent Fisheries a deposition from Mr Antoine Gregoire, identified as an interpreter from Kamloops and Adam's Lake. Gregoire refuted the charges that Native people destroyed spawn and fry, in so doing providing a glimpse of the web of Native regulation that surrounded the resource. Natives understood the importance of spawning beds and had rules, introduced to members of the community at an early age, to protect salmon reproduction:

> Antoine requests Mr Anderson to add that, so careful of the salmon are the Chiefs, they will not permit the Indians to use the pole to propel canoes in passing over the spawning shoals, after the spawn is deposited, but paddle only. Also, that in the spring, when the children sometimes seek to amuse themselves by making mimic weirs to entrap young fish, they are at once made to desist by their parents. In brief, he says that he believes firmly that the Indians act most prudently with regard to the salmon, and do all in their power to protect them.[210]

Moreover, Natives blamed the cannery boats fishing at the coast for the diminishing salmon runs. As early as 1878, Sproat reported Native 'apprehension as to the effect of the fishing carried on by the canneries at the mouth of the Fraser in diminishing the salmon in the Fraser and its tributaries.'[211] In 1879, at a remarkable meeting in Lytton at the confluence of the Fraser and Thompson rivers, the Nlha7kápmx (Thompson) elected a head chief and council, and passed a series of bylaws in an attempt to create a limited form of self-government that the Queen and her representatives in Ottawa and Victoria would recognize.[212] The bylaws included the following stricture on fishing: '(19) No person is permitted to take fish Roe, or to place fish traps entirely across the stream.'[213] They were prepared to limit their fishery, and expected the same from the cannery boats. Ten years later, however, interior groups were still blaming the canneries for preventing the fish from reaching their spawning grounds.[214] Similar complaints came from groups on the north coast. Shortly after the canneries arrived on the Nass, the people of the upper river grew alarmed at the salmon shortages: 'The Chiefs attribute the present scarcity of salmon to the fact of the fishing operations of Messrs. Croasdaile & Green, Wellwood & Co. intercepting the runs.'[215] In 1907, this remarkable statement from rOi.pellet (Blazing-stone), a Nlha7kápmx from the Cook's Ferry Band who lived in the interior at the confluence of the Nicola and Thompson rivers:

> I, from my boyhood, and my forefathers from time out of mind, have every Fall erected a weir across the Nicola River (about half a mile above the mouth) for the purpose of catching Hump-back salmon. This has never resulted in the diminution (or extinction) of these fish which have come in considerable numbers every year. The Indians all know it is not by Indians fishing, or by Indian methods of capture, that other varieties of salmon have of late years decreased in numbers. I understand the Whites have passed a law prohibiting the use of dams or weirs for catching fish. If they are to prohibit me from fishing (which is my only means of livelihood) in the only way I know how, they must support me. If they take food from me they must give me other food in place of it. I have been law-abiding all my life and I do not want to break the law now, but I must live. I intend to erect my weir this Fall, and every Fall the same as usual. It is not my intention to dam the stream entirely, and thus stop the fish from ascending to my Indian friends above, and to the spawning grounds. I will open my weir part of every day and whenever I am not using it, so as to let the fish up. It is my intention to catch what few salmon I require for the use of myself and family – This only and no more. I intend to dry a number of these fish for winter food if I can get them. I do not sell any.[216]

Natives in the interior knew the life cycle of salmon, and that overfishing could have disastrous consequences. The imbalance of power was such, however, that the rules that held meaning in Native society and that had effectively managed the resource, could not be imposed on the canneries.

Fishery Regulations, 1888

While its officers were attempting with mixed success to enforce Dominion fisheries law in the field, the Fisheries Branch in Ottawa was preparing new regulations. In November 1888, it rescinded the regulations of 1878 and replaced them with a more comprehensive set for British Columbia that, for the first time, specifically addressed the Native fishery. There were three significant additions: fishers were required to register their equipment and intended fishing location; Fisheries could limit the number of boats in a region; and under certain circumstances, Indians were not required to hold a license:

> 1. Fishing by means of nets or other apparatus without leases or licences from the Minister of Marine and Fisheries is prohibited in all waters of the Province of British Columbia;
>
> Provided always that Indians shall, at all times, have liberty to fish for the purpose of providing food for themselves but not for sale, barter or traffic, by any means other than with drift nets, or spearing.[217]

The wording of this section was ambiguous; it was unclear whether Indians were free to catch fish for food, except by drift net or spear, but were not allowed to sell fish without a licence, or whether they could catch fish for food by any means, and sell fish caught by drift net or spear without a licence. The intention was certainly the former – Natives were not to sell fish without a licence – and Fisheries clarified this when the regulations were amended in 1894.[218] The corollary of excluding the Native food fishing from the licensing requirement, however, was that any fishing by Natives for sale must be under licence. That had been the law since the licensing requirement was introduced in 1879, but it had not been enforced in much of the province, and many had argued that some or all Native fisheries were exempt. By explicitly exempting a Native food fishery, however, it was clear, in law, that Native commercial fishers had to hold a Dominion licence and abide by a set of rules that regulated the mesh size of nets, confined drift nets to tidal waters and prohibited nets in fresh waters, restricted nets to no more than one-third the width of a river, extended the fishing closure from 6 a.m. Saturday to 6 a.m. Monday, and required fishers to register their fishing boats and identify their boats and nets. The final clause of the 1888 regulations enabled the minister to limit the number of fish boats.

The food fishery was a construct: an artificial distinction with no historic or traditional roots. Ware labelled it a 'distortion,' and Newell described it as 'inventing the Indian fishery.'[219] Both descriptions are apt. Native people had caught fish for food, but also for trade and sale to other Native groups and later to non-Native traders and settlers. These new arrivals created new markets, and their technology designed to catch and process fish made new fisheries possible. These factors, combined with access to capital, meant that immigrants would participate in the fisheries. It was with law, however, that Anglo-Canadians defined the terms on which Natives would participate. The laws that governed the commercial fisheries were apparently neutral. Anyone could fish, acquire a licence or open a cannery (as did the Tsimpsean at Metlakatla). But the prior question of ownership had been shunted aside. Instead of negotiating access to a valued and owned resource, the Canadian state assumed access for all British subjects and reduced prior Native claims of ownership to a tenuous claim to a food fishery. The Native fishery had been a source of wealth, not just of sustenance, and confining it to a local food fishery was a means of reallocating the resource to the canneries.

Armed with the new regulations, Guardian McNab returned to the Nass in 1889 and seized three boats belonging to Natives who were fishing for the canneries without a licence. McNab reported that the Natives reacted strongly, with 'a great deal of loud and threatening talk.' Nevertheless, after several days they agreed to apply for licences. With licence applications in hand, McNab released the boats without collecting a fine. To do so, he reported, would have required 'a large special force,' but even without imposing a fine he believe the point had been gained.[220] Thus, by 1889 Native people around the province who were fishing to supply canneries found themselves subject to Dominion fishery regulations that Fisheries was actively enforcing. Native willingness to comply with the licensing scheme varied. Despite initial reticence, some northern Natives were prepared to purchase licences. The guardian on the Skeena reported that when he arrived two weeks into the 1889 season, Natives sought him out with their licence fees and requests for licences.[221] However, while some Natives on the Skeena were buying licences, McNab reported that those on the Nass 'adhere very tenaciously to what they consider their privileges.'[222] The issue of licensing flared again in 1891 when Fisheries proposed to raise the licence fee to $20. The increase provoked Natives to complain not only about the increasing costs, but also about the injustice of paying a fee to the Crown for their own fish.[223] The following year, the guardian on the Skeena reported that Native fishers bought licences from him when he arrived shortly after the beginning of the season. Over the course of the season he levied and collected two fines, both against Natives for fishing during a closing.[224] Other regulations provoked Native objections. When, in 1893, the guardian at Rivers Inlet attempted to enforce the regulation prohibiting fishing above the tidal boundary in the territory of the Owekeeno, he met with considerable Native resistance. 'They have the idea,' he reported, 'that because they cannot fish as high up the river as they please, their rights are being encroached on; and although they came down when ordered, yet they were saucy and slow to do so.'[225]

The regulations prohibited any sale of salmon without a licence, but despite increasing enforcement, there were still some commercial Native fisheries for which the Dominion did not press the licensing requirement. Fisheries did not pursue Natives who were trading or selling fish to other Natives for their consumption, nor did it prosecute those Natives, particularly the elderly, who peddled fish locally without a licence.[226] Sales to HBC posts in the interior such as Fort Babine also appear to have been ignored. Generally, the licensing requirement was only enforced if Natives were selling to the canneries, or were in competition with non-Native fishers, but even this was changing. In 1891, Indian Superintendent A.W. Vowell reported dissatisfaction among the Natives of the BC coast 'on account of the restrictions placed upon them as regards the taking of salmon with spoon or herring bait and offering the same, to a very limited number, for sale.'[227] He suggested that the licence fee, if enforced against Natives catching fish for local fresh markets, should be set as low as possible. Fisheries responded by announcing a permit policy that allowed Natives to 'troll for salmon in the bays and sea shores of British Columbia; but not in the estuaries or fluvial portions of rivers,' and to sell their catch for a licence fee of $1 instead of the $5 fee charged to independent commercial fishers.[228] Following the common pattern of informal exemptions for Natives from general regulations, this policy was introduced unofficially, without any change to the regulations, by letter between government departments.

Although Fisheries was increasingly vigilant, its lack of personnel and equipment and the size of the territory it had to patrol meant that its surveillance was sporadic. In 1887, the Fraser, the most heavily regulated river in the province, was patrolled by two guardians in row boats. One of them suggested that 'to protect the 70 miles of fishing ground is more than two in row boats can do efficiently,' and he requested a steamer.[229] Mowat reported the obvious: 'New regulations for salmon and trout fishing have been adopted for this province; but so far as their being carried into active operation is concerned, the matter rests entirely with the Department as to the number of guardians to be employed for their proper enforcement.'[230]

The need for a power launch on the Fraser became particularly apparent in 1889 when Fisheries instituted its most invasive regulation of the fishery. The 1888 regulations enabled Fisheries to limit the number of fish boats, and in 1889 it acted, limiting the licences on the Fraser River to 450. Of these, 350 went to cannery-owned boats and the remaining 100 to independent fishers. The following year, after pressure from independent fishers, Fisheries increased the quota to 500, allowing for 150 independently held licences.[231] The cannery licences, allotted on the basis of past pack size, cost $20 for each of the first 20 licences and $50 for every one thereafter. Independent fishers could hold only one licence each, costing $5. The experiment lasted for three years. In 1892 the limit was removed, and in 1894 the new regulations confirmed that '*bona fide* fisherman, being British subjects and actual residents of the province,' was entitled to a commercial licence for a fee of $10.[232] The guardians on the Fraser received their steam launch in 1890.

By 1893 the number of guardians assigned to patrol the fisheries had risen to fourteen, and the Fisheries 'General Service' budget for British Columbia was almost $5500.[233] There were four guardians on the Fraser River, two each on the Skeena and the Nass rivers, one on each of the Courtney and Cowichan rivers, one shared between Victoria and Esquimault, and one at each of Rivers Inlet, Burrard Inlet, and Mud Bay. In addition, special guardians were appointed occasionally to help enforce close seasons.[234]

Fishery Regulations, 1894

In 1890, Peter O'Reilly, the Indian Reserve Commissioner, was in the north, allocating reserves along the Skeena and Nass rivers. In several places, including Reserve no. 16 Tal-a haat on the Nass, he intended to secure Native fishing in waters adjacent to the reserve. Indian Affairs wrote to Fisheries asking that it not issue licences to non-Native fishers in areas adjacent to the reserves. Fisheries, in turn, asked the Department of Justice ('Justice') for an opinion on whether O'Reilly had acted within his powers. The deputy minister replied that the reserve commissioner did not have authority to grant exclusive fisheries for Indians, but that it remained for Fisheries 'to consider whether or not you might under the provisions of the "Fisheries Act," reserve from licensing to white settlers, and set apart for the use of Indians in question that part of the river which, evidently the Indian Reserve Commission wishes to have allotted to the Naas River Indians.'[235] Fisheries had authority under the *Fisheries Act* to reserve exclusive fisheries, but it refused to consider O'Reilly's recommendations and Indian Affairs' requests. It simply maintained that the reserve commissioner had no authority to grant exclusive fisheries.

Later that year, Fisheries Guardian M.K. Morrison reported that the Kitkatla who believed O'Reilly had guaranteed them their fishery, were threatening to cut cannery boat nets at Lowe's Inlet if they persisted in fishing. Chief Shukes had told Morrison:

> Judge O'Reilly gave this land and water to my people, I do not want any Whitemen to fish here please tell your chief I have fished at Low's Inlet for 8 years, it is the principal support of myself and people, I do not want to make trouble, but will do my best to hold the exclusive right for myself and people to fish this Low Inlet water, I want a paper from you Chief giving me power to do so if I cannot hold the exclusive right please tell your Chief to send me a letter to that effect – you keep the letter for me, at Essington and read it to me when it comes, I will pay my license when you come for it.[236]

Morrison also reported that Kitkatla on Banks Island had threatened to shoot anybody who lowered a net into their waters. Not wanting to provoke further a violent confrontation, the Lowe's Inlet Canning Company purchased fish directly from Native fishers, in doing so paying more than it would have paid employees to catch the fish, and shipped 6000 cases of salmon.[237] The issue was not access, but cost and who should profit from the export of salmon. The cannery operators presumed the fishery was an open-access resource, and therefore that they need only pay Natives for their labour. In this they had the support of Fisheries. Native people, by contrast, believed they owned the salmon, and wanted compensation for their resource and for their labour. Indian Affairs asked that the company discontinue its operations 'in the interests of the Indians,' but it was the lack of control over the resource rather than the cannery that was the problem. If Natives controlled their fisheries, then they could sell to a cannery or not, and the cannery would remain or move depending on the price of fish.

Charles Tupper, the Minister of Fisheries from 1888 to 1894, believed that existing 'friction' between Natives and canneries would disappear if the Indian agents and the reserve commissioner stopped informing Natives that they had rights to fish.[238] Indian Affairs, on the other hand, thought it reasonable that fisheries adjacent to reserves should be protected and that O'Reilly should continue to recommend exclusive fisheries if he thought it appropriate.[239] Based on his recommendations, Fisheries could then decide if exclusive fisheries were warranted. Tupper responded strongly. Indians had the right to fish for food, without licence, at any time; this was protected in law. If they wanted to compete with non-Native fishers by selling fish to canneries, they must do so under Dominion licence and abide by the other legal requirements in the *Fisheries Act* – 'Any other course would be unfair.'[240] If O'Reilly continued to recommend exclusive fisheries, leading Native people to believe that 'they are a privileged race, quite above the law and regulations, as regards fisheries matters,' then his Fisheries officers would be unable to enforce a law that applied equally to Native and non-Native fishers. 'I am therefore to request,' he wrote, 'that you will be good enough to cause Judge O'Reilly and the other Indian Agents in British Columbia to be instructed that they must use all their influence to make Indians under their supervision understand that in extending to them the valuable privilege they now enjoy of taking fish for their own use, whenever and howsoever they choose, such permission is not to be considered as a right, but as *an act of grace*, which may be withdrawn at any time, should it be found that it is abused or used for other purposes than those for which it is granted, or in such a manner as to embarrass the action of this Department and interfere with its officers, in the performance of their duties.'[241] The Minister of the Interior did not press the issue further.[242]

Tupper's position – that the state bestowed upon Indians a food fishery as an *act of grace* – marked the culmination of Fisheries' attempt to colonize a resource. Anderson, in the 1870s, had advocated strongly that the Dominion recognize a legal right to a Native fishery. By the end of his tenure he had begun to see the Native sale of fish as a privilege rather than a right. This was the predominant view through the 1880s, and was reflected in the regulations requiring licences for the commercial fishery. Only the Native food fishery was exempt. However, by the 1890s Fisheries began to view the Native food fishery as a privilege as well. The notion that Natives had a claim to their fisheries that underlay Dominion regulation disappeared entirely, at least in the regulations. Before he left office in 1894, Tupper amended the fishery regulations for British Columbia to reflect this view of the Native fishery. The 1894 amendment contained a provision requiring that Native people receive permission from the Inspector of Fisheries to procure fish for food:

> 1. Fishing by means of nets or any other fishing apparatus whatever for any kind of fish without licenses from the Minister of Marine and Fisheries is prohibited in any of the waters of the province of British Columbia.
>
> (a) Provided always that Indians may, at any time, *with the permission of the inspector of fisheries*, catch fish for the purpose of providing food for themselves and their families but for no other purpose, but no Indian shall spear, trap or pen fish on their spawning grounds, nor catch them during the close season, or in any place leased or set apart for the natural or artificial propagation of fish, or in any other place otherwise specially reserved ...
>
> 6. No nets of any kind shall be used for catching any kind of salmon in the inland lakes or in the fresh or non-tidal waters of rivers or streams. But Indians may, *with the permission of the inspector of fisheries*, use dip-nets for the purpose of providing food for themselves and their families, but for no other purpose.[243]

With this amendment, the Native fishery was reduced to a rump food fishery, at least on paper. It would take longer for the regulations to be enforced across the province, but they were in place. A commercial licence was available to each '*bona fide* fisherman'; businesses involved in shipping, salting, or selling fish could purchase seven licences; and cannery operators could obtain up to twenty licences. In addition, the regulations provided that 'every settler or farmer actually residing on his lands or with his family being a British subject' could purchase a 'domestic licence' for $1 (see figure 1.1). The licence enabled the holder to fish in any waters of the province, 'for the use of the owners' families and not for sale trade or barter,' subject to prescribed limits during the

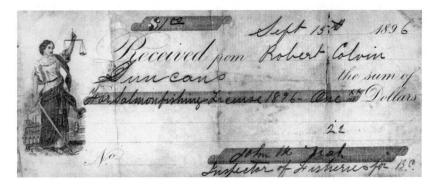

Figure 1.1 Domestic fishing licence issued to R. Colvin of Duncan's, 1896. For a $1 licence fee, all British subjects in British Columbia had virtually the same food fishing rights as Natives.

close season and a net length limit of 100 yards. Essentially, the domestic licence was a food-fishing licence, and apart from the net restriction and the possibility of a close season, for a $1 licence fee a non-Native settler had the same rights to fish for food as a Native person.

The idea that Native fishing entitlements were subject to the will of the Crown reflected larger legal understandings of the day.[244] Tupper was a lawyer and was almost certainly familiar with the decision of the Judicial Committee of the Privy Council in *St. Catherine's Milling & Lumber Co. v. The Queen*.[245] In this case, a dispute between the Dominion and Ontario over the right to issue a timber-cutting permit, the Privy Council discussed the nature of Aboriginal rights to land. Lord Watson determined that Aboriginal rights were rooted in the *Royal Proclamation of 1763* and that 'the tenure of Indians was a personal and usufructuary right, dependent on the good will of the Sovereign.' Crown title underlay Native title, the latter existing solely at the good will of the Crown. Neither consent nor compensation were required to extinguish title. Similar language appeared in court cases closer to the British Columbia fishery. In an 1886 decision regarding disputed land at Metlakatla, Chief Justice Begbie held that Indians had no rights except those that 'the grace and intelligent benevolence of the Crown may allow.'[246] Tupper's remarks were neither unusual nor exceptional by the 1890s.

In many ways this represented the closure, or perhaps the enclosure, of a resource. In the twenty years from 1874, when the Department of Marine and Fisheries began the legislative process to bring the *Fisheries Act* to British Columbia, to the *Fishery Regulations for the Province of British Columbia* of 1894, a scattered and small-scale activity had become a highly regulated and exploited industry. Although many Native people joined the industry as fishers or as cannery workers, many others resisted as their share of the catch was reduced to a food fishery at the discretion of the inspector of fisheries. Those who wanted to join the commercial fleet faced obstacles as well. Natives found work as hired hands, but had difficulty obtaining licences. The Cowichan, who had fished for generations at the mouth of the Fraser as part of their seasonal rounds, were refused licences in 1889 on the grounds that they were not a resident tribe.[247] This was part of the Dominion's policy, implemented by Indian Affairs, to promote Native self-sufficiency through agriculture and to reduce their reliance on fish, freeing the latter for the canneries. Charlie Caplin, identified as 'Chief of the Musqueam Indians' and therefore an acknowledged resident of the lower Fraser, testified before the British Columbia Fishery Commission in 1892 about his people's trouble getting licences. The commission had been appointed to review the regulation and supervision of the British Columbia fisheries, particularly the Fraser River salmon fishery. Caplin testified that his people were unable to purchase the licences they wanted. They had ten licences, but wanted more. Those with licences owned their boats and nets and fished independently, selling to the canneries. Those without licences earned less as cannery employees.

By Mr. Wilmot:
Q. Well, what is it the chief wants? – A. (After being interpreted.) He wants to tell you that it is about licences – there are lots of Indians on the same ranch as himself and they can't get licences.
Q. How is it they cannot get licences? – A. He says he don't know what is the reason, but it has been for lots of times – some Indians get licences, but he could never get one.
Q. Ask him how many Indians get licences? – A. Ten Indians get licences on his ranch.

By Mr. Armstrong:
Q. Ten Indians of his tribe? – A. Ten only.

By Mr. Wilmot:

Q. Where do they fish when they get licences? – A. They fish always on the North Arm of the Fraser.

Q. What do they fish with? – A. With gill-nets, the same as whitemen.

Q. They follow the same regulations as are given by the department for the whitemen? – A. Yes, sir.

Q. Do they pay the same fee? – A. Just the same, sir.

Q. Do they fish for their own use, or for sale to canneries? – A. They fish for sale to the canneries.

Q. Are there many other Indians besides these ten who fish for the canneries without licences? – A. Ten more fish for the canneries without licences.

Q. How do they fish without licences? – A. They work by the day, sir.

Q. Do any work on shares? – A. They always work by the day, sir.

Q. What usual price per day do they get? – A. $2 for a net-man, and $1.50 for a boat-puller.[248]

Caplin testified that he was also concerned about the size of the nets that white fishers were using. He thought they were too large to let enough salmon reach the spawning grounds and that the stocks were in danger. Even during his lifetime the runs had declined dramatically, he testified, to the point where they were dangerously low.

Further up the Fraser River, the commissioners heard similar testimony from a witness identified as 'Captain George, a native chinook Indian, of Harrison River.' Mr Tiernan, the Indian agent (who also acted as the interpreter), testified just before George that fifty Indians had wanted to appear, but he convinced them that one was enough to convey their message to the commission. When Commissioner Wilmot asked what his concerns were, George replied:

A. He says that the whole of the Indians only get forty licences, and that they are very much displeased at the number they get.

Q. What is the number of their tribe? – A. His tribe is about 120 all told, but that does not cover all – the forty licences cover all the tribes.

Q. Then their complaint is because they only get forty licences? – A. He say the white men come here and get licences and his people were here first. It is the same old story. The White men come and get licences first in preference to them, and he says they should not.[249]

Thereafter George's testimony gets superseded by argument between the commissioners and Indian Agent Tiernan. The commissioners stated that without the white man the Indians would do nothing with the fish, so they should not complain. Commissioner Higgins pointed out, 'You see if even the Indians catch less fish than the average whiteman, he gets some $200 at least for them, and if it was not for the canneries they would get nothing at all.'[250] However, it was not that Natives objected to the presence of canneries (although in some cases they did) or that they thought the entire coastal fishery should be exclusively Native. Many Native fishers were no doubt initially delighted with the canneries that provided new markets for their fish and seasonal employment. Rather, they were objecting to the loss of control of particular fisheries – those that their people had owned, managed, and exploited in some cases for centuries. They received wages for their labour, but not rent from resources that the Canadian state had assumed for itself and then allocated to the owners of capital. Twenty years later, the commissioners of the Royal Commission on Indian Affairs for the Province of British Columbia (the McKenna/McBride commission) would hear and condemn the testimony of Fisheries' officials, who attempted to justify the continuing discrimination against Native fishers. Independent fishing licences remained a tool to encourage white settlement. Indian fishers could fish under cannery licences, if canneries would hire them.

Conclusion

Into the 1870s the Pacific coast salmon fishery remained a Native fishery. Although the common law doctrine of the public right to fish had opened the tidal fisheries to all British subjects, early settlers and the colonial legislature hardly interfered. In fact, the early 1850s treaties seemed to confirm the right of Native peoples to their fisheries. Similarly, in the early stages of the commercial canning industry the Dominion government played a small role in regulating the fishery. Many Natives sold fish to the canneries, sometimes in competition with non-Native fishers, but neither the Dominion nor the province restricted the Native catch. The Native and non-Native fisheries existed side by side, unregulated by the Canadian state.

However, as the canning industry grew, so did Dominion intervention; the areas of Native control began to shrink. To be sure, Native involvement in the fishing industry remained high, a fact highlighted by Rolf Knight in *Indians at Work*, suggested in a case studies by Leona Marie Sparrow and James P. Spradley, and illustrated in the photographs compiled by Meggs and Stacey.[251] Nowhere were Native peoples more involved in the industrial, export-based, resource-extraction economy that characterized early modern British Columbia than in the fishing industry. Newell argues that 'Indians were the labour backbone of the salmon-canning industry during its chaotic rise in the late-nineteenth century.'[252] At Metlakatlha, under the direction of the Anglican missionary William Duncan and with funds raised by him in England, the Tsimpsean built and operated a cannery. There and elsewhere, Native women worked in the canneries cleaning fish and filling cans, Native men worked as fishers, and particularly in the north their wage or piece-work labour was essential to the success of the commercial canning industry well into the twentieth century. They provided flexible, industrious, and relatively inexpensive labour. Cannery operators and fisheries officers frequently asked Indian agents (Department of Indian Affairs officials) stationed along the coast to encourage Native people to work in the industry. These workers participated, however, in a fishery they no longer controlled. Dominion regulations monitored the catch for a cannery-dominated industry. The treaties, which had recognized the rights of Native peoples to continue their fisheries as formerly, were ignored, or considered to have been superseded by legislation. In the late 1880s, Fisheries isolated a portion of Native fishing, the food fishery, allowing it to remain under Native control for a few more years. The Dominion regulated the commercial industry first, and only later, when the canneries demanded greater access to fish, turned its attention to the Native food fishery.

State control of the fishery advanced unevenly along the West Coast. The Babine weir fishery in the headwaters of the Skeena River, for example, did not receive attention until the 1900s. Despite the rapid development of a canning industry at the mouth of the Skeena in the 1880s, the Babine were distant enough from non-Native population centres and the canneries to avoid state interference in their fishery until 1904. Other Native people, particularly those along the lower Fraser River where the canning industry was most active, were losing control in the early 1880s. On Vancouver Island the Dominion began asserting its control in the late 1880s. Many Native people were willing participants in the commercial canning industry, enjoying a degree of prosperity by joining the industrial workforce. However, other Native people, those with established control of a fishery and a strong sense of ownership, were determined to maintain their control, and clashed frequently and sometimes violently with Fisheries officials.

Native fishing was confined on all sides. Indians could still fish for food, but that right was increasingly circumscribed, and when they attempted to join the industrial commercial fishery they were thwarted by discriminatory licence restrictions. Licences were allotted to white fishers to encourage settlement. A few Natives received licences, but most were told they could either fish for food or work for the canneries as employees. In the early years cannery work was plentiful, but increasingly it went to immigrants. The importance of Native labour diminished, but cannery control of the resource, through the Department of Marine and Fisheries, would not. The legal capture of the resource, a process begun under the common law doctrine of the public right to fish, was complete.

CHAPTER TWO

Fish Weirs and Legal Cultures on Babine Lake, 1904–1907

At the end of the fishing season in 1904 the Department of Marine and Fisheries removed the fish weirs on the Babine River near the outflow of Babine Lake. This was the last year that the weirs would fully operate, and in comparison to the protracted dispute over the Cowichan weirs (discussed in the following chapter), the confrontation on Babine Lake burned brightly for three years and was gone. It was a shorter and, in many ways, a simpler dispute. The canneries operating near the mouth of the Skeena River needed a secure supply of fish, and the weirs on the Babine River, principal spawning ground of the Skeena sockeye, threatened that supply, or so the cannery owners believed. Through the local Fisheries officials, whom they ostensibly appointed, the cannery owners co-opted the power of the Canadian state to secure their supply of fish.

The intensity of the dispute over fish in the Babine River brings the dual roles of law into focus. The state used law, at the behest of the Skeena cannery owners, to assert its order on the Skeena and Babine river fisheries, and to justify that order. The enforcement of Canadian fisheries law on the Babine River was the power of industrial capital legitimized. Similarly, the Lake Babine people used law, their law, to resist the state's intrusion, and to justify that resistance. Two Oblate missionaries, one of whom no longer lived in the region, provided what support they could, but the small community was otherwise alone to resist and, when it appeared inevitable, to negotiate and contain such as it could the penetration of a modern nation state into their territory. Unlike the Cowichan, the Babine had neither time nor access to a sympathetic local settler society to gather the resources of the state in their defence. The result was a lopsided clash of legal cultures. Just as one fishery sought to exclude the other, so one legal culture sought to replace the other. What follows, then, is a study of the exercise of power in the colonial setting, through law.[1]

Babine Lake and Its People

Babine Lake supports many species of fish, but the focus of human activity has always been the anadromous sockeye salmon. Sockeye spawn in the fall in the Babine River above and below Nilkitkwa Lake, and in the tributaries of Babine Lake, particularly those in the North Arm (see figure 2.1). In the spring the fry migrate to Babine Lake and live in its waters for their first year. In May and June of their second year the young sockeye leave the lake and travel down the Babine and Skeena rivers to the Pacific, where over the next two years they range as far as the Gulf of Alaska, feeding on the vast array of oceanic plant life. In their fourth or fifth years they migrate back to the Babine Lake system in August and September to spawn.[2]

This yearly concentration of protein supported the people whose ancestral territory borders Babine Lake and who call themselves the Lake Babine Nation or the Ned'u'ten Nation.[3] Although their diet included plants, animals, and other fish, sockeye salmon was their dietary staple. The Babine caught sockeye with weirs in shallow waters of the Babine River and certain tributaries of Babine Lake in August and September. The locations of the weirs in the late nineteenth and early twentieth centuries were recorded by various white observers, and their maps are reproduced in figures 2.2, 2.4, 2.5. The Babine dried or smoked the sockeye in vast quantities, enough to last until the following year's harvest and longer if, as occasionally happened, the sockeye did not reappear. The preserved fish were also a valuable trade item that the Babine exchanged with neighbouring peoples, particularly those to the east on Stuart and Takla lakes, whose sockeye runs were less reliable.[4]

The Lake Babine Nation is commonly known among anthropologists as a regional group within the Athapaskan-speaking Carrier or Yinkadinee. They divide themselves into four matrilineal clans, and sometimes call themselves the 'Four Clan Nation.' The clans – Likhc'ibu (Bear), Jilhtsehyu (Frog), Gilantin (Caribou), and Likhtsemisyu (Beaver) – correspond to clans among neighbouring peoples, creating links that foster trade and marriages, and allow access to resources in other territory. The clans divide further into family groups or Houses. Within

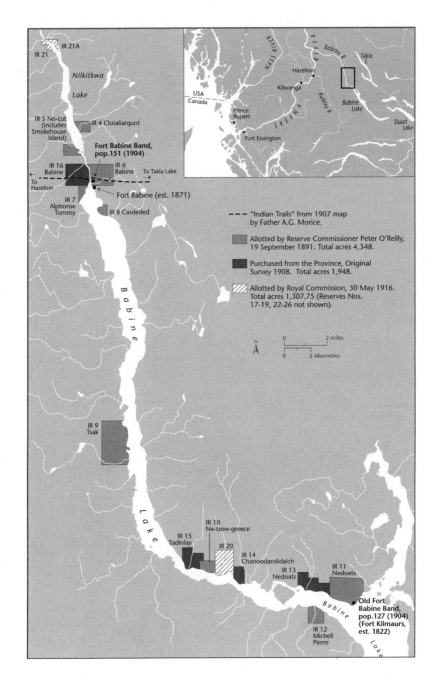

Figure 2.1   Lake Babine Villages and Reserves.

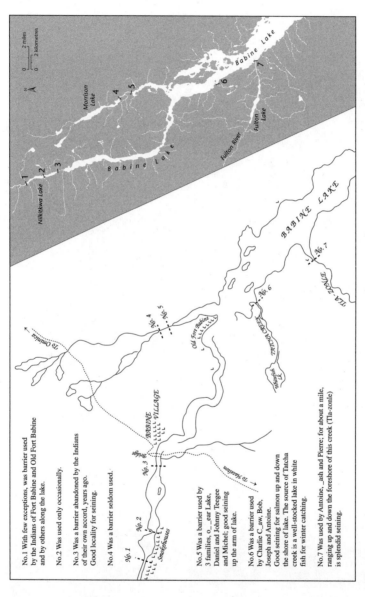

Figure 2.2 Location of weir fisheries based on a map drawn by Indian Agent R.E. Loring, 1905. According to Loring's accompanying text (missing characters are illegible in the original), members of the Fort Babine and Old Fort Babine bands used the weir at the outflow of Nilkitkwa Lake. Other weirs appear to have been used by particular families. The map on the right indicates the location of weirs identified in Loring's map.

these Houses, individuals can hold a personal crest or name that only they are entitled to use. Each name fits within a social hierarchy, and those holding the highest-ranking names are the hereditary chiefs. Not everyone holds a hereditary title; they are reserved for the nobility and acquired by holding a series of feasts or potlatches, known to the Babine as *balhats.* The more important the name, the more expensive the balhats, and the chief of the leading House within a clan usually holds the position of clan chief. The chiefs are known by their crest or name, and it is to this name and not the person that the rights associated with being a chief attach. A contemporary anthropologist, Jo-Anne Fiske, and a hereditary chief, Betty Patrick, describe the rights that accompany a name as follows: 'Each chief is known by the balhats name s/he has paid for in a series of balhats. Each chief enjoys prerogatives that are associated with and inalienable from the balhats name, such as rights to intangible property, to the performance of rituals, and to access to traditional resource territories.'[5]

Fiske and Patrick survey anthropological studies of the Carrier, all of which emphasize that the important resource-procurement sites, including traplines and fishing places, were owned by clan chiefs.[6] However, there are some differences among anthropologists about what ownership entailed. Michael Kew, working as a student in the mid-1950s, observed: 'Fishing sites were traditionally regarded as property by the Carriers; and families still retain a certain degree of exclusive right to fish in specific places.'[7] According to J.C. Hackler, also a student in the 1950s, the Likhtsemisyu or Beaver clan (he identified it as 'Laksamasyu') was the largest and most important clan within the Lake Babine Nation. They controlled three of the four Babine fish weirs that once operated on the Babine River. Furthermore, he identified Dewisimdzik (he wrote 'Deo-tsum-tsak') as the highest-ranking name within the clan, and thereby the most important title of the Babine. To take fish at the Beaver weirs, one had to receive permission from Dewisimdzik. While not disagreeing with these lines of control, Fiske and Patrick emphasize the idea of stewardship rather than ownership.[8] The fish weirs belonged to the clan. It was the responsibility of the chief to allocate individual sites along the weir or the times and order in which clan members were allowed to fish. Thus, the chief managed the resource for the people of his or her clan. Control of the resource travelled with the name, but the effect of that control was to ensure that all the clan members were provided for and that the resource remained healthy for future generations. To this end, the chief supervised the weir fishery to ensure that sufficient fish were allowed to spawn. Indian Agent R.E. Loring's description of that fishery confirms that the weir fishery was a managed fishery and that the Babine had regulations to ensure its continued viability. 'Many times,' he wrote, 'before and after fishing, also during the curing of salmon have I been below that point [the weirs at the outflow of Nilkitkwa Lake] with only here and there a post found standing to indicate the locality. The Indians did not at any time begin fishing there till 3 or 4 weeks after the salmon had begun going into the lake.'[9]

During the dispute with the Dominion government over fish weirs in the early twentieth century Tszak (Jack) William, head of the Grouse people within the Beaver clan, held the Dewisimdzik name. His wife, Hazelcho, was an important leader of Babine resistance, and is widely remembered as the woman who knocked the Fisheries officer into the river. The other prominent figure is Big George, Gwista', of the Mountain people within the Caribou clan.[10] Both Tszak William and Big George travelled to Ottawa with the Oblate missionary Father Coccola in 1906 to negotiate a resolution to their weir dispute with the Dominion government (see figure 2.3).

Big George explained to the Minister of Fisheries, L.P. Brodeur, at the first of two meetings in Ottawa that his people relied on salmon for virtually all their food, and that without weirs they could not catch enough fish to survive. He could not say how long his people had been fishing with weirs, but it was the way his father and grandfather had fished. When he was a boy the Babine built three weirs, but because their numbers were declining they had used just two weirs in the past few years, and this year they built only one. Big George explained that his people, on the chief's orders, erected the weirs every August, and removed them about four weeks later when they had caught enough fish. Everyone had their own space to fish and did so on their own accord. The chief, according to Big George, did not allocate places.[11]

Fishing rights were strongly defended against trespass; unauthorized use could result in a penalty as severe as death, and the Babine had mechanisms for settling internal disputes over the weirs.[12] William Brown, a Hudson's Bay Company trader, recounted the sketchy outline of a dispute over the weirs in 1825. One group accused another of blocking the entire river, thereby preventing the salmon from reaching Babine Lake. The dispute was settled by the middle of August with a feast held by one of the disputing parties. Once resolved, fishing began

Figure 2.3   Father Nicolas Coccola with Chief Big George (Gwista´) and Chief Tszak William (Dewisimdzik), 1907.

in earnest and by the end of October 44,000 fish had been delivered to Fort Kilmaurs on Babine Lake.[13]

The feast or balhats system was, and still is, a method of dispute resolution and of recognizing and reinforcing the authority of the hereditary chiefs. Emphasizing the communal and cooperative aspects of the balhats, Fiske and Patrick describe its role as follows:

> The legal authority of the hereditary chiefs is derived from and exercised through the balhats. It is their position within the matrilineal clan system, symbolized by the seating order in the balhats hall, that grants them the authority to interpret customary laws and to adjudicate disputes according to those laws. The names they carry confer specific obligations and privileges that are denied all others. But this is not to suggest chiefs

exercise any form of autocratic powers, for their capacity to carry through their obligations rests on their willingness to be generous to others; to show respect to one another and to their legal institutions; and to exercise wise judgments for the well-being of their lands, clans people, and future generations. When chiefs fail to behave appropriately, are found guilty of criminal offences, or show a lack of self-control they lose respect and are subject to gossip.[14]

Here is the foundation of the legal regime that was under attack in 1904. To the Fisheries officers who carried with them the laws of the Canadian state, this earlier regime was irrelevant, even illegitimate, and certainly ignored. For the 151 Babine who lived next to Fort Babine (known to Indian Affairs as the 'Fort Babine Band') and the 137 who lived on the site of the former HBC post (the 'Old Fort Babine Band') these laws, although under seige, still applied.[15]

A Permanent White Presence

The HBC established Fort Kilmaurs on the head of land between the two arms of Babine Lake in 1822 (see figure 2.1), creating a permanent white presence on the lake, and a new market for furs and fish. Some years the Babine delivered tens of thousands of fish and hundreds of furs to exchange for HBC goods. In 1871 the HBC moved its fort (then Fort Babine) to the north end of the lake, hoping to stem the flow of furs to competitors on the coast and to take advantage of the proximity to the Babine fishing sites. A sketch drawn by the HBC's Roderick Finlayson, marking the HBC claim at the north end of the lake in 1871, is reproduced in figure 2.4. Finlayson noted the location of three weirs, one at the outflow of Babine Lake opposite the village site, and two connecting Smokehouse Island.[16] Twenty and twenty-eight years later Peter O'Reilly and E.M. Skinner would also record the weir fishery attached to the island (see figures 2.4 and 2.5).

As well as creating a new market for fish and furs, the forts created permanent Native settlements where there probably had been only seasonal fishing or hunting camps. In 1879, the geologist George Dawson visited the Babine village, Wit-at, at the north end of the lake. Wit'at, from 'wit'ane keh' meaning 'site of making dry fish,'[17] was once a seasonal fishing settlement, but had become a permanent village since the HBC moved its fort. Dawson provided the following description of the Babine village: '*The Indian village* seems to have some vitality here,

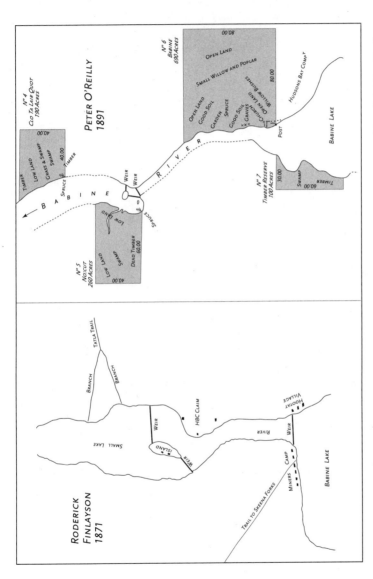

Figure 2.4 Weir fisheries based on maps drawn by Roderick Finlayson, 1871, and Peter O'Reilly, 1891. Both maps place weirs on either side of Smokehouse Island. Finlayson places a third weir in front of Wit'at Village; O'Reilly places a third weir at the inflow of Nilkitkwa Lake.

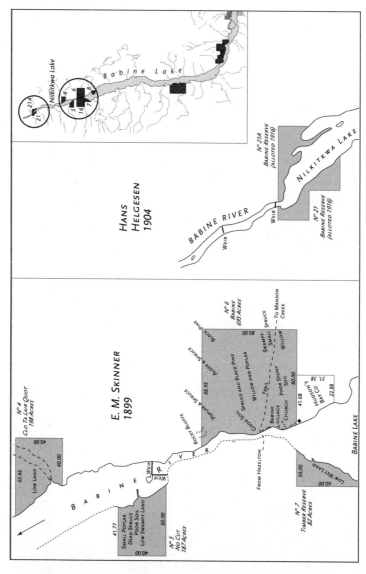

Figure 2.5   Weir fisheries mapped by E.M. Skinner, 1899, and described by Hans Helgesen, 1904. Helgesen's report seems to confirm Loring's opinion (see figure 2.2) that the Babine were no longer using the weir fishery in the short stretch of river between Babine and Nilkitkwa Lakes.

there being quite a number of small shanty-like houses, several of them new. Many salmon *caches*, standing as high [?] board erections on posts. Great quantities of salmon are annually taken here, a wicker weir with fish traps being placed completely across the river. The Indians are provided enough to keep nearly a years supply ahead and consequently have plenty to sell to trading parties of Indians.'[18]

Despite the proximity of HBC posts, the Canadian state was a relatively unobtrusive presence in Babine territory before 1904. Indian Affairs appointed R.E. Loring as the Indian agent for the newly established Babine Agency (an area that included much of the Upper Skeena, not just Babine Lake) in 1889. He travelled frequently into Babine territory, but was a transient presence, by no means controlling or even supervising Babine life. Peter O'Reilly, the Reserve Land Commissioner, arrived in 1891 to allot reserves, and he set aside 4348 acres of land for the Babine, spread over nine reserves (see figure 2.1). The sketch that accompanies his minutes of decision also locates three Babine weirs (see figure 2.4).[19] In setting land aside for the Babine, O'Reilly recognized the importance of the salmon fishery and allocated reserves accordingly. In fact, it was the only resource of any consequence that he noted in his minutes of decision. For Indian Reserve (IR) 5 he wrote: 'A small Island in the Babine river is included in this reservation; on it there are some fishdrying houses, and adjacent to it a valuable salmon fishery.' IR 6 included a village, church, small gardens in poor soil, and fronted a similarly valuable fishery:

> Babine, a reserve at the foot of Babine Lake, adjoins the Hudson Bay Company's trading post; it contains 690 acres, and on it there is a village of 28 houses with a Roman Catholic church. Mr. Loring informs me that the population amounts to 83.
>
> The soil is of poor quality, covered with small poplar and willow underbrush. With the exception of a strip along the river bank no gardens are now cultivated, the Indians being afraid of the summer frosts; in the Hudson Bay Company's garden however, immediately adjoining, no sign of frost was apparent.
>
> Salmon in large quantities are taken in the Babine river in front of the village, and white fish and lake trout are procured in the lake during the winter.[20]

Although the reserves were staked in 1891, there were few non-Babine settlers in the area and it is unlikely that Babine movement through their traditional territory was seriously hindered. Undoubtedly Babine society had been changed by its encounter with the non-Native world. The presence of an Indian agent, a person whose authority derived from external sources and who could intervene to help settle a dispute over fish (as Loring had in 1894),[21] changed power relations within Babine society. Similarly, the Oblate missionaries were an important presence since the arrival of Father A.G. Morice at the Fort St James Mission on Stuart Lake in 1885. While the Babine could not remove the HBC from their territory, they had likely welcomed the fur-trade posts as a new source of wealth. The expanded market for furs and fish could be accommodated by the Babine in ways that, to some degree, they could control. This was much less true of the direct intervention by the Department of Fisheries, which began in 1904.

Departments of the Dominion

In its dispute with the Babine over fish weirs the state was not a monolithic actor. The division was not along Dominion/provincial lines as is so often the case in the Canadian federal state, but instead between departments of the Dominion government – the Fisheries Branch of the Department of Marine and Fisheries and the Department of Indian Affairs.

The hierarchy within Fisheries in 1904 requires some explanation. At its base were the 'fishery guardians' who worked in the field enforcing the *Fisheries Act* and *Regulations*. They were assigned to a river or a relatively small region, usually just for the fishing season. In 1904 Fisheries employed two guardians on the Upper Skeena, E. Nordschow and G.F. Church, for five months at $60 a month. In 1905 Fisheries raised the rate to $75 a month. The guardians reported to a 'fishery officer,' a position occupied on the Upper Skeena by Hans Helgesen, who was based in Hazelton.[22] As a fishery officer, Helgesen was responsible for the guardians in his region, but also worked in the field enforcing the *Fisheries Act*. In 1904 and 1905 Fisheries paid him $750 for six months work ($125/month) each year. The fishery officer reported to the 'inspector of fisheries.' Before 1904 there was one inspector of fisheries for all of British Columbia, but that year Fisheries divided the province into two regions: District No. 1 included Vancouver Island and the mainland south of Bute Inlet; District No. 2 comprised the northern coast. The following year Vancouver Island became District No. 3. John T. Williams, based in Port Essington near the mouth of the

Skeena, was the inspector for District No. 2. He reported to E.E. Prince, the Dominion Commissioner of Fisheries in Ottawa, who in turn reported to the Minister of Fisheries, a position held from 1902 to 1906 by Raymond Prefontaine, and then by L.P. Brodeur until 1911.

The role of Fisheries in the dispute is relatively transparent. By 1904, fishing was big business on the Northwest Coast and the enforcement of the *Fisheries Act* reflected a business agenda, notwithstanding the rhetoric that removing the barricades was a conservation measure in the interests of all users. The fishery guardians and officers on the Upper Skeena were political appointees, nominated by the Skeena Liberal Association and appointed without vetting by Fisheries. This hiring practice created discipline problems. Responding to the Oblate missionary Father Coccola's complaint about the conduct of several fishery guardians, Inspector Williams told his department that the Liberal Association appointed the officials, and that until he had 'efficient, honest, and trustworthy Guardians,' he could not properly enforce the *Fisheries Act*.[23] Personnel concerns were exacerbated by a second factor: fishery officers received half of any fines levied for *Fishery Regulations* violations. In 1904, eight fishery guardians from the south coast wrote to the minister, complaining that this practice made it difficult to enforce the *Regulations* because the cannery operators and fishers accused them of extortion.[24]

The role of Indian Affairs was somewhat more equivocal. At its base were the Indian agents assigned to a particular band or region. Indian Agent R.E. Loring was responsible for the Babine Agency, and he operated from Hazelton. He reported to the Superintendent of Indian Affairs for British Columbia in Victoria, A.W. Vowell, who in turn reported to the Deputy Superintendent General of Indian Affairs in Ottawa. At the time of the dispute the Department of Indian Affairs was part of the Interior Ministry, Frank Oliver minister. That ministry was charged with responsibility for Indians, and in this capacity, its officers resisted the attempt to minimize the Native fishery and to characterize Native peoples as the cause of the salmon shortfall. Instead, Indian Affairs argued that Native people were entitled to fish in the manner to which they were accustomed, certainly for the purposes of food, and to buy clothing, ammunition, and other staples. Further, its agents believed, as did the Babine, that the cause of the salmon shortage was not the weir fishery, but rather the wasteful practices of the cannery operators. Indian Affairs also had budgetary concerns; every Native person it had to support reduced funds for other purposes, and it objected to policies of another department that reduced Native self-sufficiency and increased its costs. If the canneries were responsible for the shortage of fish, it argued, Fisheries should be responsible for the consequences of its poor management – in this case the compensation of Native peoples – not Indian Affairs. However, Indian Affairs was part of the Dominion government and responsible for upholding its laws. Even if its officers disagreed with a law or the policies of another department, they could not publicly denounce that department, and Indian agents often found themselves caught between what they believed to be the legitimate grievances of Natives and the demands of other branches of the Dominion government, particularly the Department of Fisheries.

Barricade Conflict, 1904

Before the mid-1870s, non-Native interest in fish on British Columbia's north coast was a relatively insignificant appendage to the fur trade or the gold rushes. This began to change when, in 1876, a San Francisco–based outfit, the Northwest Fishing Company, opened the first cannery on the Skeena River.[25] The operation was a limited success its first year, but it marked the beginning of an industrial fishery on British Columbia's north coast, connected by ships to distant markets in England, Australia, and other parts of the British Empire. From these tentative beginnings the industrial commercial fishery on the north coast grew, so that by 1904 eleven canneries operated near Port Essington at the mouth of the Skeena, supported by more than 700 fish boats and 2500 workers (see figures 2.6 and 2.7).[26] Three more canneries operated on the Nass River, making the business of canning fish a major industrial presence on the north coast.

In 1904, Fisheries began a concerted effort to eliminate a particular technology – the fish weir – from the headwaters of the Skeena River. Until then, Fisheries had left the Babine and their fish weirs entirely alone, but in 1904 it could not ignore the demands of cannery operators at the mouth of the Skeena. 'There should be a systematic and annual examination of every salmon stream up which sockeye ascend,' wrote Henry Doyle, founder and general manager of the British Columbia Packers Association, which had amalgamated much of the industry, 'in order to see that fallen trees and other natural obstructions do not impede the upward progress of fish, and that artificial barricades, such as the Indians employ are also removed.'[27]

Figure 2.6   The British American Cannery, Port Essington, 1890s.

Figure 2.7 Drying nets at Port Essington, near the mouth of the Skeena River, c. 1905.

The catch on the Skeena in 1902 set new records; the canneries shipped 155,936 cases of tinned salmon, and the value of all fish caught on the Skeena that year was $824,266.55.[28] The owners were anticipating an even better year in 1903 because, according to the evidence of one manager, the 1899 salmon run on the Skeena had been uncommonly large, but few fish were caught when the fishers struck.[29] As the salmon swam past the relatively idle canneries that year, the managers consoled themselves, expecting a big run four years later. However, the 1903 catch produced only 98,688 cases, and the value of the total catch was half the previous year's record. Cannery operators blamed the Native fish barricades in the Upper Skeena.

The 1904 season on the Skeena began with a strike. Cannery operators offered 7 cents per sockeye, Native and white fishers struck for 10 cents. In late June, Native fishers announced that they would return to their villages with their families if the canners did not increase the price. This would reduce the fishing fleet, but the canners were particularly concerned about losing the labour of Native women who worked in the canneries packing fish. White fishers, most of whom had arrived from the south for the fishing season, agreed to return south if Native demands were not met. It is not clear what position the Japanese fishers took, but it seems the canners were more concerned about retaining the cannery labour of Native women than about the striking fishers. Canners and fishers agreed on 8½ cents in early July, but not before many Natives and some whites had returned home, and editorial comment in the local newspaper revealed the importance of the Native women's cannery labour: 'It is a thing pretty well known on the Skeena that there is no dearth of actual fishermen, the trouble, it appears, being in getting labor to fill the cans. This was the lever used by the Indians during the recent trouble. The Indian women have heretofore performed that class of labor in the canneries, and of course were really standing out on behalf of their male tribespeople in a "sympathetic" strike.'[30] Their capital investments exposed by inconsistent supplies of labour and fish, the canners demanded action from Fisheries to do what it could to secure a supply of fish.

Dominion Commissioner of Fisheries E.E. Prince instructed John T. Williams, the inspector of fisheries for the Northwest Coast, to hire a guardian for the Babine River who was to 'prosecute any infringement of the Regulations and impress upon the Indians that they will not be allowed to decimate the salmon as hitherto.'[31] Williams responded, sending Fishery Officer Hans Helgesen and Fishery Guard-

ian Nordschow to Hazelton in September 1904 to investigate reports
that Natives were catching salmon by barricading the headwaters of
the Skeena. Helgesen and Nordschow reached Fort Babine at the north
end of Babine Lake on 14 September 1904 (see figure 2.8). The following
day they borrowed a canoe, hired two Native men, and proceeded
seven miles down the Babine River. There, where the water was about a
metre deep and running swiftly, they found the Babine working two
weirs about 800 metres apart, each spanning the 60-metre-wide river
(see figure 2.5).[32] With considerable admiration, Helgesen described
the weirs as 'constructed of an immense quantity of materials, and on
scientific principles.' The Babine had driven posts into the river bed at
intervals of six to eight feet to support the weir. Helgesen's description
continued:

> Then sloping braces well bedded in the bottom and fastened to the top of
> posts, then strong stringers all the way on top and bottom, in front of
> posts, then panel beautifully made of slats woven together with bark set
> in front of all, these were set firmly into the bottom, and reaching 4 feet
> above the water. This made a magnificent fence which not a single fish
> could get through.
>
> On the upper side of dam were placed 12 big traps or fish bins. Oppo-
> site holes made in the panels for fish to enter the traps, prepared with
> slides to open and shut, and if the traps did not have a sufficient quantity
> of fish in them, when the women wanted more fish on the bank, the men
> would take their canoe poles, wade out in a line and strike the water,
> making a noise which could fill the traps in a moment, then shut the slides
> down, take a canoe on each side of bin, raise the false bottom, by some
> contrivance so as to elevate the fish, then load up canoes with gaff hooks.
>
> Altogether the barricades presented a most formidable and imposing
> appearance.[33]

Helgesen reported sixteen houses filled with dried salmon and racks of
drying salmon outside. Although the run was coming to an end in mid-
September, the fishers were still catching 500 to 600 salmon a day, and
Helgesen estimated that the Babine had caught 750,000 salmon that
year. This figure is extraordinarily high, by far the highest in the historical record, and it is possible that Helgesen exaggerated the catch to
emphasize the magnitude of the perceived problem. However, there is
no doubt that the Babine had the capacity to catch immense quantities
of fish. They consumed many fish themselves and traded with other

Figure 2.8 Wit'at or Fort Babine, ca. 1905. The Oblate church looms over Fort Babine, once the seasonal fishing village of Wit'at. The buildings close to the water have been built on stilts.

Native people. It is also likely that the non-Native market for dried or smoked fish increased in the late nineteenth and early twentieth centuries. The HBC traders had been buying fish since the early nineteenth century, but the Omineca gold rush of the 1870s and the rush to the Klondike in the 1890s brought a stream of miners through Babine territory. Similarly, the flood plain of the Bulkley valley enticed white farmers into neighbouring Gitksan territory.[34] These immigrants – trappers, miners, packers, traders, and farmers who lived or worked in the region – bought salmon from the Babine for food. As more arrived the demand probably increased.[35] Furthermore, fur-bearing animals were increasingly scarce in the region, and the Babine may have been trying to compensate by increasing their trade in preserved fish.

Helgesen reported that Chief Big George was away when they arrived,[36] so he spoke with 'Chief Atio,' whom he described as 'next in command.'[37] Helgesen told Atio that he had been sent by the government to destroy the barricades; that it was in the interests of all users of the fishery, including the Babine, to allow salmon to spawn; that the law prohibited barricades because they prevented salmon from reaching the spawning grounds; that the Babine must observe the close season; that they were only allowed to fish up to one-third of the channel with nets; and that they could only catch fish for themselves and their families, but not for sale. The practice of selling fish as they had done in the past must stop. Helgesen recorded Atio's interpreted reply:

> The chief advanced many points and some of them were well taken, he said they have had an indisputable right for all time in the past, that if it was taken away the old people would starve, that by selling salmon they could always get *iktahs,* and he wanted to know to what extent the government would support them, he thought it unfair to forbid them selling fish when the cannerymen sold all theirs, and I had to promise him to tell the government to compel the canners to let more fish come up the rivers, as some years they did not get enough, that the canners destroyed more spawn than they, that formerly he could not see the water below his barricade for fish, that they were so plentiful that some of them were forced out on the beach, but latterly they had diminished, little by little every year.[38]

The Babine clearly felt they had a right to the fish for food and also for sale. They had used weirs for longer than anyone could remember, and who was Helgesen and his government to tell them that they must come down? While the cannery operators blamed the Indian fishery for fish shortages, the Babine pointed to the cannery operators. They believed the cannery fishers at the mouth of the Skeena were catching too many fish, and if more fish escaped the cannery nets, argued the Babine, more fish would reach the spawning grounds.

Notwithstanding their long-established use of fish weirs and their assertion of a right, Helgesen insisted that the Babine fishery was 'a gross breach of the law.' He threatened 'punishment or imprisonment' if they did not remove the barricades. Behind these threats lay the Dominion *Fisheries Act*. It prohibited fishing apparatus that obstructed the main channel of rivers or streams, and required that at least one third of any river or stream remain unobstructed.[39] Furthermore, it only allowed such fishing in tidal waters.[40] Anyone convicted of an offence was liable to a fine not exceeding $100 and costs, and if in default, to imprisonment for a term not exceeding three months.[41]

Eventually the Babine agreed to dismantle the weirs, but after two hours' work in cold water and the job only partially completed, they refused to continue unless they were paid for their work. Fisheries frequently hired Natives at a rate of $2 to $3 per day to clear landslides, windfalls, and other obstructions blocking rivers in the Upper Skeena.[42] Helgesen relented. He hired six of them to finish removing the weirs, conceding that it was the only way he could get the barricades down. There was little more that two Fisheries officers could do in the face of Babine opposition.

After purchasing the removal of the Babine barricades Helgesen continued through the tributaries of Babine Lake removing other barricades, that, late in the season, were largely abandoned and in various stages of collapse. He destroyed six barricades in all, and everywhere he went he explained the fisheries laws and regulations to the Native people. Next year, he told them, they would not be allowed to fish with weirs because that method of fishing destroyed the salmon stock and the law forbade it. The Babine were not persuaded. From where, they wanted to know, did the government derive its authority to make these demands? When Helgesen returned to Babine Lake from his rounds in the Upper Skeena, one Babine chief asserted a right to fish with weirs and demanded compensation if they were destroyed again. Helgesen wrote: 'To show how the Indians feel about losing their barricades I beg to call your attention to what occurred at Babine, I was asked to attend a meeting of Indians, when I was informed by one who claimed to own the barricades, that if he had been present when the barricades were destroyed they would not have been touched, that unless the government sends him $600 before the fish run next summer, the barricades would surely be constructed again, though he should die for it, this he repeated several times, and I had to promise him that I would tell the government so.'[43]

Given that the fishing season was almost over when Helgesen and Nordschow arrived at the weirs in 1904, their actions had little impact on the Babine catch. However, their presence raised concerns among the Babine. Over the ensuing winter, they informed Father A.G. Morice that a white man claiming to act on behalf of some government had forbidden their use of fish weirs, and asked him to intercede on their behalf. Morice, the Oblate missionary based at Fort St James on Stuart Lake from 1885–1903, had written extensively on the Western Dene, particularly the people of Stuart Lake, but he knew the Babine as well or better than any other white.[44] He could scarcely believe that Fisheries had forbidden the Babine to use weirs, and as his letter to Indian Affairs suggests, he thought it must be a matter of correcting a renegade official who had exceeded his authority:

Such a pretension on the part of an official – whoever he may be – appeared to me so monstrous that I refused to believe it possible and to this day I have, as you are aware, never yet acted on the Indians' suggestion. But the latter insist, and seem so earnest that I am almost inclined to suppose that some ignorant person may indeed have committed the terrible blunder of trying, through his little familiarity with matters in the northern interior, to *starve* two whole tribes of Indians, who should on the contrary be helped out of the public funds as a compensation for the loss of furs they have suffered at the hands of white parties during these few years. As to their being allow[ed] to fish only with nets, I shall not lose my time in considering that eventually [sic], since they could not then procure merely what would be necessary for their daily consumption during the fishing season, and would have literally to *starve* from the beginning of September to the middle of July.[45]

Indian Affairs forwarded Morice's letter to Fisheries, suggesting a cautious approach.[46] Fisheries replied that 'the wholesale destruction of spawning salmon, upon which the great salmon industry of the north so largely depends ... threatens most serious results to the industry.'[47] It appointed three guardians, Stuart Norrie, Charles Jones, and Harry

Frank, all of Port Essington and recommended by the president of the Skeena Liberal Association, to patrol the upper Skeena under Helgesen's command.[48] Realizing perhaps that the threat to the Babine fishery was more serious than he had imagined, Morice wrote again to Indian Affairs, indicating that the money economy was 'practically unknown' to the Babine, that the climate could not support agriculture, and that without fish to eat and trade they would not survive. In the past when the runs had failed, the Babine starved, but in the early twentieth century Morice believed conditions were even worse because fur-bearing animals were scarce.[49]

The Babine were concerned about their fishery, but believed that after the final meeting with Helgesen in 1904 they had an agreement with the government. In exchange for a guarantee not to build the weirs, the Babine expected the government to provide $600, rations for orphans and widows, and nets.[50] Although Helgesen did not think he had reached such an agreement with the Babine, he knew that if the government prohibited barricades the Babine would expect compensation. Furthermore, he thought the $600 would be money well spent.[51] Somewhat tardily, he conveyed these expectations to the Dominion government:

> I regret very much that I did not recommend in my Babine report that the Govt. should pay the Indians something in lieu of there [sic] Barricades. I said in my report of the Babine trip that an Indian who claimed the Barricades wanted the Govt. to pay six hundred Dollars. That if he got it, he would divide with the Indians of the two great Barricades that we destroyed, if he did not get that sum before the salmon run next season he would put in the barricades though he should Die for it. Now six hundred will reconcile them and I think it would be a fare [sic] way of deling [sic] with them. I know they are liable for using there [sic] barricades notwithstanding the Inspector had by letter forbid them to do so, but the Indians do not look at it in this way. And they should be treated like big children. I trust you will ask the Govt. to bestow their most favorable consideration on this matters.[52]

Indian Affairs told Fisheries as well that the Babine expected compensation from the government if they were to relinquish their right to fish with barricades. However, while Indian Affairs agreed with Fisheries that it would be best for all concerned if the weirs were removed, it was not prepared to force the issue. The Babine must be convinced, not forced, to adopt other methods of fishing. The Indian agents would do their best to arrive at an 'amicable arrangement' with the Babine; they would not compel the Babine to observe the regulations or assist Fisheries in enforcement.[53] Whatever their approach, all the government officials in the area knew that the Babine would defend the weirs with their lives if they were not compensated.

Fisheries assumed this intransigence was the work of the Oblate missionaries.[54] Father Coccola had assumed the Stuart Lake Mission in 1903 when Morice's successor lasted only a few months.[55] He travelled to Fort Babine frequently, and the Oblate church loomed over the settlement (see figure 2.8). The Oblates certainly provided assistance to the Babine and, having learned their language, often functioned as intermediaries between the Babine and the state.[56] However, while they may have guided the Babine resistance along certain channels, they were not the catalysts. The momentum came from the Babine themselves. Denying Babine agency by attributing resistance to the missionary influence was a means of denying the legitimacy of their claims.

Old Cannery Nets, 1905

On 23 July 1905 Helgesen returned to the Babine village with Fisheries Guardian James Wells and reported that they were well received.[57] They had brought a collection of used nets, given to them by the cannery operators on the coast, to distribute among the Babine. After consulting with Mr Waer, the HBC manager at Fort Babine, Helgesen compiled a list of 57 people – all those he believed were entitled to a net.[58] When he displayed the cannery nets, which were old and full of holes, the Babine refused them. Helgesen insisted that the government would not allow barricades; if they refused the nets they would have no means of catching fish. Rather than accept Helgesen's ultimatum, the Babine sought a way around the weir prohibition. A man described by Helgesen as 'the old Chief' suggested that they build weirs from each side of the river bank, leaving the centre open, or that they build a weir on one side of an island, leaving the other side open for the fish to pass upstream. This was a possibility at Smokehouse Island at the head of Nilkitkwa Lake, site of earlier Babine weirs. Helgesen rejected these proposals. The barricades must go, but he did agree to ask the government to provide the Babine with new sockeye nets every year. On the basis of this promise, the Babine apparently agreed to try the old nets.

When he left in mid-September, towards the end of the fishing season, Helgesen reported that the Babine had 40,000 dried salmon already, about 600 fish per family, and were still fishing. Helgesen believed that by the end of the season they would have enough to last the winter, and any shortfall could be alleviated by a winter catch of trout and whitefish. Pleased with his efforts to eliminate the barricades with minimal disturbance, Helgesen reported: 'The object of my appointment was to enforce the Fisheries Regulations and if possible to deter the Indians from using barricades across the various streams which have in the past prevented the salmon from reaching their natural spawning grounds, with the effect of diminishing the school of fish and the great industry and benefit derived therefrom. In my appointment the Department warned me to use caution and discretion, this I have paid strict attention to, I have given the Indians every privilege possible, without allowing them to use barricades.'[59] In his yearly report, Inspector of Fisheries Williams claimed that the enforcement work in 1905 had been a success; no barricades were erected on the Upper Skeena, and the 'illegal sale of dried salmon, that had been on the increase and had almost assumed the importance of an industry, was entirely stopped.'[60] In the estimation of its officers, Fisheries had successfully confined the Babine fishery to a subsistence food fishery, as the law required.

For the Babine, the 1905 fishery was a dismal failure. They required about three fish per person per day during the winter months, and given a population of between 300 to 400, their food requirements were approximately 1000 to 1200 fish per day.[61] Some 40,000 fish would have lasted little more than one month, and certainly did not provide any surplus for trade.[62] Despite Helgesen's assurances to Fisheries that the Babine had enough fish, they survived the winter and spring of 1905–6 only on the reserves of their 1904 catch. Father Coccola reported that by early March a number of families had little food.[63] They had not received the $600 that they thought had been promised the year before, nor had the elderly received assistance. Furthermore, the Babine could not understand why their weirs had been targeted when those used by native people on Stuart and Fraser lakes were still operating (see figure 2.9). They had been labelled cowards by their neighbours for acquiescing to the government's demands, and demanded an explanation from Helgesen.

The explanation was simple. The Babine River system was the major spawning ground of Skeena sockeye and the cannery owners who had

Figure 2.9   Fish weir at Fraser Lake with smokehouses and drying racks on the upper bank, October 1909.

invested heavily in their canneries at the mouth of the Skeena wanted the fish. Stuart and Fraser lakes were thought to be relatively minor spawning grounds in the Fraser River system and therefore of less concern to the canneries at its mouth. Fisheries allocated its resources in response to the canning industry that demanded action on the Babine but was not yet concerned about the weir fishery in the distant head-waters of the Fraser. Helgesen knew, however, that he could not pro-vide this answer. It amounted to an admission that removing the Babine fish weirs was a means of reallocating the fish to the canneries, and Helgesen felt 'compelled to stifle the truth.'[64] He told the Babine that his authority did not extend into the neighbouring watershed, but that the government would appoint officials soon. The Stuart and Fraser lake weirs would not become the focus of government attention until 1911.

Barricade Conflict, 1906

Although the Dominion *Fisheries Regulations for the Province of British Columbia* explicitly prohibited gill nets in non-tidal or fresh water,[65] a ban that certainly included the Babine River, Fisheries and Indian Af-fairs agreed that the Babine should receive new sockeye nets for the 1906 season. They did not agree on who should pay for them. Fisheries thought them the responsibility of Indian Affairs,[66] and Indian Affairs wanted more information before it agreed to pay the estimated $200: how had Fisheries determined entitlement, and where else besides the Cowichan and Upper Skeena did it intend to enforce the barricade prohibition?[67] Indian Affairs did not want to commit itself to supplying nets across the province. Fisheries assured Indian Affairs that the hard-ships caused by the barricade prohibition were localized and that Na-tive people elsewhere did not need nets. Based on these assurances, Indian Affairs bought the nets.

On 2 July 1906 Helgesen and the Indian agent, R.E. Loring, delivered 6000 feet of new sockeye nets to the Babine, cut into 100-ft. sections. The sections were too short to span the river, and the Babine refused to accept them. They intended to build weirs, and told Helgesen as much. Over the next two days Helgesen and Loring attempted to convince the Babine of 'the evil effect of killing every fish at the Dam and the consequences of violating the law.'[68] Loring promised government sup-port if, by using the nets, the Babine caught insufficient fish to last the winter. However, the Babine were adamant that the 1905 experiment with nets had failed, they had not received adequate assistance from the government, and they were not prepared to try nets or rely on promises of assistance again. Instead they asserted their right to build a weir. This caught Fisheries by surprise. After the 1905 season its officers assumed they had seen the end of 'any organized attempts' to infringe the law.[69] Helgesen and Loring left with the nets, both convinced that the Babine were acting on the advice of some unnamed white men: 'The nerve of the whole matter lies in this that the Indians there were constantly being assured both by parties on the coast and by others passing to and from Omineca that they had an indisputable right to getting fish in the way referred to, which could not be dispelled by argument.'[70]

Helgesen also believed that many of the Babine would have accepted the nets had not their leaders forbade it. In fact, at least two Babine, Donkan Pocat and Halweis, accepted sockeye nets from Helgesen and were using them on Babine Lake.[71] When the nets were found abandoned on the shores of Babine Lake, Helgesen blamed the Old Fort Babine Chief Michel, accusing him of sending four Babine to confiscate the nets. He issued summons for Michel and four other Babine to appear in Hazelton to answer charges of stealing nets. None of them appeared. Father Coccola indicated that Donkan and Halweis were simply asked to return the nets, and that Helgesen had characterized their action as stealing.[72] Whatever the characterization, it appears that Donkan and Halweis were not entitled to accept nets as compensation for something that, according to Babine law, they did not own. The Babine who owned the weirs may have believed that if some among them accepted nets from the government, the group as a whole could be construed as agreeing not to build weirs. There were divisions within Babine society, and Helgesen may have been correct that many would have used nets, although perhaps not at the expense of the weirs. However, he was certainly wrong to attribute Babine resistance to white advisers. The Babine sense of ownership and entitlement, buttressed by the missionaries who frequently acted as intermediaries, originated within Babine society, and this internal dispute reveals something of the details. Although the weirs provided the community with food and fish to trade, certain members controlled their use and thus the right to negotiate their continued existence with the state.

On 17 August 1906 when J.D. Wells reported that the Babine had built a 'barricade,' Helgesen decided Fisheries must take strong action. He applied to Stipendiary Magistrate Hicks Beach for warrants for the arrest of the six 'ring leaders' on the grounds that they had constructed weirs with full knowledge that it was illegal. Then he sent Wells, Guardian Norrie, and Constable Rosenthall, accompanied by two Natives of the 'Seecanees tribe' to dismantle the weir and to arrest the accused. Wells was in command.[73] The group arrived at Fort Babine on 21 August, and Wells hired two prospectors who happened to be at Fort Babine as constables. The following day the party of five whites and two Natives headed seven miles down the Babine River to the weirs. Wells reported that before they left the village, Chief Big George shook their hands saying in a loud voice, 'Good-bye, Good-bye,' while the women stood nearby singing a last farewell, a 'song of death.' Other Babine strongly advised the men not to go downriver for they would never come back. Nonetheless, Wells and his entourage proceeded to the barricades with their warrants, intent on arresting the leaders and destroying the barricades.

Arriving at the weirs on 22 August, Wells and his party found a large group of Babine intent on protecting their weirs. Wells announced that some of them were wanted for violating the *Fisheries Act*, and proceeded to read the warrants and make arrests in the name of the King. When officials attempted to take the men into custody, Babine who were armed with clubs rebuffed them. Whatever claims the Fisheries officials made about the law or the King, the Babine were not prepared to let government officials take their men. The officials retreated after the first day, somewhat shaken and bruised, but without serious injury. They returned the next day, this time apparently less concerned about arresting the accused than about removing the barricades. Final negotiations did not produce any agreement; the officials were determined to enforce the law, and the Babine were equally determined to defend their weir fishery. When Wells and his party approached the weirs they were surrounded by a group of Babine women, led by Hazelcho, the wife of Tszak William. She knocked Wells off his feet into the river, and then, as the Babine remember, sat on him.[74] The Babine men stood nearby, apparently ready to intervene, but not directly involved. Although the Babine had displayed their guns the night before by firing rifles into the air, none of the officials reported the Babine with any weapons other than sticks or clubs. Wet and bruised, Wells and the other officers retreated again. No Babine had been arrested and the barricades remained standing (see figure 2.10).[75] Norrie provided the following first-hand account:

Next day 22nd in Company with Wells, Rosenthal, Brisco, Spencer, and two Indians went down to Barricade to make arrests.

Figure 2.10   Members of the Lake Babine Nation with their fish weir in the background shortly after the conflict with Department of Marine and Fisheries officers.

Found over one hundred men & women all enraged and determined to resist.

Wells read the warrants to the offenders and although arrested, resisted and were speedily rescued by friends.

We were then simply driven out of camp.

They mauled us considerable Wells getting the worst.

We went into camp about a mile above and were not further disturbed through the night although they were firing their rifles and shouting all night.

Next morning got breakfast and determined to have a go at the dam. When we got there we were immediately surrounded by the same howling mob of the day before.

After a talk we gave them to understand we were going to make an attempt on the dam. They told us we would do it at our peril or words to that effect. Wells stood guard on the bank and I accompanied by Rosenthal made for the dam.

Before I could get a stick out I was surrounded by over a dozen women all armed with clubs and mobbed ashore where the men stood ready for business if we had struck down any of their women.

I received a bad blow in the small of my back which troubles me considerable yet. Wells was pushed out into the river but not otherwise hurt.

We got together eventually and started for Babine as we concluded we were powerless against their numbers.[76]

The Babine had successfully, if temporarily, resisted white authority, and word spread that the Fisheries officers, much to their embarrassment, had been handled by the Babine women. 'RED SKINS ATTACK FISHERY OFFICERS' and 'BABINE INDIANS ON WARPATH,' blared southern newspapers whose early reports were based on cannery telegrams.[77] Those concerned with asserting the authority of the Canadian state were outraged, as were those associated with the fishing industry. Helgesen, Inspector Williams, the BC Fisheries Commission, the canning industry, Stipendiary Magistrate Hicks Beach, and 'the residents of Hazelton and district' called for a militia of 100 men to enforce the *Fisheries Act*. They believed the Indians of the Upper Skeena were becoming ungovernable and the region was increasingly unsafe for whites. The Babine were flouting the law and unless the government acted decisively, displaying its power to enforce fisheries and criminal law, the salmon stock would suffer and Native intransigence would continue. They were convinced that the Babine were 'of bad character,' and that strong state action was needed. However, they also believed the immediate cause of trouble was 'irresponsible white men' who had led the Babine to believe they had a right to fish with barricades. Whatever the source, the Babine had to be disabused of these notions by a strong show of armed force to 'maintain the majesty of the Law.'[78]

Indian Affairs, on the other hand, recommended a more conciliatory approach. Its officials realized the importance of the weirs to the Babine, were sympathetic to their assertion of ownership, and recognized the existence of 'tribal laws and customs' that determined ownership of the resource. A memo on 'Babine Fishing Rights' prepared shortly after the altercation summarized Indian Affairs' approach: 'The Indians had from the early days, before the occupation of the country by whites, depended solely upon dried salmon for their food supply, that the fishery locations had been handed down from one to another through many generations, being highly valued, and not only conferred a certain envied distinction upon the owner, but were the source of considerable revenue as well. These rights ... had been undisputed and possessed for such a length of time, the title being based upon tribal laws and customs and were considered by the natives as being inalienable, that they were ... in accordance with the white man's laws and customs more or less within the domain of prescriptive rights.'[79] Indian Agent Loring suggested that instead of one hundred militia men, the government should, 'err on the side of leniency' by allowing the Babine to continue with their weirs for a few more years.[80] He recommended 'a squad of from 8 to 12 of Royal mounted police' to keep the peace in the entire region.[81] The provincial government agent in Port Simpson reported similarly that the affair 'had been greatly exaggerated,' that the Babine were 'one of the most peaceable and law-abiding tribes of Indians in the Skeena District,' that they were exercising a right 'on a river which they consider their own.' He thought the Fisheries regulations should be phased in gradually so that the Babine had time to adjust.[82] Oblate Father A.G. Morice, in Winnipeg when news of the conflict was reported across the country, wrote immediately to the Victoria press, reiterating the folly of eliminating the Babine weirs: '[I]f the fisheries department really wants to take away from the original inhabitants of the North their chief means of support in order to enrich a few cannery men, who can live without the same, they are in honor and sheer justice bound to make a treaty with the said aborigines and furnish them with some other means of subsistence, as has been done with the Indians of the Northwest, who were deprived of their daily bread – buffalo, the equivalent of salmon to our own aborigines.'[83]

Surrender and Trial

Six Babine were accused of obstructing the passage of fish, contrary to the *Fisheries Act*, and assault, contrary to the Criminal Code. Others were charged with stealing a net and failure to appear, and there was a warrant for the arrest of Chief Big George as well.[84] According to Canadian law, they were outlaws. Helgesen and Loring returned to Babine village on 8 September in an attempt to persuade the Babine to remove the barricade and surrender the accused. Loring promised government support if it were required, and Helgesen used a mixture of persuasion and threat, explaining 'the law upon the subject, and the consequences of its violation.'[85] After deliberating overnight, the Babine refused. The threats and offers of support were neither serious nor generous enough for them to agree to remove their weir. They did, however, indicate a willingness to negotiate. From hiding, Chief Big George sent a telegram to Indian Affairs, offering to open the barricades on weekends, the close time for the cannery boats on the coast – an arrangement that had worked on the Cowichan River: 'Will government agree allow us put in salmon barrier opening same from twelve noon Saturday to six p-m. Sunday twelve foot space we wish meet wishes of government but means starvation, authorities wish to arrest us. Will give ourselves up without resistance answer Hazelton.'[86] Eight days later Indian Affairs, whose officials were apparently uncertain about the appropriate response, replied to this offer in a cryptic fashion – obey the law, but we will see what Fisheries has to say about the matter: 'Telegram seventeenth received. On no account resist the law. Am consulting Fisheries Department re salmon barrier.'[87]

On 26 September the day after receiving the telegram from Indian Affairs, nine Babine including Chief Big George surrendered, on the advice of Father Coccola. They were held in custody in the Hazelton jail while officials from the Ministry of Fisheries and Indian Affairs met in Ottawa to discuss developments. From this meeting came a flurry of telegrams to British Columbia. Fisheries sent instructions to Williams on 27 September to release those held in custody on suspended sentences as a guarantee for future good behaviour. Fisheries also informed Coccola of these instructions. The ministers in Ottawa believed the Babine had surrendered in good faith, on the assumption that the government would negotiate an equitable resolution, and they recognized the need for a diplomatic solution. Apparently Williams did not receive the telegram before the trial, or perhaps he chose to ignore instructions. On 28 September the prisoners appeared in court before Stipendiary Magistrate Hicks Beach and two justices of the peace, Stephenson and Helgesen (who remained a Fisheries officer).

The accused gave statements to the court, but their meaning was debated. Helgesen interpreted them as guilty pleas, but Coccola suggested the Babine did not understand the procedure and had not intended their statements as admissions of guilt.[88] Such misunderstanding did not seem to concern the bench. It found six of the accused guilty on two separate charges: unlawfully obstructing streams, for which they were fined $20 and required to pay $11.75 in costs or one month in jail, and obstructing officers in discharge of their duties, for which they were fined $100 or six months in jail. Two others were convicted of stealing fishing nets and were sentenced to one month in jail. Chief Big George had been charged with inciting riotous acts, but the bench found no evidence to support a conviction and he was acquitted.[89] The convicted were held in custody in Hazelton and then transported to the jail in New Westminster, where they arrived on 9 October.

Opinions about the trial and punishment varied widely among white settler society. Father Coccola, who had encouraged the Babine to surrender and assured them that they would be treated fairly, later described the hearing as a 'sham trial.'[90] Similarly, an editorial in Vancouver's *Province* newspaper condemned the result as 'an outrage against justice to these native peoples which would condemn the Government as guilty of the most treacherous and tyrannical conduct.'[91] An anonymous letter to the editor described the affair as 'a reproach to Canadian law and justice in the eyes of humanity, and a blot on the page of Canadian history.'[92] Official opinion in Ottawa was also concerned. Learning that the Babine had been convicted, and before the Babine were transported to New Westminster, the Minister of Fisheries sent instructions to Magistrate Hicks Beach to remit the full penalty imposed on the Babine for the offences under the *Fisheries Act*. Indian Affairs wrote to the Department of Justice to petition for the release of the Babine who were convicted of theft and obstructing officers under the Criminal Code.[93]

Helgesen, however, reluctant to show any weakness when dealing with Indians, opined that releasing the Babine was a mistake. He believed that insurrection was the inevitable result of a 'coaxing policy.' Unless the Babine were punished for their 'lawless acts,' they would drive whites from the region: '[S]hould the Babines be released in the present instance and justice be defeated, it will be a menace to white men amongst them in future.'[94] J.D. Wells, who had been unceremoniously dumped in the river and was later convicted of plying those Babine released from the New Westminster jail with alcohol and fined $50 under the *Indian Act*,[95] shared Helgesen's views. In a letter to the editor he stated bluntly that the action against the weirs was meant to secure fish for the canneries. 'It is not a case of starvation,' he wrote, 'that is the silliest balderdash. It is purely a case of proprietary rights over territory claimed as theirs; further, a contempt of the whiteman's government.'[96] These views were shared by others, and when combined with the reporting of a double murder in Hazelton and news that the accused, Native trapper Simon Peter Gun-a-noot, was still at large, a sense of unease and insecurity was created among some in the settler population.[97] Nonetheless, officials in Ottawa opted for a negotiated settlement. The interred Babine were pardoned and released on 11 October. Indian Affairs sent another telegram to Coccola recommending that he accompany Chief Big George, Indian Agent Loring, and Fisheries Inspector Williams to Ottawa to consult with the ministers on the fishery dispute. The Babine accepted the invitation and, accompanied by Father Coccola, Chief Big George and Tszak William travelled to Ottawa in October (see figure 2.5).

Ottawa Meetings

Chief Big George, Tszak William, and Father Coccola met with Minister of Fisheries L.P. Brodeur and Minister of the Interior Frank Oliver on 25 October 1906. Coccola's account begins as follows: 'We were shown through the city and at four o'clock we found ourselves in a large room. The Minister of Interior at the head of a long table, I was offered a seat to his right, my two Indians, trembling close to me and the rest of the table occupied by members of the Indian Department and Fisheries; at one end stenographers. At first the Minister of the interior was cross and sharp in questioning the Indians, I being the interpreter. The two poor men were naturally excited, all in perspiration, but I was interpreting with calm giving them a look of encouragement.'[98] The transcript does not convey the emotion Coccola remembered. The meeting began with Oliver and Brodeur questioning Big George about the

Babine's fishing practices and about that summer's catch. He replied that they caught very few fish: 'We began to put the barricades but the white men, the Fish Commissioners, came and they prevented us from fishing and many people were terrified and were afraid of getting into trouble. Some others did some little fishing. For my part I could not do any fishing because I had to keep people in order.'[99]

Brodeur and Oliver then explored the possibility of using nets. Did the Babine know that whites were prohibited from fishing in non-tidal waters, but that the government might allow the Babine to fish in the river if they considered using nets? Big George explained that they had tried nets in 1905, but only caught enough food to last until March. The salmon, he explained, could see the nets in the clear water of the Babine and would swim around them. It was simply not possible to catch enough fish to last the winter with short nets, and this is why they had refused the sockeye nets this year, even though they were new. The ministers considered various other means that the Babine could support themselves without fishing. Furs had once been an important source of income, but fur-bearing animals were scarce. Cannery employment was an option, but the canneries were at the mouth of the Skeena and Coccola discouraged the idea: 'It ruins the morals of the Indians. It would be better for them to die at home. They are always in debt. Never come home with money. Their money is always left down there.'[100] Another possibility was agriculture. Was there agricultural land? If so, would the Babine consider farming as an alternative to fishing? Coccola reported that there was some land, but it belonged to the government, not the Babine. The ministers continued to explore ways to secure the self-sufficiency of the Babine while, at the same time, reduce their reliance on fish. If the Babine could be taught to farm, then more fish would be available for the canneries. Big George said they planted a garden every year, but it produced little because of the cold. The meeting ended with questions from the ministers about the barricade incidents and the arrests.

A second meeting was held in Brodeur's office on 6 November. This time Williams and Helgesen were present, and they spent much of the meeting attempting to justify their actions to Brodeur and Oliver. Their partisanship is evident – they were expounding the views of the industrial fishery. Williams began by outlining the extent of the salmon-canning industry at the mouth of the Skeena, the amount of capital invested, and the need to preserve that investment by ensuring that Native fish weirs would not compete for the salmon:

This industry is very valuable; we consider it the principal industry of British Columbia.

Now we claim that the most important part of the fishery protection service on the Skeena River is the protection of the spawning grounds. We claim that it is absolutely necessary that the salmon should get to their spawning grounds in order to enable them to propagate, otherwise they will undoubtedly be exterminated. The Department is now spending large sums of money blasting away obstructions in the rivers, and opening up spawning areas, but what is the use of this expenditure if the Babine Indians are allowed to catch and kill the fish before they reach the spawning grounds.[101]

Williams equated the barricades with any other 'natural' obstacle that should be removed. Brodeur asked whether the barricades reduced the fish stock, noting that the Babine had fished with weirs since time immemorial, yet there were lots of fish in the river when the cannery operators arrived fifteen years ago. How then were the barricades the problem? Helgesen answered that Babine were now catching more fish than they had before the arrival of whites. They were now selling fish to the white trappers, traders, and miners, as well as using them for food:

The case is this, – in olden times the Indians were alone. The Indians got an ample supply, all they cared for. Mind, no one but the Indians in the country, – probably one or two at the Hudson Bay Post, that used the salmon. Now the country is full of packers, prospectors, miners, foresters, etc., and they all buy salmon, more or less. They buy sockeye salmon.

The Babine Indians like to kill every fish that comes along, they mean so many dollars to them. They pounce upon a school of fish which formerly they did not want, – they did not want it they could not dispose of it. The part which they don't use they sell now. It is most damaging upon the school of fish.[102]

Chief Big George countered, claiming they caught fewer fish with the single weir now in operation than with the three they once used. He did confirm that the Babine sold salmon to the HBC, which in turn sold the fish to the Stuart Lake people, but in this the HBC was simply facilitating trade between Native peoples.

Brodeur then asked his officers to state the fisheries law that prohibited barricades,[103] that referred to Indians,[104] and that governed fishing in non-tidal waters.[105] He concluded that the *Fisheries Act* and *Regulations* prohibited fishing with both barricades and nets in fresh water, and he wondered why the Babine were being offered gill nets to replace their barricades when the nets were illegal as well. The *Regulations* allowed Indians, with the permission of the Inspector, to use dip nets for the purposes of food, but they prohibited gill nets in fresh water. Williams replied: 'The way I looked at it was this, sir, it was for their food. You want the strictly legal aspect of the case? We went a little beyond the strict interpretation of the law, but we kept to the spirit of the law.'[106] Williams and Helgesen thus appear to have arrived at the following position: barricades must be prohibited, but the Babine should be allowed to use gill nets, although illegal, to catch their winter supply of food. If Indians fished as Indians, in their view to support meagre subsistence, then they might use nets in fresh water to catch salmon. If Indians fished as white men, that is, to sell, then they must fish as white men fished. Brodeur asked if the Indians were required to pay licence fees and the following exchange illustrates the different positions:

> Mr. Williams: – Not one single cent in any shape or form. All we wish is that if they are going to be white men let them fish as white men do; If Indians, who fish for their winter supply of food, we will give them any kind of nets they want.

> Mr. Brodeur: – Will they not require some clothing? How do you expect that they will provide clothing if they cannot sell fish?

> Mr. Williams: – Let them come down to the Canneries and work as all other Indians do, not loaf. The Babine Indians must realize that they must work as the other Indians do, they cannot be spared.[107]

Just before the Ottawa conferences, Alex Noble, a cannery operator at Port Essington, offered Fisheries 'an industrial point of view' that coincided with the position taken by Williams and Helgesen. Noble set out the three basic factors of production: capital, labour, and land (in this case, fish). He claimed that more than half a million dollars had been invested on the Skeena, that the industry paid three thousand workers a similar amount annually, and that the thirteen Skeena canneries required 1,600,000 fish.[108] To protect that capital investment, the cannery owners demanded that the Government enforce the law and remove the barricades.

Removing the barricades secured not only a supply of fish, but also a pool of dependent labour. Without barricades, the cannery operators hoped the Babine would turn to the canneries for work, the men as fishers and the women in the canneries. By 1901 the fishing industry on the Skeena employed more than 2500 people on the boats and in the canneries.[109] In 1905 the number for the entire northern coast was 5740 cannery workers and fishers.[110] Native people were an obvious source of labour, and in many ways were ideal for the isolated north-coast canneries. Fishing was seasonal work, and it was difficult to attract white settlers to the north for a few months' work. Native peoples, by contrast, lived in the region and were accustomed to supporting themselves between fisheries. The Fraser River Canner's Association claimed that the industrial salmon fishery provided Native people on the coast with the largest portion of their income – $750,000 in 1905.[111] Active recruitment notwithstanding, labour shortages during the fishing season were frequent. The Fisheries Inspector's Report for 1881 reveals that despite extensive Native employment the canneries were still looking for workers: 'At present the services of all the young men among the Indians who are accessible, and who have more or less been habituated to the work, have been eagerly sought by the canners. It should, I opine, be made a special object by the Indian Agents, stationed along the coast, to encourage the young men around them to devote themselves, during the season, to this industry – profitably alike to those who may engage in it, and to those who employ them.'[112] This was not an isolated shortage. John McNab, fishery guardian for the Skeena and Nass, reported in 1888 that a lack of Native labour was a problem given the defection of skilled Tsimpsean fishers from Metlakatla to Alaska. Most of these employees worked at piece rate, based on the number of fish caught or tins filled, and the cannery operators frequently complained about labour shortages. By paying piece rate, the canneries could almost always use more fishers. Once the licence fee had been paid, it did not matter how many were fishing if you were paying for the number of fish caught.

By the early twentieth century, however, the composition of the labour force had changed. White fishers received independent licences, and the canneries used Japanese fishers. Native fishers were less important than they had been, but Native women's labour inside the canneries had assumed increasing importance, as the strike on the Skeena at the beginning of the 1904 season revealed.[113] The rhetorical stance taken by Williams and Helgesen, suggesting the Babine should go to the coast to work for the canneries as did other Natives, high-lighted the effort to secure a labour force and a supply of fish.

Seeing the issue for what it was – a question of allocation and not of conservation – the Minister of the Interior, Frank Oliver, suggested that the Babine should be entitled to catch a fixed number of fish, enough to cover their food needs, with their weirs. Having reached this threshold the Babine would remove their weirs, but could continue to fish with nets and sell the catch in order to purchase clothing and other essentials.[114] Oliver did not want the weir prohibition to push more Natives into a welfare dependency relationship with Indian Affairs, increasing its costs. Williams, Helgesen, and Fisheries Commissioner E.E. Prince objected to this proposal on the grounds that if the Babine were al-lowed to use weirs, other Natives would want to do the same. Further-more, allowing the barricades would require extensive supervision. It was simpler to reallocate fish by prohibiting fish weirs. The issue was unresolved, and the conference ended, as had the first one, with a discussion of the August barricade incident. No decision was made, and no agreement reached.

On 8 November, two days after the meeting at Fisheries, Oliver wrote to Brodeur, arguing that, as British and Canadian government policy, Natives had a 'first right to their ordinary means of livelihood,' or a right to compensation if they were deprived of their resources.[115] Fisheries, he suggested, was concerned solely to protect the interests of cannery owners, and was ignoring the rights of the Babine. If the interests of the cannery operators were to prevail, the Babine must be compensated, and Oliver made it clear that the costs should be born either by the canneries or by Fisheries: '[T]he Indians are clearly enti-tled to compensation, either directly at the hands of the canners or on the part of the Government which assumes to subordinate the evident necessities of the Indians to the supposed interests of the canners.'[117]

Then the Babine, through Coccola, offered to relinquish their barri-cades in exchange for nets, arable land, farm implements, and an in-dustrial school. The terms were as follows:

'Babine Indians' Proposition':

We are willing to relinquish barricades on Babine lake if in return the Government furnishes us:
1. With sufficient netting, i.e., hundred feet for each family, or each individual man or woman depending on himself for support; the nets to

be replaced by Government when out of use or so damaged as to render fishing unpracticable.

2. With sufficient arable land, say, 460 acres in front of Babine village on the opposite of the river and 1000 acres to be found on Babine Lake shore where some families are already located, or adjoining Old Fort Reserve.

3. Two ploughs, 2 mowers and horse rakes, 2 pairs of harnesses for each band. Grass seeds and grain sufficient for the amount of land and garden seeds like potatoes, &c.

4. One industrial school in the district.[117]

The weirs had been conceded, and Fisheries now believed it had something to work with. Brodeur, in a letter to Oliver, responded to the accusations of collusion between Fisheries and cannery owners, claiming that the removal of barricades was not a question of cannery domination, 'but of the perpetuation of a national asset' that should not be threatened by 'the primitive and destructive method[s]' of the Babine.[118] Enforcing the law was in everybody's interest, argued Brodeur, including the Babine's, but particularly of the Natives who sought employment as fishers or cannery workers at the coast. Why should their right to 'lucrative employment' be sacrificed in the interests of the Babine? The right to fish had been re-cast as the right to lucrative employment. Brodeur then proposed a draft of what was to become the Dominion's version of the 'Babine Barricade Agreement.' His version omitted the specifics contained in the Babine proposition regarding net length, acreage of arable land, and farm implements, and it made no mention of an industrial school, but the general outline was similar:

1. It was agreed, in the best interests of all concerned, and in a special endeavour to meet the wishes of the Indians, that the Department of Marine and Fisheries would be willing to relax its Fishery Regulations to such an extent as to admit of a sufficient amount of netting being prosecuted on the River to enable the Indians to obtain their requisite food supply, the cost of the nets supplied from time to time as necessary, to be borne by the Department of Indian Affairs; each head of a family or each individual Indian supporting himself or others, will be furnished with sufficient netting for his needs; the Department of Marine and Fisheries agreeing to provide instruction in the best manner of using the nets in order to obtain a proper food supply;

2. The Department of Indian Affairs agreeing to send the Reserve Commissioner early next spring to the Babine Indians, with instructions to

ascertain what additional agricultural lands they require, and to adjust their land holdings so as to give them suitable land for farming;

   3. The Department of Indian Affairs further agreeing that Reserve Commissioner Vowell will be instructed to make a special study on the spot, of the needs of the Babine Indians, and to suggest such measures as, in his opinion, will assist in providing for their future support;

   4. Also, that the Officers of both Departments will cooperate to carry out this arrangement, in order to avoid further difficulties;

   5. In consideration of these terms, the Indian Chiefs agree to abandon the use of barricades, to accept these conditions, to abide by the law, to assist the Officers of both Departments in the discharge of their duties and to assist the Departments in carrying out such measures as may be adopted in the best interests of the Indians.[119]

Fisheries would 'relax its Fisheries regulations' to allow the Babine to procure fish with nets if Indian Affairs agreed to provide nets and land, and the Babine agreed to relinquish their weirs. This version of the agreement, which has become known as the 'Barricade Treaty,' appears in subsequent correspondence between Fisheries and Indian Affairs and seems to have been generally acceptable to both departments. There is no evidence that Chief Big George or William Tszak signed this version, and evidence of their consent to these specific terms is slim. Whether or not anything had been signed the Babine chiefs returned home believing they had made a treaty with the Dominion, although probably on the terms they had proposed and not on Fisheries' subsequent proposal.

Implementing the Agreement

Different understandings created problems of implementation. The two Dominion departments continued to disagree over the specific terms and over who should bear responsibility for the costs. Discussions between Fisheries and Indian Affairs continued into the following year, with the result that the Babine began to wonder if the terms would be honoured. Indian Affairs was still trying to retain a limited barricade fishery for the Babine; otherwise, the costs to compensate the Babine and ensure their self-sufficiency would be too high. Further, Oliver expressed concern that the cost of additional land to compensate the Babine fell entirely on his Department when in fact Fisheries should be responsible because it was demanding the weirs' removal for the benefit of one of its interest groups – the canneries. In an attempt to extricate Indian Affairs from shouldering the cost, Oliver suggested there was never any promise to provide the Babine with additional land, but only to 'adjust' their existing reserves. Given the stalemate between the provincial and Dominion governments over reserve allocations, providing additional land for the Babine meant that Indian Affairs had to purchase it from the province. Brodeur responded that compensating Indians was the prerogative of Indian Affairs and he did not want to trench on that prerogative. Further, he reiterated that his department had made a significant concession by agreeing not to prosecute the Babine for using gill nets on the river, even though nets were illegal. He was not prepared to allow fish weirs of any description.

Another sticking point was the sale of net-caught fish. On this issue, Brodeur reluctantly, but only temporarily, conceded to Indian Affairs that the Babine be allowed to sell some of their catch: 'Since it appears to be a fact that the Indians have hitherto to some extent trafficed [*sic*] in the food fish they have taken, I would not be disposed at the moment to interfere with the extent to which this traffic has prevailed; but this concession, so far as it may bind in future the policy of the Department, must be distinctly understood as conditional upon whatever action it is deemed advisable for the Government to take upon the recommendation which will shortly be submitted by the British Columbia Fishery Commission.'[120] On the basis of this concession, Indian Affairs agreed to buy nets and additional agricultural land.[121] In February 1907, Fisheries sent the following instructions to Williams and to Coccola:

> The solution of this matter involves:
>   1. The prohibition of barricades;
>   2. The permission of netting by the Indians as above explained in lieu of barricades, subject of course to the regular statutory close times;
>   3. Net fishing in Babine Lake during the winter through the ice, as suggested and explained by Fishery Overseer Helgesen, the Officers of this Department under your control to furnish full and necessary instructions to the Indians, as to the manner and method of using the nets; and
>   4. The Department of Indian Affairs to supply the nets to be used by the Indians, and to make all possible arrangements to secure agricultural land for their use.[122]

Farm implements, seed, and schools were missing, and the sale of fish was not explicitly permitted or forbidden. Restrictions on net fishing and the proposed ice fishing were new. The later was Helgesen's idea, and part of his attempt to reduce the Babine sockeye catch. He believed that if the Babine caught white fish in winter they could sustain themselves without needing to catch and store large quantities of sockeye in August and September. It fit his vision of a Babine subsistence economy that neither interfered nor competed with the industrial commercial fishery at the coast.

By June 1907, the Dominion had not taken any visible steps to honour the agreement, whatever its terms. With the fishing season looming, the Babine were concerned that nothing had happened. Father Coccola wrote to the Minister of Fisheries, stating that no land had been conveyed and that none of the promises had been fulfilled. He warned of impending trouble, 'for the Indians at the suggestion of some white people are more or less under the impression that we sold, at our interest, to the canneries and department of Fisheries their natural rights and are in a state of restlessness.'[123] Indian Affairs had authorized the purchase of nets in April, but when Helgesen delivered them in July the Babine were dissatisfied with the length. In response to the seriousness of the situation, Helgesen ordered additional nets, and this eased tensions. Indian Affairs also provided seed grain and agreed to provide relief for those requiring assistance.[124] At the end of the season the fisheries guardian, G. Spinning, reported that the Indians had caught enough fish and were 'jubilant' with their new nets.[125] Inspector Williams informed Fisheries of the additional nets after the fact, adding rather gratuitously that, '[t]he Babine Indians have always been a bombastic, trouble some and lazy lot of Indians, and will remain so to the end of the chapter.'[126] At least with regard to the nets, however, the Babine had successfully demanded that the Dominion comply with their understanding of the agreement.

The next year, Indian Affairs surveyed and purchased from the province an additional 1948 acres that it added to the Babine reserves (see figure 2.1).[127] The new reserves all bordered Babine Lake and extended existing reserves. One of the new reserves, IR 16, was a mirror image of an earlier reserve, IR 6, and it gave the Babine control of the land on either side of the river at the outflow of Babine Lake, an old weir site. These new reserves, unlike others allotted to the Babine or to neighbouring peoples by Peter O'Reilly in 1891 and later by the royal commission in 1916, were intended to compensate the Babine for their weirs. IR 16 was particularly important because it secured access from either side of the river to the gill-net fishery that Fisheries had insisted upon and that the Babine had agreed to undertake. Thus, these reserve allotments involved more than just setting aside land; they were part of an agreement that included nets and a guarantee that the fisheries law would not be enforced against the Babine net fishery.[128]

In 1908, Helgesen reported that the Babine had caught sufficient fish for their winter supply and that although their nets were rotten and needed replacing, they 'seemed more satisfied and pleased than on any former occasion.'[129] When Overseer Stewart Norrie travelled through the region towards the end of August 1908 he observed that the former barricade site was deserted. The buildings that were once there had been stripped and the Babine had built six smokehouses at various locations just below the outflow from Babine Lake. With the introduction of nets, the fishing and processing that had once been concentrated at the weirs had dispersed by 1908. What had once required the collective efforts of the group was becoming the work of smaller family units (see figure 2.11). In 1909, Indian Affairs spent $700 to replace the nets issued in 1907, and Norrie, Indian Agent Loring, and Guardian Charles Pearce distributed 83 nets and lines to the Babine.

Having agreed to allow the Babine to sell fish caught with nets on the Upper Skeena pending the report of the British Columbia Fisheries Commission, the Department of Fisheries got the recommendation it expected when the commission released its report in 1908. The commissioners briefly surveyed the barricade disputes on the Cowichan and Babine rivers and concluded that the sale of fish from these locales must stop. If Natives were to sell fish, they had to catch them under the appropriate commercial licence. The food-fishery concession must not expand to allow sales. According to the commissioners, '[t]o be lenient in one locality and rigid in another is fatal, and all the Indian tribes should be treated with the same uniform regard for their real interests, and with a regard for the stupendous national and commercial interests involved.'[130]

Despite the apparent calm, the Barricade Treaty would continue to be a thorn in the side of fisheries officials in the region. In 1909, Overseer Norrie wrote that providing the Babine with nets was the source of considerable jealousy among Gitksan at Hazelton and in the Bulkley Valley. They threatened to start fishing with barricades if it would force the government to give them nets as well. Norrie attributed these difficulties to the weakness the Dominion had shown, first when it released the Babine convicted of fisheries violations, and then when it

Figure 2.11   Sockeye salmon fishery on the Babine River, 1923. Note the nets piled into the front of one of the rowboats.

provided nets: 'I can trace this course of unrest right back to our Babine troubles, they saw the law despised, the Government Officials humiliated and assaulted, and instead of being punished, they have been rewarded, naturally they think they must commit some depradation before they can expect to be rewarded also.'[131] Nonetheless, in 1911 Indian Affairs spent $700 to purchase new nets.

Conclusion

In 1910, at a gathering in the home of Inspector of Fisheries Williams, the owners and managers of the canneries that relied on the Skeena sockeye publicly thanked the retiring Fisheries officer Hans Helgesen. The canners gave Helgesen a gold-headed walking stick, a purse of gold containing $650, and a copy of their public address, which they had all signed. As reported in the *Trade Register*:

> The address expressed the thanks of the cannerymen for the active and important part taken by Mr. Helgesen in obtaining the permanent prohibition of the 'Babine Barricades,' and added, 'We realize that through your efforts, combined with those of the department, this terrible engine of destruction to the salmon has been obliterated for all time. As a result, with the strict enforcement of the weekly close season, an abundance of salmon is allowed to reach the spawning grounds, and also enables the Indians in the interior to obtain a more abundant supply for their needs.
>
> 'We are also of the opinion that the present magnificent run of salmon, a run, we believe, unprecedented in the history of the Skeena River canneries, is due in a great measure to the removal of these barricades, and we trust that the department will continue to remove other obstructions until they make the Skeena river the grandest salmon stream on the coast.'[132]

The canneries had secured their supply of fish, and the owners rewarded the government official for effectively enforcing the law that prohibited weirs. Moreover, the needs of the Indians had, in the canners' opinion, been amply satisfied.

When Chief William of the Fort Babine people and Chief Michel of the Old Fort Babine testified to the Royal Commission on Indian Affairs for the Province of British Columbia (the McKenna-McBride commission) in 1915, the commissioners heard from a desperately poor people. The fur-bearing animals were scarce, they were unable to catch enough salmon to feed themselves, and their crops were frequently killed by a late-spring or an early-fall frost. The Dominion had intended to minimize their salmon catch, while at the same time secure access to other resources so that the Babine could provide for themselves. Nine years after the Barricade Treaty, the Babine chiefs made it clear to the commissioners that the resources were inadequate. They sought more agricultural land and wanted their hunting territories included in their reserves, but their focus was salmon. The Babine wanted their fishing territories protected and enough timbered land to fuel the smokehouses that preserved the fish. The commissioners refused most Babine requests for additional land, but they did increase their reserves by 1282 acres, including land that bordered traditional fishing grounds along the lake and river. Two reserves on either side of the Babine River near an old weir site at the outflow of Nilkitlkwa Lake, IR 21 and IR21A, were granted as a fishing station and for farming and timber supply (see figure 2.1).

Small plots of land bordering the lake or river, however, did not provide sufficient resources unless they were accompanied by guaranteed access to the fishery. Whatever the Babine had been told by Peter O'Reilly when he allotted reserves in 1891, or whatever the Babine believed they had been promised as part of the 1906 agreement, they now had insufficient access to fish. The commissioners reserved more land to the Babine, but this did not increase their allocation of salmon. Fisheries allowed the cannery catch on the coast to grow while further restricting the Babine catch to a limited net food fishery. The fishing sites may have been secured from white settlement, but the Babine were still required under the *Fisheries Act* to *conserve* fish for the canneries. Justified on the basis of establishing and preserving a particular economic order, and legitimized with law, the removal of the Babine weirs had secured for the Skeena River canneries a supply of fish and a flexible, although increasingly neglected and impoverished, labour force.

CHAPTER THREE

The Law Runs Through It: Weirs, Logs, Nets, and Fly Fishing on the Cowichan River, 1877–1937

In contrast to the transparent efforts of capital and state to eliminate the Lake Babine weir fisheries and to capture the Skeena sockeye runs, the conflict over fish weirs on the Cowichan River demonstrates the complexity of a continuing colonial encounter and of the role of law in shaping that encounter. Spread over sixty years, while a settler society established its control and the Cowichan people struggled to retain some control, the dispute over weirs reveals state law both as an instrument of colonial power and as an avenue, albeit limited, of resistance. The Canadian state sought control of the river, channelling its use and its resources to lumber mills and fly fishers, and away from the Cowichan people. It did so with law, and in the process denied the legitimacy and efficacy of Cowichan law. The Cowichan, for their part, defended their legal traditions, insisting that human use of the river and the fish in it were allocated under and subject to Cowichan laws. The result of sixty years of struggle, however, was a river subject to the laws of the Canadian state. The Cowichan built their last weir in 1936, a symbolic end of the last vestiges of Cowichan control. They were confined to a meagre subsistence fishery, supervised by the state, on what had been their river.

To focus on the result, however, is to miss the processes of colonialism at work. Weirs had been prohibited on British Columbian rivers under Canadian law since 1877, yet the Cowichan continued to build them for sixty years, often with support from the local settler population and the Department of Indian Affairs, and sometimes with permission from the Department of Fisheries. Constructed at a distance, the formal terms of Canadian law were modified not only by Cowichan resistance and accommodation but also by the presence of a local settler society, and to understand the processes of colonialism, particularly the role of law in remaking a people and a territory, is to understand the local historical detail. The Cowichan families who controlled the weirs defended their long and continuing weir fishery. Other Cowichan, particularly those with uncertain access to the weirs under Cowichan law, preferred to use nets and spears in the lower river where tides limited the effectiveness of weirs. Immigrant working-class fishers selling fresh fish in the Victoria markets advocated a gill net fishery in Cowichan Bay. Cannery fishers sought permission to fish with seine nets. Victoria's elite, the tourist industry, and railway interests imagined the river as an angling and hunting preserve, and Fisheries stocked the river with Atlantic salmon to enhance sport fishing. Until a railway spur was built to Cowichan Lake in the early twentieth century, logging companies used the river to run logs to mills at the coast, destroying the weirs and fish habitat and eroding valuable farmland.

The uses of the Cowichan River were many and varied, and often conflicting. Although Native and non-Native interests frequently clashed, the conflict did not always follow this cultural divide, and elements within both groups sought broader alliances to keep competing users off the river. The enduring conflict, nonetheless, remains between the claims of the Cowichan and the Canadian state over ownership and control, and over the legitimacy of different but increasingly intertwined legal traditions. The protracted struggle over fish weirs on the Cowichan River reveals those traditions, starkly contrasted over sixty years in opposition to each other.[1]

The Cowichan River and Its People

From headwaters in Cowichan Lake, the Cowichan River winds forty-seven kilometres east through the narrow and fertile flood plain of the Cowichan Valley on Vancouver Island to the ocean. The river is at its lowest from July to September, before rising with the fall rains and cresting with the winter rains of December and January. Chinook, coho, and chum salmon spawn in the river or its tributaries, as do steelhead trout. All anadromous, these fish live their early lives in fresh water, migrate to the ocean, and return to their natal streams to spawn and to die. These four fish, with different but interconnected life cycles, became the focus of dispute between the Cowichan people and the Canadian state for control of the river.

The Cowichan lived in as many as fifteen winter villages along the lower course of the Cowichan and Koksilah rivers and around Cowichan

Bay. Six villages appear repeatedly in the historical record of the late nineteenth century and their locations and relative size are mapped in figure 3.1: Somenos (S'amuna'), Quamichan (Kwa'mutsun), Comiaken (Qwumi'yuqun), Khenipsen (Hinupsum), Koksilah (Hwulqwselu), and Clemclemeluts (Lumlumulu<u>ts</u>). The Cowichan spoke Hul'qumi'num, closely connected to dialects spoken on the lower Fraser River,[3] and had strong cultural and familial ties with many of the surrounding Central Coast Salish peoples. Seasonal rounds took them well beyond the Cowichan Valley to neighbouring islands in the spring and to the mouth of the Fraser River for much of the summer.

There is little in the historical or ethnographic record about these villages and their changing social organization in the nineteenth and twentieth centuries as the Cowichan responded to the arrival of European traders, to the devastation of recurring epidemics, and later to settlers and to industry.[4] This is in part because the Cowichan chose not to share information about their laws and social structures with outsiders. In an 1886 visit to the Cowichan, the ethnographer Franz Boas found great difficulty eliciting any information. One Cowichan man at Somenos told him that '[t]he whites look upon the Indians not as humans but as dogs, and he did not wish anyone to laugh at things that were their laws, such as painted houses and articles used for celebrating their festivals.'[5] More recently, the Cowichan have chosen to tell their story to a wider audience in *Those Who Fell from the Sky: A History of the Cowichan Peoples.*[6] There is, as well, enough in the historical record and the general literature on the Central Coast Salish to suggest an outline of the social organization within and between the Cowichan villages.[7]

Anthropologist Wayne Suttles describes the family (consisting of husband, wife, and minor children, possibly plural wives, dependent older relatives, and slaves) as the basic social unit of the Coast Salish. It would have occupied a section of a winter house, kept its own stores, cooked and eaten independently, and possibly travelled to its own resource procurement sites in summer. Members of this relatively small unit were connected to other Central Coast Salish through dense kinship ties that produced reciprocal rights and obligations.

A household, as the next level of social organization, 'was composed of several families related either through males or females, who cooperated economically and socially.'[8] The activities of the household were directed by a core of blood relatives, or a kin group, all of whom were descended from some 'notable ancestor.' From this ancestor the members of the kin group inherited the rights to resources, names, dances,

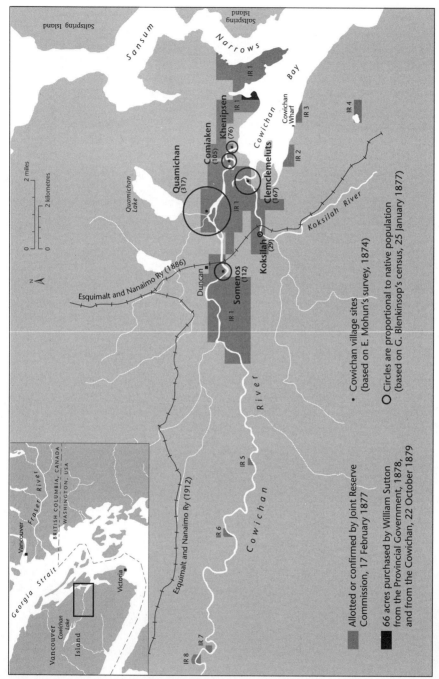

Figure 3.1 Cowichan Villages and Reserves.

songs, and ceremonial objects. Although membership was extensive in theory, '[i]n practice, the management of resources remained in one house and tended to become concentrated in the hands of an elite, through a preference for primogeniture modified by a policy of restricting technical, ritual, and other information to children who showed special aptitude.'[9] The leading men of the kin group, according to Suttles, were probably identified as chiefs of the local group.

A winter village may have been occupied by a local group, or by several houses that included several kin and local groups.[10] Much like the families within a household, the houses within a local group or village would cooperate to gather resources, defend their winter village, and join in ceremonial activity. The degree of cooperation between the six Cowichan winter villages would have varied considerably. They joined together to cross the Strait of Georgia each summer to their Fraser River fishing sites, but then would fish independently. Similarly, the chiefs of the powerful kin groups within the villages would direct the building of weirs at established locations along the Cowichan River in the spring and fall. The villages would also combine to defend or expand their territory.

The most comprehensive though as yet unpublished study of Cowichan marine resource use is David L. Rozen's, 'The Ethnozoology of the Cowichan Indian People of British Columbia.'[11] Rozen's informants provided Cowichan names for each species of salmon and trout, for the different runs of each species, and for the different stages of their life cycles. Chinook were considered the most important salmon and were the first to run in the Cowichan's seasonal cycle. A winter run appeared in January or February, intensifying through March and April, and a second run would appear in the late spring and early summer. In late June or early July, the Cowichan crossed the Strait of Georgia to a summer village near the mouth of the Fraser, where they caught and dried sockeye salmon and collected edible plants in the surrounding territory to augment their winter food supply. In September they returned to fish on the Cowichan River.

Through the fall the Cowichan used twelve or more weirs in the river to catch salmon and steelhead trout, some of which they smoked and stored (see figures 3.2 and 3.3).[12] They were joined by people from the winter villages on the Chemainus River, just north of the Cowichan Valley, who also held fishing sites on the Cowichan River.[13] Chinook salmon would arrive first, congregating in Cowichan Bay in August and September, migrating to the middle and upper reaches of the

Figure 3.2 View of the downstream side of the fish weir at Quamichan, ca. 1866. One lattice-work panel has been removed to allow fish and a canoe to pass through.

Figure 3.3 View of the upstream side of the fish weir at Quamichan, ca. 1866. Small openings in the lattice-work panels allowed fish into the pens, where they could be speared or netted.

Cowichan River with the first fall rains, and spawning in the latter half of October. Steelhead would begin to run at the same time, but their spawning activity would not peak until March or April. Coho would gather in Cowichan Bay from late September to early November, running with the chinook in mid-October, peaking in November, and continuing through December. The chum would follow a similar pattern, slightly later. They would begin running in October and peak in late November, spawning in the lower portions of the main stems of the river.[14] The Cowichan weir fishery continued until the late fall rain raised the level of the river to the point where the weirs could no longer withstand the current and the debris.

The three salmon species – chinook, chum, and coho – migrate once to the ocean and return once to spawn, but steelhead trout travel within the river for several years before migrating to the ocean. They spend their first summer in natal streams, migrating to the warmer water in the lower reaches of the Cowichan for the winter. They repeat the cycle in their second year. In the spring of their third year they migrate to the ocean. This migration pattern meant that a young steelhead could pass through the weirs several times before returning to spawn as a mature fish in its fourth year.

Access to resources, including fish, was controlled by a system of property rights. As a general observation about the rights of access among the Coast Salish, Suttles found that '[w]eirs and traps for salmon seem usually to have been built by a whole community, perhaps under the direction of the head of an extended family, but with no distinction in access. However, the houses standing at the weir sites, which were necessary for smoking the catch, were owned by individuals or extended families.'[15] Access to the weirs among the Cowichan may have been somewhat more controlled by particular families, although community members were not excluded. Rozen suggests that a Cowichan headman directed the building of a weir. These were high-status people who not only held the right to build a weir, but were usually the head of a house or a family as well. The headman selected a location for a weir and from four to six members of his family to help build it. The weir belonged to its builders, and once it was built they speared or netted the fish in the traps from the top of the weir. The weirs worked best in shallow water during low run-off, and the Cowichan prized sites a short distance above rapids (see figure 3.4). If the weir were located on the lower river, the builders were required to let enough fish through for the upper weirs. When the builders had taken their fill,

Figure 3.4   Fishers on a large Cowichan weir just above rapids, ca. 1900.

others could use the weirs, but once a weir had been constructed, the headman had a right to rebuild in the same location the following year. The wicker screens were removed, but the upright poles were left in the water to validate the claim.[16]

Suttles, in describing the class system among the Coast Salish, argues that '[a]t one time, most villages consisted each of a single lineage which regarded itself as descended from an ancestor left on the site by the Transformer, or dropped from the sky.'[17] When villages grew to accommodate other families, the ancestry of the original family conferred rights to the village site, fishing sites, and other productive places. This explained, in part, the emergence of a division between an upper and lower class. Suttles argues that defined classes existed among the Coast Salish, but that the class structure resembled an 'inverted pear' rather than a pyramid. Most people belonged to an upper or respectable class, fewer to a lower or worthless class, and fewer still were considered slaves. As evidence of the importance of these origin stories, the lower classes were those who 'had lost their history,' meaning that they had no claim to productive resource sites or other privileges. Those with recognized lineage controlled access to resources and to whatever surplus might be produced, while those unrelated to the owner might suffer poverty.

Lineage controlled access within villages, but it also provided the basis for excluding outsiders from the resource unless they had familial ties. The Cowichan were entitled to build the weirs because, according to their legends, they were the descendants of the first people to build weirs on the river.[18] In Cowichan lore, the first person to fall from the sky, a man named Syalutsa, moved with his wife and children to a place on the Cowichan River, the site of the village at Somenos. Once at their new home, they discovered there were no fish. Syalutsa built a weir, but still there were no fish. He fished every day for a long time, but always returned home empty-handed. One day Syalutsa took his baby daughter in her cradle-basket to the river. He tied the basket behind the weir with a long cedar-bark rope and left her to drift on the current. When he returned the next morning, the cradle was floating on the water, but his daughter had disappeared. The trap behind the weir, however, was full of salmon. The baby girl had been transformed into a salmon. She had been sacrificed so that the salmon would spawn in the Cowichan River and provide her people with food forever. The Cowichan, it is said, are descendants of Syalutsa and the other first people who fell from the sky, and because of this they have a right to the salmon.[19]

Land, Logs, Weirs, and a Settler Society

In early 1877, the Joint Indian Reserve Commission (JIRC) camped for a month near Quamichan village to investigate Cowichan concerns, to confirm previous reserve grants, to consider settler purchases and pre-emptions, and to take a census of Native people before allotting what was intended to be the final settlement of Cowichan reserves. The census taker, George Blenkinsop, recorded 831 people in the six Cowichan winter villages (see figure 2.1),[20] and the commissioners discovered considerable unrest among them.

Governor James Douglas had purchased land from natives on the Saanich peninsula to the south and at Nanaimo and Port Hardy to the north, but no agreement had been made with the Cowichan. Instead, Douglas, who described the Cowichan as 'the most numerous and warlike of the Native tribes in Vancouver's Island,'[21] launched gunboat expeditions in 1853 and 1856 to capture and, after cursory trials, to execute several Cowichan who had allegedly murdered early settlers.[22] A few settlers trickled into the valley in the 1850s, but it was not until 1862 that Douglas thought the Cowichan sufficiently subdued for him to sanction the first organized party of settlers to sail from Victoria to the Cowichan. The settlers arrived in August with Douglas, their belongings towed into Cowichan Bay by a gunboat, and encountered considerable opposition from the Cowichan, who insisted that the government purchase their land before allowing settlement.[23] One who accompanied the expedition recounted the combination of promises, bluster, and violence with which Douglas secured land for the settlers: 'When the settlement was first planted in Cowichan Valley in August 1862, certain definite promises were made to the Indians by Governor Douglas in person. He told them in the presence of the settlers that in the ensuing Autumn he would return to Cowichan, have a gathering of all their tribes and make them suitable presents. This promise was never fulfilled. The Lamalchas [of nearby Kuper Island] unhappily became troublesome, three of there [sic] number were hanged, and the Governor did not think it would be expedient *then* to carry out his original intention.'[24]

Not only did Douglas not return to fulfil his promises, but the allocation of reserves in the Cowichan Valley before Confederation is beset with confusion, multiple and inaccurate surveys, settler purchases and pre-emptions, cut-offs, and growing Cowichan discontent.[25] In 1871, the Chief Commissioner of Lands and Works sent an incomplete schedule of reserves to the Colonial Secretary in London, indicating a single reserve for the Cowichan Tribes of 2675 acres, surrounding much of the lower river.[26] On the basis of Blenkinsop's 1877 census listing 831 Cowichan, they had a meagre 3.2 acres per person. The Cowichan expected more, and when the JIRC arrived in 1877 the broken promises had not been forgotten. Reserve Commissioner Gilbert Malcolm Sproat recorded their grievances.[27] Settler encroachment on Cowichan land was a continuing concern, but so was access to the Fraser River fishery. The Cowichan had heard that their summer village and fishing station on the lower Fraser had been purchased by whites and wanted to know if this was true. Sproat acknowledged that the land had been sold. The absentee owner had not objected to the Cowichan's seasonal presence – Sproat estimated that 1000 Natives had fished from the site during the 1877 season – but Sproat thought conflict was inevitable and there was nothing he could do given that the land had already been purchased. He and the other reserve commissioners confirmed and extended the existing reserve in the Cowichan Valley, creating a comparatively large, contiguous reserve for all the villages that largely surrounded the lower reaches of the Cowichan River, two small reserves on Cowichan Bay, one surrounding Dougan Lake, and four small reserves further upstream on the Cowichan River that the commissioners identified as fishing stations – 6030 acres in total (see figure 2.1). These upstream fishing stations were intended to protect weir fisheries.

In 1878, Sproat returned to find that the province had sold 60 acres of the reserve to a settler, William Sutton, who intended to build a lumber mill. Sproat blamed 'the unbusinesslike inaction of the Provincial government,' which had all the necessary documents in its possession and should have known that this was reserve land and not available for sale.[28] He was, however, more concerned about the Cowichan weir fishery than about the land. Running logs from Cowichan Lake to the mill would damage the weirs, interfering with the Cowichan's fishery, something that the JIRC had promised would not be disturbed. Sproat insisted that the government secure the Cowichan's consent and compensate them for the disruption of their fishery: 'In connection both with the clearing of the River and the requirements of the proposed saw mill in getting saw-logs down the River, I may remind you of the absolute necessity of thoroughly explaining to the Indians the effect of these operations upon their numerous fishing weirs, and of obtaining their intelligent consent to such operations and their agreement with your approval to receive compensation for any injury to their weirs.'[29]

These comments precipitated an extended discussion between Indian Affairs and Fisheries over the applicability of the *Fisheries Act* to Native peoples in British Columbia. Fisheries argued that the *Act* prohibited weirs and that they must be removed. Indian Affairs defended the Cowichan's use of weirs as both a right and a necessity. The result of this intra-departmental debate was a practical, if informal, exemption for Native peoples. Fisheries announced that Natives were subject to the *Act*, but instructed its officials to exempt them when not fishing among whites.[30]

The lumber mill remained a problem. Sutton claimed a $28,000 investment and hoped some amicable arrangement could be reached.[31] The Indian superintendent for British Columbia, Israel Wood Powell, believed the Cowichan were unlikely to surrender the land. He suggested erasing the reserve grant from the reserve commissioner's Minutes of Decision; the land was of little value to the Cowichan, he argued, and with the mill they would be able to purchase lumber more cheaply. The provincial attorney general George A. Walkem approved, and Powell wondered whether Indian Affairs would consent as well?[32] Sproat was astonished. Nothing was more certain, he argued, to reinforce distrust among Native people of white government than such duplicitous action and he pressed for a negotiated solution. The mill was likely useful to the Cowichan, but they were in the best position to judge its value and that of their land and fish weirs. Tact and maybe a little money would settle the conflict, but only 'if the people had confidence.' 'There has been,' he wrote, 'too much man of war business on the coast and too little plain kindly dealing.' The taking of Cowichan land, illegally and improperly, with no regard to the weir fishery was too much like the former and the honour of the Crown was at stake.[33]

Indian Affairs instructed Powell to negotiate, and on 22 October 1879 the chiefs of the Comiaken, Quamichan, Clemclemeluts, Somenos, and Khenipsen villages made their marks on an '*Agreement* between the undersigned Chiefs of the Cowichan tribes of Indians resident in the Cowichan District and William Sutton of the same place. Gentleman.'[34] The agreement, witnessed by Powell but not signed by anyone other than the chiefs, conveyed the land to Sutton in exchange for his payment of $200. The matter seemed closed, but the agreement, as written, was not what the Cowichan chiefs had understood. They had wanted lumber wagons instead of the money, perhaps because Indian Affairs would have held the money in trust. Five wagons (one for each band) would cost approximately $350, and Powell promised to ask Indian

Affairs to cover the additional cost. It eventually agreed, but only as a cost 'incurred in order to encourage the Indians at following agricultural pursuits,' and not as an obligation arising from the agreement.[35]

Sproat's initial concern – that running logs would damage the fish weirs and interfere with the Cowichan right to fish as formerly – had been forgotten. Perhaps the issue had been raised, but the Cowichan had not been prepared to bargain about their weirs. Or perhaps compensation for the damage to the weirs had been included. The Koksilah people, whose weirs on the Koksilah River would not have been affected by logs on the Cowichan, were not a party to the agreement, and the final cost of settling the improper sale was approximately $350, well above the $66 that Sutton had paid the provincial government for the land one year earlier. The damage to the Cowichan fishery and to Cowichan and settler land from the logs, however, would far exceed either sum. Loggers drove thousands of logs, millions of timber feet, down the river in the short period between the summer's low water and the winter's high water, the principal season of salmon migration. Log-jams were frequent, particularly in the canyons, and often required dynamiting. Once loosed, the logs and water swept down the river, threatening road and railway bridges, causing extensive damage to the riverbed, and killing the migrating salmon and trout. Bazil Kier, then a young logger, recounted a 1906 log drive, reputedly the largest to descend the river, where dynamite was used to break a log-jam, and then, '[a]s the river was cleared of logs we moved camp to the Scutts [Skutz] falls and the logs made a thunderous noise going over the falls and with thousands of salmon jumping trying to get up the river. It was quite a sight and made up for the hardships.'[36]

Complaints from both the Cowichan and settlers about the log damage appeared almost immediately after logging began. Powell wrote to Indian Affairs in 1881, providing a sketch of how the logs had altered the riverbed and eroded farm land between Somenos and Quamicham.[37] The damage seemed particularly devastating in the early 1890s, beginning with a run in 1890 that swept over much of the Cowichan flood plain, destroying houses and farm buildings, eroding good soil, and stranding logs the length of the main Cowichan reserve. 'At the large [log] jamb near the junction of the Cowichan and Koksilah Rivers,' wrote Indian Agent W.H. Lomas, 'the River has cut itself an entirely new channel by which one Indian has lost between $300 and $400 worth of personal property besides land, barns and house.'[38] In 1891, he requested that Indian Affairs file for an injunction to prevent the lumber companies from running logs until they had properly protected the riverbanks. It would take two more years of damaging log runs (one report estimated that the logs had eroded one hundred acres of Cowichan reserve)[39] before the Supreme Court of British Columbia granted the injunction in December 1893.[40] Settlers were also concerned about the log runs, and in what is described as a 'large and influential meeting of the residents in Cowichan district' they resolved to press the government for funds to build suitable barriers so that logs could be run 'without risk or damage to private property.'[41] The injunction was lifted in 1898, however, and the Cowichan River would remain a log run into the twentieth century.

Logs in the river were just one of the intrusions of a settler society. Between 1862, when the first organized group of white settlers arrived with gunship escort in the Cowichan Valley, and the first fisheries prosecutions in the mid-1890s, Cowichan settler society had firmly established itself. Settlers on Vancouver Island, as Richard Mackie suggests, began with the 'terrible advantage' of a devastating smallpox epidemic that swept British Columbia between April and December 1862.[42] He estimates that more than one-third of an already depleted Native population on Vancouver Island perished that year, opening land for White settlement as never before. Missionaries provided vaccines and their strong presence in the Cowichan Valley may have meant that the Cowichan suffered less than many groups, but other diseases would continue to take considerable toll.[43]

In 1877, the JIRC recorded 529 adult Cowichan in the valley. The provincial voters' list of that same year, which excluded Natives, women, and children, listed 85 eligible voters.[44] Extrapolating from the voters' list, approximately 160 adult settlers lived in the Cowichan Valley in 1877, about one-third of the adult Native population.[45] These settlers had come to farm (72 of the 85 settlers in the voters' list were described as farmers and two as gentlemen) and farming required land, Cowichan land. In the early years, relations with the Cowichan were fraught with tension and violence, caused in good measure by settlement without prior purchase from or compensation to the Cowichan. The Cowichan demanded that the Crown purchase their land even as it was being settled from under them. This situation produced considerable tension, still unresolved, but felt most keenly in the early years by the minority of white settlers whom the Cowichan considered squatters. Cattle were killed, settlers were nervous, and in 1864, thirty-eight of the recently arrived settlers petitioned Governor Kennedy for government protection.[46]

Farming required labour as well as land, particularly in a forested country that had to be cleared before it could be ploughed, and despite tensions, Natives were an obvious source. Many were hired to transport goods and people, to clear land, and to work as farmhands, particularly at harvest time. Chinook, the pidgin language of the fur trade, became the language of work between Natives and whites in these early settler communities before the missionary schools introduced English.[47] Although the pattern was less common than it had been in the fur trade, Native women married some of the earliest settlers.[48]

As opportunities grew, the Cowichan increasingly integrated into the wage economy. Some Cowichan farmed on the reserves, selling their produce in local markets, others worked as farmhands, as packers, for the lumber companies, and in the coal mines. The salmon fisheries, however, remained their focus. The traditional summer migration to fishing grounds on the lower Fraser continued, but the Cowichan now sold their catch to the canneries or worked for wages as fishers and cannery workers. Lomas reported in 1881 that his agency was 'almost entirely deserted, men, women and children having found paying employment at the salmon canneries on the Fraser.'[49] Employment prospects fluctuated with the Fraser salmon run, but when it was available, wage work was an attractive addition to the seasonal Cowichan migration. With the end of the sockeye run on the Fraser, many Cowichan moved south into the Washington Territory to work for wages in the hop fields before returning to Vancouver Island for the fall, their income providing a boost to the local economy.

This seasonal movement replicated traditional migrations, but the Cowichan now participated in the industrial economy, working for money. This transition was not without considerable dislocation. The combination of white settlement, fish and game laws, saw-logs, and wage-labour migration forced an increasing number of elderly Cowichan who could not participate in the wage economy to turn to Indian Affairs for assistance.[50] Their age-old patterns of subsistence were no longer possible as the land and people were made over to fit the new industrial economy, or to provide space for farmers or, as it will become apparent, to offer sport for a wealthy few.

As a result of these formal and intimate connections between individual Cowichan and settlers, however, and despite the unresolved land question, local settlers remember coexisting with the Native community on good terms.[51] Lieutenant Verney, commander of the HMS *Grappler* and frequent visitor to the valley, reported in 1863 that '[t]he Cowichan Indians are, on the whole, very peaceable, and well disposed

towards the settlers, who treat them with kindness and consideration.'[52] Clashes erupted over land, and a letter from Archibald Dods, a
farmer, to the provincial attorney general expressed another view of
the colonial encounter. Complaining of 'Indians trespassing' on his
land, Dods wrote that '[t]hey have a hundred times more respect for a
gunboat than all the talk in creation.'[53] The Cowichan do not recall a
harmonious relationship either,[54] but as settlement grew and settler
society consolidated control, its concerns about Cowichan insurrection
diminished. By 1894 a railway traversed the valley, the adult settler
population in the valley was approaching 500, Duncan was becoming
something of a regional centre, and a settler society was comfortably
established on British Columbia's south coast.[55] In this context, the
Native became viewed as the trusted neighbour and labourer, not the
threatening savage. Once secure in their possession of land, the settlers,
largely of British extraction, came to see industrial logging operations,
railways, and canneries as the primary threats to their way of life, not
Cowichan hunting and fishing. In fact, Dominion efforts to limit
Cowichan fishing only provoked a Cowichan reaction that concerned
the local settler population, which remembered earlier unrest, much
more than the activity itself. By the 1890s, a significant segment of
settler society supported the Cowichan in their limited use of the weirs
as a food source and for local sale. This is an important part of the
context in which the Department of Fisheries, based in Ottawa, and its
local officials attempted to enforce Canadian fisheries law, and I shall
return to it when I evaluate the failed prosecutions of the 1890s.

Protests, Prosecutions, and the Sport Fishery

One element of the English settler society enveloping the Cowichan
Valley did not support the Cowichan weirs. Close to Victoria and
renowned for its steelhead, the Cowichan River had become the local
elite's favourite fly-fishing stream. When the Esquimalt & Nanaimo
Railway (E&NR) was completed in 1886, the Cowichan Valley became
that much more accessible, and sport fishers and those involved in the
tourist industry sought to preserve the Cowichan as a fly-fishing para-
dise – one to delight the readers of Izaak Walton's *The Complete Angler*,
the seventeenth-century book that was immensely popular in North
America in the late nineteenth century.[56] Sport fishing, particularly fly
fishing, long a favoured and fiercely protected activity of England's
landed gentry and, in the nineteenth century, an important element

of an increasing tourist industry, would command the Department of Fisheries' attention. It would accommodate fishing for other purposes – food, fresh market, canning – around the sport fishery on the Cowichan River.

The impact of sport fishing on Native fisheries is underplayed in the existing literature. Historian Michael Thoms, in the only sustained analysis of the sport and Native fisheries in British Columbia, describes how an elite fly-fishing club manoeuvred to evict Native fishers from their age-old fisheries at Pennask Lake near Kamloops in the 1920s and 1930s.[57] It succeeded by purchasing the land around the lake and then using the law of trespass to make the lake its own. Surrounded by Indian reserve in its lower reaches and therefore impossible to girdle with private property, the Cowichan River required direct intervention from public officials to capture its fish for sportsmen.

In 1885, Inspector of Fisheries George Pittendrigh received a complaint about the Cowichan weirs from an avid sportsman who was also the lieutenant-governor, C.F. Cornwall. Pittendrigh went immediately to investigate and found several recently erected weirs in the age-old fishing sites of the Cowichan. Age-old or not, he insisted that to preserve their food supply and to protect the fish the Cowichan must open the weirs weekly for 48 hours beginning at 6 a.m. Saturdays. Pittendrigh acknowledged that the weirs by themselves might not be a problem – long Cowichan use was evidence that weirs and fish could coexist – but with other users taking fish by other means, it was now necessary as a conservation measure to enforce the law. The Cowichan were to *conserve* fish for other users.[58]

In 1887, Indian Agent Lomas filed his report as the first fisheries guardian on the Cowichan River.[59] Better attention was being paid to the fishery closures, he reported, and the compromise that required the Cowichan to open their weirs on weekends, confirmed by the new inspector of fisheries, Oliver Mowat, appeared to be holding. The Cowichan Council, elected representatives from the villages, was less sanguine.[60] It met in June 1888 to consider how to secure the Cowichan supply of fish and to express concern about the growing number of commercial seiners who were catching the schooling fish that appeared in Cowichan Bay in the early fall and were selling them in the Victoria markets. The council passed a resolution to 'protest against the granting of licences to fish with seines or Gill nets in Cowichan Bay as the same is only done during the time that the river is too low to admit of the fish ascending to their spawning grounds, and thus last year the fish were all taken, before the Indians had a chance of catching their winter food, which has caused much distress among the Cowichan Indians.'[61] Lomas suggested that if Fisheries decided to grant this 'favour,' it should do so on the condition that the Cowichan relinquish their 'right' to use weirs. The right, he claimed, was held by only two or three families in each kin group.[62] Fisheries replied that several seine licences had already been issued for the season and would not be rescinded, but that new territorial limits for seine fishing would minimize the problem by keeping the nets away from the mouth of the river.[63] In September 1889, the minister announced that all salmon fishing within the Cowichan River estuary must occur beyond a line drawn due north from the Cowichan wharf (see figure 3.1).[64] Then, in November 1890, Fisheries banned salmon fishing with seine nets in British Columbia.[65]

The Cowichan fishery on the Fraser was also increasingly threatened. Those who travelled to the Fraser and to the Washington Territory for seasonal employment, mostly young men and women and their children, or who found work in the Island lumber mills were relatively well paid. Those who could not travel were increasingly destitute, according to Lomas, because of the fish and game laws:

> All the younger men can find employment on farms or at the sawmills and canneries, and many families are about leaving for the hop fields of Washington Territory; but the very old people who formerly lived entirely on fish, berries and roots, suffer a good deal of hardship through the settling up of the country. The lands that once yielded berries and roots are now fenced and cultivated, and even on the hills the sheep have destroyed them. Then again, the game laws restrict the time for the killing of deer and grouse, and the fishery regulations interfere with their old methods of taking salmon and trout.[66]

When the Fraser salmon runs were light or the hops failed, however, those who relied on the wage economy also suffered. Imagining that the Cowichan would evolve into stout farming stock, Lomas thought that in the long run this was a good thing. The uncertainty of wage labour would encourage them to cultivate their reserve land and become a land-based farming community.

When Fisheries limited the number of licences on the Fraser in 1889 to 450, 350 of which went to cannery boats, the Cowichan, who had fished with their own boats and nets and sold their catch to the canneries, could no longer purchase licences. Vigorous protest from the independent fishers increased the available licences for non-cannery boats to 150, but the Cowichan would not receive any. Lomas requested licenses for the Cowichan,[67] but John McNab, the new Inspector of Fisheries, replied that the Cowichan earned 'a good livelihood' from selling fish to the local markets in Victoria and Nanaimo, and did not need a Fraser River licence.[68] Lomas wrote again, stating that the Cowichan had been fishing on the Fraser for generations, that they had paid for licences in the past, and that some owned boats and nets worth several hundred dollars. Would Fisheries reconsidered?[69] Ignoring the long-established Cowichan fishery on the Fraser, McNab replied that if the Cowichan received licences, then Natives from around the province would insist on licences for the Fraser as well. The Cowichan were 'favourably situated' on Vancouver Island and had no need of Fraser salmon, which were to be reserved for 'the Fraser River Indians' and so that 'freezing establishments and other fish curing industries may be systematically and successfully conducted.'[70] The provincial government had sold the Cowichan fishing station on the Fraser to a white settler, and some years later Fisheries closed their access to that same fishery (except if they were willing to work as cannery employees) by refusing to sell them licences.

In January 1894, Lomas found commercial gill nets from the Fraser River on the Cowichan River, but could not determine who owned or set them. He asked McNab for instructions, and was informed that it was his duty to seize them. If they were Cowichan nets, McNab replied, 'it was exceeding the permit granted to them as it was not in my opinion, that they should use commercial fishing nets, for catching fish in the Rivers for their own use during the close time.'[71] Despite lingering questions about ownership, several Cowichan men were charged and, if convicted, they faced fines of $20 and costs, or between eight days and one month in jail in default.[72] The prosecution failed, however, because the Crown had no evidence that the Cowichan were catching the fish to sell. Since 1888, the *Regulations* had allowed Native people, at all times, to fish for food, 'but not for sale, barter or traffic.'[73]

Officials in Ottawa were not pleased with McNab's work, and required that he pay the costs of the prosecution. Was he not aware, the deputy minister demanded to know, that the *Regulations* allowed Indians to fish for food, and that it did not matter that they were using commercial nets if they were fishing for food?[74] McNab suspected, however, that the Cowichan were selling fish to white merchants for the Victoria markets. He was convinced that he had acted correctly, believing if nothing else that it was irresponsible for a fisheries officer to leave unclaimed nets in the water, a deadly practice for fish.[75]

The prosecutions stirred the Cowichan to action. Despite the acquittals, nets had been confiscated and the Cowichan felt increasingly harassed. They met with church and government officials later in 1894 to protest the intervention.[76] Lomas endorsed the protest, and there were no further prosecutions in 1894. McNab decided, however, that he needed a guardian on the Cowichan River who was prepared to enforce his understanding of the law, and he dismissed Lomas from the 'position which requires him to enforce regulations which in his opinion are so objectionable.'[77]

In 1895, McNab refused to issue permits for a Cowichan weir food fishery and he instructed James Maitland-Dougall, the new guardian, 'to see that no dams or other obstructions were erected by the Indians or others.'[78] The Indian Superintendent, A.W. Vowell, objected. The Cowichan food fishery, he argued, was being closed 'to supply inexhaustible sport for the Angler who, at times, takes from 10 to 30lbs of fish a day merely for recreation,' and begrudges the Cowichan their fishery.[79] The Cowichan built a weir nonetheless, and in June Maitland-Dougall charged Jack Quilshamult from Somenos with unlawfully maintaining a fish weir and unduly obstructing the passage of fish in the Cowichan River.[80] Lomas, who was still the Indian agent, appeared with Quilshamult at a preliminary hearing before two justices of the peace, Edward Musgrave and W.H. Elkington. Musgrave, an outspoken member of the Vancouver Island Fish & Game Protection Society, was a vigorous opponent of the weirs.[81]

Lomas argued four points to this presumably unreceptive bench. First, the weirs may temporarily delay fish, but did not prevent migration to the spawning grounds. Second, in 1877 the JIRC had promised that the Cowichan's right to take salmon would always be protected. This had been confirmed by a verbal agreement, witnessed by Lomas, with then Inspector of Fisheries Mowat in 1887, when the Cowichan had agreed to open their weirs on weekends. Third, the Cowichan had never surrendered their right to obtain food with their traditional methods. And finally, even though the Cowichan had once used as many as twenty weirs, the runs had remained healthy, proving that the weirs did not block the migrating fish.[82] Lomas asked for a 17 June trial date so that he could consult with Indian Affairs and the provincial attorney general. According to Lomas, the justices of the peace thought that any agreement with the JIRC had been extinguished by the subsequent regulations. The only option for the Cowichan, they believed, was to request a food fishing permit from the inspector of fisheries, and they granted Lomas time to secure this permit.

Lomas was concerned that the Cowichan would retaliate against a conviction by refusing anglers and hunters access to their reserve lands. This was a credible threat, for the Cowichan Indian Reserve no. 1 surrounded much of the lower river and many prime hunting and fishing sites (see figure 3.1). He turned to the province, but the attorney general replied that fishing in the Cowichan River was a Dominion responsibility.[83] McNab would not accommodate the weir fishery either. The oral agreement with the JIRC never had any force, he argued, and if it did the Cowichan must still fish 'by lawful methods.' The *Fisheries Act* prohibited weirs, and McNab indicated he had no authority to relax the law; the case would be decided 'according to the laws in force when the offence was committed,' and he had no doubt that the Cowichan would be convicted.[84] Given the loose enforcement of the *Act* and *Regulations* by his predecessors, McNab's insistence on the letter of the law was a new development. Furthermore, he was incorrect. Even where Native food fishing conflicted with the *Act*, the *Regulations* enabled him to grant food-fishing permits.[85] He choose not to.

Unable to secure an agreement with Fisheries, Lomas requested a further adjournment to allow Quilshamult to hire legal counsel, and the trial was rescheduled on the condition that the Cowichan remove their weirs pending its outcome.[86] The Cowichan retained a Victoria barrister, S. Perry Mills, and asked Lomas for a meeting at the Indian Affairs office in Duncan. He declined, apparently not wanting to appear too closely associated with the Cowichan's position, although until that point he had organized their legal defence.

Three days before trial the Cowichan met at the Quamichan schoolhouse and unanimously adopted eight resolutions, which they sent to Indian Superintendent Vowell. In a strongly worded statement that rejected Dominion jurisdiction over their fisheries, the Cowichan asserted a *right* to the fish, to their fishing methods, to hunt game, and to land. Furthermore, their history with the river proved they were capable of managing the fishery, whereas white fishers were damaging the stock and the Dominion should regulate their activities more closely. The resolutions began:

1. We always had the right to take any fish, by any means, at any time, in

any of the waters of British Columbia, and we want to preserve that right in its entirety.

We formerly did not protest against the Fishery Regulations – except last year – because their true sense was unknown to us.

2. We claim that the fish is our property; we own it by natural right, and therefore we consider as unjust all Government Regulations depriving us totally or partly of that right. Our history proves that we do not destroy the fish. On the other hand it is evident that the white population does destroy it. The protective regulations then should embrace the white people only, not the Indians. We do take fish for our own daily use, to have a living, and we make use of all the fish we take; the white population on the contrary takes fish mostly for pleasure's sake, and usually destroys the small fish by throwing it away ...

3. Now that we are aware of the object of what we claim to be unjust regulations, we strongly protest, and we are decided to keep hold of our natural rights, were we to suffer imprisonment.[87]

On 26 June Quilshamult appeared before Musgrave and Elkington for trial.[88] The substance of the charge, however, was never tried. Mills argued that the hearing had been improperly adjourned, the justices of the peace concurred, and the charges were dismissed.[89] Mills doubted that any other defence would have succeeded, something he thought unjust, and he recommended that the government change the law to allow a Native weir food fishery. The Cowichan weir fishery, he argued, had been expressly reserved to them by the JIRC and should not be interfered with.[90]

On the day of the trial, the Cowichan had posted signs warning against trespass on their reserves, effectively limiting non-Native access to much of the lower river. Two days later a letter from 'A Cowichan Indian' appeared in the *Victoria Daily Times*. It publicized the Cowichan's pre-trial resolution that they would risk imprisonment to defend their rights. Was not their sustenance more important, the author asked rhetorically, than the sport fishery? Given the uncertain wage income from the Fraser canneries and Washington hop-fields, did they not need their weir fishery to survive the winters? And even had they secure incomes from other sources, why should they be expected to compromise their fishing rights? In a powerful challenge to the government's disregard of their fishing rights, the author wrote:

And suppose we were all farmers with plenty of food and clothing; does that by labouring acquired deprive us of our immemorial right of fishing? Since when does Mr. Dunsmuir lose his right to the benefits of his E.& N. railway belt because his Wellington mines pay him more than a hundred-fold? Why he should lose all his rights and have nothing, besides enough to keep body and soul together, like us poor Indians.

Regarding the recent amendments to the *Regulations*, the author continued:

We learn that our paternal government by an act of parliament has deprived us of the right of fishing at any time of the year for our daily food. We look upon it as unjust and a most shameful act, and we do not hesitate to say publicly that we will not submit to it. The idea that a few sportmens, the instigators of such inequitous law, should be allowed to come from all parts of the country to catch in our rivers and lakes hundreds of pounds of fish for mere pleasure's sake, impudently exhibit their grand catches before us now starving Indians, who have the first right to the fish, and seemingly say with a smile of arrogance on their face: '*Saaiwash, look out. Don't you catch a fish in the river. There's the lock-up!*'[91]

After this courtroom setback Fisheries took no further action in 1895. Maitland-Dougall reported that both Lomas and Mills asked him not to prosecute again until they made arrangements with Indian Affairs and Fisheries. The Cowichan set off to work on the Fraser. Musgrave and Elkington had dismissed the charges, but the former certainly expected further action. When Fisheries failed to prosecute again that year, the Fish and Game Protection Society expressed its disappointment with the lack of action, claiming that the weirs were 'the worst sort of obstruction to the run of both salmon & trout.' To help stop the 'illegal fishing' it offered its members as 'honorary inspectors,' and then it proposed that Fisheries extend the area and season for rod fishing.[92]

The Dominion Fisheries Commissioner, E.E. Prince, a product of a St Andrew's education and a professor of zoology and comparative anatomy, intervened.[93] In August 1896, accompanied by Maitland-Dougall and Lomas (to interpret), he visited the Cowichan River to investigate the weirs. Prince observed that much of their reserve was not being farmed, and that except for a few old people most of the Cowichan earned high wages on the Fraser and in the hop-fields. In his opinion, '[f]ew white settlers [were] so fortunately placed.' He concluded his survey of the river with a three-pronged attack on the Cowichan fishery: the fishery was illegal, unnecessary, and primitive.

> It is an outrage that so fine a river should be injured by the idle & well-to-do Indians. For a certain no. of days per week the gates could be lifted with each; but my own view is that no such barriers should be allowed. Ex-Inspector McNab on other rivers caused them to be removed & in some cases personally Destroyed them. These weirs are:
>
> (1) A violation of the Act c 95. s 14 ss 4&5[94]
> (2) Unjustifiable as the Indians on the whole are well off & have good land
> (3) Unnecessary as other methods of fishing would suffice.[95]

Indian Affairs continued to impress upon Fisheries the need to relax the regulations, but Fisheries adopted Prince's position: the Cowichan claims of hardship were exaggerated and they should obey the law.[96]

In 1897, Maitland-Dougall prevented the Cowichan from erecting weirs before they left for the Fraser in June, and when they returned he again warned them against the practice. In response, the Cowichan drafted a statement denouncing the Dominion law. The weir prohibition, they asserted, was both 'unjust and unlawful,' and the destructiveness of their technology was a 'myth.' Their land had never been purchased by any government, and their right to fish as formerly had been promised them by the Hudson's Bay Company, former governments, and the JIRC.[97] They offered to remove the weirs two days each week – a compromise that had worked in the past.[98] Fisheries replied that the Cowichan had no grounds for claiming these 'exceptional privileges.'[99]

Opinions varied, however, even among the sport fishers. In response to accusations that he favoured the sport fishery, Prince replied that the law was intended 'solely to prevent the extermination of fish,' and in fact not all sport fishers supported his approach.[100] In 1897, a deputation of twenty-four 'sportsmen' told Prince, much to his astonishment, that the weirs did not hurt the fishing, that the Cowichan treated them well, and they wished Fisheries would not interfere, a view that Prince reported was shared by official circles in Victoria. They were more concerned about the damage caused by running logs down the river.[101] Prince attributed this 'sympathy' to a belief that Natives had certain rights by virtue of their previous occupation of the land, and to a fear that the Cowichan would retaliate if these rights were challenged. He believed such sympathy misplaced. The Cowichan were well provided for, he argued, and the best way to prevent retaliation was to act forcefully.[102] The approach preferred by Indian Affairs, to gradually integrate the Native population by turning them to agriculture, was misguided: 'The B.C. Indians are essentially a *fishing race* & to make them farmers is as *hopeless* as trying to make tea-planters of Esquimaux.'[103] The Cowichan would remain fishers, Prince thought, but they must abide by Dominion laws designed to protect the fish.

The laws, however, were designed to protect fish for particular users, and Native people were not among the favoured few. Fisheries had begun to stock the Cowichan River with Atlantic salmon for the sport fishery, but the program was foolish, argued Prince, if the fish were caught in Native weirs.[104] Other rivers and lakes draining the east coast of Vancouver Island were similarly stocked, but the planted fish were meant to enhance the lucrative sports fishery, not Native fishing.

The next year, 1898, Indian Affairs attempted to catalogue Indian fishing privileges across the country. It asked its Indian agents for a detailed report about reserved fisheries, fishing privileges, and Native concerns.[105] Lomas reported that no fisheries in the Cowichan Agency had been 'properly reserved for the Indians, and their former modes of taking salmon for their own use, and for peddling to the white people is now stopped.'[106] This intervention, he continued, was 'a great injustice to them, as they were promised by the Indian Reserve Commissioners that their right to fish as formerly should always be respected.' He noted a long list of grievances and recommended that Fisheries not interfere with the weirs, that it relax the close season, and that the Cowichan be allowed to sell fish as formerly. But Fisheries was moving in the opposite direction. Guardian Maitland-Dougall continued to seize nets,[107] and in March 1898 he reported that the Cowichan, with the assistance of Lomas, had again posted signs on their reserves threatening to refuse access to the river to white anglers.[108] Hearing this, Commissioner Prince instructed McNab 'to employ such aid and take such measures' necessary to remove the weirs,[109] and he reconsidered the Fish and Game Protection Society's proposal to employ sports fishers as honorary inspectors on the Cowichan River.[110] McNab, anticipating charges and no doubt recalling the procedural defence of Quilshamult's lawyer in the 1895 trial, requested that Fisheries hire legal counsel to prosecute the Cowichan weir fishery. Prince thought it unnecessary: 'If the prosecution is before an honest magistrate and the evidence sufficient, a conviction will likely be secured as well without as with counsel.'[111]

In March, Maitland-Dougall charged Quilshamult again with constructing a weir contrary to the *Fisheries Act*.[112] In response, the Cowichan announced they would prevent all sports fishers from approaching the river through their reserves. Faced with this ultimatum, Musgrave, who had demanded that the weirs come down, wrote to Fisheries claiming that this action would greatly harm the sports fishery, and that he had been mistaken about the damage caused by the weirs. He asked the Department not to interfere with the weir fishery;[113] Indian Affairs asked Fisheries to stay the prosecution.[114] Lomas convinced Maitland-Dougall and the justices of the peace to adjourn the case until 16 April, by which time he hoped that Fisheries would respond.[115] Fisheries did not respond, but the prosecution was no more successful than earlier attempts to secure a conviction. The justices of the peace dismissed the case on the grounds that the weir did not unduly obstruct fish.[116] The debate over weirs continued in departmental correspondence[117] and in the local press,[118] but the Cowichan had won important recognition that their weirs could coexist on the river with fish.

These cases and the events surrounding them reveal something about the strategies of power and resistance. Fisheries, led by Prince in Ottawa and McNab in British Columbia, launched a discursive attack against the weir fishery, invoking both law and science. Under the *Fisheries Act* weirs were illegal; they had to be removed. Crown sovereignty was assumed. Parliament was the legitimate source of authority and its laws applied to the Cowichan. Validated by their legal pedigree, the laws prohibiting weirs were also defended by appeals to science. The weirs were a primitive, scientifically unsound method of fishing to be removed, argued Prince, for the benefit of all fishers, including the Cowichan. Violations called for sanctions, and it was a fisheries officer's duty to enforce the law, not to exercise discretion by exempting Native fishers from the laws that applied to all.

Indian Affairs, for its part, generally supported the Cowichan, but found itself in an increasingly untenable position. Lomas was no longer both Indian agent and fisheries guardian, but the contradictions inherent within Indian Affairs made his job as Indian agent almost as difficult. On the one hand, Lomas consistently defended the Cowichan fishery from Fisheries officials who would eliminate it. On the other hand, as an official of the Dominion government he was responsible for encouraging Natives to abide by its law. The tension between these two positions became evident when Lomas, who initially had helped to organize the Cowichan legal defence, refused to let them meet in his offices until after the 1895 trial. He was, I suspect, trying to maintain a semblance of detachment, perhaps even of objectivity, while marshalling resources of the Canadian state to defend the Cowichan against that state.

The Cowichan responded to the discursive attack within the same discourses of law and science, and outside them. The arguments were not new, but the court proceedings gave them a forum and a wider audience. Legal entitlement arose, they and their supporters argued, from two sources: long, uncontested use that predated white settlement, and an agreement with the JIRC that the Canadian state would not interfere with their fisheries. Prior Cowichan use was uncontested, although Fisheries denied that this conferred a right to continuing use. Exactly what the JIRC had promised, or had the authority to promise, was disputed, but the Cowichan certainly believed, as did Lomas, that their right to continue fishing had been guaranteed, and they could point to the earlier treaties with neighbouring peoples and subsequent arrangements with successive fisheries inspectors over opening times that also suggested continuing recognition of a right. The Cowichan also challenged the Crown's assumption of sovereignty with a sovereign discourse of their own. They asserted jurisdiction over the fishery, arguing that they had never ceded it to the Crown or anyone else. This assertion had strong pedigree in Anglo-Canadian law; it lay behind the Douglas Treaties of the 1850s and the whole treaty-making process from Upper Canada west, a process set out in the *Royal Proclamation of 1763*.[119] This argument, at the core of Cowichan resistance, fit uncomfortably in the courts of a province that denied the existence of Native title and had refused to negotiate treaties with most Native groups. As a result, it is somewhat muted in the historical record. It was not a position that Indian Affairs could emphasize in supporting the Cowichan fishery, but it appears in the statements drafted on behalf of the Cowichan by various Catholic and Methodist missionaries.

The Cowichan also argued within what might be identified as a discourse of traditional ecological knowledge that the weirs did not damage fish stocks and that they could manage a sustainable catch. Their history of intensive fishing and healthy fish stocks provided ample support, and the court confirmed this view in the 1898 trial; the weirs did not unduly obstruct fish. The Cowichan and Indian Affairs would refer to this decision to rebuff claims from Prince and other Fisheries officials that the weirs were destructive.[120] In fact, the Cowichan blamed Fisheries for failing to enforce Canadian law against sport fishers who took fish in increasing numbers. The Cowichan could manage their fishery; Fisheries should focus its attention on white fishers.

The results of the trials are also revealing. When Musgrave had an opportunity in 1895 as justice of the peace to convict Quilshamult for constructing a fish weir, he dismissed the charges because of a procedural failing, his own. If the law was simply a tool for settler society to recreate a territory and a resource in its own image, this was the opportunity. Yet, Musgrave deferred to the formal requirements of the law rather than use his position of authority to restrict the Native fishery. It seems, however, that Musgrave may have been influenced by other Cowichan strategies of resistance, particularly the refusal to let whites have access to the river through the Cowichan reserve. The Cowichan encountered the law of trespass when they tried to move through or when their animals strayed on alienated land, but now they used it to their advantage, posting 'no-trespassing' signs on the boundaries of their reserve to limit non-Native access to the river. Limited access was a serious concern, particularly to anglers and hunters, and the threat caused Musgrave, the most outspoken local opponent of the weirs, to reverse temporarily his opposition. The weirs, he claimed during the 1898 trial, were not as damaging as he once thought.

The 1895 charge against Quilshamult for obstructing fish was dismissed because of a procedural failing. In 1898, however, he was acquitted of the same charge because the justices of the peace held that the weirs did not unduly obstruct fish. The result was the same for the accused in either case; Quilshamult was free to go without fine or incarceration, but the two decisions had very different meanings. In the first instance the law protected the procedural rights of the individual. Quilshamult, as an individual and, in the eyes of the law, a subject of the Queen, was entitled to all the procedural rights of a 'free born Englishman.' The decision could stand without reference to the collective rights of the Cowichan to their weir fishery. In the second case, however, the court considered the Cowichan's weir technology and found it unobjectionable. Quilshamult was acquitted because the justices of the peace deemed the weirs an acceptable fishing technology that did not unduly obstruct fish. Although an individual victory for Quilshamult, it was also a vindication of the Cowichan fishery and would become useful as such when the Cowichan sought to defend their weirs. The Cowichan won on the merits of their technology, in effect their ability to manage the resource, and not on the procedural rights of an individual. Canadian law, it appears, armed fisheries officers with the authority to remove the Cowichan weirs, but the Cowichan could influence the local interpretation of the law to strengthen their claims against other users and the state.

To understand these decisions further, one must consider the local context. The first observation is that some combination of settler fear of Cowichan unrest and, at the same time, settler support for the Cowichan fisheries delayed prosecution. The extent of the delay is difficult to ascertain, but it took ten years from Fisheries' first intervention in 1885 to lay formal charges against the weir fishery. It is also difficult to separate the relative impacts of the settler society's fear of the Cowichan from its support for the Cowichan fisheries. Cowichan resistance had been effective; it had delayed settlement in the valley and secured for the Cowichan a relatively large, contiguous reserve surrounding much of the lower river. Even as the balance of power shifted to the settler society and its governments in the late nineteenth century, the Cowichan could still cause considerable inconvenience and create unease by refusing settler access to the reserves. The impact of these strategies of resistance should not be underestimated, but neither should the degree of support among the local settler population for the continuing Cowichan fisheries. In 1889, Lomas had expressed concerns about Fisheries' insistence that Natives purchase licences if they were selling fish in local markets. He indicated that although the law prohibited sales without a licence, he knew 'of no instance of an Indian being punished for selling salmon but this is simply because Indians are the chief and only reliable providers for the fresh fish markets on the Coast, and the feeling of the inhabitants is so much against the regulation that scarcely any Justice would take an information against an Indian under it.'[121]

In 1896, 285 'residents, Indian Chiefs and Indians of the Cowichan District' sent a petition to Indian Affairs setting out six points: the Cowichan claimed the right to catch fish for food; until recent legislative changes, they had always enjoyed this right; they could not live without salmon; they did not destroy the fish; if their rights were restricted, then the Dominion government must provide support; and, the Cowichan had always been law-abiding and kind to the white population.[122] On these grounds the petitioners asked that Indian Affairs re-establish the Cowichan's rights and privileges to their weir fishery.[123] It is unlikely that local magistrates and justices of the peace would have been immune to such strong local sentiment when considering the weir-fishery prosecutions.

How is one to explain this sentiment? Settlers in the Cowichan Valley had, from the beginning, sought to reproduce an English society in their corner of the Empire. Lieutenant Verney recounted a conversation in 1862 with one of the newly arrived settlers who told him, 'We will have nothing foreign here, every thing here shall be English, thoroughly English, and first of all we must have our church.'[124] The church, St Peter's Anglican, was erected by volunteer labour in 1866–7 and was well attended.[125] Historian Jean Barman remarks on the Britishness of settlement in British Columbia in the later nineteenth and early twentieth centuries, particularly in the Kootenays, Okanagan Valley, Gulf Islands, and the Cowichan Valley, where the emerging landscapes evoked for many the English countryside.[126] Historical geographers Cole Harris and Robert Galois describe the settlement in the Cowichan Valley in 1881 as 'English and Anglican.'[127] The English pretensions attracted some and dissuaded others, but a sense of connection to the 'Old Country' remained strong.[128] The call to arms in 1914 produced an enthusiastic response, and the focus for the next four years in the Cowichan district as in much of the rest of the Empire remained on their boys who were fighting and dying in northern France.

The sense of empire and of the place within it of the Vancouver Island farmer is captured in two engravings reproduced on the same page at the beginning of the Columbia Mission Reports for 1897, a record of the Church of England's missionary activity for that year in British Columbia (see figure 3.5). Vancouver Island is positioned on the globe in location to other points of empire. Australia, New Zealand, and Hong Kong are connected by shipping lines, as is the emerging power in the East, Japan. A railway traverses North America connecting the West with the East Coast, with spurs to San Francisco, the American midwest and eastern seaboard, and a shipping line from Halifax to Liverpool completes the link to the British Isles. Vancouver Island was positioned within the Empire as part of an emerging world economy. Below that engraving is another titled the Canadian Settler's 'Homestead.' A farmer ploughs an expensively fenced field in front of a hamlet dominated by a church spire. Two cows languish in the foreground, while a rabbit bounds from the tracks of an approaching passenger train. Placed in the corner so as not to disrupt the pastoral tranquillity, the train reaffirms both that this is an age of progress and

Figure 3.5   Vancouver Island and the farmer's field positioned in the Empire.

that this place is connected to empire and the world economy. Bare, rolling hills recede into the background, and tucked behind the deciduous tree that dominates the foreground is a coniferous tree, a reminder, perhaps, of the work involved to clear and farm the land. The fact that this print hardly represents the homesteader's experience is less important than the aspirations it reveals – to recreate, although at some considerable distance, the comfortable familiarity of rural England.

These aspirations were part of what David Demeritt has identified as an *arcadian* discourse that 'celebrated the moral virtues and personal benefits of country living.' Arcadianism, he continues, 'extolled the picturesque landscape and held it out as a historic relic to be preserved from the destruction wrought by progress and the relentless onslaught of industrial capitalism.'[129] It was only one of the visions of agriculture that shaped rural British Columbia (Demeritt includes agrarianism and the Country Life Movement), but it was prevalent among the Cowichan Valley settlers of the late nineteenth century.[130] Natives, once subdued, fit within the English picturesque as the somewhat exotic peasant labourer, their weirs a historic relic and reminder of a pre-capitalist society. An etching of the 'Indian Village of Quamicham,' based on a drawing by Captain Porcher of the Royal Navy and printed in the Columbia Mission Reports, 1888–9, provides a sense of the Native and the landscape in transition towards an English picturesque (figure 3.6). In the foreground, three Natives, one on horseback, with a dog, herd two cattle and two laden donkeys. They appear to be living a life somewhere between the traditional economy of seasonal rounds and the pastoral, agrarian lifestyle urged on them by missionaries and Indian agents. Behind them, two canoes traverse the river, one beached in front of the shed-roofed traditional winter houses. Behind these, and confirming the sense of a people in transition, are the gable-roofed, single-family dwellings that missionaries were entreating Natives to build and use instead of the multi-family longhouses.

The Cowichan had long used a weir in front of the Quamichan village, and it is captured in an 1899 painting by Josephine Crease, daughter of the former provincial attorney general and supreme court judge Henry Crease[131] (figure 3.7). Painted with the soft strokes of a watercolour brush, a deciduous tree frames the Cowichan River that flows through the middle of the painting. The river is divided by a weir, which supports a person who is perhaps fishing. Behind the weir are the gable-roofed buildings of the Quamichan village. The weir is not out of place in the painting, nor was it out of place in the English

Figure 3.6 'The Indian Village of Quamicham, District of Cowitchen (from a drawing by Capt. Porcher, RN).'

construction of nature. Indians were part of that nature, and perhaps a necessary part for its authentic representation in North America. Their fishing technology, the weir, fit within the recreated English country-side much more readily than did the industrial desecration of a logging camp or a cannery. It was this sentiment, that Native people were part of the place and their technology part of the landscape, that contrib-uted to the settler support of the Cowichan fisheries.[132]

Cannery Boats and Tourism

In 1888 the Cowichan council had asked Fisheries not to license seine and gill-net fishers in Cowichan Bay who were catching fish for the

Figure 3.7   Watercolour painting, attributed to Josephine Crease, of the Cowichan River with weir and fisher at Quamichan Village, 1899.

local fresh markets. In 1895, they confronted a commercial fishery on
an altogether larger scale. Thirteen cannery boats from the Delta Cannery on the Fraser River appeared with gill nets. The expedition was
unsuccessful, partly because a daytime gill-net fishery was ineffective
in the clear waters at the mouth of the Cowichan (fish could see and
avoid the nets) and partly because Fisheries had interrupted the unlicensed fishing.[133]

When the cannery fishers reappeared on Cowichan Bay in 1898 they
brought drag seines.[134] Lomas forwarded Cowichan complaints that
boats with large seine nets and small mesh were fishing salmon in
Cowichan Bay for the canneries. McNab reported that he had issued
coho seine-net licences for Cowichan Bay to five fishers, 'who are all

old residents, and have been British subjects and property owners for many years in B.C.' He also recognized, however, that 'poachers' who travelled the coast in large boats, setting nets and catching salmon, were beyond the reach of the land-based fishery guardians.[135] The Cowichan were incensed, not only because Fisheries granted seine licences while attacking their weir fishery, but also because they were unable to participate in this lucrative fishery. Seine nets were expensive, and the canneries, while providing nets to Japanese and white fishers, would not give any to the Cowichan. Maitland-Dougall thought he secured promises from the cannery operators in 1898 to supply them with nets for the following season,[136] but none were forthcoming, and to make matters worse there was extensive seine-net fishing near the mouth of the river by Japanese and other cannery fishers.[137]

In 1899, the Cowichan sent a petition to Fisheries, signed by Comiaken Chief Joe Kukhalt, requesting permission to use purse seines in the bay. Kukhalt noted that the Fraser cannery operators, who once thought chum an inferior fish, were now paying seven cents a fish, and the Cowichan could develop a viable commercial purse-seine fishery.[138] However, the *Fisheries Act* prohibited purse seines,[139] and given the sport-fishing lobby on the Cowichan River, Fisheries refused his request.[140] A petition the following year from twenty-four local gill netters to allow them to fish closer to the mouth of the river was also denied to forestall further complaints from the 'resident Indian communities.'[141] Net fishing inside a line stretching north from the Cowichan wharf remained prohibited to all fishers (see figure 3.1), but the gill- and seine-net fisheries for coho and chum beyond this line continued.

At the Nanaimo hearings of the 1902 British Columbia Salmon Commission, appointed to investigate the protection and future development of the salmon-fishing industry, the Cowichan voiced concerns about seines and gill nets. In a letter to the commission Quamichan Chief Suhiltun requested that fishing in Cowichan Bay be reserved for residents of the Cowichan district, Native and white. Kukhalt requested half-price licences for Natives and free access to fish for food.[142] C.M. Tate, the Methodist missionary, interceded for the Cowichan, demanding to know why non-natives could fish with modern implements while Native fishing was restricted to traditional practices. Fisheries officers confiscated Cowichan gill nets in the river, while at the same time issuing drag-seine permits to white fishers in Cowichan Bay. Why the double standard?[143] The British Columbia Fishermen's Union raised its voice in support of the Cowichan. John Elliott, a settler who had married into a Quamichan family, and a member of the Cowichan local of the Fishermen's Union, testified before the commission about the declining wages earned by Cowichan fishers on the Fraser. Japanese and American fishers were taking their jobs, in part because the Cowichan were staying on their reserves long enough to plant their crops and were missing the opening of the fishing season.[144] Further-more, the seine nets of other non-local union members threatened their Cowichan River fishery. The union advised Fisheries to stop issuing seine licences to non-local members,[145] and Fisheries prohibited all net fishing within Cowichan Bay later that year.[146]

The Cowichan riverine fishery remained under surveillance as well. In 1902, Guardian Colvin found three set nets in the river, and spent several nights in the bush in March hoping to catch the person respon-sible.[147] The mayor of Victoria, Charles Hayward, had also decided that the illegal weir fishery must end. Although the area was well beyond his jurisdiction, he sent a detective sergeant from the Victoria City Police to investigate. The officer found several weirs in the river, the remains of nets on the banks, and fear among the locals that enforce-ment of the law would bring reprisals. He concluded that 'the Fishery law has never been enforced nor fish protected.'[148] Hayward then went himself, with a photographer, to document the Cowichan weirs. He was president of the Tourist Association and believed the industry was suffering because the weirs were destroying the lucrative angling busi-ness. One correspondent estimated that the 'fish in our lakes and rivers are worth on an average in the sporting sense $5.00 for every trout and salmon that is taken.'[149] The problem, Hayward argued, was the lack of will among Fisheries officers to enforce the law.[150]

When Fisheries did not act on his complaints, Hayward announced that he had evidence that the Cowichan were illegally selling fish. This prompted an investigation. Fisheries Inspector Sword, accompanied by another member of the Victoria police, travelled to Duncan to investi-gate the charges. They discovered that the wife of a hotel-keeper in Duncan, newly arrived in the region, had purchased two salmon from an Indian woman. Fishery Overseer Galbraith informed her of the $100 fine for possession of illegally caught fish. The fish, however, had no spear or net marks, and the woman told the purchaser that they had been caught in salt water. Fisheries allowed local sale of salmon caught by trolling. Sword expressed his exasperation with the whole affair, suggesting that Fisheries ignore future complaints from Hayward and temper Galbraith's excessive zeal to remove the weirs.[151] Hayward

demanded immediate action from Fisheries; failing that he would institute 'such proceedings as may be necessary to bring the offenders to
justice.'[152] Fifty-seven residents of the Cowichan district followed this
with a petition, initiated by Musgrave, demanding similar action against
the 'illegal fishery.'[153]

The Dominion appointed another commission to investigate. Senator
Templeman, Indian Superintendent Vowell, and Inspector of Fisheries
Sword held hearings in Duncan and Victoria in early August 1902.
Musgrave denounced the weirs. Overseer Galbraith advocated strict
enforcement of the law and blamed the guardians on the Cowichan for
failing to eliminate the weir fishery.[154] Otherwise, the vast majority of
those who testified, including many who had signed Musgrave's petition, told the commission that running logs down the river caused
more harm to the fishery than the weirs. In fact, many supported the
Cowichan and their weir fishery. John N. Evans, Reeve of Duncan and
resident of the region for thirty years, testified: 'I do not attribute the
decrease [in fish] to the weirs but to the destructive character of the
Anglo Saxon race.'[155] Opinion within the settler society remained
divided.

In 1905, a new paper – the *Cowichan Leader* – appeared in Duncan. Its
title suggested progress, but it was also a reference to the short section
of lightweight line that connects the heavier fly-fishing line to the fly.
The Cowichan was renowned for its fly fishing, and the Canadian
Pacific Railway sought to capitalize on that reputation (see figure 3.8).
That year it purchased the E&NR, including the land grant with significant property in the Cowichan Valley, and sought to increase ridership
and to enhance the value of its property by creating fish and game
reserves to lure the sports-minded tourist and settler. The weir fishery
and Cowichan hunting were problems that needed to be resolved
before the CPR could begin developing the reserves.[156] Fisheries had
continued to stock the Cowichan with sport fish (79,000 steelhead fry
in 1901/2; 30,000 trout fry and 20,000 Atlantic salmon fry in 1904/5),[157]
and it renewed efforts to remove the weirs. Earlier in the season,
Indian Agent Robertson intercepted Fisheries Guardian Colvin, who
was about to act on instructions to remove the weirs. Robertson warned
of violence if the weirs were destroyed and he asked for a delay to
resolve the situation.[158] Indian Affairs officials in Ottawa reminded
Fisheries that the Cowichan would expect compensation to remove
their weirs.[159] Once again, the Cowichan and Fisheries reached a
compromise: the Cowichan would keep the weirs open on weekends

Figure 3.8   Esquimalt & Nanaimo Railroad train crossing the Cowichan River, ca. 1900.

and would remove them entirely before they left in early July for the Fraser River fishery.[160]

The CPR purchase piqued interest elsewhere. In 1906 *Rod and Gun and Motor Sports in Canada*, a outdoor sporting magazine, featured the Koksilah River:

> The Koksilah is the grave of many reputations. Unconquered and unconquerable Isaac Waltons have gone there and come away vanquished, crestfallen, and crushed. They have gone with magnificent, costly tackle and brilliant reputations in the piscatorial world, and they have been deprived of both tackle and reputation by the trout of that, to some, most attractive of fishing streams.[161]

The Cowichan River appeared in the magazine the following year. 'It is a stream,' wrote the same correspondent, 'named after one of the most war-like tribes of Indians on the British Columbia Coast.' Once the site of raids and battles and the source of mysterious stories, the Cowichan River and its people were now known and tamed:

Now, however, the merry, joyous, hospitable Cowichan sings out an invitation to the white fisherman with his modern equipment of Greenhart, patent reel, fly-book and French wicker basket. He is as welcome as the brown man, who sits and watches with a certain amount of stolid interest the efforts and manoeuvres of his white brother to lure those 'beauties' to the surface.[162]

If the 'thoroughly *Englishly* austere trout of the Koksilah river' presented one challenge, the trout of the Cowichan, 'perfect Irishmen for conviviality,' presented another and the author recommended anglers to a particular fly, the 'Cowichan Coachman.'

The 'brown man' was not an incidental observer. Native guides were integral to the sport fishery, not only because they knew the river, its dangers, and its bounty, but also because they were an essential part of the sport fisher's authentic wilderness experience, or so the CPR believed. Its promotional literature, in an effort to attract the fly fisher who sought unadulterated nature, featured the Native guide in a supporting role to the pioneer adventurer. As late as 1941, the CPR suggested that fishers on the Cowichan 'hire an Indian canoe man through the Indian Agent at Duncan,'[163] and the following account from one of the many books on sport fishing describes what was probably common practice:

One of my pleasantest fishing trips was up the Cowichan river in Vancouver Island. After three hours' train journey from Victoria, through magnificent scenery, H.B.H. and myself reached Duncan's and embarked on our canoe to make our way up the river to Cowichan Lake, out of which the Cowichan river flows. We had two Red Indians to pole the canoe, which was about twenty-five feet long, scooped out of a single tree. They were both dour-looking fellows, without the paint and feathers of romance, and answering to 'George' and 'Joe.'[164]

Bill Parenteau, in his study of Natives in the Atlantic salmon fishery, describes 'the transformation of Native people from active resource users to cultural commodities – there to enhance the wilderness experiences of the fly fisherman.'[165]

The CPR's vigorous promotion of fish and game reserves coincided with renewed interest from the provincial government. The province had passed a *Game Protection Act* in 1898,[166] and in 1905 it created a Department for the Protection of Game and Forests and an office of the

Provincial Game and Forest Warden. The warden's first report emphasized the need to enforce existing game and fisheries laws, particularly
against Indians who, he argued, were the principal culprits and showed
insufficient respect for the law.[167]

The CPR continued to press for abolition of the weirs. In 1906, its
chief game warden for the E&NR line, Mr Heald, produced a report on
fishing in the region. The Cowichan River, he concluded, was the most
valuable sport-fishing river, but it could be improved. The best fishing
sites should be 'set apart as a preserve, and improved by placing rocks,
both as "lies" for the fish and to prevent netting.' Further, he commented that it was 'utterly hopeless' to expect an improved sport
fishery until the law was enforced.[168] Identified by the CPR as 'a hunter
of world-wide fame,' Heald believed that the 'Indians are the chief
sinners in the matter of fish' and that '[i]n the Cowichan river and other
fishing streams the destruction of fish by Indians is appalling.'[169] To
encourage effective prosecution, the CPR gave Overseer Galbraith, stationed in Victoria, a pass on the E&NR. It was not renewed in 1907, and
Galbraith reported that he had to buy tickets to investigate complaints
from the Fish & Game Club.[170] That year he made monthly visits to the
Cowichan to investigate the weir fishery and to report on the stocks of
Atlantic salmon, which he claimed had been devastated by Cowichan
fishing.[171] Inspector of Fisheries Edward G. Taylor, responding to the
CPR complaints, reported that there were few incidents of illegal fishing by Natives and that the incidents were diminishing every year.
Furthermore, it was a slow process to change the views of Native
peoples: 'The Indian does not consider his methods for taking fish
illegal; but look upon them as his right, and we cannot expect to change
his views on this delicate subject (the way to obtain his food) in one
year.' Taylor wrote that Heald would be better advised to look to
destructive logging practices for the cause of diminishing fish stocks.[172]

Although privileging the sport fishery, Prince had always thought
that the Cowichan River could support a commercial fishery as well. In
1907, he proposed that Fisheries offer an exclusive right to net salmon
in Cowichan Bay to the Capital City Canning & Packing Company of
Victoria for nine years, the maximum length allowed under the *Fisheries Act*.[173] In exchange the company would pay a yearly fee of $50, and
build and operate a salmon hatchery. Prince justified the lease on the
grounds that potentially valuable commercial fish, particularly chum
salmon, were not being caught because nets had been prohibited in
Cowichan Bay. The lease would allow Fisheries to manage the commer-

cial catch without endangering the sports fishery, which was not interested in chum. The Cowichan had requested a similar lease in 1899, but Fisheries had refused on the grounds that the riverine fishery needed protecting. Now it proposed to grant an exclusive lease to that same fishery to a Victoria company. The following vague provision was to be included in the lease: 'Provided that the said lease does not interfere in any way with any fishing privileges that may have been conceded to Indians and that the said lessees in utilizing the privileges conveyed by this lease adopt no measure which will antagonize the local Indian tribes, and that the said lessees will afford the Indians every reasonable opportunity of obtaining employment in the fishing, canning, or other operations carried on in connection with the said lease.'[174] Indians had their food fisheries and could work as cannery employees; they were excluded from ownership and management of the commercial fishery. Local settlers did not want a commercial monopoly either and they denounced the lease. The provincial government, concerned about the sport fishery and its jurisdiction, disapproved as well and Capital City did not receive its lease.[175]

Seine and gill-net fishing had been expunged from the bay, but the Cowichan weirs remained. This result stemmed from a combination of several factors. The Cowichan used legal and ecological arguments to buttress their case that the weirs should remain, and the 1898 finding of the local court that the weirs did not unduly obstruct fish certainly helped. Other Native peoples around the province, particularly the Lake Babine, used similar arguments but lost their weirs. The Cowichan had other things in their favour. First, they were simultaneously feared and supported by elements of the local settler population, who were inclined to see logging and industrial fishing as a greater problem than the weirs. Second, no cannery relied on the Cowichan River as its primary source of fish. Anglers sought to protect the river and effectively denied the canneries a foothold from which the industry might have established itself. Somewhat paradoxically, the sport fishery, a riverine fishery like the weir fishery, shielded the Cowichan from a direct attack by the industrial canneries. The uneasy coincidence of interest between sports fishers and the Cowichan, combined with considerable local settler support, protected the weir fishery. Sport fishers, however, were unpredictable allies, inclined to turn against the Native fisheries when the cannery threat subsided. When combined with the interests of a growing tourist industry, the sport fishery became a formidable opponent, equally adept at appropriating Native fisheries and transforming ownership into the uncertainties of paid employment, in this case as guides.

In June 1913 the provincial Department of Fisheries forwarded the following complaint to the Dominion: 'Both forks Cowichan River entirely blocked Indian weirs. Impossible any fish over half pound to pass up. Prospects sport this summer and autumn absolutely nil unless action taken.'[176] The following year the Cowichan Conservation Association, unhappy with Fisheries' failure to remove the weirs, demanded that 'the present fishery officer at Sahtlam be removed and that an officer be appointed who can understand and can deal with the Indians more successfully.'[177]

Royal Commissions

On 27 May 1913 the Royal Commission on Indian Affairs for the Province of British Columbia held hearings at Comiaken. After an opening statement from Commissioner McKenna, five Cowichan chiefs – Suhiltun (Quamichan), Kukhalt (Comiaken), Tsulpi'multw (Khenipsen) (see figure 3.9), Queoqult (Clemclemeluts), and Kutsowat (Koksilah) – replied. Their testimony and that of eleven other Cowichan followed.[178] Virtually all those who testified raised concerns about the fishery and about the constant harassment from fisheries officers. Comiaken Chief Kukhalt emphasized the surveillance and intervention that effectively stopped their food fishery and prevented them from selling to the local fresh-fish market: 'At all times of the year we are in trouble and they will not let us fish at all. The constables are always watching us, no matter when we fish, or what we fish with.'

One year before the hearings, the Superintendent of Fisheries W.A. Found, acting on rumours of twenty to thirty nets in the river, had instructed local officials that 'violations of the law should be at once put an end to, and the desireability of seeing that such an important spawning river as the Cowichan is not netted is so obvious as to require no further comment.'[179] Chief Inspector of Fisheries Cunningham replied that the reports were greatly exaggerated, but that nine nets had been destroyed between March and April.[180] Shortly after the hearings, Inspector Taylor investigated complaints that Cowichan weirs were completely obstructing the fish. He found two weirs in place on a Saturday and ordered them destroyed. The Cowichan protested strongly and Taylor agreed to meet with them. They demanded, according to Taylor, permission to operate at least one weir. He agreed, but on the

Figure 3.9   Khenipsen Chief Charlie Tsulpi'multw addressing the Royal Commission on Indian Affairs for the Province of British Columbia, 26 May 1913.

following condition: the weir had to be open for three days each week, from 6 a.m. Saturday to 6 p.m. Monday. Taylor considered this interim arrangement satisfactory, but reported that the Cowichan 'were very hostile indeed.'[181]

In 1914, in an open letter printed in the local newspaper, the 'Chiefs of the Cowichan' informed the white population that they were no longer allowed to cross Cowichan land and that any who attempted to do so would be prosecuted for trespass. Employing an 'appeal to fair play and to all those who are animated with feelings of fair play,' designed to resonate with an English angler's sense of sport, the Cowichan did what they could to close the river to the sport fishery.[182] In another letter, the Cowichan informed the commissioners that they had placed their trust in the process when they had testified the year before. Since testifying, however, their weirs had been destroyed without notice and their trust had been abused.[183] The commissioners convened a meeting in April with Dominion and provincial fisheries officials and representatives from Indian Affairs to consider Indian fishing rights. No Cowichan were present.[184] The Dominion fisheries officials believed the weirs were damaging the fishery, that the Cowichan continually violated any compromise agreement, and that the extremely valuable sport-fishing interests needed protecting. Cunningham noted the 'large investment in summer homes' built to accommodate sport fishers in the Cowichan Valley.[185] Officials from Indian Affairs, by contrast, pointed out that the weirs had become the source of trouble again only since Fisheries interfered the previous year. The problem was not the weirs, but rather the law. Earlier commissions had promised the Cowichan that their fishery would not be disturbed, and this should be recognized by broadening the current regulations. Inspector Ditchburn of Indian Affairs suggested a further compromise: the Cowichan might agree to open the weirs three days each week.[186] There was some discussion about allowing the Cowichan to use nets if they agreed to remove their weirs, as the Lake Babine people had agreed in 1906, but nobody seemed convinced that this could work on the Cowichan. The meeting concluded with a decision to hold another meeting, this time in Duncan with the Cowichan present.

Inspector of Fisheries Taylor chaired the July 2nd meeting, attended by 120 Cowichan, the Catholic missionary, representatives of the Cowichan Anglers Association, and several local settlers not affiliated with the anglers. David Silsemult presented a petition on behalf of the Cowichan, claiming recognition of their rights: 'We are gathered here not to ask for any privileges, but to protest against the injustices, that have been done to us, for the last year or two, we are here to put before you our just claims and we hope you give them your consideration.'[187] The petition accompanied the testimony of seven prominent Cowichan representing the six Cowichan villages, all of whom strongly protested any interference with their rights.[188] They used weirs and nets to catch salmon and trout, and they had a right, recognized since Governor James Douglas's time, to continue fishing in this manner. The chiefs produced a section of a weir as evidence that the weirs simply impeded the fish, but did not stop them. Father Scheelen spoke for the Cowichan, arguing that they had a right to fish without a licence, and furthermore that they should be allowed to sell their catch. Members of the Cowichan Anglers Association testified that the weirs prevented the migration of salmon and trout, and recent poor years were evidence of that. The president, L.C. Rattray, suggested that instead of weirs the Cowichan should be allowed to use gill nets in Cowichan Bay. If the weirs must remain, he recommended a three-day opening each week and 2.5 inches between slats in the weirs. Non-angling members of the white community told the committee that the weirs were not the cause of any recent shortfall and that they should be allowed to remain. Nets, they argued on the other hand, should be prohibited. W.H. Hayward, the local member of the provincial legislature, pointed out that relations between whites and Native had been good until Fisheries destroyed the weirs last year. Why continue to strain relations when the weirs were not a problem?

More than a month after the meeting the commission issued its report. Following what appeared to be the wishes of the local, non-angling settler community, it recommended that nets should be prohibited in the Cowichan River, but that four weirs be allowed in the following manner:

> The Indians be granted the privilege of placing three weirs in the Cowichan River, one at Quamichan, one at Somenos, and another at a point to be decided upon, and one in the Koksilah River.

> That the lattice work of the weir provide for open spaces of not less than 2½ inches in width.

> That the weirs be open for the free passage of fish from Friday at 6 p.m. in each week to the following Monday at 6 a.m. and the opening shall be not less than 15 feet in width in the centre of the weir.[189]

Failure to comply with these terms would result in a fine or imprisonment under the *Fisheries Act*. The report did not mention the sale of weir-caught fish, stipulating neither that sale was prohibited nor that it should be allowed. The Cowichan had been clear that they were asserting a right and not asking for privileges, but the commission was equally clear in its report that it was granting a privilege: 'That in view of the privileges, above granted, it is distinctly understood that the use of nets of any kind is strictly prohibited and will not be condoned.'[190]

In later years, this report became the standard against which the Cowichan weir fishery was measured. Correspondence within the Department of Fisheries describes the 1914 recommendations as an agreement, suggesting that the Cowichan respect the terms to which they had agreed. However, apart from a suggestion that the Cowichan agreed to increase the wicker mesh to 2.5 inches, there is no indication that they agreed to these terms or thought them fair. The terms of the report were drawn up after the meeting and there are no signatures of the Cowichan chiefs on anything except petitions of protest.

The following year, Fisheries showed some flexibility towards the Cowichan sale of weir-caught fish. At another commission meeting to discuss 'Fishing Privileges of Indians in B.C.,' Inspector Taylor reported that the Cowichan requested a permit to sell fish. He acceded to the request, given that 'they were in very poor circumstances,' and directed Indian Agent Robertson to dispense licences allowing for local sale. Commissioner McKenna dubbed it a 'Peddler's licence,' to distinguish it from a commercial licence that allowed sale to the canneries, and did not indicate any concern about the practice.[191] The discussion then turned to the 'agreement' of the previous year. Taylor reported that apart from a few wicker meshes that were too small, the Cowichan had respected its terms. However, pressure from the Angler's Association to remove the weirs continued, and Cunningham continued his efforts to maintain property values at the expense of Cowichan food fishing. Members of the association, he reported, 'say they have property up there which is assessed as high as a thousand dollars an acre and in their opinion the river is far more important to them than the few fish that the Indians catch for food.'[192] In their final report setting out the reserves for the Cowichan agency, the Royal Commission did not mention the weir fishery.

Sport-fishing interests, despite opposing the weirs, would continue to invoke the Native fishery when cannery interests threatened. In 1916, Fisheries granted a purse-seine licence to an American firm allowing it to fish for salmon from Saltspring Island near Cowichan Bay. The fish were shipped south of the border for canning, which raised the ire of local residents. In 1917, a Canadian subsidiary of that same company proposed to build a cannery near Cowichan Bay if it were granted a similar purse-seine licence for chum salmon. It promised to use local, white unskilled labour to build and operate the cannery. 'Asiatics' would be excluded. The Duncan Board of Trade struck a fisheries committee to consider the matter and it produced a long report condemning the proposal.[193] The concerns were many, including fears that the proposed cannery was a front to export salmon to idle canneries in Washington state. The principal concern, however, was to conserve fish, particularly the coho that would invariably be caught with the chum, for the 'established fishing interests.' These included the Native food fishery (the committee forwarded a copy of the report to Indian Affairs) and the commercial handliners that Fisheries had begun to license in Cowichan Bay for local sale, but particularly the sport fishery, which offered 'attractions of the greatest value in securing tourist travel and its resultant benefits.' Fisheries granted the licence nonetheless, and the following year the Board of Trade fought another proposal to licence a chum fishery within Cowichan Bay to supply a fish-freezing plant. 'There can be no doubt,' wrote the editor of the Daily Colonist in Victoria, 'that irreparable damage will be done to one of the best and most famous resorts in British Columbia for sporting fishermen if the licence is upheld.'[184] A Fisheries' report concluded that 'as is the case of a number of issues on this coast the Cowichan Indian is brought into the argument for effect only,'[195] and it was at least partially correct. While the Board of Trade invoked the Native fishery to exclude foreign commercial interests, it continued to attack the Cowichan fishery.

A 1919 royal commission appointed to investigate fisheries management in the waters around Vancouver Island held hearings in Duncan.[196] F.C. Elliot, counsel for the Duncan Board of Trade, filed seven charges against Fisheries officers with the commission alleging dishonesty, bias in the awarding of licences, and inefficiency. Witnesses complained that the law was not enforced against Native fishers; the mayor of Duncan, Thomas Pitt, testified that wagonloads of Indian-caught fish were carted to the train station; Elliot alleged that Chief Inspector for Fisheries Taylor 'had stifled a prosecution brought against the owner of a weir,' and Fisheries official George Cathcart claimed he had been assaulted by several Cowichan when he attempted to remove their weir. The Cowichan were eventually persuaded to remove the weir, he testified, but they promptly rebuilt it.[197]

Seven Natives testified to the 1919 commission at Nanaimo, six from the Cowichan and one from Chemainus. C.F. Davie acted as their legal counsel, and in a letter to the *Cowichan Leader* before the hearings Davie expressed his opinion that the Cowichan were legally entitled to fish with weirs. The editor, apparently unaware of the preceding history, replied that 'Mr. Davie and the Indians have become connected with this "fish fight" at a comparatively recent date,' and that in his opinion the weirs were 'contrary to law.'[198] Louis Underwood, a Cowichan, testified to some of that history. He produced a gill net made from grasses by an Indian woman for his grandfather fifty years earlier. Underwood himself used commercial net made of twine, but the exhibit was evidence that the Cowichan had long used nets, particularly in the lower river where weirs were less effective. Comiaken Chief Joe Kukhalt reiterated the need for nets and urged that Fisheries allow his people 'to catch and sell fish in moderation as a means of livelihood.'[199] Chiefs Schallen (probably Suhiltun or his son Modeste) and Bill Golasulok of Quamichan testified to the importance of their weir fishery and of nets when the water was high. 'They had no intent of breaking the law, and only asked that they fish in their own precincts,' for food and sale to the local while population, 'without molestation' from fisheries officers.[200] After the hearings Fisheries cancelled the seine licence it had granted to an American firm in 1916, but the underlying issues of access were unresolved.

Reverse Onus, Prosecutions, Nets, and Weirs

In 1917, Fisheries amended the *Special Fishery Regulations for the Province of British Columbia* to emphasize that Indian food-fishing permits only allowed the catching of salmon for food purposes. In fact, after 1917 any Native sale of fish created a presumption that the seller had caught the fish under a food-fishing permit:

> 2. An Indian may, at any time, with the permission of the chief inspector of fisheries, catch fish to be used as food for himself and his family, but for no other purpose ...
> (a) Proof of a sale or of a disposition by any other means by an Indian of any fish shall be prima facie evidence that such fish was caught by the

said Indian, and that it was caught for a purpose other than to be used as for food himself or his family, and shall throw on the Indian the onus of proving that such fish was not caught under or pursuant to the provisions of any such permit.[201]

This reverse onus applied only to Indians; non-Native commercial fishers had to carry their licences when fishing, but it was only the Native commercial fishery that was illegal unless proven otherwise. Those purchasing fish caught under a food-fishing license were also guilty of an offence.[202]

Fisheries officers continued to remove nets and destroy weirs, but they did not prosecute the Cowichan. Instead they prosecuted the Chinese merchants who, they alleged, purchased fish from the Cowichan to resell in the Victoria markets. Near the end of January 1924, Fisheries Overseer Easton arrested a Chinese merchant, Hong Lee, whom he caught transporting a load of Cowichan-caught steelhead to markets in Victoria.[203] The stipendiary magistrate and former fisheries officer, James Maitland-Dougall, set the trial for 6 February, and released Lee on bail. Lee was charged with purchasing fish from an unlicensed fisher, contrary to the *Fisheries Act*, which prohibited those engaged in the storing or processing of salmon from buying fish from unlicensed fishers.[204] He sold the fish in fresh markets, however, and because he was not engaged in the storing or processing of salmon the section did not apply. Lee was also charged with purchasing fish caught under an Indian food-fishing permit, contrary to the *Regulations*.[205] The Cowichan, however, had not received a permit to use nets in the river. The fish were caught illegally, but because they had not been caught under a food-fishery permit, the section prohibiting the sale of fish caught under permit did not apply either. This time Fisheries hired a lawyer to prosecute the accused, but it was no more successful. Maitland-Dougall acquitted Lee on both charges.

The acquittal precipitated demands to change the law,[206] and in 1925 Fisheries amended the *Regulations* as follows:

15.b.(6) Any person buying any fish or portion of any fish, caught under such permit [Indian food-fish permit] shall be guilty of an offence against these regulations, and any person buying any fish or portion of any fish from an Indian, which fish was caught without a permit in an area for which permits are not granted, shall be guilty of an offence against these regulations.[207]

Although the amendment did not specify any particular fish, fisheries officials were most concerned about protecting the steelhead on the Cowichan River, the preferred fish of sports fishers, and they sought to confine the Cowichan to a chum fishery. The sports fishers were not interested in chum, so Fisheries began issuing permits to the Cowichan to catch chum for food with drift nets in Cowichan Bay.[208] Nets were still prohibited in the river, but the Cowichan could now apply for limited chum licences in the bay.

The weirs remained a difficult issue for Fisheries, but most disputes were resolved by returning to the 1914 'agreement.' Chief Inspector of Fisheries Motherwell believed the Cowichan would voluntarily relinquish any claim to use weirs, perhaps within the next two or three years.[209] He grossly underestimated the depth of the Cowichan's sense of entitlement, and in 1926 Fisheries renewed its efforts. The Indian agent reported that '[w]ithout warning and just as the fall run commenced the law was enforced ... On one occasion the Fishery patrol men went so far as to take two spears from Indians, break them and throw them in the river.'[210] This should not have surprised the Indian agent; Fisheries had employed similar tactics for years, but the Cowichan continued to build weirs at Quamicham and Somenos. By 1929 the Associated Boards of Trade of Vancouver Island thought they had waited long enough for the weirs to be removed and they passed a resolution that the weirs open from noon Friday to noon Monday and that the slats should be at least three inches apart. Motherwell announced, however, that the terms of the 1914 'agreement' would not be changed.[211]

The window of opportunity for weirs in the fall was relatively short. In some years there were only a few weeks before the late fall and winter rains raised the level of water in the Cowichan River to the point where the weirs would be swept away by the current and the accumulated debris. If the rains came early or too suddenly, the Cowichan could face difficulties securing their winter supply. In 1930, the water level rose dramatically in early November, largely eliminating the weir fishery. To prevent suffering, and realizing that it would be impossible to enforce a net prohibition, J.F. Tait, the new Supervisor of Fisheries for Vancouver Island, formally recognized what had been established practice and he issued permits to allow a Cowichan net fishery in the river to catch chum for their winter supply of food.[212] His officers continued to confiscate nets and prosecute Cowichan when they sold river-caught fish, particularly steelhead. In 1930 fisheries officers seized nine nets and prosecuted two Cowichan. A third, an 'old blind Indian' who was peddling fish in Duncan, was released with a warning.[213]

The formal recognition of a net fishery in the Cowichan River proved a mixed blessing for the Cowichan. In 1932, a large group of Cowichan met with Fisheries at the Indian Affairs office in Duncan. According to Tait, the majority favoured relinquishing the weirs in exchange for nets. Indian Agent A.H. Lomas had reported in 1930 that of the 650 Cowichan then living on the reserves 'possibly 50 heads of families or less participate' in the weir fishery, but it was not clear how many of the total population this represented.[214] Those who wanted nets instead of weirs were opposed, claimed Tait, by a group of influential leaders, and '[t]he issue was confused by Indian orators who advocated unrestricted rights in fishing, hunting and many other matters.'[215] For Tait the issue was not whether the Department of Fisheries had authority to regulate the Cowichan fishery, but how best to regulate that fishery. He assumed jurisdiction. Cowichan claims of sovereign control 'confused' the issue, which was how to remove the weirs. He thought this could be achieved by encouraging the Cowichan to use nets, but the Cowichan resisted, arguing that it was for them to decide whether to use weirs or nets, or both. Nothing was resolved at the meeting, but Tait was undeterred. He believed the majority of Cowichan prefered nets over weirs.

In the fall of 1932 the water in Cowichan River was low and fish could not ascend until the rains came in late October. As the water rose and the salmon moved into the river, fisheries officials sought to keep the Cowichan from building weirs in an effort to reduce their catch of chinook and coho salmon. In return, the officials assured the Cowichan that they would receive net permits during the chum salmon run in November.[216] The net permits were granted, and Fisheries also supplied sixteen Cowichan with used gill nets that it had confiscated for *Fisheries Act* violations at Port Alberni. The nets had little commercial value, but portions of them could be used in the river to catch chum.

Tait supplied these nets in an effort to accentuate divisions within the Cowichan over the weirs. Those who lived or had fishing rights in the lower three villages (Khenipsen, Comiaken, and Clemclemeluts) wanted nets, which were more effective in the tidal waters of the lower river than weirs. Comiaken Chief Kukhalt had testified to the need for nets in the lower river at the 1919 commission. The Cowichan at Quamichan and Somenos, however, were not prepared to relinquish their weirs. Quamichan chiefs had testified in 1919 that nets could augment weirs, but not replace them. Fisheries sought to exploit this division. At a meeting in February 1933, Tait presented a choice of weirs or nets. He had hoped to orchestrate a morning vote in favour of nets, but claimed it was blocked by influential leaders. In the afternoon fewer Cowichan returned. Those who stayed away realized, perhaps, that Tait was interested primarily in his agenda to remove the weirs. Those who did return wanted nets, but not at the expense of the weirs. Tait thought that some Cowichan had been coerced into changing their statements. He recommended that the permits not be issued in the spring, at least until after the steelhead run had passed.[217]

In the fall of 1933, once the chinook had passed upstream, Fisheries again issued permits allowing the Cowichan to catch chum with nets. Tait remained convinced that a closely monitored net fishery in the river was the most ecologically sound and practicable method of convincing the Cowichan to give up their weirs. He thought that the move away from weirs had already begun,[218] and he did what he could to exacerbate divisions between the Cowichan on the lower and upper river.[219] In 1934, Tait received a petition signed by 103 Cowichan requesting that Fisheries abolish the weirs: 'We, the undersigned Indians of the Cowichan Indian Reserves, hereby petition that the weirs on the Cowichan and Koksilah rivers be done away with, as there are so few that are able to get fish from this means, and that we be given the privilege to catch fish for our food supply by means of nets, gaffs or spears.'[220] Shortly thereafter, Tait received a counter-petition signed by 108 Cowichan insisting that Fisheries should allow the weirs to remain. He dismissed this petition, believing the majority wanted to fish with nets. A few influential leaders, he concluded, were preventing an agreement to abolish weirs because they controlled the weirs and thus the access to fish. He considered Chief Modeste and John Elliott from Quamichan the primary culprits.[221]

Tait changed his strategy. Instead of encouraging nets, he prohibited their use in the river for any purpose. This would illustrate the benefit of nets, he thought, and convince the majority of Cowichan to reject the weirs.[222] Except for a few compelling cases of need, Fisheries did not issue net permits in 1934 or 1935. It reverted to the terms established in 1914, allowing two or three weirs during the week, but prohibiting nets. When Guardian Purvey found a weir in place one Friday evening in July 1934, he seized the panels and held them for almost one month until Indian Agent Graham intervened.[223] Graham also believed that the weirs benefited only a few Cowichan and were the source of 'a great deal of dissatisfaction and jealousy.' He asked Fisheries to produce a proposal outlining how the government would secure Cowichan access to a food fishery if they agreed to relinquish their weirs. Tait thought the weirs should be abolished, and that Graham's proposal appeared too much like bargaining over something to which the Cowichan had no rights. Motherwell, nonetheless, responded to Graham's request for a proposal by offering the following terms, if the Cowichan agreed to relinquish their weirs:

1. That the Indians be permitted the use of gillnets, at the discretion of the local Fishery Officer, when the main chum run appears in the Cowichan River.

2. That nets be permitted at certain other times of the year but only under the specific authority of the local Fishery Inspector as to times, localities and dimensions of gear.

3. That permits for the use of spears and dip nets be fairly freely issued, which is a continuation of the present privilege.

4. That permission be given each fall during the chum salmon run for the use by the Indians of a purse seine in Cowichan Bay, inside the boundaries, for the purpose of their own food requirements; these operations, of course, to be under the direct supervision of the local Fishery Inspector.[224]

Graham apparently thought the terms reasonable, but there is no indication that the Cowichan agreed to them. Several meetings were held in an attempt to secure their consent, but according to fisheries officials, on each occasion 'a final agreement was prevented by a small majority who were able to dominate the meetings.'[225] With or without Cowichan consent, Fisheries decided to proceed. It instructed Motherwell not to renew the weir permits in 1936 and to implement the net fishery. Before these instructions were conveyed to the officers in the field, the Cowichan erected one weir. Fisheries determined that, for this last year, it was best left alone, but that the weirs would not be built again.

At a meeting in June 1937, Cowichan from Somenos and Quamicham repeated the need for both weirs and nets, but Tait would not be convinced. They also asked for permits entitling them to fish year round, including Saturdays and Sundays for those who worked during the week. Tait told them that 'the permit system purposed the taking of fish only by those actually in need, and not by Indians who were employed in competition with white men, and drawing regular wages.'[226] By this Tait meant that Cowichan working in the wage economy were now ineligible even for a food-fish permit. Those deemed in need by Fisheries could use gill nets, dip nets, spears, and gaffs to catch fish, but Fisheries would not issue a weir permit.[227]

After the meeting Fisheries clarified what permits it would issue to the Cowichan. All permits were for food fishing only and would be issued free. In the late summer and early fall permits would be available from the Indian agent to 'all needy Indians' to catch salmon during weekdays with spear, gaff, or dip net. The inspector of fisheries had discretion to issue gill-net permits. All fish caught during the summer and early fall would be 'for consumption fresh.' In the late fall, the Cowichan would be allowed to fish with gill nets, spear, or gaffs, 'to obtain all the chums they require for smoking and salting for winter use.'[228] From late December until the end of the steelhead run, permits would 'be issued sparingly to only those Indians who might be found to be actually in want.' Fisheries would take similar care in issuing permits during the summer when the chinook were running.[229] The weirs were not rebuilt, marking the symbolic end of what had been a sixty-year struggle for control of the river.

Conclusion

The Cowichan successfully defended their weirs longer that any Native group in the province, but after sixty years the Canadian state finally displaced Cowichan law with its own. The battle had been fought on the river, over appropriate fishing technology, but it had been waged with law, both Dominion and Cowichan. The Dominion had constructed its fisheries policy in law, thereby legitimizing the threat and use of force against those who disputed its preferred allocation. On several occasions members of the Cowichan were charged with fisheries offences, arrested, and tried. On numerous other occasions, less visible in the historical record, fisheries officers seized nets, removed weirs, or threatened Cowichan fishers with the *legal* consequences of continuing to fish, including fines and jail, and the destruction of Cowichan property, namely, weirs and nets. This continuing harassment was, perhaps, more intrusive and ultimately more effective than the formal court appearances that the Dominion consistently lost. Nonetheless, law was the principal device with which the state legitimized and effected the capture of the resource.

At the same time, Dominion law, including the common law, provided a surprising diversity of tools for Cowichan resistance. Although several Cowichan were prosecuted for fisheries offences, I have found no evidence that any was ever convicted for building a weir. Frequently assisted by the local Indian agent and missionaries, individual Cowichan successfully defended themselves in local courts on procedural grounds and on the merits of their fishing technology to sustain fish stocks. Fisheries could not secure a conviction, and each failed prosecution strengthened the Cowichan's position that they had a legal entitlement to fish. Although not choosing to enter the Canadian legal space of the courtroom, the Cowichan turned that space to their advantage, forcing Fisheries to negotiate the terms of a continuing weir fishery. Aware that their prosecutions would only lead to acquittals that would strengthen rather than diminish Cowichan claims, fisheries officials declined to prosecute, but continued to confiscate nets and destroy weirs. The formal face of law in the local setting – the courts – provided little support for the fisheries officials, who removed their challenge to the Cowichan fisheries from the courts to the riverbanks. Observation, confiscation, and harassment became the controls of choice, followed by attempts to accentuate divisions within Cowichan society. This was done with the authority of law, but outside the local legal forum of the court.

The Cowichan were able to make such effective use of Canadian law because they were increasingly surrounded by a settler society that was, in parts, fearful of Cowichan unrest and sympathetic to Cowichan claims. Once securely established, this English settler society viewed industrialization as a greater threat to its ways of life than the Cowichan weir fishery. Settlers blamed logging for the destruction of fish stocks and Fisheries for provoking unrest among their Cowichan neighbours by its repeated attempts to destroy weirs. These settlers, after all, were the ones most inconvenienced by the no-trespassing signs that the Cowichan erected on their reserve boundaries to prevent white access to the river. This local public opinion was reflected more in the legal arena and the decisions of local magistrates who lived as part of the settler society than in the political arena, which with its base in Ottawa was far removed from local influences.

The courts proved useful to the Cowichan, but their resistance was rooted in Cowichan law. On the basis of a fundamental sense of entitlement drawn from within Cowichan teachings, the Cowichan defended their weirs from repeated challenges by officials of the Canadian state. Cowichan law served the same basic purposes as Canadian fisheries law. It provided a structure for managing human access to the resource, allocating fish among particular users by regulating the time, place, and method of harvest. At its heart were the stories and myths that described kinship connections back to an original ancestor from the mythical age. That these foundational myths were not recognized by the state as a legitimate source of authority did not make this alternate system of regulation any less real, but it did cause the Cowichan to recast their claims in a language that the officials of the state could understand. The Cowichan and their allies presented a rights-based claim that emphasized 'natural rights' and the binding nature of earlier agreements with government officials. Although the authorship of various letters and petitions is difficult to establish, the language of 'natural rights' was likely the work of Catholic missionaries who had been an important presence in the Cowichan Valley since the 1850s. Similarly, the language of binding agreements was probably introduced by sympathetic government officials or lawyers steeped in nineteenth-century ideas of contracts as reciprocally binding promises.[230] This evolution of Cowichan claims may have been responsible, in part, for the frequent charges by political authorities that the rights-based claims of Natives to land and resources were new, fabricated by meddlesome missionaries and trouble-making sympathizers. The Cowichan claims were undoubtedly re-characterized in response to the challenges posed by the Canadian state, and in this sense reinvented. Although expressed differently and in new settings, however, the claims were not new. Their expression might have changed, but Cowichan legal forms had long articulated rights of access.

There is little doubt, however, that state power reduced the effectiveness of Cowichan traditions. The Department of Fisheries marginalized the Cowichan and other Native fisheries to the point where only people on the edge of destitution, as determined by Indian Affairs, could receive a food-fishing permit. The Cowichan could work for the canneries and many did, but when a Cowichan chief applied for a commercial licence, for example, he was refused, only to see Fisheries issue a lease to a Victoria-based firm. In this environment, Cowichan law as a source of authority declined. The availability of new technology, particularly the long and deep commercial gill nets, further diminished the importance of weirs within the Cowichan economy and consequently the interest in fighting for them. They were controlled by certain families, and were a useful technology only on certain portions of the river. They had once been the focus of community activity in the fall, but that declined as other Cowichan began using nets more extensively in the lower river and bay. The divisions that existed in Cowichan society were accentuated by fisheries officers in their efforts to remove the weirs. In the end, the Canadian state regulated the weirs out of existence, but not without a half-century of determined Cowichan resistance, and never with the Cowichan's consent.

If there is any doubt about the salience of an analysis that emphasizes the cultural divide between colonizer and colonized, and the role of law in an unfolding relationship, one need only consider recent developments. In 1973, members of the Cowichan built a weir at Quamichan in symbolic protest (see figure 3.10). The weir had been approved by a Cowichan vote, but the band council refused to endorse the protest. Fisheries officials observed the operation but did not intervene or lay charges, and after several days of fishing the weir was dismantled.[231] In September and October of the following year, however, Fisheries charged nine Cowichan for fishing or being in possession of fish on the Cowichan River during the close season.[232] They were convicted at trial, and their appeals to the British Columbia Court of Appeal (BCCA) and the Supreme Court of Canada (SCC) were dismissed. Only Justice Brian Dickson in his dissenting judgment in the SCC would have acquitted the Cowichan on the grounds that an Aboriginal food fishery should have priority over any other fishery.[233]

In the intervening years between 1937 and these convictions, Cowichan resistance had not disappeared, but the history of the conflict over fish on the Cowichan was gradually forgotten or suppressed. Cowichan efforts to hire a lawyer in the 1940s to test their fishing rights in court were curtailed when Indian Affairs refused to release band-council funds.[234] Determined to maintain some control over their fisheries, the Cowichan passed a bylaw in 1956, pursuant to the *Indian Act*, for 'Preservation, Protection and Management of Fish.' It required that all non-band members obtain a permit from the band council before fishing in the Cowichan reserve. Almost thirty years later, in 1983, the Cowichan would replace that bylaw with another, more comprehensive, set of regulations. The 1983 bylaw required that non-Cowichan obtain a licence from the band council before fishing in 'Cowichan Indian Band Waters,' defined as 'all waters situated upon or within the boundaries of reserves established for the use and benefit of the Cowichan Indian Band,' and it set limits on the fishing of band members.[235] In 1984, another Cowichan, John Louie Jimmy, was charged

Figure 3.10 Joe Elliott, great-grandson of John Elliott (see pp. 161–2) and son of Gordon Elliott, who was one of the organizers of the protest fishery, at seven years old, standing on the protest weir built on the Cowichan River in September 1973.

and convicted with having a steelhead caught on the Cowichan River in his possession, contrary to the *Fisheries Act* and the *British Columbia Sports Fishing Regulations*. He was convicted in the provincial court, but acquitted on appeal to the county court, and the BCCA dismissed the Crown's appeal, citing the 1983 Cowichan bylaw and the judgment of Justice Dickson in *R. v. Jack*.[236] These charges, court appearances, and judgments reveal a continuing clash between the Cowichan and the Canadian state over ownership and jurisdiction.

CHAPTER FOUR

Law and Colonialism

'Colonialism' describes the processes of military, economic, and cultural domination employed by a state to bring territory and people within its sphere of control. It involves the transfer of cultural and economic institutions from one society to another, and results in the appropriation of land and resources. Sometimes colonialism leads to colonization, the more or less systematic settlement of the territory by members of the colonizing society and the eventual transfer of authority to the settler society. In other circumstances, the imperial state maintains administrative control, extracting resources and labour but not encouraging settlement, and eventually withdraws, leaving a transformed indigenous society. The circumstances of settler and administrative regimes differ considerably, but in both contexts the varied tactics or strategies of power used to assert control have ranged from gunboats and infantry to cultural definition. Somewhere in between, combining both violence and discourse, one finds law.

Law was at the forefront of European colonialism in the late nineteenth and early twentieth centuries. Not only was it a vehicle through which colonizing powers secured control of other territories and people, but at a basic level it justified the colonial projects. In their imperial expansion, Europeans believed they brought civility to supplant savagery, Christianity to banish superstition, progress to supersede stasis, and law to replace anarchy. Law, like the Christian gospels, was a contribution from the metropolitan country to its 'uncivilized' colony.[1] In *knowing* and representing the *other* as savage and superstitious, living in anarchy, Europeans could, with confidence, impose their civility, religion, and law. With knowledge of the other came power over the other, and although power was expressed in many forms, law was a principal conduit.

Particularly for the English, law justified the colonial project. Law was about order, and establishing a much-heralded English legal order was thought to be an unmitigated good. Colonial administrators or the settler societies they established had little doubt that imposing English legal norms secured the well-being of British nationals, but was also justified as a means of improving the human condition. The common law was England's cultural treasure, the rule of law the pinnacle of English constitutional achievement. Judge-made law in ordinary courts distinguished English law, and even the English, from the civil codes and state tribunals of the nation states of continental Europe and their inhabitants. Individual liberties, it was thought, were protected more effectively from arbitrary official action by the accumulation of judicial decisions than by the generalities of a written constitution. In his influential *Law of the Constitution* (1885), A.V. Dicey wrote:

> We may say that the constitution is pervaded by the rule of law on the ground that the general principles of the constitution (as for example the right to personal liberty, or the right of public meeting) are with us the result of judicial decisions determining the rights of private persons in particular cases brought before the Courts; whereas under many foreign constitutions the security (such as it is) given to the rights of individuals results, or appears to result, from the general principles of the constitution.[2]

In territories claimed for the British Crown, particularly those that became settler colonies, establishing English law was essential to the colonial project.[3]

Where necessary, European colonial powers used other, blunter instruments of force, including gunboats and infantry, to secure control. Pervasive violence, so powerfully portrayed in Frantz Fanon's *The Wretched of the Earth*, lingered in the background of every imperial enterprise, supporting the power of the colonial state, ready to defend European nationals and their property.[4] I shall return to Fanon and to the particular violence of the colonial encounter shortly, but it was not only violence that secured the European position. Less obviously sources of power, the numerous cultural assumptions about family, dress, language, work, and the apparently mundane details of an ordinary life reproduced particular hierarchical relations between colonial rulers and subjects. Edward Said, in his immensely influential study *Orientalism*, managed to portray 'the formidable structure of cultural domination' that enveloped the West's relationship with the Middle

East. It was this cultural domination – the ability to name, to label, to categorize an other – that permeated the relationship, Said argued, confirming at every level a Western superiority and an Oriental inferiority. Culture was not, in Said's study, 'merely decorative or "superstructural,"' but a source of great and under-examined power in the West's relationship with the East.

Neither violence nor cultural domination can be excluded from a study of law. Backed by infantry and navy guns, and supported by a powerful set of cultural assumptions, the British established their economic, political, and social order in distant territories with law. Law was the instrument through which Britain both seized and justified its control of colonial lands, remaking people and resources to fit within its economic sphere as a source of raw materials and labour, a market, or as a destination for a convicted, unwanted, or 'excess' population. In the hands of its settler societies, law became the means to assert a particular order that would reproduce much of what had been left behind in Britain.

Produced and enforced by the state, law was understood by the British in the late nineteenth century as a means of securing order and obedience with rules rather than violence. It was a strongly centralist model, captured most enduringly by John Austin's mid-nineteenth-century definition of law as the command of the sovereign.[5] Austin's jurisprudential contribution was to combine judge-made law and legislation into a unified theory of law.[6] Law emanated from the state, whether directly through legislative enactment, or indirectly from judges appointed by the state. It could be discovered by applying certain formal tests, and was recognizable as law because it was backed by the force of the state. Some have suggested that this was an overly formal and deficient understanding of law in nineteenth-century Britain; that despite an increasingly centralized law under state control, remnants of age-old customary law continued to function, and that the emergence of administrative bodies posed a challenge to the hegemony of the ordinary courts.[7] Nonetheless, an 'ideology of legalism' prevailed in the legal profession and beyond.[8] Law stood apart, distinct from politics or policy, to be determined by formal legal tests. It was ordered, coherent, and it sought to produce order.[9] Martin Chanock, in his study of law in colonial Africa, describes the British perception of law in the late nineteenth century as follows:

The British model of civilised government was one in which the state secured obedience and order by command; not a command which enforced itself by capricious terror, but a rule-bound command. Nineteenth-century British jurisprudence emphasized that law came from the state but that it restrained power; that it was the main means of control in social order; and that the alternative was anarchy, which was not a good thing. Law was seen to be essentially about order and obedience, rather than about the expression of social solidarity, the facilitation of market relations, the legitimation of power, the manipulation of symbols, the definition of inalienable rights, or the expression of class interests, all of which have been the foci of other traditions of explanation.[10]

Chanock's study is part of a growing body of work to describe the interplay of European and indigenous legal forms in late-nineteenth and early-twentieth-century colonial Africa and Asia. He and others have pointed out that colonialism usually involved not only the capture of land and resources, but also the large-scale transfer of laws and legal institutions from the European state to the colonized territory. To understand the colonial processes, one must explore the intersecting legal systems. Other themes emerge.[11]

Greatly outnumbered by the indigenous population in most of their empires, the small cadre of colonial officials could not administer European law across these territories. Attempts to do so could have disastrous consequences. The British, for example, retreated from an attempt to formalize land ownership to facilitate tax collection in India when they discovered their polices had, in short order, produced the Bengal famine of the late 1760s.[12] In his powerful collection of essays *Colonialism and Its Forms of Knowledge: The British in India*, Bernard Cohn describes the extension of 'officializing' procedures that enabled the British state to control its own population, but also that of its colonies. The British state took control of India, he argues, 'by defining and classifying space, making separations between public and private spheres; by recording transactions such as sale of property; by counting and classifying their populations, replacing religious institutions as the registrar of births, marriages, and deaths; and by standardizing languages and scripts.'[13] And later, '[t]he conquest of India was the conquest of knowledge.'[14] The gathering of legal knowledge was an important part of this process. Cohn describes the British effort first to learn and control language in India through dictionaries and grammar texts, and then to codify Indian law by producing an equivalent of *Blackstone's Commentaries*. Colonial officials concluded, in part because of the famine, that it was both impossible and unwise to extend British law to India, and therefore attempted to catalogue the 'ancient Indian constitution' in a legal code that could be printed and disseminated for magistrates to enforce. The creation of a state capable of fulfilling these administrative tasks was, Cohn argues, an invention without precedent in British constitutional history, and certainly not one for which the earlier colonial experience in the Americas had prepared it.

European colonial powers in much of Africa and Asia established dual legal systems – one for the colonizer and one for the colonized. The former, administered by Europeans, applied to European nationals, replicated the commercial laws of their home country, and enabled them to conduct business in the colonial territory under a familiar legal regime designed to protect individual property. The latter, often described as 'customary law,' applied to the indigenous peoples who staffed and frequently administered the customary law courts. European law was paramount – unacceptable indigenous customs could be outlawed under the 'repugnancy principle' – but otherwise the systems were separate. Although systems of customary law had roots in the pre-colonial social order, many have argued that the legally recognized 'custom' was a product of the colonial encounter and a part of the colonizer's efforts to integrate the colonized within the European economic sphere.[15] In fact, some reject the language of duality or pluralism, arguing that such terms convey parity that 'misrepresent[s] the asymmetrical power relations that inhere in the coexistence of multiple legal orders.'[16] From this perspective, the formally recognized systems of customary law were another colonial institution that 'transformed conceptions of time, space, property, work, marriage, and the state' in the interests (usually economic) of the colonial power.[17]

Similar processes were, or had been, at work in Europe from the eighteenth century.[18] Sources of wealth emerged that were not directly connected to land. Contract replaced status as the principal tool of social organization, and law and state were engaged in remaking relations between people, land, and resources, to fit an emerging industrial capitalism.[19] Particular social relations, such as master and servant or husband and wife, were defined, categorized, and reproduced in law, and were, not surprisingly, generally responsive to the interests of a male ruling class. As England's constitutional struggles of the seventeenth century receded, Douglas Hay argues, law displaced religion as the legitimate source of authority.[20] Neither the priest nor the monarch could command as they once had; they were no longer legitimate sites of coercion. Law, in the forms of statute and common law, had become the legitimate source of authority. The legitimacy of law, however, was not something that could be assumed; legitimacy had to be maintained through the administration of law. This was done in rural England, Hay argues, not only through the terror inspired by an increasingly bloody penal code but also by the combined workings of majesty, justice, and mercy – the tools of the assizes courts. By the court's ceremonial splendour (majesty), the periodic hangings of a member of the landed gentry (justice), and the frequent commutation of sentences (mercy), the ruling class were able to maintain the widespread perception of legitimacy in a violent legal system that protected their property. Thus, it was on the thin shoulders of law, as ideology, that the ruling class was able to rule. Hay suggests that 'the criminal law, more than any other social institution, made it possible to govern eighteenth-century England without a police force and without a large army,'[21] and not only because it instilled fear with violence.

Notwithstanding the gross imbalance of power between rulers and ruled in eighteenth-century England, E.P. Thompson, in his much-cited conclusion to his study of the struggle for use and control of Windsor Forest, concluded that law was never simply the tool of the ruling class. Law, he suggested, provided an arena for struggle, for resistance as well as oppression.[22] Thompson interprets *The Black Act* of 1723, passed by the British Parliament to protect the King's forests by, among other things, making poaching a capital offence, as the site of conflict between the property rights of the land-owning gentry and the customary rights of peasant foresters and farmers. Sometimes the foresters were hanged for killing deer, catching fish, cutting turf, or taking timber or for defending these 'unauthorized' uses of the forest. Other times they successfully defended charges of theft by appealing to customary uses recognized by local forest law. The conflict was sustained not only by competing economic interests or material need, but also by competing visions of legal entitlement. As Thompson argued in a later work, '[m]any of the classic struggles at the entry to the industrial revolution turned as much on customs as upon wages or conditions of work.'[23] Legal claims, often made in terms of customary uses or customary rights, were particularly prominent in what Thompson describes as the '*rebellious* traditional culture' of the eighteenth century.[24] Some customs were, of course, newly conceived or articulated, a defensive response to property rights newly defined by the landed gentry in statute.[25] Law, Thompson argued, was contested ground. Describing it as the 'handmaiden' of the ruling class, while accurate to a point, is incomplete:

> We reach, then, not a simple conclusion (law = class power) but a complex and contradictory one. On the one hand, it is true that the law did mediate existent class relations to the advantage of the rulers; not only is this so, but as the century advanced the law became a superb instrument by which these rulers were able to impose new definitions of property to their even greater advantage, as in the extinction by law of indefinite agrarian use-rights and in the furtherance of enclosure. On the other hand, the law mediated these class relations through legal forms, which imposed, again and again, inhibitions upon the actions of the rulers.[26]

Though they are highly evocative and compelling, one must be careful in applying Thompson's and Hay's analyses beyond eighteenth-century England. Law, as ideology, functioning both to recreate the social order and to legitimize that order, emerged from particular historical circumstances, most immediately the conflict and constitutional struggle in seventeenth-century England. Transporting an analysis of a peculiarly English institution to the colonial setting, where the economic relations were fundamentally different and society was divided more obviously by culture and then by class, must be done with care. England was riven by class distinctions and diverse local cultures, but in comparison to the cultural chasm between colonizer and colonized overseas the differences at home were of a smaller order. Language (if not accent) and religion were shared broadly, as was a connection to the Crown. Law and state became strong centralizing forces, but they did so among people who were part, if marginalized, of the British polity. David Neal, in his study of Australia as a penal colony, argues that even among the transported convicts the ideology and legitimating force of the rule of law remained 'convincing and important.'[27] Indigenous peoples in the colonies, however, although nominally British subjects, did not share this common cultural ground. Hay and Snyder argue, as a result, that in administrative colonies in Africa and Asia, the rulers (Europeans) and ruled (indigenous peoples) assumed that European law would reflect the interests of the colonial masters; '[t]he ideology of the rule of law was thus practically absent in many if not most colonies.'[28]

There is little doubt that law and state functioned differently in the colonial settings, particularly in their relation to indigenous peoples.

English law in Britain's colonies was both entirely foreign to that population and particularly important for maintaining social control. This is Peter Fitzpatrick's point when he suggests that law in the colonial setting 'lacks the support of the detailed and tentacular non-legal controls that operate in the West and which go to create a self-determining, and self-regulating subject,' and therefore it assumes a greater role.[29] In his study of colonial Papua New Guinea, Fitzpatrick argues that whereas law and state in the first world were 'oriented towards the elimination of pre-capitalist modes,' in the third world they were 'oriented towards the conservation and continuing exploitation of the traditional mode.'[30] Law and state sustained the traditional society and economy in the colonial setting, constructing customary law to shield indigenous societies from the frontal assault of industrial capitalism. The colonial power's interest in maintaining a nominally traditional sector lay primarily in subsidized labour; supporting a meagre subsistence economy was one means of ensuring a dependent and inexpensive indigenous labour force. Customary law, when formalized in state institutions, had the further effect of formalizing many of the pre-existing tribal, religious, gender, and other divisions in the indigenous society, thereby hindering the emergence of a working-class consciousness that might have challenged the capitalist colonial authority. The result, argues Fitzpatrick, was that 'the law and state continue[d] to be particularly and predominantly responsive to the interests of the only coherent and potent class element affecting it, the metropolitan bourgeoisie.'[31] Shielding the traditional required sustained effort. It was not enough, as with pre-industrial Europe, to remove pre-capitalist relations. Law and the state, Fitzpatrick suggests, continually intervened to keep the capitalist and traditional economies separate, allowing the latter to create an inexpensive pool of labour, yet integrated so that capital had access to that subsidized labour. The result is that 'law and state have a role that is more structurally central and structurally enduring in the third world.'[32]

It is not the division and integration of so-called traditional and capitalist economies that is Fitzpatrick's contribution. Rather, it is his highlighting the role of law in this process. Fanon similarly emphasizes the particular role of the officers of the law and the military in the colonial setting, providing some examples of Fitzpatrick's 'detailed and tentacular non-legal controls' that function in the metropolitan centre to bewilder and to obscure the exercise of power, something that is laid bare in the colony:

The colonial world is cut in two. The dividing line, the frontiers are shown by barracks and police stations. In the colonies it is the policeman and the soldier who are the official, instituted go-betweens, the spokesmen of the settler and his rule of oppression. In the capitalist societies the educational system, whether law or clerical, the structure of moral reflexes handed down from father to son, the exemplary honesty of workers who are given a medal after fifty years of good and loyal service, and the affection which springs from harmonious relations and good behaviour – all these esthetic expressions of respect for the established order serve to create around the exploited person an atmosphere of submission and of inhibition which lightens the task of policing considerably. In the capitalist countries a multitude of moral teachers, counsellors and 'bewilderers' separate the exploited from those in power. In the colonial countries, on the contrary, the policeman and the solider, by their immediate presence and their frequent and direct action maintain contact with the native and advise him by means of rifle-butts and napalm not to budge. It is obvious here that the agents of government speak the language of pure force. The intermediary does not lighten the oppression, nor seek to hide the domination; he shows them up and puts them into practice with the clear conscience of an upholder of the peace; yet he is the bringer of violence into the home and into the mind of the native.[33]

By locating the police station and naming the policeman, Fanon gives a space and identity to a principal instrument of colonial power – the law – and he emphasizes its particular violence in the colonial setting. This violence is not confined to the past or to administrative colonies. In a trenchant critique of the continuing colonization of Australia, Jeannine Purdy argues, following Fanon, that the violence of law depends 'on which side of the colonial divide one stood,' and, importantly, one stands.[34] She points to the increasing incarceration of Aborigines that accompanied the mining and agricultural expansion in Western Australia in the second half of the twentieth century as evidence of law's violent complicity.

Fanon does not, however, differentiate the power of the law and the military in the passage reproduced above, and this is where some, although perhaps not Purdy, would part company. In the English tradition at least, legal institutions sought to maintain a broadly held perception of legitimacy, a need that differentiated them from the military. To produce and reproduce this legitimacy in Britain, the law could not be a totalizing power (Hay and Thompson's point), but neither was it in the colonial setting. As James C. Scott has argued in his studies of class relations in a Malay village,[35] and more generally,[36] the colonized were not passive bystanders, caught inside a legal straightjacket, unable to respond. Instead, they consistently directed and managed change, such as they could, for their benefit. Sometimes this meant using European law to limit the excesses of settler brutality. Other times it meant co-opting the power of the state to affect relations within indigenous societies, enabling some to advance their interests at the expense of others. Indigenous people did not, of course, experience colonialism equally, a point nowhere made more strongly than in Ranajit Guha's remarkable essay 'Chandra's Death.'[37] Helping to create and then working within a collective of *Subaltern Studies* scholars who sought to challenge the elitism of Indian historiography,[38] Guha in this essay presents the extraordinary struggle of a woman, with the help of her female relatives, to avoid the consequences of a forbidden pregnancy. Chandra dies in a failed abortion, condemned by local custom, caste, and gender, but in her struggle and in the solidarity of women against a feudal patriarchy, Guha finds choice and the barest threads of agency. Law, 'the state's emissary,' constructs this death as murder; family members who tried to help become defendants in a criminal trial.[39] The law of a colonial state reproduced an indigenous society in the image of its own elite or in that of the colonizer, but it also created unintended spaces of resistance, forced compromise, and was a source of power at least to certain members of the indigenous society. Sally Engle Merry provides the following summary of the law and colonialism literature:

> Taken together, the works under review show that European law was central to the colonizing process but in a curiously ambiguous way. It served to extract land from precolonial users and to create a wage labor force out of peasant and subsistence producers. Yet, at the same time, it provided a way for these groups to mobilize the ideology of the colonizers to protect lands and to resist some of the more excessive demands of the settlers for land and labor. Moreover, the law provided a way for the colonial state to restrain the more brutal aspects of settlers' exploitation of land and labor. Thus, the legal arena became a place of contest among the diverse interest groups in colonial society. The contest included struggles between traditional leaders and new educated elites of the colonized population as well as colonial officials, missionaries, and settler populations. It was an unequal contest, however, in which colonial officials and settler populations exerted vastly greater power than colonized groups. The use

of law in colonial processes therefore parallels other state efforts to assert control through law, efforts often undermined by patterns of non-compliance and appropriation by the subjugated.[40]

In the literature on law and colonialism, then, there are several important observations. First, law was central to the colonial project, both as a source of control and as a justification for that control. Second, legal pluralism rather than legal centralism characterized the colonial setting; European and indigenous legal forms operated in the same territory, creating intersecting spheres of social control.[41] Third, law in the colonial setting played a different, perhaps more intrusive and sustained, role than it did in the metropolitan country. Finally, although both European and customary law channelled resources to the benefit of the colonial power, law was not only an oppressive instrument of power. It was that, but more. Law was a source of power that could be used to affect social relations within the indigenous society, for the benefit of some and to the detriment of others. It also provided space where the colonized might limit the excesses of colonial control. Though it could not remove the colonial power, law and legal argument might ameliorate oppression. This may have been especially true in British settler societies, where law and the ideology of the rule of law were particularly important elements in the settlers' self-identity.

Law and Colonialism, and British Columbia

Violence, or its prospect, was never far from the imposition of English law in nineteenth-century British Columbia. The gunboat expedition in 1853 led by Governor James Douglas to capture, try, and execute the Cowichan murderers of the Scottish shepherd Peter Brown, an event that Hamar Foster describes as 'the first, unequivocal application of English criminal law and procedure to an Aboriginal person accused of murder' in British Columbia,[42] is an early example. The procedure may have emulated an English criminal trial, but the setting (the deck of a Royal Navy gunboat) and the jurors (naval officers) were part of a theatre of power as much as of law. Douglas was certainly attempting to impose English law over a territory and people as immigrant settlement expanded from its toehold on the Saanich Peninsula of southern Vancouver Island, but this was an exercise of military power still only thinly mediated by that law. Violence accompanied the extension of settlement north from Victoria in the 1850s and early 1860s,[43] and Royal

Navy gunboats continued to patrol the Northwest Coast until 1890, providing the necessary firepower to subdue a difficult frontier and extend English law. The gunboats, argues historian Barry Gough, were 'the armed might of the fragile system of magistrates and police superintendents that were extending English law on this populous Indian frontier.'[44] After 1890, a sufficiently developed system of magistrates, police, courts and jails, and occasionally the militia, continued their task.

Choosing a somewhat different emphasis, Tina Loo argues that nineteenth-century immigrants to British Columbia 'were concerned less with countering the possibility of violence and crime with English law and its institutions than they were about structuring a particular kind of social, political and economic order and privileging a particular set of values.'[45] The order they sought and the values they espoused are encapsulated, suggests Loo, in a discourse of nineteenth-century English laissez-faire liberalism. Law and the state were asked to create the 'standardization, uniformity, certainty, and above all rationality' that Europeans sought to secure their economic futures.[46] Her study begins with the 'Club law' of the Hudson's Bay Company, turns to the miner's law that arrived with the gold rushes of the late 1850s and 1860s, and concludes with imposition of state law on the Chilcotin people in 1864 and the formation of a colonial identity. It is in her final chapter that Loo explores the resistance born of domination and, drawing upon Thompson, the possibility that law creates a 'discursive space' that can be harnessed to challenge the state. Law, she suggests, with its assertion of equality, could transcend the material interests of white British Columbia, creating the possibility of justice for Native people. Her case study of the Bute Inlet Massacre – where eighteen railway workers were killed in 1864 and eight Chilcotin Indians were arrested for their murder – is perhaps not the best example of the emancipatory possibilities of law's discursive spaces. The eight were tried and five were hanged, notwithstanding the procedural irregularities of their capture (they surrendered under false pretences). The arrests and trials appear as little more than the transparent exercise of state power, unconstrained by legal procedure. Loo concludes as much in a later version of the same essay: 'The Chilcotins' otherness, it seemed, prevailed; the need for Terror outweighed the need for British Justice.'[47]

The record is mixed: the laws of immigrant British Columbia were, through their violent imposition, meant to counter violence, but also to construct a liberal political, economic, and social order. Some Natives used this new locus of power, attaching their interests to the successful enforcement of Anglo-Canadian law. Others resisted its imposition, using, among other things, the discursive spaces of Anglo-Canadian law. In 'Dan Cranmer's Potlatch: Law as Coercion, Symbol and Rhetoric in British Columbia, 1884–1951,' Loo argues through a study of the enforcement of the potlatch prohibition that the legal process is revealed 'as a system of rhetoric or a way of arguing,' and as such, it contributed to the varied strategies of resistance Native people employed to deflect and circumvent the potlatch law.[48] The legal process narrowed the realm of argument, defining what questions were important or irrelevant to the resolution of any particular case, often to the detriment of Native peoples. But the narrowing of debate does not determine the outcome or diminish the importance of argument. The law produces space for argument that, when creatively employed, 'not only allows the powerless to resist the oppression of the powerful,' argues Loo, but 'also gives them a means to transform their own relationships.'[49] In another essay Loo explores this last possibility, that state law could be deployed by Native people to transform relationships with other Natives. Native individuals, she suggests, used state law for their material advantage (reward or payment), to rid their communities of troublemakers, or to gain status within their communities through association with the Crown.[50] Similarly, I have argued elsewhere that Native communities, not just individuals, attempted to use state law and an association with the Queen to structure a relationship with the local government of a white settler society based on the rule of law.[51] Extending this analysis one step further, Merry argues that Hawaiian kings sought to impose a Western legal system on their subjects in the mid-nineteenth century to prove their 'civilization' to European states in an effort to remain autonomous and sovereign.[52]

The work of Loo and others suggest that the themes which Merry highlights in her survey – the centrality of law in the colonial process and the possibility of indigenous resistance – resonate strongly within an analysis of colonial settler societies and in British Columbia in particular. In general, however, historical studies of law and colonialism in North America have paid little attention to the extensive work on law and colonial processes in Africa and Asia, principal sites of postcolonial study.[53] Similarly, those interested in law and colonialism in Africa and Asia have ignored late-nineteenth and early-twentieth-century North America. Why have there been few connections?

Part of the answer lies in the important differences between settler and administrative colonies. The presence of a settler society that would soon outnumber the indigenous population distinguishes British colonies such as Canada, Australia, and New Zealand from most of Africa and Asia. These settler societies assumed that the laws of the home country applied to them and, by extension, to the indigenous people who assimilated and then to all the original inhabitants. Their presence and insistence on the common law tradition inserted English law more deeply into relations between colonizer and colonized than in administrative colonies, where dual legal systems were more common.

Another part of the answer, however, lies in a blindness to the persistence of North America's colonial past. Law and colonialism scholars use 'colonialism' most frequently, sometimes implicitly, to describe nineteenth- and early-twentieth-century European forays into Africa and Asia. Thus, it was possible for Merry to remark that the study of legal pluralism, once confined to an analysis of intersecting indigenous and European legal forms in colonial and postcolonial societies, was now being applied to '*noncolonized societies*, particularly to the advanced industrial countries of Europe and the United States.'[54] By this she meant that the concept of legal pluralism had resonance beyond colonial settings, and was being used to describe relations between dominant and subordinate groups, as well as various forms of unofficial ordering in developed countries.[55] The use of 'noncolonized' to describe the United States is unfortunate, but also suggests why little attention has been paid to North America.[56] Merry's recent book, *Colonizing Hawai'i: The Cultural Power of Law*, exposes a hitherto shrouded example of American overseas expansion. She works deeply into a colonial and postcolonial literature, and the study is infused with comparisons to European, particularly British and French, penetration into Africa and Asia. The comparisons are important and telling, but so are the colonial encounters in continental North America, particularly in its west and north. Apart from a handful of sentences in the introduction, one of which suggests that the colonial strategies developed in North America were applied to Hawai'i, Merry ignores continental colonial processes.[57] While one window is opened on the role of law in a colonial past, another remains closed.

British Columbia's formal designation as an independent colony ended when it joined the Canadian confederation, itself a larger colony, in 1871, just as the race for Africa among European nation states was under way. The formal change in status from colony to province, however, did not alter the fact that the colonial processes designed to bring the territory and the indigenous peoples under settler control were only just beginning. Just as it moved south from Europe into Africa and Asia, or across the Pacific from the United States, industrial capitalism penetrated the spaces of British Columbia, integrating them into empire and a global economy. Although direct political ties to Britain diminished after Confederation, many settlers still thought of themselves as British and certain institutions maintained imperial connections. This was particularly true in law, where the Judicial Committee of the Privy Council in London remained a court of last resort in Canada until 1949.

Other law and colonialism scholars have gone further, dismissing North America's colonial past as irrelevant and assuming that the interesting legal innovations, such as the systems of 'customary law,' occurred elsewhere, predominantly in Africa or Asia. Cohn's important point – that the creation of a state capable of recording and controlling vast quantities of information (including languages, legal systems, and histories), and with it controlling other peoples, emerged from the British experience in India – does not lead to his conclusion that the processes of domination and assimilation occurred quickly and completely in the Americas. 'The indigenous populations encountered in North America,' he argues, 'were quickly subjugated, relocated, or decimated, and even though there continued to be, from the colonial perspective, a "native problem," it was a military and political one, requiring little in the way of legal or administrative innovation.'[58]

To describe Native people as 'quickly subjugated' in the territory that became Canada, given the extensive history of a Native/European fur trade, is inaccurate. As many have pointed out, Native people were trading partners, allies, enemies, employees, wives, sexual partners, and much else. In varying contexts, relations between Europeans and Natives were military and political, but also legal and even personal.[59] Perhaps in comparison to the prodigious task of ruling hundreds of millions of people in India, the North American experience may seem relatively inconsequential. Certainly, it was less an issue with the Colonial Office in London, which, by the mid-nineteenth century, was more concerned with how best to devolve responsible government to its white settler colonies in North America than with governing Native peoples. However, the assumption that the only interesting legal innovation took place elsewhere is wrong. The interaction between Natives and Europeans created a panoply of compromise, accommodation, and innovation. Richard White has argued that a social, political, and legal 'middle ground' emerged in the seventeenth century between French and Native cultures in the *pays d'en haut* (the Great Lakes basin). Given a rough balance of power and the need to explain one's actions in terms that could fit within the cultural imperatives of the other, argues White, a cultural 'middle ground' developed that was neither French nor Native, but hybrid. After the British consolidated control of North America and the French retreated in 1761, the middle ground diminished with the British need for Native allies. It had all but vanished in the early nineteenth century as American settler society spread across the Appalachians and west to the Mississippi.[60]

The lack of law-and-colonialism analysis in North America, or the denial of its relevance to late-nineteenth-century studies of imperial domination, may reflect an eastern North American perspective. Although pockets of resistance remained, European- and American-based legal institutions were secure in the east by the early nineteenth century. The balance of power had shifted to the point where the earlier cultural and legal hybrids existed only on the margins. This shift occurred much later in the west and in the north. Hamar Foster has argued that disputes between traders and Natives were settled 'more in keeping with Indian than with English methods' well into the nineteenth century.[61] Similarly, John Phillip Reid, in a series of articles on legal relations in the Oregon Territory (an area that until 1846 included most of what is now British Columbia) argues that European and American traders drew heavily upon Native principles of dispute resolution to help structure and order inter-cultural relations.[62]

Cole Harris disputes these claims, arguing not against considerable Native agency, but warning of an overemphasis on *law* and suggesting that European efforts to manage violence in the fur trade are better understood (and were understood by the traders) as 'sporadic, local, and highly visible power.'[63] 'The fur trade,' he argues, 'was built on terror and violence that, as much as possible, was implacable and witnessed.'[64] The spectacle of violence during the western fur trade, therefore, was not accompanied by the legitimizing discourses of rights and law that surrounded the violent imposition of state law in Britain or the later imposition of state law in a settler society. Despite their argument about the prevalence of Native law in the western fur trade, both Foster and Reid hesitate to assert that European traders understood Native law or attempted to legitimize their actions in its terms, and they can only speculate about how Natives understood the violence directed towards them.

The fur trade in British Columbia did not produce an enduring cultural and legal middle ground, such as the one created by Algonquin and French in the *pays d'en haut* of the seventeenth century. There is, however, work which suggests that Native legal forms were not ignored by some elements of the settler society that followed the fur trade into British Columbia. Jo-Anne Fiske argues that Native laws were much in evidence in Native/settler relations in northern British Columbia until late in the nineteenth century.[65] The missionaries, whose influence in Native society far exceeded that of local magistrates, used their knowledge of 'Indian law' to resolve or diffuse disputes between Natives and settlers. It was not until the 1880s, argues Fiske, that Indian law was transformed by the state into 'privileges' granted under Canadian law, and she traces the discursive transformation into the twentieth century, where 'Indian law' became 'oral tradition' to be considered by courts as evidence but not as law.

Notwithstanding the marginalization of indigenous legal tradition as the nineteenth century drew to a close, legal innovation between indigenous and settler societies is not simply a historical relic, but a continuing process. Although a process fraught with the difficulties of an impoverished Anglo-Canadian legal imagination[66] (which struggles to recognize the legitimacy of the other legal tradition) and a huge imbalance of power, legal innovation continues. Aboriginal rights as they have developed in the Canadian context, argues Jeremy Webber, are the product of the meeting of two legal systems – indigenous and European.[67] To search for their origins exclusively within either indigenous or European law is to miss the formative interaction between the two. This interaction has produced and continues to modify a particular legal innovation – constitutionally entrenched Aboriginal rights – that bears heavily on contemporary relations.[68]

In the preceding chapters, then, I have described the role of law in one part of the colonial project – the capture of Native fisheries in late-nineteenth and early-twentieth-century British Columbia. How can one understand the colonial processes at work in British Columbia's fisheries in light of analyses of experiences elsewhere?

Anglo-Canadian Law and the British Columbia Fishery

In the 1870s, industrial capital penetrated British Columbian spaces. In combination with labour and fish, it created an oar and sail–powered gill-net fishery, located in the tidal waters near the mouth of the province's major rivers, that supplied nearby canneries with salmon for export to markets around the world. Access to the fisheries was presumed. The common law doctrine of the public right to fish created an open-access fishery, effectively guaranteeing non-Native access to the resource; Natives became employees, subject to the law of master and servant, in a fishery that they had once owned. To secure their capital investments, the cannery owners sought a guaranteed supply of fish and a flexible labour force. Unable to achieve these on their own, however, they enlisted the state and it, through increasingly comprehensive fishing regulations, reproduced a particular set of relations that secured the pre-eminence of the canneries in the fishing industry. Fish became an industrial resource; Native people became an industrial labour force.

Centralized bureaucratic management designed to secure the capital investment of cannery operators replaced the locally generated and understood rules that had regulated and allocated the fishery. It was with law that the state created an *Indian food fishery* to open the resource to non-Native interests. The food fishery allowed Natives to catch fish for food with various methods, and at certain times and places that were prohibited to non-Natives. It created a traditional economy, separating a Native fishery from the industrial or sport fishery. It was, however, a traditional fishery that had no precedent in Native society.[69] Native people certainly fished for food, but their fisheries were never so categorized or limited. The Indian food fishery in British Columbia was a product of late-nineteenth-century state regulation. It was the device with which the state constructed a 'traditional economy,' marginalizing native control and, at the same time, integrating Native peoples into the global economy as subsidized labour. When they worked, fishers and cannery workers were relatively well paid, but the work was seasonal and it fluctuated year-to-year with the salmon runs. As the cost of fishing technology grew and canneries consolidated in the early twentieth century, and as settlers arrived in British Columbia to work in the fisheries, the importance of Native labour diminished. Canneries hired Japanese to fish and Chinese to work in the canneries, and the state granted independent licences to whites to encourage their settlement.[70] Even though their participation in the fishing industry remained higher than in any other industry in the province, Native fishers were systematically restricted. If the need for law to create a flexible labour force for the canneries diminished as the non-Native population grew, the constructed Indian food fishery continued to limit Native control of the resource. Non-Natives may no longer have wanted Native labour, but they still wanted the fish.

The links between the canning industry and the Dominion Department of Marine and Fisheries were many and obvious, including the de facto appointment of local fisheries officers in some parts of the province. The officers on the Skeena River, including Babine Lake, were cannery-appointed, and the attack on the Babine weirs was a transparent example of state appropriation of a resource for industrial capital. The state, through regulation, reallocated fish from the Babine to the canneries. Nonetheless, senior officials in Ottawa were more removed from the canning industry than were local officials, and rejected accusations that they were cannery puppets. The Department of Fisheries was an independent institution with its own agenda that, while broadly supportive of the canning industry, was not entirely subservient to it. Senior officers professed an independent interest in maintaining the long-term health of fish stocks, and were not above questioning the work of local officials when they appeared to be acting too aggressively on behalf of the canneries or the sport fishery. But the record is mixed. If on the Babine the Minister of Fisheries tried at times to restrain overzealous officers, on the Cowichan the Commissioner of Fisheries, E.E. Prince, attempted to impose his vision of the correct balance between Native, cannery, and sport fisheries, often at odds with local sentiment. The general outline of fisheries law may have suited the cannery owners, but they often disagreed about the detail. Initially, at least, they were a fractious group, in competition for fish and employees, wanting to protect their drifts and labour force from each other, as the 1877 court cases reveal. They did agree, however, that competing users of the fish must be limited and that efforts should be taken to enhance fish stocks. In this they had the support of Fisheries.

The conflict over fish on the Cowichan River reveals that the colonizing pressures emanated not just from the cannery owners, but from the fly-fishing community as well. Fly fishing was less obviously a commercial enterprise. With hunting, it was the quintessential leisure activity of the English landed gentry. It was bound to an ethos of sport and fair play, catalogued by Izaak Walton in *The Compleat Angler*,[71] and it defined a particular connection with 'nature' that was both individual and masculine.[72] In late-nineteenth-century North America, the angler's nature included Indians, although not as fishers but as guides who paddled the self-styled explorer to prime fishing sites.[73] Fishing clubs, if they could raise the funds, might also purchase land around small lakes to secure exclusive rights of fishing, thereby preventing Native access to long-established fisheries.[74] Notwithstanding the sport's regal pedigree, local tourist boards and industrial giants such as the CPR did not let Fisheries forget that fly fishing could also be a business proposition and that it needed protection from both the commercial fleets and Native fishing. Where privatizing a lake or river was not possible within the parameters of Anglo-Canadian law, as with the Cowichan, these commercial interests urged the state to regulate the non-angling fishery with licensing requirements, technology restrictions, and close times. On the Cowichan River the state targeted the Cowichan weirs, eventually removing them from the river, although not without an extended struggle.

The Cowichan weirs came down, just as the Babine weirs had done thirty years earlier. Perhaps most importantly, fisheries officials, cannery owners, and fly fishers, despite their differences, shared a set of cultural assumptions about progress, civilization, and the law. These shared discourses reproduced a set of relationships that excluded Native people from control of their fisheries. The province's large rivers were dominated by the canning industry; some of the smaller rivers and lakes were controlled by fly fishers. Native people participated as workers, but their ownership of the resource was denied and their laws regulating its use were ignored. Even in instances of protracted Native struggle, where Natives repeatedly asserted in their terms a right to fish, Dominion officials attributed the resistance to white agitators, particularly missionaries, whom they accused of fermenting trouble among Native peoples with rights talk. Whites were seen as the agents of unrest; Native agency was discounted. The fisheries had been regulated by Native peoples, but not in a manner recognizable to the Canadian state. The perceived absence of law justified, for Dominion officials, the imposition of state law.

At a general level, this much is clear: the state used law to remove the West Coast salmon fisheries from Native control. Anglo-Canadian legal forms reproduced particular relationships between people and their use of resources that redirected control of salmon fisheries away from Native people. With law, the Canadian state captured a resource. Of course law was by no means the only form of power. On the one hand, it was buttressed through most of the nineteenth century by gunboats, and on the other, particular laws were justified by appeals to other constellations of knowledge. In this regard, science and a scientific discourse grew increasingly important in the late nineteenth century. The newly emerging field of fisheries science, with university-trained practitioners such as the Dominion Commissioner of Fisheries, Professor E.E. Prince, assumed an important supporting role by providing a seemingly neutral or objective basis on which to judge different fisheries. Prince, for example, would denounce the weir fisheries as illegal and primitive, that is, scientifically unsound, the one accusation confirming the other. It was not science, however, that confronted Native peoples, but laws made in the name of science, progress, capital, and/or sport. Fisheries officers used these and other discourses to justify their actions, but in dismantling fish weirs they were enforcing the law, and it was the law that provided the principal justification for their actions.

When one probes the details of application and enforcement of the law, however, its role is much more ambiguous and uncertain. Law is a site of conflict, flexible in one instance, rigid the next, and sometimes operating in the particular to support rather than diminish Native resistance. Replacing one system of resource allocation and social control with another is not so neat and tidy as it appears from a distance.

The early application of Anglo-Canadian fisheries law under A.C. Anderson was so flexible that one is hard pressed to describe the fishery as subject to the rule of law. The *Fisheries Act* appears to offer occasional guidance, but little more. Myriad forms of power were at work, transforming people into wage labour and fish into an industrial resource. Law was but one form, and in Anderson's day it was seldom used in direct attacks on Native fisheries that for the most part continued to operate unhindered, although certainly not unchanged as Natives responded to new markets and commercial opportunities. In these early years, the state's legal forms sat in the background, structuring relationships without much direct intervention. When called upon, however, law explicitly constructed a particular relationship. The master and servant cases on the Fraser River in 1877 provide one illustration. Native people were constructed by the local police courts as cannery employees, and jailed for continuing to act as traders. The law acted sharply and quickly to delimit a new relationship between capital and labour. Having established the terms of this new relationship, law receded again into the background, less to operate as a hammer than to limit what was thought possible.

Through the 1880s and 1890s, fisheries officers grew increasingly interventionist, enforcing restrictions on Native fisheries around the province that had previously been ignored. On the Cowichan River, the law closed around those Cowichan unable or unwilling to join the wage economy, restricting their access to fish, animals, and land. But just as some Cowichan were able to modify their traditional fishing, gathering, and semi-agricultural seasonal cycles to accommodate the wage economy of the late nineteenth century, so they were able to use the imposed legal system to defend their interests. Despite repeated attempts, Fisheries was unable to secure a conviction against the Cowichan for weir fishing. The person of Edward Musgrave, an ardent and outspoken critic of the weirs and of Fisheries' failure to enforce the law, provides a wonderful illustration of the paradoxical effect of Dominion law on the Cowichan fishery. As a justice of the peace hearing a charge against a Cowichan man for building a weir, Musgrave and his fellow JP dismissed the charge because they had improperly granted a second adjournment to allow the accused time to secure legal counsel. Law had a space of its own – constraining both the power of the state from which it emanated and that of the local justice of the peace – that could be used to protect individual rights. Natives and their supporters used that space defensively to protect themselves and, by extension, their fisheries. The local courts confirmed the procedural rights of individuals, but in the Cowichan Valley they also confirmed the fish weir as a valid fishing technology. The Cowichan successfully defended each attack by the state in its own forum. Each failure by the state weakened its claim that the weirs were a conservation hazard; each Cowichan victory gave legitimacy to their claims of unextinguished right and effective traditional management. The state's legal institutions confined Cowichan resource use, denying any collective management or ownership of their fisheries, but the local legal forum provided space for Cowichan resistance.

It is important, therefore, not to reduce the various forms of Anglo-Canadian law that surrounded the West Coast salmon fishery in the late nineteenth-century to instruments of cannery owners or fly-fishing clubs. As Loo has suggested, law and a belief in the rule of law were central to the colonial identity of nineteenth-century British Columbians. Law and order were, in the eyes of the settler society, what distinguished it from both savage Indian life and the unconstrained and therefore dangerous freedom of American society. British settlers sought to reproduce a British order, so far as they could, through law. That legal order dispossessed Native people of land and resources, but it did so in a manner that was, at times, constrained by legal forms. When it proved a hindrance, law could be and was cast aside to reveal the opportunistic use of power in a radically unequal relationship. In a society, however, whose self-identity turned in large measure on the rule of law, law could only be cast so far. That these limits were tested in late-nineteenth-century British Columbia, particularly in settler society's relationship with Native peoples, cannot be in doubt. But neither can one ignore the fact that Anglo-Canadian legal forms did, from time to time, have a space of their own that allowed for Native resistance in the most unlikely of circumstances.

Native Law

However much Native peoples used Anglo-Canadian legal tools, their resistance was rooted in a sense of ownership derived from their culture and their laws. Native law governed the use of local fisheries, performing the same functions as Canadian fisheries law – defining and determining access to and ownership of particular fisheries. The Canadian state used licences and leases to allocate the fishery; Native societies determined ownership through a collection of familial and clan ties recognized in the feasts. But whereas state law was centralized and generalized, Native law was local and intensely specific. The state created regulations that applied across the province, largely oblivious to local difference and only tenuously connected to the actual fisheries. Native people, by contrast, could point to a name, the holder of which had the right to fish from a particular rock, cast a net in a certain portion of a river, or direct the building of a weir just above the rapids. These radically different management systems co-existed in British Columbia as the conflict over fisheries attests, but once the wealth of the fishery became apparent to non-Natives, the state replaced the local with the central, the specific with the general, and reallocated the fisheries in the process.[75]

It is undeniably difficult to recapture Native legal forms, both as they operated before the state inserted its law into the fisheries, and as they responded to the intrusion. Sufficient records do not exist, at least in a form accessible to a non-Native legal historian with no anthropological or ethnographic training. The efforts of the salvage ethnographers of the late nineteenth and early twentieth centuries provide some detail of traditional Native fisheries, but good as they were, their work grants a timeless quality to Native cultures that betrays the dynamic, innovative, and responsive societies which struggled to assert themselves in rapidly changing circumstances over which they had little control. These ethnographers were interested in capturing something before it was lost; the study of the transforming cultures around them would be left for later anthropologists. Those studies, particularly as they relate to the ownership and allocation of resources, remain rare, in part because sources are scarce, but also because the state was so effective in imposing its legal order and suppressing the forms that preceded it.

While it may be difficult to describe fully the aboriginal systems of resource management, it is less difficult to banish a common misconception by describing what they are not. Native fisheries were not without law. When the Dominion Minister of Public Works described to the Canadian parliament an unfettered, open-access fishery on the Pacific coast in 1871, he was describing the state of Anglo-Canadian fisheries law, not the state of the fishery and certainly not the nature of Native fisheries law. Native regulation ranged from an injunction on polling a canoe through spawning grounds to the length of time a weir could remain, to ownership of important sites, to the preparation of the first fish caught every year. The regulations were so numerous that in one story told by the people who lived around the lower Columbia River, Coyote, the trickster and transformer, despaired ever being able to catch enough salmon. Certain sites were owned by individuals; others were generally open to members of a specific community, usually connected through kinship ties. That access to certain fisheries was less strictly controlled or held by extended communities rather than specific individuals should not, however, lead to a general assumption that these were unregulated, open-access fisheries. In his study of Aboriginal property rights, Peter Usher concludes that the often-used metaphor of the unregulated commons to describe Native fisheries misrepresents not only the commons, but also the locally regulated fisheries:

> The commons without law, restraint, or responsibility is thus a metaphor not for aboriginal tenure systems, but rather for laissez-faire industrial capitalism and the imperial frontier: precisely the historical contexts of the depletion of the whale fishery, the sturgeon fishery, the salmon fishery, the buffalo, and the passenger pigeon. Consider, for example, the salmon fishery – the classic case for biologists and economists alike of the evils of

common property. In fact, the open access that has prevailed for so many decades resulted from the expropriation of historic, local tenure systems, and their deliberate substitution by an economic free-for-all in which the spoils went to those whose capital was best able to transform fish into money.[76]

Put slightly differently by another group of scholars, the degradation of resources under an open-access regime occurs 'often as a consequence of the destruction of existing communal land-tenure and marine-tenure systems,' and can frequently be traced to colonial rule.[77]

Any system of regulation, including Native systems, must respond to new technology. Regulations that had effectively governed the community-based fish weir, for example, would have to adjust when commercial gill nets made individual fisheries an efficient alternative. The adjustment would advantage some and disadvantage others; transitions were often painful, but that does not mean that they were not possible. Anthropologist Michael Kew has posited a pre-contact evolution of fishing technology that changed methods of production and, as a result, the allocation of fish and the web of regulation that surrounded Native fisheries.[78] Although Native societies had achieved a certain balance with their environment to support a significant population for centuries, they were by no means static. They had created institutions that enabled them to deal with great abundance and periodic scarcity. Wayne Suttles, in a widely accepted argument, has suggested that among the Coast Salish the potlatch was at the centre of a prestige economy that, by promoting continuous exchange, increased the variety and quality of food available to any local group, providing some insurance against periodic and inevitable local shortages.[79]

There is a growing body of scholarship on traditional ecological knowledge (TEK) that seeks to document and explain the extensive collection of practices and beliefs that constitute the relationship of a local community, particularly an indigenous community, to its environment. Scholars in this field usually contrast what they document to the work of scientists who study an environment, or a particular feature of it, independently of the long-established human communities for whom that environment provides a livelihood.[80] One of its prominent practitioners, Fikret Berkes describes TEK, usually associated with 'non-industrial or less technologically advanced societies,' as 'a cumulative body of knowledge and beliefs, handed down through generations of cultural transmission, about the relationship of living beings (including humans) with one another and with their environment.'[81] Berkes's studies of the James Bay Cree fisheries in Canada's subarctic provide an example of this emerging field. He began in the 1970s with a null hypothesis that the Cree fish 'in a haphazard manner, catching what they can,' and therefore that the sustainable fishery was a function of a small population and not of resource management. The evidence he gathered, however, indicated that the Cree carefully managed their fisheries and that 'social practices regulating the fishing intensity, locations, and the minimum mesh size provided a control against overfishing of stocks.'[82] He has since located this work in a body of scholarship that considers the management of common-property resources (i.e., resources where access is difficult to control and use by one reduces what is available to others) and the nature of communal property. This literature emphasizes that local communities, working within communal property regimes, can manage common-property resources such as fish sustainably. Communal property does not necessarily create a 'tragedy of the commons.'[83]

The work of Berkes and others reveals TEK as a foundation upon which rights of access to and use of fisheries were built in many indigenous communities. A recent study of the 'Ehattesaht Traditional Fisheries Systems' on the west coast of Vancouver Island provides another glimpse into the comprehensive and intensely local nature of these rights that were based around kinship ties. The authors provide the following example:

A head chief of 27 chiefs did not own any rivers. Therefore, he proposed marriage into a high ranking family that owned a river well known for its runs of chum and tyee (Chinook) salmon. The owner of the river consented to the marriage. Once married into the family, the head chief acquired the rights to fish the river except for three very specific places:

– the mouth of the river, where the fresh and salt water meet;
– a large deep pool three miles up the river, for gaffing of salmon; and
– a small tyee creek with a lake behind it, where the watersheds meet.

The head chiefs were also not permitted to harvest berries along the banks of the river. This demonstrates that the head chief did not gain ownership by marriage; only access to fish.[84]

This level of management and control is a long way from Berkes's null hypothesis and from the assumptions of many government officials in the late nineteenth-century of an unregulated fishery.

Without equating the forms of Native law to E.P. Thompson's 'moral economy,' a term he uses to describe the 'legitimising notion' that underscored the food riots in eighteenth-century England, there are some striking parallels. Thompson argued that the food riot was more than simply the instinctive reaction of a hungry English peasantry. Instead, 'the men and women in the crowd were informed by the belief that they were defending traditional rights or customs; and in general, that they were supported by the wider consensus of the community.'[85] Thompson was reacting against what he saw as an 'abbreviated view of economic man,'[86] one that ignored the complexity of crowd behaviour by reducing the agency of the English poor to the reactions of hungry people. What was remarkable about the riots, argued Thompson, was the restraint and order of the crowd as it set about rectifying an unjust price for bread. Riotous perhaps, the eighteenth-century English crowd was disciplined by strong notions of right.

It is tempting to use Thompson's 'moral economy' when considering Native resistance to the Canadian state's fisheries laws. Just as the English peasantry did, Native people believed they were defending traditional rights, and there are powerful legitimizing notions running through their actions. The Babine, for example, displayed ritual, pageantry, and controlled violence led by women in defence of their weirs. What is remarkable is not their resistance, but their discipline in responding, as a community with its own norms, laws, and forms of governance, to the challenges posed by the Canadian state. This discipline emerges when the two Babine who accepted nets from the government in 1906 were required to return them. Those with the authority to negotiate, De wisim dsik (Tszak William) and Gwista' (Chief Big George), travelled to Ottawa, where they apparently conceded the fish weirs if the Dominion met certain conditions regarding the provision of nets, land, farm implements, and schools.

Assertions of right are everywhere in the historical record and are confirmed again and again by the actions of Native peoples. However, Thompson urges caution when transporting the idea of a moral economy beyond 'the given field-of-force of Eighteenth century English relations.'[87] For the reasons discussed earlier in this chapter in the context of law as ideology, a cautious approach is warranted.

Thompson's analysis is compelling, nonetheless, in part because it folds considerable attention to local cultures into a broader analysis of radically unequal relations of power. He argues that the food rioters succeeded in causing authorities to regulate the market and lower the price of bread, if only temporarily, when the broader community endorsed their action. If that community believed the actions of the rioters to be 'just,' that is, to be based on earlier customs, traditions, or laws that the authorities should respect, then the rioters might succeed. Without that support, they were isolated, unlikely to succeed, and in danger of being hanged. Appeals to the local and traditional were successful in radically unequal power relations when the appeals gained broad support. Understood this way, Thompson's work helps to explain the longevity of the Cowichan weirs and the rapid removal of the Babine weirs. The Cowichan managed to keep their weirs for as long as they did, in part, because they were able to forge a consensus in the local settler community that they were entitled to the weirs. This was an important difference between their situation and that of the Babine, whose visible support within settler society came only from two Oblate missionaries. Apart from a transient mining population and the HBC post manager, virtually no whites lived along Babine River or Lake. A few settlers were arriving in the neighbouring Bulkley valley, but the canneries on the coast were the dominant presence. The Babine faced the canneries themselves, without a local white community that might have tempered cannery dominance. The Cowichan, by contrast, felt themselves increasingly constrained by white settlers, their fences, and their laws. Nonetheless, the local settler community was much more diverse than the vocal sport-fishing interests would indicate, and its support of Cowichan resistance, or lack of support for state intervention, helped to sustain the weir fishery in the context of radically unequal power. The Cowichan were able to harness that support, thereby sustaining their weir fishery. Instead of state law tempering settler brutality (one of the general points arising from studies of law and colonialism in both settler and administrative colonies), in this case the local settler community, although the great beneficiaries of state law, mitigated the brutality of that law.[88]

With or without local support, however, Native resistance to Dominion regulation was born of Native systems of resource allocation that were produced and reproduced in Native legal cultures. Although the success of Native resistance depended, at least in part, on support from within settler society, ideas of right and entitlement did not, as Dominion and provincial officials often claimed, originate from their white supporters. They were, instead, a product of Native laws.

Conclusion

'There is no single Act in the whole of Canada that raises more problems between authorities and Indian people than the *Fisheries Act*.'[89] These comments of Judge Cunliffe Barnett in the British Columbia Provincial Court at Williams Lake in 1979 suggest the extent of the conflict that continues between Natives and the Canadian state over access to and control of fisheries. The law that surrounds fish, constructing particular fisheries, remains a principal site of conflict. The confrontation over the lobster fishery off the East Coast following the Supreme Court of Canada's *Marshall* decisions reveals this all too clearly.[90]

It is impossible to escape Canadian law when one considers relations between First Nations and Canadian society in early-twenty-first-century British Columbia. From the provisions in the *Indian Act* to the Canadian constitution, and the decisions of the Supreme Court of Canada (SCC), law surrounds the contemporary relationship. If one wants to justify a historical study in terms of its contemporary relevance, then it is not difficult regarding a history of the state's regulation of Native fisheries. The 'Indian food fishery,' a category constructed in the nineteenth century to limit Native fishing, continues to linger in Canadian law. In fact, recent SCC decisions formalized the division.

In *Sparrow*, Fisheries charged a Musqueam chief with using a net that violated the *Fisheries Act*.[91] The SCC, notwithstanding its strong affirmation of Aboriginal rights in the case, constructed the case around food fishing, and pronounced that the Aboriginal food fishery had priority over any other fishery. The commercial fishery was left for another day, to be categorized differently.[92] That day came with the decisions of the Supreme Court in the *Van der Peet* trilogy.[93] In considering the charges under the *Fisheries Act* against a Stó:lō women, Dorothy Van der Peet, who had sold a few salmon, the court recognized the possibility of an Aboriginal right to a commercial fishery, but did not find that such a right existed in that case. In *Gladstone*, one of the triology, the SCC concluded that the Heiltsuk of the central coast had an Aboriginal right to a commercial herring fishery, but it then expanded the grounds on which the Crown could infringe that right.[94] Thus, although the SCC has recognized the priority of an Aboriginal food fishery, and the possibility of priority for an Aboriginal commercial fishery, the distinction between a food and a commercial fishery is entrenched for the foreseeable future in Canadian courts.

Beyond the courts, the distinction is beginning to blur. Following *Sparrow*, Fisheries implemented an Aboriginal Fisheries Strategy that recognized the right of several First Nations, including the Stó:lō, to harvest limited quantities of fish for food or for sale. These allocations are vigorously contested, both by the Stó:lō, who find them insufficient, and by non-Native commercial fisheries, who believe them too generous. It is access to fish that is being contested, but that contest is framed by categories defined in law.

Other legal categories created or imported into nineteenth-century British Columbia transformed fish to fit into tins or to be caught on the end of a dry fly, and Native people into pieceworkers or guides. Some remain with us today. The law of master and servant and the spectre of imprisonment for breach of employment contract have disappeared, but the common law doctrine of the public right to fish remains as a means to limit Aboriginal rights in Supreme Court jurisprudence.[95] The public right to fish is also central to the legal challenges of various non-Native commercial fishing organizations to the Aboriginal commercial fisheries.[96]

A principal difference between the conflict over weirs on the Cowichan and Babine rivers one hundred years ago (or even the decision of Barnett J. in 1979) and the current disputes over fish, is the constitutional entrenchment of Aboriginal and treaty rights. The content and meaning of those rights are hotly contested, but their existence can no longer be denied. The local struggles continue; Natives still appear in local courts to face charges for *Fisheries Act* offences, but they do so in the light of constitutional protection for recognized rights. The events in the Cowichan Valley in the late nineteenth century, however, suggest the possibilities of resistance but also the limits of state law, even constitutional law, when imposed upon a group of people that will not accept its terms. Whether from fear of Cowichan unrest or a belief in the justness of Cowichan claims among the settler society, the state did not have much success imposing its fisheries law in the local courts. Similarly, the Supreme Court of Canada, which appears to have led public opinion or at least provincial governments and local courts (including provincial appellate courts) in recognizing Aboriginal rights, may not be prepared to lead much further. And even if it is prepared to lead, local resistance could well reduce the impact of its decisions.

It is increasingly impossible, nonetheless, to ignore Native law as we move, with halting steps, towards some manifestation of contemporary legal pluralism. Native declarations of right, of ownership, and of jurisdiction are not new claims, as is often assumed. They precede the attempt by the Canadian state to wrest control of the fisheries from Native people, and come to light in the historical record when the state challenged for control. That Native people are reasserting these claims today should not surprise anyone familiar with the history of the struggle over fish. The Canadian state's legal capture of British Columbia's fisheries came at the expense of Native legal forms that, while subdued and altered, never disappeared. The knots that have tied the nets of colonialism are slowly, perhaps surely, coming undone.

Notes

Introduction

1 Ronald Dworkin, *Law's Empire* (Cambridge, Mass.: Harvard University Press, 1986), 13.

2 Included within one mid-nineteenth-century English definition of *fishery* is the notion of right: 'A Fishery is properly defined as the right of catching fish in the sea, or in a particular stream of water; and it is also frequently used to denote the locality where such a right is exercised.' Patterson on the Fishery Laws (1863), cited in *Reference as to the Constitutional Validity of Certain Sections of the Fisheries Act, 1914* [1928], S.C.R. 457, at 472.

3 The unfortunate and ahistorical myth of the commons, following Garrett Hardin's influential essay 'The Tragedy of the Commons,' *Science* 162 (1969): 1243–8, is that they are unregulated. In the fisheries context, see Arthur F. McEvoy's 'Toward an Interactive Theory of Nature and Culture: Ecology, Production, and Cognition in the California Fishing Industry,' *Environmental Review* 11 (1987): 289–305; and *The Fisherman's Problem: Ecology and Law in the California Fisheries, 1850–1980* (Cambridge: Cambridge University Press, 1986). More generally see David Feeny et al., 'The Tragedy of the Commons: Twenty-Two Years Later,' *Human Ecology* 18 (1990): 1–19; and Bonnie J. McCay and James M. Acheson, eds., *The Question of the Commons: The Culture and Ecology of Communal Resources* (Tuscon: University of Arizona Press, 1987). J.M. Neeson, *Commoners: Common Right, Enclosure and Social Change in Common-field England, 1700–1820* (New York: Cambridge University Press, 1993), examines the web of regulation that enveloped the English commons.

4 Crisca Bierwert, *Brushed by Cedar, Living by the River: Coast Salish Figures of Power* (Tucson: University of Arizona Press, 1999), 248–64, provides a

revealing discussion of the modern commercial Stó:lō fishery on the Fraser River and its regulation.

5 E.P. Thompson, *Customs in Common: Studies in Traditional Popular Culture* (New York: New Press, 1993), 6, describes custom as the 'rhetoric of legitimation' in eighteenth-century England. Tina Loo, 'Dan Cramner's Potlatch: Law as Coercion, Symbol, and Rhetoric in British Columbia, 1884–1951,' *Canadian Historical Review* 78 (1992): 125–65, develops the idea of law 'as a system of rhetoric or a way of arguing' in British Columbia in the context of the potlatch prohibition.

6 There is a vast international literature on these subjects, much of it building upon the highly influential work of Michel Foucault, including *Discipline and Punish: The Birth of the Prison*, trans. Alan Sheridan, 1977 (New York: Vintage Books, 1995) and *Power/Knowledge: Selected Interviews and Other Writings, 1972–1977*, ed. Colin Gordon (New York: Pantheon, 1980). In the colonial context, Edward Said, *Orientalism* (New York: Vintage, 1978) is a foundational text. Daniel W. Clayton, *Islands of Truth: The Imperial Fashioning of Vancouver Island* (Vancouver: UBC Press, 2000) writes Vancouver Island into and out of this literature.

7 There is an emerging literature on Traditional Knowledge and Traditional Ecological Knowledge that seeks to represent the accumulated knowledge of indigenous peoples of their local environments. See, for example, Julian T. Inglis, ed., *Traditional Ecological Knowledge: Concepts and Cases* (Ottawa: International Program on Traditional Ecological Knowledge, 1993); Fikret Berkes, *Sacred Ecology: Traditional Ecological Knowledge and Resource Management* (Philadelphia: Taylor & Francis, 1999); and the discussion in chapter 4.

8 There is a vast literature on the potlatch, including Homer G. Barnett, 'The Nature of the Potlatch,' *American Anthropologist* 40 (1938): 349–58; Helen Codere, *Fighting with Property: A Study of Kwakiutl Potlatching and Warfare, 1792–1930* (Seattle: University of Washington Press, 1950, 1966); Philip Drucker and Robert F. Heizer, *To Make My Name Good: A Reexamination of the Southern Kwakiutl Potlatch* (Berkeley: University of California Press, 1967); and Wayne Suttles, *Coast Salish Essays* (Vancouver: Talonbooks, 1987).

9 Philip Drucker, *Cultures of the North Pacific Coast* (San Francisco: Chandler Publishing, 1965), 56.

10 Drucker and Heizer, *To Make My Name Good*, 133.

11 See Douglas Cole and Ira Chaikin, *An Iron Hand upon the People: The Law against the Potlatch on the Northwest Coast* (Vancouver: Douglas & McIntyre, 1990).

12 The recent study by Jo-Anne Fiske and Betty Patrick, 'C'is dideen khat' *When the Plumes Rise: The Way of the Lake Babine Nation* (Vancouver: UBC Press, 2000), is perhaps as close to such a study as exists. I refer to it extensively in chapter 3.

13 For surveys of the important historical sources and of ethnographic research on the Northwest Coast see Wayne Suttles, 'History of Research,' and Wayne Suttles and Aldona Jonattis, 'History of Research in Ethnology,' in Suttles, ed., *Handbook of North American Indians*, Vol. 7, *Northwest Coast* (Washington: Smithsonian Institution, 1990), 70–2, 73–88.

14 June Starr and Jane F. Collier, 'Introduction: Dialogues in Legal Anthropology,' in Starr and Collier, eds., *History and Power in the Study of Law: New Directions in Legal Anthropology* (Ithaca: Cornell University Press, 1989), 6. See also Laura Nader, ed., *Law in Culture and Society* (Berkeley: University of California Press, 1969).

15 Pierre Clastres, *Society against the State: The Leader as Servant and the Humane Uses of Power among the Indians of the Americas* (New York: Urizen Books, 1974).

16 This does not necessarily mean they were well managed. In her discussion of the eighteenth-century English common, Neeson recognizes that not all commons were well managed, but in a pointed critique of the political economists who denounced common right and lauded the virtues of enclosure through legislation if necessary, she argues that '[g]ood husbandry was not born of Act of Parliament.' A commons could be well managed, and many were. *Commoners*, 116. Similarly, sound management of the Pacific fishery did not begin with the *Fisheries Act* and *Regulations*.

17 Richard White, *The Organic Machine* (New York: Hill and Wang, 1995), 89.

18 For extensive descriptions see C. Groot and L. Margolis, eds., *Pacific Salmon Life Histories* (Vancouver: UBC Press, 1991).

19 Wilson Duff, *The Upper Stalo Indians of the Fraser River of B.C.*, Anthropology in British Columbia, Memoir no. 1 (Victoria: Royal BC Museum, 1952).

20 See Steven Romanoff, 'Fraser Lillooet Salmon Fishing,' and Dorothy I.D. Kennedy and Randy Bouchard, 'Stl'atl'imx (Fraser River Lillooet) Fishing,' in Brian Hayden, ed., *A Complex Culture of the British Columbia Plateau: Traditional Stl'atl'imx Resource Use* (Vancouver: UBC Press, 1992).

21 See Richard Somerset Mackie, *Trading beyond the Mountains: The British Fur Trade on the Pacific, 1763–1843* (Vancouver: UBC Press, 1996), 191–201, 221–30.

22 Keith Ralston, 'Patterns of Trade and Investment on the Pacific Coast, 1867–1892: The Case of the British Columbia Salmon Canning Industry,' *BC Studies* 1 (1968–9): 37–45; Dianne Newell, 'Dispersal and Concentra-

tion: The Slowly Changing Spatial Pattern of the British Columbia Salmon Canning Industry,' *Journal of Historical Geography* 14 (1988): 22–36. On the cod fishery, see Harold A. Innis, *The Cod Fisheries: The History of an International Economy* (New Haven: Yale University Press, 1940).

23 E.P. Thompson, *Whigs and Hunters: The Origin of the Black Act* (New York: Pantheon Books, 1975).

24 See the marvellous collection of essays in Thompson, *Customs in Common*.

25 E.P. Thompson, *The Poverty of Theory and Other Essays* (London: Merlin Press, 1978) (emphasis in original).

26 To use Thompson's frequently cited characterization of the relation between law and society in *Whigs and Hunters*, 261.

27 Legal anthropologists have defended isolating the 'legal' as they created a sub-discipline within social anthropology, but they are careful to situate their studies of law historically and culturally, paying particular attention to asymmetrical power relations. See Starr and Collier, 'Introduction.'

28 J.W. Hurst, *Law and Economic Growth* (Cambridge, Mass.: Belknap Press, 1964), viii; cited by David H. Flaherty, ed., *Essays in the History of Canadian Law*, Vol. 1 (Toronto: The Osgoode Society, 1981), 7.

Chapter 1: Legal Capture

1 Canada Sessional Papers, 1873, Annual Report of the Department of Maine and Fisheries ('Fisheries Annual Report') 1872, app. Q, 177.

2 The fishery would inspire Alexander Begg's unrealized proposal of the late 1880s to bring impoverished Scottish crofters to British Columbia, principally Vancouver Island; British Columbia Archives (BCA), MS-1640, copied from the Scottish Record Office AF files 51/151–6 and 51/55.

3 *British North America Act*, 1867, s. 91(12).

4 Statutes of Canada, 1868, c. 60.

5 Garrett Hardin, 'The Tragedy of the Commons,' *Science* 162 (1969): 1243–8.

6 Reuben Ware, *Five Issues, Five Battlegrounds: An Introduction to the History of Indian Fishing in British Columbia, 1850–1930* (Chilliwack: Coqualeetza Education Training Centre, 1983).

7 Geoff Meggs, *Salmon: The Decline of the British Columbia Fishery* (Vancouver: Douglas & McIntyre, 1991, 1995), 74–80.

8 Geoff Meggs and Duncan Stacey, *Cork Lines and Canning Lines: The Glory Years of Fishing on the West Coast* (Vancouver: Douglas & McIntyre, 1992).

9 Dianne Newell, *Tangled Webs of History: Indians and the Law in Canada's Pacific Coast Fishery* (Toronto: University of Toronto Press, 1993).

10 Ibid., 6–8.

11 Alicja Muszynski, *Cheap Wage Labour: Race and Gender in the Fisheries of*

British Columbia (Montreal and Kingston: McGill-Queen's University Press, 1996), 9.

12 Ibid., 223.

13 Bill Parenteau, '"Care, Control and Supervision": Native People in the Canadian Atlantic Salmon Fishery,' *Canadian Historical Review* 79 (1998): 1–35.

14 Victor Lytwyn, 'Ojibway and Ottawa Fisheries around Manitoulin Island: Historical and Geographical Perspectives on Aboriginal and Treaty Fishing Rights,' *Native Studies Review* 6 (1990): 1–30; John J. Van West, 'Ojibway Fisheries, Commercial Fisheries Development and Fisheries Administration, 1873–1915: An Examination of Conflicting Interest and the Collapse of the Sturgeon Fisheries of the Lake of the Woods,' *Native Studies Review* 6 (1990): 31–65; Lise C. Hansen, 'Treaty Fishing Rights and the Development of Fisheries Legislation in Ontario: A Primer,' *Native Studies Review* 7 (1991): 1–21; Leo G. Waisberg and Tim E. Holzkamm, 'The Ojibway Understanding of Fishing Rights under Treaty 3: A Comment on Lise C. Hansen, "Treaty Fishing Rights and the Development of Fisheries Legislation in Ontario: A Primer,"' *Native Studies Review* 8 (1992): 47–55; Lise C. Hansen, 'A Rejoinder to Waisberg and Holzkamm,' *Native Studies Review* 8 (1992): 57–60; Roland Wright, 'The Public Right of Fishing, Government Fishing Policy, and Indian Fishing Rights in Upper Canada,' *Ontario History* 86 (1994): 337–62; J. Michael Thoms, 'Illegal Conservation: Two Case Studies of Conflict between Indigenous and State Natural Resource Management Paradigms,' MA thesis, Trent University, 1995.

15 Frank Tough, *'As Their Natural Resources Fail': Native Peoples and the Economic History of Northern Manitoba, 1870–1930* (Vancouver: UBC Press, 1996).

16 For an anthropological entry into this literature see Daniel L. Boxberger, *To Fish in Common: The Ethnohistory of Lummi Indian Salmon Fishing* (Lincoln: University of Nebraska Press, 1989).

17 Joseph E. Taylor III, *Making Salmon: An Environmental History of the Northwest Fisheries Crisis* (Seattle: University of Washington Press, 1999). See the fine bibliographical essay at the end of the book.

18 Arthur McEvoy, *The Fisherman's Problem: Ecology and Law in the California Fisheries, 1850–1980* (Cambridge: Cambridge University Press, 1986).

19 Wayne Suttles, *Coast Salish Essays* (Vancouver: Talonbooks, 1987), 45.

20 Philip Drucker, *Cultures of the North Pacific Coast* (San Francisco: Chandler Publishing Co., 1965), 9–10.

21 Hugh W. McKervill, *The Salmon People* (Vancouver: Whitecap Books, 1967, 1992).

22 For a survey of the patterns of resource ownership see Allan Richardson,

'Control of Productive Resources on the Northwest Coast of North America,' in Nancy M. Williams and Eugene S. Hunn, eds., *Resource Managers: North American and Australian Hunter-Gatherers* (Washington: American Association for the Advancement of Science, 1982), 93–112.

23 Drucker, *Cultures*, 47.

24 Wayne Suttles, ed., *Handbook of North American Indians*, Vol. 7, *Northwest Coast* (Washington: Smithsonian Institution, 1990), 4.

25 The distinction between ownership of fishing sites and that of general resource areas that include a salmon stream is suggested by Berringer, 'Northwest Coast Traditional Salmon Fisheries: Systems of Resource Utilization,' MA thesis, University of British Columbia, 1982, 191.

26 Philip Drucker, 'Rank, Wealth and Kinship in Northwest Coast Society,' in Tom McFeat, ed., *Indians of the North Pacific Coast* (Ottawa: Macmillan, 1978), 140 (emphasis in the original).

27 Gilbert Malcolm Sproat, *The Nootka: Scenes and Studies of Savage Life* [1868], ed. and annotated by Charles Lillard (Victoria: Sono Nis Press, 1987), 59.

28 Steven Romanoff, 'Fraser Lillooet Salmon Fishing,' and Dorothy I.D. Kennedy and Randy Bouchard, '*Stl'atl'imx* (Fraser River Lillooet) Fishing,' in Brian Hayden, ed., *A Complex Culture of the British Columbia Plateau: Traditional* Stl'atl'imx *Resource Use* (Vancouver: UBC Press, 1992), 470–505 and 256–354.

29 Sam Mitchell in Romanoff, 'Fraser Lillooet Salmon Fishing,' 244.

30 Kennedy and Bouchard, '*Stl'átl'imx* Fishing,' 314. Marilyn G. Bennett, in her study of the 91 Indian bands living on the Fraser River system in the early 1970s, discovered that 21% of those surveyed believed that fishing places were family-owned; 43% believed they were band-owned; 19% believed they were owned by all Indians; and 13% said they were open to anyone. *Indian Fishing and Its Cultural Importance in the Fraser River System* (Fisheries Service, Pacific Region, Dept. of the Environment and Union of British Columbia Indian Chiefs, April 1973), 17.

31 Aubrey Cannon, 'Conflict and Salmon on the Interior Plateau of British Columbia,' in Hayden, *A Complex Culture*, 506–24.

32 Robert Tyhurst, 'Traditional and Comptemporary Land and Resource Use by *Ts'kw'ayláxw*,' in Hayden, *A Complex Culture*, 355–404, has attempted to document and map resource use and ownership along the middle Fraser.

33 Franz Boas, 'Introduction' to James Teit, *Traditions of the Thompson River Indians of British Columbia* [1898] (New York: Kraus Reprint, 1969), 6.

34 See Franz Boas, *Chinook Texts* (Washington: Government Printing Office, 1894), 92–106.

35 Franz Boas, ed., *Folk-Tales of Salishan and Sahaptin Tribes* (New York: Kraus

Reprint Co., 1969), 70–1. See Taylor, *Making Salmon*, for an analysis of the Native fisheries on the Columbia River system.

36 Kennedy and Bouchard, 'Stl'átl'imx Fishing,' 275–6; Franz Boas, *The Indian Tribes of the Lower Fraser River* (London: n.p., 1894), 3; Teit, *Traditions of the Thompson River Indians*. Terry Glavin, *Dead Reckoning: Confronting the Crisis in Pacific Fisheries* (Vancouver: Greystone Books and David Suzuki Foundation, 1996) begins chapter 4 with a Shuswap version of the Coyote myth and investigates its meaning in chapter 5.

37 For a discussion of the collection and interpretation of myth in British Columbia, particularly of James Teit's work among the Nlha7kámpx, see Wendy C. Wickwire, 'To See Ourselves as the Other's Other: Nlaka'pamux Contact Narratives,' *Canadian Historical Review* 75 (1994): 1–20.

38 T.T. Waterman and A.L. Kroeber, 'The Kepel Fish Dam,' in *American Archaeology and Ethnology*, Vol. 35, *1934–1943* (New York: Kraus Reprint, 1965), 50.

39 Michael J. Kew and Julian Griggs, 'Native Indians of the Fraser Basin: Towards a Model of Sustainable Resource Use,' in Anthony H.J. Dorcey, ed., *Perspectives on Sustainable Development in Water Management: Towards Agreement in the Fraser River Basin* (Vancouver: UBC Westwater Research Centre, 1991), 35.

40 Ibid., 36.

41 From an undated manuscript by A.C. Anderson, reproduced in Michael Kew, 'Salmon Availability, Technology, and Cultural Adaptation in the Fraser River Watershed,' in Hayden, *A Complex Culture*, 176–221, app. 2 (emphasis added). Kew suggests the manuscript probably dates from 1860.

42 See also Newell, *Tangled Webs*, 28–45.

43 Taylor, *Making Salmon*, 36.

44 Ibid., 27.

45 Kew, 'Salmon Availability,' 201–6.

46 Randall F. Schalk, 'The Structure of an Anadromous Fish Resource,' in Lewis R. Binford, ed., *For Theory Building in Archaeology: Essays on Faunal Remains, Aquatic Resources, Spatial Analysis, and Systemic Modeling* (New York: Academic Press, 1977), 241.

47 See Robert T. Boyd, *The Coming of the Spirit of Pestilence: Introduced Infectious Diseases and Population Decline among Northwest Indians, 1774–1874* (Seattle: University of Washington Press, 1999); Cole Harris, *The Resettlement of British Columbia* (Vancouver: UBC Press, 1997), 3–30; and Boyd's response to Harris, 'Commentary on Early Contact-Era Smallpox in the Pacific Northwest,' *Ethnohistory* 43 (1996): 307–28.

48 Gordon W. Hewes, 'Indian Fisheries Productivity in Pre-Contact Times in
    the Pacific Salmon Area,' *Northwest Anthropological Research Notes* 7 (1973):
    133–55. For the Columbia River see J.A. Craig and R.L. Hacker, 'The
    History and Development of the Fisheries of the Columbia River,' *Bulletin
    of the Bureau of Fisheries* 49 (1940): 150; and Randall F. Schalk, 'Estimating
    Salmon and Steelhead Usage in the Columbia Basin before 1850: The
    Anthropological Perspective,' *Northwest Environmental Journal* 2 (1986):
    1–29. Schalk argues that Craig and Hackler underestimate salmon con-
    sumption because their population estimates are low, and that Hewes
    underestimated per capita annual consumption. He also suggests that
    competition among spawning salmon in crowded spawning beds could
    actually reduce reproduction (22, n. 5). Taylor, *Making Salmon*, 20–4, 42,
    provides a good summary of the various positions on pre-European
    contact fish consumption, and also suggests that the decline in the Native
    population had other ecological effects (particularly a reduction in control-
    led burns) that complicate any direct correlation between Native harvest
    and salmon stocks. For estimates of Native consumption on the Fraser, see
    Glavin, *Dead Reckoning*, 102–6.
49 Canada Sessional Papers, 1880, Fisheries Annual Report 1879, 300. The
    'exclusive European supply' caveat was probably meant to exclude un-
    used cannery fish that were given to Natives. This figure remained con-
    stant in the inspector's annual report until it was lowered in 1885 to
    $3,257,500 (Canada Sessional Papers, 1886, Fisheries Annual Report 1885,
    297).
50 Hudson's Bay Company Archives (HBCA) D.4/125, fos. 62–3, McDonald
    to Governor and Council, Northern Development, 10 February 1831, cited
    in Richard Somerset Mackie, *Trading beyond the Mountains: The British Fur
    Trade on the Pacific, 1763–1843* (Vancouver: UBC Press, 1996), 224.
51 See Richard Somerset Mackie, 'Colonial Land, Indian Labour and Com-
    pany Capital: The Economy of Vancouver Island, 1849–1858,' MA thesis,
    University of Victoria, 1984, 221. For estimates of the commercial harvest
    that involved Europeans see M.P. Shepard and A.W. Argue, 'The Commer-
    cial Harvest of Salmon in British Columbia, 1820–1877,' *Canadian Technical
    Report of Fisheries and Aquatic Sciences* 1690 (1989).
52 Mackie, Colonial Land, 33–4; Hamar Foster, 'British Columbia: Legal
    Institutions in the Far West, from Contact to 1871,' *Manitoba Law Journal* 23
    (1996): 317.
53 In order of their appearance: Lytwyn, 'Ojibway and Ottawa Fisheries';
    Wright, 'Public Right of Fishing'; Peggy Blair, 'Solemn Promises and *Solum
    Rights*: The Saugeen Ojibway Fishing Grounds and *R. v. Jones and*

Nadjiwon,' Ottawa Law Review 28 (1996–7): 125–43; Mark D. Walters, 'Aboriginal Rights, *Magna Carta* and Exclusive Rights to Fisheries in the Waters of Upper Canada,' *Queen's Law Journal* 23 (1988): 301–68; P. Blair, 'Taken for "Granted": Aboriginal Title and Public Fishing Rights in Upper Canada,' *Ontario History* 92 (2000): 31–55.

54 See *R. v. Gladstone*, [1996] 2 S.C.R. 723; 4 C.N.L.R. 65, para. 67: 'While the elevation of common law Aboriginal rights to constitutional status obviously has an impact on the public's common law rights to fish in tidal waters, it was surely not intended that, by the enactment of s.35(1), those common law rights would be extinguished in cases where the Aboriginal right to harvest fish commercially existed ... As a common law, not constitutional, right, the right of public access to the fishery must clearly be second in priority to Aboriginal rights; however, the recognition of Aboriginal rights should not be interpreted as extinguishing the right of public access to the fishery.'

55 Newell, *Tangled Webs*, 46.

56 The common law of fisheries embodies the two fundamental principles that, according to Peter Usher, govern the ownership of and access to wildlife under state management in the nineteenth and twentieth centuries: 'One is that fish and animals in their wild sense are considered to be incapable of private ownership, and can be possessed only through capture. The other is that all citizens should have equal opportunity of access to these resources' ('Aboriginal Property Systems in Land and Resources,' in G. Cant, J. Overton, and E. Pawson, eds., *Indigenous Land Rights in Commonwealth Countries: Depression, Negotiation and Community Action* [Christchurch: Dept. of Geography, University of Canterbury, 1993], 41). In a case study from the American eastern seaboard, Bonnie J. McCay argues that the commitment to open-access fisheries in the New World grew from a determination not to replicate the class-based privileged access in the Old World ('The Culture of Commoners: Historical Observations on Old and New World Fisheries,' in B.J. McCay and J.M. Acheson, eds., *The Question of the Commons: The Culture and Ecology of Communal Resources* [Tucson: University of Arizona Press, 1987], 195–216). Walters ('Aboriginal Rights') suggests, however, that the doctrine was interpreted somewhat differently in American and Canadian courts.

57 Foster, 'British Columbia: Legal Institutions,' 298.

58 There are many texts on English fish and water laws, including Lord Chief Justice Hale, 'De Juris Maris et Brachiorum Ejusdem,' in F. Hargrave, ed., *A Collection of Tracts Relative to the Law of England, Vol 1, Part 1* [1787] (Abington: Professional Books Ltd., 1982), 1–44; Joseph Chitty, *A Treatise on*

the Game Laws and on Fisheries [1812] (New York: Garland Publishing, 1979); H.J.W. Coulson and Urquhart A. Forbes, The Law Relating to Waters, Sea, Tidal and Inland (London: Henry Sweet, 1880); and Stuart A. Moore and Hubert Stuart Moore, The History and Law of Fisheries (London: Stevens and Haynes, 1903). For Canada, see Gerard V. La Forest, Water Law in Canada: The Atlantic Provinces (Ottawa: Information Canada, 1973).

59 Hale, 'De Juris Maris,' 11.

60 Chitty, Game Laws, 272 (emphasis in original). Walters, 'Aboriginal Rights,' 313–26, provides a good analysis of the Magna Carta and the public right to fish.

61 See Lawrence Juda, International Law and Ocean Use Management: The Evolution of Ocean Governance (London and New York: Routledge, 1996), for the historical development of territorial waters in international law and for his argument that a developing fisheries science and new fishing technology was a catalyst for change in marine law and policy through the nineteenth century. Nicholas Everitt, Shots from a Lawyer's Gun (London: Everett & Co., 1910), 28–51, provides an engaging narrative portraying the complexity of the Crown's ownership of the foreshore.

62 LaForest, Water Law, 196.

63 1914 A.C. 153.

64 Wright, 'Public Right of Fishing,' 337.

65 Ibid., 343.

66 National Archives of Canada (NAC), Department of Justice, RG 13, vol. 2368, file 4/1866, W.F. Whitcher, Head of Fisheries Branch, Department of Crown Lands, Province of Canada, to Alexander Campbell, Commissioner of Crown Lands, Province of Canada, 23 January 1866; NAC, Department of Indian Affairs (DIA), RG 10, vol. 612, 215, W.H. Draper, Attorney General, Province of Canada, to J.M. Higginson, Supt. Gen. Indian Affairs, Province of Canada, 16 April 1845; NAC, DIA, RG 10, vol. 323, pp. 216, 134–5, James Cockburn, Solicitor General, Province of Canada, Memorandum, 8 March 1866.

67 Walters, 'Aboriginal Rights.'

68 Blair, 'Taken for "Granted"'; J. Michael Thoms, PhD thesis, Dept. of History, UBC (in progress).

69 La Forest, Water Law, 196.

70 As Blair ('Solemn Promises,' 128) argues in the Ontario context, and I demonstrate in British Columbia, this position was much contested by Native peoples, but also within government, particularly by the DIA.

71 NAC, DIA, RG 10, vol. 1972, file 5530, Whitcher to Fisheries Overseers, 17 December 1875.

72 The records of the Joint Indian Reserve Commission and the Indian Reserve Commission are held by the DIA in its Vancouver Regional Office. P. O'Reilly's allocations in 1881 on the Fraser and Nass rivers are recorded in the Federal Collection of Minutes of Decision, Correspondence and Sketches, vol. 8, P. O'Reilly (Indian Reserve Commissioner), May 1881 to January 1882, file 29,858, vol. 2 [Indian Land Registry no. B-64,643], and vol. 9, P. O'Reilly (Indian Reserve Commissioner), January 1882 to July 1882, file 29,858, vol. 3 [Indian Land Registry nos. B-64,644 (pp. 1–130) and B-64642 (pp. 149–294)]. Thanks to Anne Seymour for helping me navigate through this extensive and well indexed collection.

73 NAC, DIA, RG 10, vol. 3766, file 32,876, Whitcher to Vankoughnet, 9 December 1881.

74 Ibid., Macdonald to A.W. McLelan, Acting Minister of Marine and Fisheries, 20 December 1881.

75 Ibid., A.W. McLelan to J.A. Macdonald, 30 January 1882.

76 DIA, Vancouver Regional Office, Federal Collection of Minutes of Decision, Correspondence and Sketches, vol. 10, P. O'Reilly (Indian Reserve Commissioner), June 1882 to February 1885, file 29,858, vol. 4 [Indian Land Registry no. B-64645], 133, Vankoughnet to Whitcher, 12 January 1883.

77 Ibid., 129–31, Whitcher to Vankoughnet, 5 January 1883. For a more thorough treatment of the connections between reserves and fisheries see Douglas C. Harris, 'Indian Reserves, Aboriginal Fisheries and Anglo-Canadian Law,' forthcoming; see also Newell, *Tangled Webs*, 55–62.

78 HBCA, A.37/42 fos. 13–14, Hudson's Bay Company, *Colonization of Vancouver's Island* (London, 24 January 1849). In an earlier draft the Colonial Office proposed that the HBC control the fishery as well, but that was thought to give the company too much control.

79 BCA, Colonial Office Correspondence (CO), 305, pp. 151–65, James Douglas to Captain J. Sheppard, HMS Inconstant, Fort Nisqually, 28 May 1849.

80 Hartwell Bowsfield, ed., *Fort Victoria Letters: 1846–1852* (Winnipeg: Hudson's Bay Record Society, 1979), 43, Douglas to Archibald Barclay, HBC Secretary, 3 September 1849. Hamar Foster includes this passage at the beginning of 'The Saanichton Bay Marina Case: Imperial Law, Colonial History and Competing Theories of Aboriginal Title,' *UBC Law Review* 23 (1989): 629–50.

81 *R. v. White and Bob* (1964), 52 D.L.R. (2d) 481 (S.C.C.), affirming 50 D.L.R. (2d) 613 (B.C.C.A.). Treaties were signed with the groups now known as the Esquimalt, Songhees, Beecher Bay, Sooke, Tsawout, Tsartlip, Pauquachin, Tseycum, Namaimo, and Kwakiutl First Nations.

82 Wilson Duff, 'The Fort Victoria Treaties,' *BC Studies* 3 (1969): 4; Foster, 'Saanichton Marina,' 632–4.

83 Copies of the treaties are contained in *Papers Connected with the Indian Land Question, 1850–1875, 1877* (Victoria: Queen's Printer, 1987), 5–11.

84 Newell, *Tangled Webs*, 47.

85 NAC, DIA, RG 10, vol. 3662, file 9756, pt. 1, Sproat to E.A. Meredith, Minister of the Interior, 30 July 1878.

86 Ibid., Sproat to the Deputy Minister of the Interior, 6 November 1878.

87 Ibid., Sproat to Powell, 22 April 1878.

88 In the BC Supreme Court, *Saanichton Marina Ltd. v. Tsawout Indian Band* (1987), 18 B.C.L.R. (2d) 217, Meredith J. framed the treaty right to fish in the following terms: 'I conceive that the right of the Band is to insist that the whole of the Bay continue to be used as a fishery as stipulated in the Deed. That is to say that other uses which might derogate from use as a fishery cannot be permitted to intrude ... The marina would reduce the size of the fishery and thus be in derogation of the rights of the Band.'

89 Thirty years later J.A. Macdonald, the Prime Minister and Superintendent General of Indian Affairs, would instruct the Indian Reserve Commissioner Peter O'Reilly to allocate 'exclusive fisheries' with the reserves.

90 Douglas to A. Barclay, 16 May 1850, cited in Duff, 'Fort Victoria Treaties,' 7–8.

91 BCA, GR-0673, Colonial Office Correspondence, 306/1, *An Act for the Preservation of Game*, 20 April 1859.

92 *An Act to amend an Act for the Preservation of Game*, R.S.B.C. 1871, c. 12.

93 The British parliament had consolidated English salmon law in 1861 with the *Salmon Fishery Act* (1861) 24 & 25 Vict. c. 109. The Colonial Office probably sent Douglas an extract of the 1860 report on the Scottish salmon fishery by the Select Committee of the House of Lords that recommended a central board to regulate the fishery. Great Britain, House of Commons, Parliamentary Papers, 1860, vol. 19, Reports from Committees, Salmon Fisheries.

94 BCA, GR-1486, Colonial Office, CO, 60/10, pp. 366–7, James Douglas to the Duke of Newcastle, 31 August 1861.

95 John Lutz, 'Work, Wages and Welfare in Aboriginal–Non-Aboriginal Relations, British Columbia, 1849–1970,' PhD thesis, University of Victoria, 1994, 256.

96 Ibid., 257–8.

97 See James E. Hendrickson, ed., *Journals of the Colonial Legislatures of the Colonies of Vancouver Island and British Columbia, 1851–1871, Vol. 3, Journals of the House of Assembly, Vancouver Island, 1863–1866* (Victoria: Provincial

Archives of British Columbia, 1980), 70–2, 215; *Vol. 4, Journals of the Executive Council, 1864–1871, and the Legislative Council, 1864–66, of British Columbia*, 23–4, 227–8. Also *The British Colonist* (Victoria), 2 July, 10 August, and 5 October 1863.

98 Allan Pritchard, ed., *Vancouver Island Letters of Edmund Hope Verney, 1862–1865* (Vancouver: UBC Press, 1996), 220, Verney to his father, 1 September 1864.

99 Ibid., Pritchard, 'Introduction,' 24.

100 Great Britain, House of Commons, Parliamentary Papers (hereafter Parliamentary Papers), 1863, vol. 28, Reports from Commissioners, Report of the Royal Commission on the operation of the act relating to trawling for herring on the coasts of Scotland.

101 Parliamentary Papers, 1866, vol. 17, Reports from Commissioners, Report of the commissioners appointed to inquire into the sea fisheries of the United Kingdom.

102 Larry A. Nielsen, 'The Evolution of Fisheries Management Philosophy,' *Marine Fisheries Review* 38 (1976): 15–23.

103 For a study of the correlation between treaties and fisheries legislation in the Ontario context, and an argument that the fisheries legislation that followed the Mississauga treaties was intended to protect their treaty rights, see Thoms, PhD thesis.

104 Duff, 'Fort Victoria Treaties,' 5, 29–30.

105 Duncan Stacey, 'Technological Change in the Fraser River Canning Industry,' MA thesis, University of British Columbia, 1970. A shorter published version appears as *Sockeye and Tinplate: Technological Change in the Fraser River Canning Industry* (Victoria: BC Provincial Museum Heritage Record no. 15, 1982). See also Ralston, 'Patterns of Trade,' 40.

106 Canada Sessional Papers, 1874, Fisheries Annual Report 1873, app. 5, p. 205.

107 Ibid., 1875, 219. Cicely Lyons, *Salmon: Our Heritage. The Story of a Province and an Industry* (Vancouver: British Columbia Packers Ltd., 1969), describes Ewen as the 'Father of Salmon Canning in British Columbia.' See the picture of Ewen on the inside cover. For a history of the Californian fishery, see McEvoy, *The Fisherman's Problem*.

108 Statutes of Canada, 1874, c. 28.

109 Order-in-Council, May 1876, *Canada Gazette*, vol. 9, 1513.

110 *Fisheries Act*, Statutes of Canada, 1868, c. 60. On the 1857 *Act*, see Hansen, 'Treaty Fishing Rights.'

111 Canada Sessional Papers, 1875, Fisheries Annual Report 1874, Report of the Commissioner of Fisheries, 31 December 1874, p. lxiv.

112 *Fisheries Act*, Statutes of Canada, 1868, c. 60, s. 13(8). For descriptions and drawings of the spear-like implements named in the section, see Stewart, *Indian Fishing*. According to Parenteau ('"Care, Control and Supervision"'), allowing Natives to continue spear fishing undermined efforts to 'civilize' them through agriculture, and on the East Coast the minister issued only a few exemptions in the late 1860s and early 1870s.
113 Canada Sessional Papers, 1877, Fisheries Annual Report 1876, p. 343 (his emphasis).
114 *Daily British Colonist* (Victoria), 21 December 1877, reprinted in the Fisheries Annual Report, 1893, cxii.
115 *Mainland Guardian* (New Westminster), 14 July 1877.
116 Henry Keith Ralston, 'John Sullivan Deas: A Black Entrepeneur in British Columbia Salmon Canning,' *BC Studies* 32 (1976–7): 64–78. Ralston raises the issues of race and racism, but concludes that it is difficult to gauge the degree of discrimination Deas suffered.
117 *Mainland Guardian*, 28 July 1877. The details of O'Reilly's decision are not provided.
118 Ibid., 25 July 1877.
119 Ibid., 11 July 1877.
120 British Columbia Sessional Papers, 1905, 5 Ed.7, Prefontaine to Fulton, 12 January 1905.
121 *Mainland Guardian*, 17 November 1877.
122 Canada Sessional Papers, 1894, Fisheries Annual Report 1893, p. cxiii, memorandum of a meeting held at the Colonial Hotel, New Westminster, 17 December 1877.
123 *Journals of the Legislative Assembly of British Columbia, 1878*, 55.
124 NAC, DIA, RG10, vol. 3651, file 8540, 303–4, Anderson to Minister of Fisheries, 3 January 1878.
125 Canada Sessional Papers, 1878, Fisheries Annual Report 1877, p. 295. Anderson refers to a letter of 12 June 1876.
126 Ibid., 1877, Fisheries Annual Report 1876, 343.
127 Ibid., 1878, Fisheries Annual Report 1877, 295, Anderson to the Hon. A.J. Smith, Minister of Marine and Fisheries, 27 September 1877.
128 NAC, DIA, RG 10, vol. 3651, file 8540, W.F. Whitcher to Deputy Minister of the Interior, 15 November 1877.
129 Order in Council, 30 May 1878, *Canada Gazette*, vol. 11, p. 1258.
130 Canada Sessional Papers, 1894, Fisheries Annual Report 1893, p. cxvi. T.R. McInnes to A.J. Smith, 24 June 1878.
131 Ibid., Smith to Anderson, 24 June 1878.
132 Ibid., cxxii, Clement F. Cornwall, Lieutenant-Governor, 20 February 1882.

133 At the insistence of the province, which thought the JIRC too expensive and unnecessary, Anderson (the Dominion representative) and Archibald McKinley (the provincial representative) were not reappointed. The province reluctantly agreed to allow Sproat (the joint appointee) to continue on his own in 1878.

134 NAC, DIA, RG 10, vol. 3662, file 9756, part 1, Sproat to E.A. Meredith, Minister of the Interior, 30 July 1878. Twenty years earlier, Sproat (*The Nootka*, 145), had written of the west coast of Vancouver Island that 'fish is, to man, here what the corn crop is in England, or what the potato crop was in Ireland.'

135 The province informed Sproat: 'You will avoid disturbing them in their proper and legitimate avocations whether of the chase or of fishing, whether pastoral or agricultural.' NAC, DIA, RG 10, vol. 3633, file 6425-1, C. Good, Deputy Provincial Secretary to Sproat, 26 October 1876. The Dominion instructed him 'not to disturb the Indians in the possession of any villages, *fishing stations*, fur-trading posts, settlements or clearings which they may occupy and to which they may be specially attached, and [the Indians] should rather be encouraged to persevere in the industry or occupation they are engaged in, and with that view should be secured in the possession of the villages, fishing stations, fur-posts or other settlements or clearings which they occupy in connection with that industry or occupation.' Minister of the Interior to Sproat, 25 August 1876 (emphasis added).

136 BCA, GR 494, box 1, file 1, Provincial Secretary of British Columbia to A. McKinley, 23 October 1876; NAC, DIA, RG 10, vol. 3633, file 6425-1, D. Laird, Minister of the Interior, to A.C. Anderson, 25 August 1876.

137 'Report of the Government of British Columbia on the subject of Indian Reserves,' in *Papers Connected with the Indian Land Question*, suppl., 7.

138 For a much fuller discussion of the importance of fish in the allocation of reserves, and consideration of recent Supreme Court of Canada decisions see Douglas C. Harris, 'Indian Reserves, Aboriginal Fisheries and Anglo-Canadian Law in British Columbia,' forthcoming; see also Newell, *Tangled Webs*, 55–62.

139 NAC, DIA, RG 10, vol. 3662, file 9756, pt. 1, Sproat to Meredith, 30 July 1878.

140 Canada Sessional Papers, 1879, Commissioner of Fisheries Report 1878, p. 293. In *R. v. Lewis* [1996] 3 C.N.L.R. 131, a case involving the fishing rights of the Squamish people adjacent to their Cheakamus Reserve, Justice Iacobucci of the Supreme Court of Canada determined that 'the Crown's policy was to treat Indians and non-Indians equally as to the use of the

water and not to grant exclusive use of any public waters for the purpose of fishing' (141). Fisheries' instructions to Anderson suggest that, in the early years of enforcement, at least the first part of this statement is wrong. Fisheries exempted Native people from the fisheries legislation.

141 NAC, DIA, RG 10, vol. 3662, file 9756, pt. 1, Powell to Supt. Gen. Indian Affairs, 9 July 1878.

142 BCA, Attorney General, GR 429, box 1, file 7, 89/78, Chief Justice Begbie to Attorney General Walkem, 26 June 1878.

143 NAC, DIA, RG 10, vol. 3662, file 9756, pt. 1, Mills to Smith, 18 July 1878.

144 Ibid., Commissioner of Fisheries Whitcher to Deputy Minister of the Interior Meredith, 5 August 1878.

145 Ibid., Whitcher to Meredith, 15 June 1878.

146 Canada Sessional Papers, 1879, Fisheries Annual Report, 1878, p. 293.

147 Ibid., 299.

148 BCA, Attorney General, GR 429, box 1, file 7, memo by provincial Attorney General Walkem, 2 July 1878.

149 Anderson chronicled his experiences in 'A History of the Northwest Coast,' 1878 (archived at UBC Special Collections). For his thoughts on Native peoples see 'Notes on the Indian Tribes of British North America, and the Northwest Coast,' *The Historical Magazine* 7 (1863).

150 Canada Sessional Papers, 1878, Fisheries Annual Report 1877, pp. 303–4, Anderson to Minister of Fisheries, 3 January 1878.

151 Ibid., 1879, Fisheries Annual Report, 1878, p. 296.

152 Ibid.

153 NAC, DIA, RG 10, vol. 3662, file 9756, pt. 1, Sproat to Meredith, 15 June 1878.

154 Canada Sessional Papers, 1879, Fisheries Annual Report, 1878, p. 296.

155 Ibid., Report from the Deputy Supt. Gen. of Indian Affairs, p. 69, J.W. Powell's 'Report of Indian affairs in the Victoria Superintendency for the year ended 30th June, 1878' (emphasis added).

156 NAC, DIA, RG 10, vol. 3657, file 9361, Sproat to Supt. Gen. of Indian Affairs, 4 February 1878.

157 Ibid., Sproat to Supt. Gen., 6 May 1878; Whitcher to Deputy Supt. Gen. of Indian Affairs Vonkaughent, 12 September 1878.

158 Newell, *Tangled Webs*, 52.

159 Hamar Foster discusses master and servant law briefly in two articles: 'British Columbia: Legal Institutions' and 'Mutiny on the *Beaver*: Law and Authority in the Fur Trade Navy, 1835–1840,' in Dale Gibson and W. Wesley Pue, eds., *Glimpses of Canadian Legal History* (Winnipeg: Legal Research Institute, 1991), 15–46.

160 See Paul Craven, 'The Law of Master and Servant in Mid-Nineteenth-Century Ontario,' in David Flaherty, ed., *Essays in the History of Canadian Law*, Vol. 1 (Toronto: The Osgoode Society, 1981), 175–211. For England see the recent article by Douglas Hay, 'Master and Servant in England: Using the Law in the Eighteenth and Nineteenth Centuries,' in Willibald Steinmetz, ed., *Private Law and Social Inequality* (Oxford: Oxford University Press, 2000), 227–64. For a comparative analysis see Craven and Hay, 'The Criminalization of "Free" Labour: Master and Servant in Comparative Perspective,' *Slavery and Abolition* 15 (1994): 71–101.

161 See Daphne Simon, 'Master and Servant,' in John Saville, ed., *Democracy and Labour Movement: Essays in Honour of Donna Torr* (London: Lawrence & Wishart, 1954), 160–200, for a discussion of master and servant law, its origins, and the process of reform in England to 1875.

162 Paul Craven, '"The Modern Spirit of the Law": Blake, Mowat, and the Breaches of Contract Act, 1877,' in G. Blaine Baker and Jim Phillips, eds., *Essays in the History of Canadian Law*, Vol. 8, *Essays in Honour of R.C.B. Risk* (Toronto: The Osgoode Society, 1999), 142–70, argues that the 1877 act to repeal criminal sanction for breach of contract left open the possibility that provinces could maintain criminal sanctions into the twentieth century.

163 Geo. IV c. 34.

164 *Mainland Guardian*, 18 July 1877.

165 Edmonds, a businessman, politician, and public official, was in 1877 the sheriff for the New Westminster district. He had no formal legal training. See J.B. Kerr, *Biographical Dictionary of Well-Known British Columbians: With a Historical Sketch* (Vancouver: Kerr & Begg, 1890), 156–9.

166 Bole had arrived in New Westminster in 1877, the first lawyer to settle on mainland British Columbia. See Kerr, *Biographical Dictionary*, 107–8.

167 *Mainland Guardian*, 18 and 21 July 1877.

168 Ibid., 25 September 1877.

169 Hay, 'Master and Servant in England.'

170 Craven and Hay, 'Criminalization of "Free" Labour,' 72.

171 *Mainland Guardian*, 10 February, 23 June, 1 August, 22 September 1877.

172 The principal figures in this debate are Rolf Knight, *Indians at Work: An Informal History of Native Labour in British Columbia, 1858–1930* (Vancouver: New Star Books, 1978, 1996) and Robin Fisher, *Contact and Conflict: Indian–European Relations in British Columbia, 1774–1890* (Vancouver: UBC Press, 1977, 1992). See also John S. Lutz, 'Work, Wages and Welfare,' 83–95, for his estimates of Aboriginal labour in the canning industry.

173 *Mainland Guardian*, 11 August 1877.

174 Canada Sessional Papers, 1878, Fisheries Annual Report 1877, p. 306.

175 *Mainland Guardian*, 18 August 1877. See 22 September and 14 November 1877 for reports on other canneries. See also Muszynski, *Cheap Wage Labour.*

176 Philip Drucker, *The Native Brotherhoods: Modern Intertribal Organizations on the Northwest Coast* (Washington: U.S. Govt. Printing Office, 1958), 123.

177 *Mainland Guardian*, 26 September 1877.

178 Hendrickson, *Journals of the Colonial Legislatures, Vol. 5, Journals of the Legislative Council of British Columbia, 1866–1871*, 567–8.

179 John Lutz, 'After the Fur Trade: The Aboriginal Labouring Class of British Columbia, 1849–1890,' *Journal of the Canadian Historical Association* (1992): 81. Lutz, *Work, Wages and Welfare*, chap. 10, does take care to chronicle the dispossession of Native resources.

180 *Mainland Guardian*, 3 July 1878.

181 For a map of the British Columbia canneries, including their dates, see Edward N. Higginbottom, 'The Changing Geography of Salmon Canning in British Columbia, 1870–1931,' MA thesis, Simon Fraser University, 1988. See also Newell, *Tangled Webs*, 16–20; and Newell, 'Dispersal and Concentration: The Slowly Changing Spatial Pattern of the British Columbia Salmon Canning Industry,' *Journal of Historical Geography* 14 (1988): 22–36.

182 Order-in-Council, 11 June 1879, *Canada Gazette*, vol. 12, 1616.

183 Canada Sessional Papers, 1883, Fisheries Annual Report 1882, p. 190.

184 BC Sessional Papers, 1905, p. F-46, Prefontaine to Fred J. Fulton, 12 January 1905.

185 *Mainland Guardian*, 10 March 1883.

186 Canada Sessional Papers, 1878, Fisheries Annual Report 1877, p. 290.

187 *Journals of the Legislative Assembly of British Columbia*, 1878, 15.

188 Canada Sessional Papers, 1894, Fisheries Annual Report 1893, pp. cxxiii–cxxvii, 'Report on Salmon Culture by the British Columbia Board of Trade,' 20 January 1882.

189 Ibid., p. cxxi.

190 Ibid.

191 The Board of Trade report included the following statement: 'Another important reason for guarding against a dimunition of the salmon supply exists in the fact that a large Indian population depends upon it as its main article of support. This does not apply only to the Indian residents on rivers, but also to those on the coast, on islands, and in parts of the interior, as the river Indians catch and dry large quantities of salmon which they barter with other Indians who cannot obtain this essential

article for themselves, and should salmon become extinct in the rivers, or be so seriously reduced in quantity as to cause destitution among the Indian population, it would be a serious matter for the Government to provide means of support for those Indians' (p. cxxvi).

192 Canada Sessional Papers, 1879, Fisheries Annual Report 1878, p. 293.

193 Ibid., 1882, Fisheries Annual Report 1881, 203.

194 NAC, DIA, RG 10, vol. 3651, file 8540, Anderson to Minister of Fisheries, 3 January 1878.

195 *Johnson's Dictionary of the English Language* (London: 1882).

196 *A New English Dictionary* (Oxford: Clarendon Press, 1909). This was the first edition of what became the *Oxford English Dictionary* in 1933.

197 Ibid. (emphasis added).

198 This distinction is noted elsewhere. Henry Reynolds, *The Law of the Land* (Ringwood: Penguin Books Australia Ltd, 1987), 140, describes British officials referring to Aboriginal rights, while their colonial counterparts in Australia spoke of granted privileges. In the aftermath of the enclosures in eighteenth-century England, J.M. Neeson, *Commoners: Common Right, Enclosure and Social Change in Common-field England, 1700–1820* (New York: Cambridge University Press, 1993), 184, argues that commoners were required to ask permission to gather the wood, berries, nuts, and grain that were now behind fences; '[t]hey were gathering as a privilege not a right.'

199 Ware, *Five Issues, Five Battlegrounds*, 18.

200 See Cole Harris, *Making Native Space: Colonialism, Resistance, and Reserves in British Columbia*, forthcoming. See also Robert E. Cail, *Land, Man and the Law* (Vancouver: University of British Columbia Press, 1974); Fisher, *Contact and Conflict*; Paul Tennant, *Aboriginal People and Politics* (Vancouver: UBC Press, 1990); Hamar Foster, 'Letting Go the Bone: The Idea of Indian Title in British Columbia, 1849–1927,' in Hamar Foster and John Mclaren, eds., *Essays in the History of Canadian Law*, Vol. 6, *British Columbia and the Yukon* (Toronto: The Osgoode Society for Canadian Legal History, 1995), 87–127.

201 Canada Sessional Papers, 1886, Fisheries Annual Report 1885, p. 275.

202 Ibid., 1887, Fisheries Annual Report 1886, p. 248.

203 Statement of Rev. A.E. Green, 27 November 1888, *Letter from the Methodist Missionary Society to the Superintendent-General of Indian Affairs respecting British Columbia Troubles: with affidavits, declarations, etc.* (Toronto, 1889), appendix p. 14.

204 Canada Sessional Papers, 1888, Fisheries Annual Report 1887, p. 253.

205 Wilson Duff, ed., *Histories, Territories, and Laws of the Kitwancool*, Anthro-

pology in British Columbia, Memoir no. 4 (Victoria: Royal British Columbia Museum, 1959, 1989), 36.

206 Canada Sessional Papers, 1889, Fisheries Annual Report 1888, p. 243.

207 Ibid., pp. 249–50.

208 This dispute over licences on the Nass bears unmistakable similarity to the dispute between the Dominion and Ontario governments over the right to issue timber licences that led to the leading nineteenth-century case on Native rights in Canada, *St. Catherine's Milling*. In that case the province objected to the Dominion's granting of a timber licence on Crown land, just as the Nisga'a were objecting to the granting of a Dominion fisheries licence on Nisga'a land.

209 Douglas to the Colonial Office, 15 July 1857, cited in Barman, *The West Beyond the West*, 64.

210 Canada Sessional Papers, 1878, Fisheries Annual Report 1877, pp. 297–8.

211 NAC, DIA, RG 10, vol. 3662, file 9756, pt. 1.

212 See Douglas Harris, 'The Nlha7kápmx Meeting at Lytton, 1879, and the Rule of Law,' *BC Studies* 108 (1995/6): 5–25.

213 Federal Collection of Minutes of Decision, Correspondence and Sketches, Vol. 2, Letterbook no. 3, Gilbert Malcolm Sproat, February 1879 to September 1879, copy held by DIA, Vancouver Regional Office.

214 NAC, DIA, RG 10, vol. 3802, file 50,341.

215 Ibid., vol. 3766, file 32,876, Memorial of the Chiefs of the Upper Nass Villages to Powell, August 1881.

216 NAC, DIA, RG 10, vol. 11,021, file 538C.

217 Order-in-Council, 26 November 1888, *Canada Gazette*, vol. 22, 956. Except for a short section closing the trout fishery from 15 October to 15 March, all the remaining provisions pertained only to the salmon fishery. They were as follows:

2. Meshes of nets used for capturing Salmon shall be at least six inches extension measure, and nothing shall be done to practically diminish their size.

3. (a) Drifting with salmon nets shall be confined to tidal waters, and no salmon net of any kind shall be used for Salmon in fresh waters.

(b) Drift nets shall not be used so as to obstruct more than one-third of any river.

(c) Fishing for salmon shall be discontinued from 6 o'clock a.m. on Saturday to 6 o'clock a.m. on the following Monday ...

4. (a) Before any salmon net, fishing boat or other fishing apparatus shall be used, the owner or persons interested in such net, fishing boat or

fishing apparatus shall cause a Memorandum in writing setting forth the name of the owner or person interested, the length of the net, boat or other fishing apparatus and its intended location, to be filed with the Inspector of Fisheries who, if no valid objection exists, may, in accordance with instructions from the Minister of Marine and Fisheries, issue a fishery license ...

(b) All salmon nets and fishing boats shall have the name of the owner or owners marked on two pieces of wood or metal attached to the same ...

5. The Minister of Marine and Fisheries shall, from time to time, determine the number of boats, seines, or nets, or other fishing apparatus to be used in any of the waters of British Columbia.

It had been the policy in Upper Canada since 1859 to exempt Indians from licence fees if they were catching fish for domestic consumption, but the close seasons still applied. See Hansen, 'Treaty Fishing Rights,' 6–7.

218 Order-in-Council, 3 March 1894, *Canada Gazette*, vol. 27, 1579.
218 Ware, *Five Issues, Five Battlegrounds*, 7; Newell, *Tangled Webs*, 62.
220 Canada Sessional Papers, 1890, Fisheries Annual Report 1889, p. 257.
221 Ibid., 1891, Fisheries Annual Report 1890, p. 187.
222 Ibid., 1892, Fisheries Annual Report 1891, p. 167.
223 NAC, DIA, RG 10, vol. 3849, file 75,317, Department of Fisheries to the Department of Indian Affairs, April 1891.
224 Canada Sessional Papers, Fisheries Annual Report, 1893, p. 285.
225 Ibid.
226 NAC, DIA, RG 10, vol. 3828, file 60,926, Mowat to John Tilton, Deputy Minister of Fisheries, 17 October 1889.
227 Ibid., vol. 3849, file 75,317, A.W. Vowell to L. Vankoughnet, Deputy Supt. Gen. Indian Affairs, February 1891.
228 Ibid., S.P. Bauset, Acting Deputy Minister of Fisheries, to L. Vankoughnet, 4 February 1891.
229 Canada Sessional Papers, 1888, Fisheries Annual Report 1887, p. 257.
230 Ibid., 1889, Fisheries Annual Report, 1888.
231 *Fishery Regulations for the Province of British Columbia*, Order-in-Council, 14 March 1890, *Canada Gazette, vol. 23*, 1903. See the discussion in Meggs, *Salmon*, 32–47.
232 Ibid., Order-in-Council, 3 March 1894, *Canada Gazette, vol. 37*, 1579.
233 BC Sessional Papers, 1905, Prefontaine to Fulton, 12 January 1905.
234 Canada Sessional Papers, 1894, Fisheries Annual Report 1893, p. cxxxvi.
235 NAC, DIA, RG 10, vol. 3828, file 60,926, Robert Sedgwick, Deputy Minister of Justice to John Tilton, Deputy Minister of Fisheries, 15 August 1890.

236 Ibid., M.K. Morrison, Fishery Guardian to Thomas Mowat, Inspector of Fisheries, 21 August 1890.
237 Canada Sessional Papers, 1891, Fisheries Annual Report 1890, Supplement no. 1, app. F, British Columbia, p. 179. Each case contained the industry standard of 48 one-lb. tins.
238 NAC, DIA, RG 10, vol. 3828, file 60,926, Charles Tupper, Minister of Marine and Fisheries to Edgar Dewdney, Minister of the Interior, 3 August 1891.
239 Ibid., L. Vankoughnet, Deputy Supt. Gen. Indian Affairs, to Dewdney, 7 August 1891.
240 Ibid., Tupper to Dewdney, 24 August 1891.
241 Ibid. (emphasis added).
242 Ibid., Dewdney to Vankoughnet, 27 August 1891.
243 Order-in-Council, 3 March 1894, Canada Gazette, vol. 27, 1579 (emphasis added).
244 E.P. Thompson, Customs in Common: Studies in Traditional Popular Culture (New York: New Press, 1993), 160–1, describes customary uses in England becoming 'less of right than by grace' by the end of the eighteenth century.
245 (1888), 14 App. Cas. 46 (J.C.P.C.); denying an appeal from the Supreme Court of Canada (1887), 13 S.C.R. 557; upholding the lower court decisions of the Ontario Court of Appeal (1886), 13 O.A.R. 148, and Chancellor Boyd at trial (1885), 10 O.R. 196 (Ch.). In 1873, under the terms of Treaty 3, the Ojibway ceded part of their land to the Dominion Government. A portion of that land was subsequently included within the provincial boundaries of Ontario. The Dominion Government issued a permit to the St. Catherine's Milling & Lumber Co. to cut timber within the ceded lands, and Ontario disputed the right of the Dominion Government to issue the permit. The Dominion argued that by virtue of section 91(24) of the BNA Act, 1867 it had jurisdiction over 'Indians and land reserved for Indians.' The Privy Council held that on the basis of the Royal Proclamation of 1763, which reserved land for Indians, the Dominion did have jurisdiction over the territory, but once the Indian title was ceded under treaty, the province acquired the beneficial interest. For discussions of the legal arguments, court decisions, and political context see Donald B. Smith, 'Aboriginal Rights in 1885: A Study of the St. Catherine's Milling or Indian Title Case,' in R.C. Macleod, ed., Swords and Ploughshares: War and Agriculture in Western Canada (Edmonton: University of Alberta Press, 1993); and Sidney L. Harring, White Man's Law: Native People in Nineteenth-Century Canadian Jurisprudence (Toronto: Osgoode Society for Canadian Legal History, 1999).

246 *A.G. and I.B. Nash v. John Tait (4 Metlakatla Indians)*, Begbie Bench Books, vol. 13, 28 October 1886 (BCA), cited in Foster, 'Letting Go the Bone,' 66.
247 See discussion in chapter 3.
248 Canada Sessional Papers, 1893, British Columbia Fishery Commission 1892, Minutes of Evidence, p. 130.
249 Ibid., p. 392.
250 Ibid., p. 395.
251 Knight, *Indians at Work*, 179–206. Leona Marie Sparrow, 'Work Histories of a Coast Salish Couple,' MA thesis, University of British Columbia, 1976. James Spradley, *Guests Never Leave Hungry: The Autobiography of James Sewid, A Kwakiutl Indian* (New Haven: Yale University Press, 1969). Meggs and Stacey, *Cork Lines*.
252 Newell, *Tangled Webs*, 53–4, 66–97.

Chapter 2: Fish Weirs and Legal Cultures on Babine Lake

   1 The dispute over fish weirs on the Babine is little discussed in the existing literature. The only published account longer than a few pages appears in Geoff Meggs, *Salmon: The Decline of the British Columbia Fishery* (Vancouver: Douglas & McIntyre, 1991, 1995), 74–80. Dianne Newell includes a brief account in *Tangled Webs of History: Indians and the Law in Canada's Pacific Coast Fisheries* (Toronto: University of Toronto Press, 1993), 91–4. For unpublished accounts see Barbara Lane, 'Federal Recognition of Indian Fishing Rights in British Columbia,' prepared for the Union of B.C. Indian Chiefs, April 1978; Brendan O'Donnell, 'Indian and Non-Native Use of the Babine River: An Historical Perspective' (Dept. of Fisheries and Oceans, Native Affairs Division, Issue 2, Policy and Program Planning, August 1987); and Jos C. Dyck, '"And Then We Will Mind the Law": The Enforcement of Federal Fisheries Regulations in British Columbia and the Resistance of Native Fishers, 1894–1916,' MA thesis, Simon Fraser University, 1994.
   2 D.A. Levy and K.J. Hall, *A Review of the Limnology and Sockeye Salmon Ecology of Babine Lake* (Vancouver: UBC, Westwater Research Centre, 1985).
   3 Jo-Anne Fiske and Betty Patrick, *'C'is dideen khat' When the Plumes Rise: The Way of the Lake Babine Nation* (Vancouver: UBC Press, 2000), is the principal source for the following discussion. June McCue, who holds the name of Neklh in the Bear Clan, provided many comments and much general encouragement. Her recent LLM thesis, 'Treaty-Making from an Indigenous Perspective: A Ned'u'ten-Canadian Treaty Model' (University

of British Columbia, 1998), provides a framework for contemporary treaty negotiations between the Ned'u'ten Nation and the Canadian state. See also Margaret L. Tobey, 'Carrier,' in June Helm, ed., *Handbook of North American Indians, Vol. 6, Subarctic* (Washington: Smithsonian Institution, 1981); J.C. Hackler, 'Factors Leading to Social Disorganization among the Carrier Indians at Lake Babine,' MA thesis, San Diego State, 1958; Michael Kew, 'Notes on Indian Communities on Babine Lake,' 1954; archived at Special Collections, UBC; and Wilson Duff, *The Indian History of British Columbia*, vol. 1, *The Impact of the White Man* (Victoria: Royal British Columbia Museum, 1969).

4 Although only a few kilometres apart, Stuart Lake and Babine Lake drain in opposite directions. Stuart Lake empties into the Fraser River and is hundreds of kilometres further up that system than Babine Lake is up the Skeena River system. Consequently, the sockeye run on the Babine was more reliable and abundant that the Start run, and the HBC fort on Babine Lake regularly supplied neighbouring Fort St James with fish.

5 Fiske and Patrick, *When the Plumes Rise*, 50.

6 Ibid., 127–33.

7 Kew, *Notes*, 6.

8 Arthur J. Ray, 'Fur Trade History and the Gitksan-Wet'suwet'en Comprehensive Claim: Men of Property and the Exercise of Title,' in Kerry Abel and Jean Friesen, eds., *Aboriginal Resource Use in Canada: Historical and Legal Aspects* (Winnipeg: University of Manitoba Press, 1991), 301–15, makes a similar argument based largely on William Brown's records at Fort Kilmaurs.

9 NAC, DIA, RG 10, vol. 6972, file 901/20-2, pt. 1, R.E. Loring to A.W. Vowell, 1 April 1905.

10 Hackler, 'Social Disorganization,' 44, identifies Big George as *Dewisimdzik*, but this is refuted by several Babine chiefs. See Fiske and Patrick, *When the Plumes Rise*, 49.

11 NAC, Dept. of Marine and Fisheries (DMF), RG 23, file 583, pt. 1, transcript, Ottawa conference, 25 October 1906, pp. 3–8.

12 Given that access to resources is at stake, the nature of ownership is not only of anthropological interest but is contested today within the Lake Babine Nation. Fiske and Patrick, *When the Plumes Rise*, 207, comment about the divisions within the contemporary society: 'While at least one hereditary chief argues that the fishery was always a resource controlled by *Likhtsemisyu*, with final authority and control over revenues accruing to the chief whose lands surround the traditional fishing ground, others assert the opposite. They suggest that a communal right was vested in the village as a whole, and they differ as to whether or not residents of Fort

Babine, the closest village, retained any advantages over the residents of the Old Fort.'

13 HBCA, B 11/a/3, Fort Kilmaurs Journal, 8 and 12 September 1825.

14 Fiske and Patrick, *When the Plumes Rise*, 57.

15 Population figures from Canada Sessional Papers, 1905, DIA Annual Report 1904, 215.

16 BCA, A/C/20/Vi3F, Ft. Victoria Correspondence Outward, Roderick Finalyson to O'Reilly, Gold Commisioner, 29 May 1871. The post is widely reported to have moved to the north end of the lake in 1835, but this is incorrect. The HBC did not use Finalyson's survey, instead building its post just south of the Babine village that Finlayson labelled 'Hootat' village. Thanks to Robert Galois for providing this reference.

17 Fiske and Patrick, *Where the Plumes Rise*, 40.

18 BCA, B/G/47, George Dawson diary entry, 29 June 1879 (emphasis in original). Thanks to Robert Galois for providing this reference.

19 Federal Collection of Minutes of Decision, Correspondence & Sketches, vol. 13, P. O'Reilly (Indian Reserve Commissioner), May 1889 to October 1894, file 29858, vol. 7 [Indian Land Registry no. B-64648]. Copy held by the DIA Vancouver Regional Office.

20 Ibid.

21 NAC, DIA, RG 10, vol. 3571, file 126, pt. A, Loring to A.W. Vowell, Supt. of Indian Affairs, 24 September 1894.

22 Helgesen, a member of the legislative assembly in the 1880s, described himself as a fisherman at the November 1906 conference at the DMF in Ottawa. In 1905 and 1906, in partnership with John Witty and Albert A. Argyle, he held foreshore fishing-station leases on the southwest coast of Vancouver Island, Metchosin District; BCA, GR 1402, box 5, file 20, and box 6, file 14.

23 NAC, DMF, RG 23, file 23, Inspector Williams to R.N. Venning, Assistant Commissioner of Fisheries, 19 January 1907.

24 Ibid., file 1469, pt. 1, Fisheries Guardians to Raymond Prefontaine, Minister of Marine and Fisheries, 22 August 1904.

25 Canada Sessional Papers, 1877, DMF Annual Report (Fisheries Annual Report) 1876, 339. For a short description of each cannery operating on the north coast see Gladys Young Blyth, *Salmon Canneries: British Columbia North Coast* (Lantzville: Oolichan Books, 1991). For cannery locations, including dates, see the maps in Edward N. Higginbottom, 'The Changing Geography of Salmon Canning in British Columbia, 1870–1931,' MA thesis, Simon Fraser University, September 1988. See also Newell, *Tangled Webs*, 17.

26 Canada Sessional Papers, 1906, Fisheries Annual Report 1905, p. 219.

27 UBC, Special Collections, Henry Doyle Papers, Doyle to Prefontaine, 15 August 1904.
28 Canada Sessional Papers, 1904, Fisheries Annual Report 1902, p. 212.
29 NAC, DMF, RG 23, file 2235, pt. 2, Peter Wallace, Wallace Brothers Packing Company, Claxton, Skeena River, to the Honourable William Sloan, MP for Skeena, 11 April 1905.
30 Skeena District News (Port Essington), 11 July 1904. The strike is also reported on 27 June and 4 July.
31 NAC, DMF, RG 23, file 23, E.E. Prince to J.T. Williams, 17 September 1904.
32 Canada Sessional Papers, 1906, Fisheries Annual Report, p. 206.
33 Ibid.
34 Robert Galois, 'The History of the Upper Skeena Region, 1850 to 1927,' Native Studies Review 9 (1993–4): 142.
35 Evidence Submitted to the British Columbia Fisheries Commission (Victoria: Times Publishing and Printing Co., 1906), 419 and 208, testimony of John T. Williams and Peter Wallace, 18 November 1905. Helgesen corroborates this view in the Ottawa meeting of 6 November 1906.
36 HBCA, B.11/a/7, Babine Post Journals 1899–1905, record that Big George left Fort Babine on 7 September packing goods, and did not return until 22 September.
37 NAC, DMF, RG 23, file 583, pt. 1. At the Ottawa conference, 25 October 1906, the person Helgesen identified as Chief Atio is identified as Tszak William. However, later in the conference Chief Big George stated that Atio was not a chief but just an elderly man present at the weirs whom Helgesen decided to consult.
38 Canada Sessional Papers, 1906, Fisheries Annual Report, p. 207. Iktahs is a Chinook word for basic supplies such as flour, sugar, ammunition, etc. Joseph E. and Anne D. Forester, Fishing: British Columbia's Commercial Fishing History (Saanichton, BC: Hancock House Publishers Ltd, 1975), 210–14, reproduce a long section of Helgesen's report and conclude: 'The laws were upheld – ancient rights were not.'
39 Fisheries Act, R.S.C. 1886, c. 95, s. 14:

    (4) The main channel or course of any stream shall not be obstructed by any nets or other fishing apparatus; and one-third of the course of any river or stream, and not less than two-thirds of the main channel at low tide, in every tidal stream shall be always left open and no kind of fishing apparatus or material shall be used or placed therein ...
    (5) No net or other device shall be so used as entirely to obstruct the passage of fish to or from any of the waters of Canada, by any of the

ordinary channels connecting such waters, or prevent their passage to and from accustomed resorts for spawning and increasing their species.

40 *Fisheries Act*, R.S.C. 1886, c. 95, s. 8(5), as amended by 52 Vic., c. 24, s. 1.

41 Ibid., s. 18, as amended by 57–8 Vic., c. 51, s. 7; 61 Vic., c. 39, s. 3.

42 NAC, DMF, RG 23, file 2235, pt. 2, appendix to Helgesen's report of 24 November 1905.

43 Canada Sessional Papers, 1906, Fisheries Annual Report, p. 211. The identity of this person is unclear. Helgesen appears to have known Big George and would likely have identified him if it were him.

44 Morice indicated that the letters came from 'the head chief of the Babine tribe,' but he does not indicate whom that was. For an account of Father A.G. Morice's remarkable life as a missionary, linguist, historian, and cartographer, see David Mulholland, *The Will to Power: The Missionary Career of Father Morice* (Vancouver: UB Press, 1986). For Morice's own version, published under the pseudonym 'D.L.S.,' see *Fifty Years in Western Canada: The Abridged Memoirs of Father A.G. Morice, O.M.I.* (Toronto: Ryerson Press, 1930).

45 NAC, DMF, RG 23, file 583, pt. 1, p. 167, Morice to Vowell, 2 July 1905 (emphasis in original).

46 Ibid., F. Pedley, Deputy Supt. Gen. Indian Affairs, to F. Gourdeau, Deputy Minister of Fisheries, 14 July 1905.

47 Ibid., Gourdeau to Pedley, 31 July 1905.

48 NAC, DMF, RG 23, file 23, E.E. Prince, Dominion Commissioner of Fisheries, to J.T. Williams, Inspector of Fisheries, 23 June 1905. Harry Frank did not accept the commission and was replaced by J. Wells.

49 Ibid., file 583, pt. 1, Morice to Indian Supt., 15 July 1905. Minister of Fisheries Brodeur claimed at the November 1906 meeting that Morice went to Ottawa to intercede on behalf of the Babine.

50 Ibid., Coccola to Pedley, 6 September 1906.

51 Fisheries spent $1150 on another tributary of the Skeena in 1905 to remove a log-jam. NAC, DMF, RG 23, file 2235, pt. 2.

52 NAC, DMF, RG 23, file 23, Helgesen to the Honourable William Sloan, MP for Skeena, 3 May 1905.

53 Ibid., file 583, pt. 1, Pedley to Gourdeau, 15 June 1905.

54 Ibid., file 23, E.E. Prince, 'Memo. re: Indian Obstructions, Skeena River B.C.,' 21 June 1905.

55 Coccola wrote an account of his life that has been published in a book edited by Margaret Whitehead, *They Call Me Father: Memoirs of Father Nicolas Coccola* (Vancouver: UBC Press, 1988). A biography of Coccola

appeared in serial form every Thursday in *The Cranbrook Courier* from January to April 1927. For a version of the weir dispute that places Coccola firmly in the centre, see the entries for March 31 and April 7 1927.

56 Brett Christophers, *Positioning the Missionary* (Vancouver: UBC Press, 1998), describes the relation between the Nlha7kápmx and the Anglican missionary at Lytton, J.B. Good, noting that the Nlha7kápmx initially perceived him as useful in their relations with the larger white settler society, but they later turned to the representatives of the Queen for assistance, specifically Gilbert Malcolm Sproat, the Indian Reserve Commissioner. See also Douglas Harris, 'The Nlha7kápmx Meeting at Lytton, 1879, and the Rule of Law,' *BC Studies* 108 (1995/6): 5–25.

57 NAC, DMF, RG 23, file 3031, Helgesen to Williams, 30 July 1905.

58 Ibid., file 583, pt. 1, Helgesen to Williams, 19 October 1905.

59 Ibid., file 3031 (or file 2235, pt. 2), Helgesen to Williams, 24 November 1905.

60 Canada Sessional Papers, 1907, no. 22, Fisheries Inspector's Report, District no. 2, 1905, p. 31.

61 NAC, DMF, RG 23, file 583, pt. 1, Coccola, transcript, Ottawa conference, 6 November 1906, p. 16.

62 There is no record of any trade in salmon in the HBC Fort Babine journal for 1905.

63 NAC, DMF, RG 23, file 583, pt. 1, Coccola to Pedley, 8 September 1906.

64 Ibid., file 3031, Helgesen to Williams, 24 November 1905.

65 Order-in-Council, 3 March 1894, *Canada Gazette*, vol. 23, p. 1903, *Fishery Regulations for the Province of British Columbia*:

> s. 6   No nets of any kind shall be used for catching any kind of salmon in the inland lakes or in the fresh or non-tidal waters of rivers or streams. But Indians may, with the permission of the inspector of fisheries, use dip-nets for the purpose of providing food for themselves and their families, but for no other purposes.

66 NAC, DMF, RG 23, file 3031, R.N. Venning, Assistant Commissioner of Fisheries, to Prince, 15 August 1905.

67 Ibid., file 583, pt. 1, Pedley to Gourdeau, 15 September 1905.

68 Ibid., file 3031, Helgesen to Williams, 19 October 1906.

69 Ibid., Williams to Prince, 5 January 1905.

70 NAC, DMF, RG 23, file 583, pt. 1, Loring to Vowell, 27 August 1906.

71 Ibid., Helgesen to Williams, 19 October 1906. The names appear as 'Duncan' and 'Hall' in NAC, DMF, RG 23, file 583, pt. 1, Loring to Vowell, 27 August 1906, and as 'Duncan Paquet' and 'Hal Louis' in the transcript of the Ottawa conference, 6 November 1906, p. 27.

72 NAC, DMF, RG 23, file 583, pt. 1, transcript, Ottawa conference, 25 October 1906, p. 13.

73 Ibid., Helgesen summarizes Wells's report in a letter to Williams, 21 October 1906.

74 Fiske and Patrick, *When the Plumes Rise*, 143–4.

75 NAC, DMF, RG 23, file 583, pt. 1.

76 BCA, GR 429, 1906, box 13, file 4, 2578/06.

77 *Daily News* (New Westminster) and *Daily Colonist* (Victoria), 30 August 1906.

78 NAC, DMF, RG 23, file 583, pt. 1, Venning memo 'Trouble with Babine Indians,' 18 September 1906.

79 Ibid., memo of 30 August 1906 summarizing letter from Vowell, 7 February 1905.

80 Ibid., Loring to Vowell, 27 August 1906.

81 Ibid., 30 August 1906.

82 BCA, GR 429, 1906, box 13, file 4, 2578/06, Provincial Government Agent in Port Essington to the Deputy Attorney General of British Columbia, 15 September 1906, provides one example of a calmer response:

'I found that the reports which had reached the Coast had been greatly exaggerated and that, although a technical assault had been committed, there was not, nor had there been at any time, any serious danger of the Babines or any other of the Skeena tribes going on the warpath.'

83 *Daily Colonist* (Victoria), 9 September 1906.

84 NAC, DMF, RG 23, file 583, pt. 1, Loring to Vowell, 30 August 1906.

85 Ibid., Helgesen to Williams, 19 October 1906.

86 Ibid., Acting Deputy Supt. Gen. Indian Affairs to Deputy Minister of Marine & Fisheries, 18 September 1906, reproducing contents of the telegram dated 17 September 1906.

87 Ibid., Deputy Supt. Gen. Indian Affairs to Deputy Minister of Fisheries, 27 September 1906, reproducing contents of telegram.

88 Ibid., transcript, Ottawa conference, 26 October 1906, p. 12.

89 *The Province* (Vancouver), 29 September 1906. Thanks to Matthew Evenden for sharing his notes and for alerting me to this and other newspaper accounts in the Scrapbooks of the Fraser River Canners' Association, Papers of the International Pacific Salmon Fisheries Commission, UBC Special Collections.

90 Archives Deschâtelets, Ottawa, 'Reminiscences of the Rev. Father Coccola,' dictated by Father Coccola while in St Paul's Hospital in Vancouver, August–September 1924, recorded and transcribed by Deny Nelson.

91 *The Province* (Vancouver), 29 September 1906.

92 *The World* (Vancouver), 6 October 1906.

93 NAC, DMF, RG 23, file 583, pt. 1, J.D. McLean, Acting Deputy Superintendent General, to the Deputy Minister of Justice, 4 October 1906.

94 Ibid., Helgesen to Williams, 6 October 1906.

95 *The World* (Vancouver), 20 October 1906.

96 Ibid., 7 November 1906.

97 See David Ricardo Williams, *Trapline Outlaw: Simon Peter Gunanoot* (Victoria: Sono Nis Press, 1982).

98 Whitehead, *They Call Me Father*, 145.

99 NAC, DMF, RG 23, file 583, pt. 1, transcript, Ottawa conference, 25 October 1906, p. 3.

100 Ibid.

101 Ibid., transcript, Ottawa conference, 6 November 1906, p. 3.

102 Ibid., p. 6.

103 *Fisheries Act*, R.S.C. 1886, ss. 14(4) and (5).

104 Ibid., s. 14(8), and *Fishery Regulations for the Province of British Columbia*, 1894, ss. 1(a) and 6.

105 *Fisheries Act*, R.S.C. 1886, s. 8(5), as amended 52 Vic., c. 24, s. 1.

106 NAC, DMF, RG 23, file 583, pt. 1, transcript, Ottawa conference, 6 November 1906, 13. In fact, the *Regulations* allowed the Fisheries Inspector to issue food-fishing permits for a weir fishery.

107 Ibid., p. 15.

108 NAC, DMF, RG 23, file 583, pt. 1, Alex Noble of Port Essington to Deputy of Marine and Fisheries, 23 October 1906.

109 Canada Sessional Papers, 1903, Fisheries Inspector's Report 1901, p. 178.

110 Ibid., 1906, Fisheries Inspector's Report 1905, pp. 220–2.

111 NAC, DMF, RG 23, file 583, pt. 1, Fraser River Canners' Association to the Minister of Marine and Fisheries, 30 October 1906.

112 Canada Sessional Papers, 1882, Fisheries Inspector's Report 1881, p. 220.

113 On this point more generally see Alicja Muszynski, *Cheap Wage Labour: Race and Gender in the Fisheries of British Columbia* (Montreal and Kingston: McGill-Queen's University Press, 1996).

114 NAC, DMF, RG 23, file 583, pt. 1, transcript, Ottawa conference, 6 November 1906, p. 21.

115 Ibid., Oliver to Brodeur, 8 November 1906.

116 Ibid.

117 NAC, GR 2759, B9870, f. 881-1, pt. 1, attached in a letter from Coccola to DIA, received 10 November 1906.

118 Ibid., Brodeur to Oliver, 23 November 1906.

119 Ibid.

120 NAC, DMF, RG 23, file 583, pt. 1, Brodeur to Oliver, 14 January 1907.

121 Ibid., Indian Affairs to Brodeur, 9 February 1907.

122 Ibid., Fisheries to Williams, 19 February 1907, and to Coccola, 21 February 1907.

123 Ibid., Coccola to Minister of Fisheries Brodeur, 10 June 1907.

124 Ibid., Deputy Supt. Gen. Indian Affairs to Deputy Minister of Marine and Fisheries, 20 July 1907.

125 Canada Sessional Papers, 1909, Fisheries Annual Report 1907–8, p. 219.

126 NAC, DMF, RG 23, file 583, pt. 1, Williams to Assistant Commissioner of Fisheries, 23 July 1907.

127 Department of Mines and Resources, Indian Affairs Branch, 'Schedule of Indian Reserves in the Dominion of Canada, Part 2, Reserves in the Province of British Columbia,' 31 March 1943. Copy held by DIA, regional office, Vancouver.

128 These distinctions are potentially important given the recent Supreme Court of Canada decision in *R. v. Nikal*, [1996] 3 C.N.L.R. 178, where Justice Cory held that the Wet'suwet'en at Moricetown did not have an exclusive fishery on the Bulkley River because the Crown had never intended to grant an exclusive fishery when it allocated the reserve. Peter O'Reilly allotted the Wet'suwet'en reserve in question on 18 September 1891, the day before he allotted reserves for the Babine. The reserve included both banks of the river, and the presumption under common law is that the owner of land bordering on a river owns the riverbed to the mid-point and the right to fish above it (*ad medium filum aquae*). The fishing rights may be severed from ownership, and Cory J. ruled that because the Crown had never intended to grant an exclusive fishery with the reserve, the Wet-suwet'en could not claim exclusive fishing rights. Cory J. also held that the Bulkley River was navigable and that the *ad medium filum aquae* presumption did not apply to navigable rivers in British Columbia. The Crown allotted the Babine reserves in 1908, however, as part of an arrangement to secure to the Babine a net fishery.

129 NAC, DMF, RG 23, file 583, pt. 1, p. 542, Helgesen, 12 October 1908.

130 *Dominion–British Columbia Fisheries Commission, 1905–7. Report and Recommendations* (Ottawa: Government Printing Bureau 1908), 66.

131 NAC, DMF, RG 23, file 583, pt. 1, p. 551, Norrie to Williams, 6 July 1909.

132 *Trade Register*, 22 August 1910; copy found in University of British Columbia, Special Collections, Papers of the International Pacific Salmon Commission, Fraser River Canner's Association Scrapbooks, 5 August 1910 to 21 August 1911, p. 8. See also Meggs, *Salmon*, 74–80.

Chapter 3: The Law Runs Through It

1 Historians have paid some attention to Cowichan protests. See R.M. Galois, 'The Indian Rights Association, Native Protest Activity and the "Land Question" in British Columbia, 1903–1916,' *Native Studies Review* 8 (1992): 1–34; Daniel P. Marshall, *Those Who Fell from the Sky: A History of the Cowichan Peoples* (Duncan: Cowichan Tribes, 1999), 146–61. The dispute over fish on the Cowichan River, however, has been remarkably little discussed. See Jos C. Dyck, '"And Then We Will Mind the Law": The Enforcement of Federal Fisheries Regulations in British Columbia and the Resistance of Native Fishers, 1894–1916,' MA thesis, Simon Fraser University, 1994; Brendan O'Donnell, 'Indian and Non-Native Use of the Cowichan and Koksilah Rivers: An Historical Perspective' (Dept. of Fisheries and Oceans, Native Affairs Division, Issue 8, Policy and Program Planning, July 1988); and Marshall, *Those Who Fell from the Sky*, 134–45.

2 See Marshall, *Those Who Fell from the Sky*, 56–8. See also the map in Wayne Suttles, 'Central Coast Salish,' in W. Suttles, ed., *The Handbook of North American Indians*, Vol. 7, *Northwest Coast* (Washington: Smithsonian Institution, 1990), 453–75.

3 See Thomas Hukari, ed., *The Cowichan Dictionary of the Hul'qumi'num' Dialect of the Coast Salish People* (Duncan, B.C.: Cowichan Tribes, 1995); Charles Hill-Tout, 'Report on the Ethnology of the South-Eastern Tribes of Vancouver Island, British Columbia,' *Journal of the Royal Anthropological Institute of Great Britain and Ireland* 37 (1907): 363–4.

4 For what is available, see Barbara Lane, 'A Comparative and Analytic Study of Some Aspects of Northwest Coast Religion,' PhD thesis, University of Washington, 1953.

5 Ronald Rohner, ed., *The Ethnography of Franz Boas: Letters and Diaries of Franz Boas Written on the Northwest Coast from 1886 to 1931* (Chicago: University of Chicago Press, 1969), 54.

6 Marshall, *Those Who Fell from the Sky*.

7 The principal work is Wayne Suttles, *Coast Salish Essays* (Vancouver: Talon Books, 1987). For a brief review of other sources see Suttles, *Handbook of North American Indians*, 475. See also the bibliography in Marshall, *Those Who Fell from the Sky*.

8 Suttles, *Handbook of North American Indians*, 464.

9 Ibid.

10 Ibid.

11 David L. Rozen, 'The Ethnozoology of the Cowichan Indian People of British Columbia, Vol. 1: Fish, Beach Foods, and Marine Mammals' (unpublished, 1978). Archived at the *Xwi7xwa* Library, First Nations

House of Learning, UBC. Rozen gathered his information in the mid-1970s, relying heavily on interviews of Cowichan elders, particularly Abraham Joe, K'eyexkinem, born 1905. See also Edward S. Curtis, *The North American Indian*, vol. 9 (New York: Johnson Reprint Corp., 1913), 39–41.

12 Rozen, *Ethnozoology*, 126–7, indicates the location of six weirs on the lower Cowichan River and seven weirs on the upper river, each with a designated headman. Hilary Stewart, *Indian Fishing: Early Methods on the Northwest Coast* (Vancouver: J.J. Douglas, 1977), 99–110, provides descriptions and illustrations of various weir fisheries.

13 Suttles, *Handbook of North American Indians*, 455. Lane, *Northwest Coast Religion*, includes the inhabitants of these villages in her study of the Cowichan.

14 Leonard M. Bell and Ronald J. Kallman, *The Cowichan-Chemainus River Estuaries: Status of Knowledge to 1975* (West Vancouver, BC: Fisheries and Marine Service Pacific Environment Institute, Environment Canada, 1976), provide a detailed examination of the Cowichan River estuary.

15 Suttles, *Coast Salish Essays*, 20.

16 The rules governing the construction and use of the Cowichan weirs appear generally consistent among other peoples who used weir technology. See Patricia Ann Berringer, 'Northwest Coast Traditional Salmon Fisheries: Systems of Resource Utilization,' MA thesis, University of British Columbia, 1982, pp. 74–84, 195.

17 The following paragraph is drawn from the first two essays in Suttles, *Coast Salish Essays*.

18 Marshall, *Those Who Fell from the Sky*, 9–23.

19 This story is recounted by Rozen from his principal informant, Abraham Joe, in *Ethnozoology*, 28–9, 112–13. Rozen spells the first person's name *Siyóletse*.

20 NAC, DIA, RG 10, vol. 3635, file 7936, George Blenkinsop, 25 January 1877. Quamichan had 317 residents; Somenos, 112; Clemclemeluts, 167; Koksilah, 29; Comiaken, 105; and Khenipsen, 76. Blenkinsop also recorded 6 goats, 55 horses, 437 cattle, 11 sheep, 528 pigs, 56 oxen, 1091 fowls, 3 turkeys, 2 geese, and 10 ducks.

21 Cited in Robin Fisher, *Contact and Conflict: Indian–European Relations in British Columbia, 1774–1890* (Vancouver: UBC Press, 1977, 1992), 55.

22 See Barry M. Gough, *Gunboat Frontier: British Maritime Authority and Northwest Coast Indians, 1846–1890* (Vancouver: UBC Press, 1984), 50–6, 61–8; Marshall, *Those Who Fell from the Sky*, 97–102.

23 Allan Pritchard, ed., *Vancouver Island Letters of Edmund Hope Verney, 1862–1865* (Vancouver: UBC Press, 1996), 81–9, 133–8.

24 The Anglican Superintendent of Indian Missions for Vancouver Island,

Rev. Alexander Charles Garrett to the Surveyor General, reproduced in Elizabeth Blanche Norcross, *The Warm Land* (Duncan: E.B. Norcross, 1959), 15.

25 O'Donnell, 'Indian and Non-Native Use,' 4–21; Marshall, *Those Who Fell from the Sky*, 104–26.

26 *Papers Connected with the Indian Land Question, 1850–1875* (Victoria, BC: Queen's Printer, 1987), 102–6, B.W. Pearse to the Colonial Secretary, 16 October 1871.

27 NAC, DIA, RG 10, vol. 3662, file 9756, pt. 1, G.M. Sproat 'Rough Memorandum on Cowichan Reserves' to the Provincial Attorney General, February 1878.

28 Ibid., Sproat to Supt. Gen. Indian Affairs, 26 April 1878. The province did not formally recognize the Cowichan reserve until 1938, by Order-in-Council 1036.

29 Ibid., Sproat to Indian Superintendant Powell, 22 April 1878.

30 See discussion in chapter 1.

31 NAC, DIA, RG 10, vol. 3662, file 9756, pt. 1, Sutton to McDonald, 29 March 1879.

32 Ibid., Powell to Supt. Gen. Indian Affairs, 21 May 1879.

33 Ibid., Sproat to Supt. Gen. Indian Affairs, 26 July 1879. Sproat had paid both the colonial government and the Nootka for the land on which he built a sawmill in the 1860s; Sproat, *The Nootka: Scenes and Studies of Savage Life* [1868], ed. and annotated by Charles Lillard (Victoria: Sono Nis Press, 1987), 7.

34 NAC, DIA, RG 10, vol. 3662, file 9756, pt. 2.

35 Ibid., pt. 1, Dep. Supt. Gen. Indian Affairs to Powell, 22 November 1879.

36 John F.T. Saywell, *Kaatza: The Chronicles of Cowichan Lake* (Sidney: Cowichan Lake District Centennial Committee, 1967), 25.

37 NAC, DIA, RG 10, vol. 8310, file 974/8-3-3-1(1). O'Donnell, 'Native and Non-Native Use,' 43–4, 49–53, 57–9, provides extended extracts from the primary material.

38 Ibid., vol. 7885, file 36,152-8, Lomas to Vowell, 23 March 1891.

39 BC Sessional Papers, 1893, 283, Davie to Sir John Thompson, 18 November 1892.

40 Canada Sessional Papers, 1895, DIA Annual Report 1894, Lomas to Supt. Gen. Indian Affairs, 24 September 1894.

41 *Victoria Daily Colonist*, 10 February 1894.

42 See Richard Somerset Mackie, *The Wilderness Profound: Victorian Life on the Gulf of Georgia* (Victoria: Sono Nis Press, 1995), 46.

43 Indian Agent W.H. Lomas wrote is his 1882 report: 'I am happy to be able

to report that the number of deaths during the year, although large, has been much less than that of the previous year, being confined chiefly to very young children who have suffered from epidemics of scarlet fever and whooping cough, and to young men, several of whom have died this year from lung diseases.' Canada Sessional Papers, 1883, DIA Annual Report 1882, p. 53. The impact of continuing epidemics is explored in Mary-Ellen Kelm, *Colonizing Bodies: Aboriginal Health and Healing in British Columbia, 1900–1950* (Vancouver: UBC Press, 1998).

44 BC Sessional Papers, 1878, pp. 193–5, 'List of Persons Entitled to Vote in the Electoral District of the Cowichan.' The list includes eligible voters between Shawnigan Lake and Chemainus. I have included only those whose residence is listed as Comiaken, Cowichan, Quamichan, and Somenos.

45 From the 1881 census, Cole Harris and Robert Galois indicate that the average male-to-female ratio in British Columbia was 3:2, but that in the Cowichan Valley 'males only marginally outnumbered females.' Cole Harris, *The Resettlement of British Columbia: Essays in Colonialism and Geographical Change* (Vancouver: UBC Press, 1997), 138, 142.

46 Norcross, *The Warm Land*, p. 15.

47 Ibid., 34; Margaret W. Bishop, *And So They Came to Cowichan* (Victoria: Robinson Press, 1975), 7. My great-grandfather Joseph Colebrook Harris arrived in the Cowichan Valley in 1892, a 21 year old fresh from the Agricultural College in Guelph, to farm. He stayed the better part of four years and attempted to turn a swamp into farmable land. His reminiscences, written in the 1940s, include many accounts of Native participation as labourers in the rural economy and the continuing use of Chinook. BCA, MS 1094.

48 Norcross, *Warm Land*, 1, recorded that one of the earliest settlers, John Humphreys, who arrived before the settlers in 1862, married the daughter of the Quamichan chief.

49 Canada Sessional Papers, 1882, DIA Annual Report 1881. One of the early settlers in the Cowichan Valley, Lomas taught at the Somenos school from 1864 and was the Indian catechist for the Church of England from 1867 to 1874. See David R. Williams, *One Hundred Years at St. Peter's Quamichan* (Duncan, BC: Duncan Print-Craft, 1977), 71–80.

50 Canada Sessional Papers, 1894, DIA Annual Report 1893, p. 117, report from Lomas.

51 Norcross, *Warm Land*, 34, and Bishop, *Cowichan*, 7.

52 Pritchard, *Vancouver Island Letters*, 136, Verney to his father, 5 May 1863. Verney credited the early work of the Roman Catholic church, including

Bishop Modeste Demers, for the relatively peaceful relations. Father Peter Rondeault had been in the valley since the late 1850s and had erected a Roman Catholic Indian mission church, St Ann's, before the settlers arrived.

53 *Papers Connected with the Indian Land Question*, 132–3.
54 Marshall, *Those Who Fell from the Sky*, 104–65.
55 This figure is based on the voters' list for the Cowichan-Alberni Electoral District, 30 May 1894, where approximately 225 adult males are listed as residents in the Cowichan Valley. BC Sessional Papers, 1894, pp. 1363–70.
56 Izaak Walton, *The Complete Angler*, ed. Jonquil Bevan (Oxford: Clarendon Press, 1983).
57 J. Michael Thoms, 'A Place Called Pennask,' *BC Studies* [forthcoming].
58 NAC, DIA, RG 10, vol. 3713, file 20,618, Pittendrigh to Powell, 28 April 1885.
59 Canada Sessional Papers, 1888, Fisheries Annual Report 1887. Lomas continued in his roles as Indian agent and fisheries guardian until 1894, when the conflicts between the positions became too great and he was dismissed from Fisheries service.
60 W.H. Lomas recorded the creation of this elected council in 1881, Canada Sessional Papers, 1882, DIA Annual Report 1881, p. 160. The 'elected' members were almost certainly hereditary chiefs.
61 NAC, DIA, RG 10, vol. 3801, file 49,287, 'Resolutions passed by Cowichan Indian Council June 4th 1888.'
62 Ibid., Lomas to Powell, 18 June 1888.
63 Ibid., Deputy Minister of Fisheries to Powell, 5 July 1888.
64 Order-in-Council, 28 September 1889, *Canada Gazette*, vol. 23, p. 546.
65 Order-in-Council, 7 November 1890, *Canada Gazette*, vol. 24, p. 876. In its 1894 amendment of the *Fishery Regulations*, Fisheries prohibited all commercial net fishing for salmon in British Columbia except by drift net; Order-in-Council, 3 March 1894, *Canada Gazette*, vol. 27, p. 1579. See chapter 1.
66 Canada Sessional Papers, 1888, DIA Annual Report 1887, p. 105.
67 NAC, DIA, RG 10, vol. 3828, f. 60,926, Lomas to McNab, 26 January 1892.
68 Ibid., McNab to S.P. Bauset, Acting Deputy Minister of Fisheries, 29 February 1982.
69 Ibid., Lomas to A.W. Vowell, Indian Superintendent, 31 March 1892.
70 Ibid., McNab to Bauset, 21 April 1892.
71 NAC, DMF, RG23, file 583, pt. 1, McNab to Deputy Minister, 17 February 1894.

72 A justice of the peace or fishery officer also had discretionary authority to reduce any penalty if 'the offence was committed in ignorance of the law, or that because of poverty of the defendant the penalties imposed would be oppressive.' Revised Statutes of Canada 1886, c. 95, s. 18(1).

73 Order-in-Council, 26 November 1888, *Canada Gazette*, vol. 22, p. 956.

74 NAC, DMF, RG 23, file 583, pt. 1, Deputy Minister to McNab, 1 March 1894 and 27 March 1894.

75 Ibid., McNab to Deputy Minister, 9 March 1894.

76 Ibid. Bishop Bermens and the Honourable Theo. Davie presided at the meeting; Indian Superintendent Vowell and Indian Agent Lomas endorsed the protest. See letter from Father Geolbs VanGoethem, 23 June 1895.

77 NAC, DMF, RG 23, file 1600, pt. 1, McNab to Deputy Minister, 17 June 1894.

78 Ibid., file 1469, pt. 1, McNab to Deputy Minister, 25 April 1895.

79 Ibid., Vowell to Deputy Supt. Gen. Indian Affairs, 28 May 1895.

80 Ibid., Lomas to Vowell, 10 June 1895. The defendant's name appears in the *Victoria Daily Colonist*, 28 June 1895.

81 Musgrave brought his family from Ireland to Saltspring Island in 1885, and then in 1892 to the Cowichan Valley, where he established a farm. Although of Irish decent, he had spent much of his life ranching in Argentina. See the entry for his son, John Musgrave, in E.O.S. Scholefield, *British Columbia from the Earliest Times to the Present, Vol. IV* (Vancouver: S.J. Clarke Publishing, 1914). In 1889, J.C. Harris, then an 18-year-old recently arrived from England, lived for a few months with the Musgraves on Saltspring Island. 'Mr Musgrave,' he remembered, 'was rather overwhelming ... very much the old aristocrat and very autocratic in appearance and nature.' BCA, MS-1094.

82 NAC, DMF, RG 23, file 1469, pt. 1, Lomas to Vowell, 10 June 1895.

83 Ibid., Deputy Attorney General, Arthur G. Smith, to Vowell, 12 July 1895.

84 Ibid., McNab to Vowell, 12 June 1895.

85 The regulations made under the authority of the *Fisheries Act* had 'the same force and effect' as the *Act*, 'notwithstanding that such regulations extend, vary or alter any of the provisions of this Act respecting the places or modes of fishing or the times specified as prohibited or close seasons.' Statutes of Canada 1886, c. 95, s. 16.

86 NAC, DMF, RG 23, file 1469, pt. 1, Lomas to Vowell, 17 June 1895.

87 Ibid., file 583, pt. 1. The resolutions were recorded 'in substance,' by Father Geolbs VanGoethem and sent to Vowell, 23 June 1895. The claims of ownership were undoubtedly Cowichan in origin, but the appeal to 'natural rights' was probably the priest's addition.

88 Brief accounts of the trial appear in the *Victoria Daily Times*, 27 June 1895, and the *Victoria Daily Colonist*, 28 June 1895.

89 *Summary Convictions Act*, S.B.C. 1889, c. 26, s. 47, allowed for adjournments, but for not more than one week, and the trial had been adjourned for sixteen days.

90 NAC, DMF, RG 23, file 583, pt. 1, Mills to Tupper, 2 July 1895.

91 *Victoria Daily Times*, 29 June 1895 (emphasis added).

92 NAC, DMF, RG 23, file 583, pt. 1, James Ewing Bridgman, Secretary, to the Minister of Maine and Fisheries, 19 December 1895. This was common practice to relieve an overburdened and underfunded Fisheries department elsewhere, particularly on the East Coast, where salmon clubs provided guardians, many of them vested with magisterial powers, to protect rivers on which they held an exclusive lease. See Bill Parenteau, '"Care, Control and Supervision": Native People in the Canadian Atlantic Salmon Fishery, 1867–1900,' *Canadian Historical Review* 79 (1998): 1–35.

93 Prince had been appointed in 1893 to bring a scientific approach to fisheries management. See Kenneth Johnstone, *The Acquatic Explorers: A History of the Fisheries Research Board of Canada* (Toronto: University of Toronto Press, 1977), 24.

94 These sections prohibited obstructing the main channels of streams and prohibited nets or other devices that obstructed entirely the passage of fish.

95 NAC, DMF, RG 23, file 583, pt. 1, Prince memorandum, 4 September 1896.

96 Ibid., Deputy Minister Marine and Fisheries to Deputy Supt. Gen. Indian Affairs, 10 June 1897.

97 NAC, DIA, RG 10, vol. 3908, file 107,297-1, Lomas to Vowell, 9 October 1897.

98 NAC, DMF, RG 23, file 583, pt. 1, Louis Gabouri, 'Spokesman of and at the request of the Cowichan Indians,' to W.W.B. McInnis, MP, and Rev. Maxwell, 22 September 1897.

99 Ibid., Deputy Minister Marine and Fisheries to McInnes, MP, 4 October 1897.

100 Ibid., Prince memo included with a letter dated 30 November 1897.

101 Ibid., Prince 'Memo re Conference with Anglers in Victoria, B.C. re Cowichan River,' 22 June 1897.

102 NAC, DMF, RG 23, file 1469, pt. 1, Prince 'Memo re Indian disturbances,' 8 February 1897.

103 Ibid. (emphasis in original).

104 Ibid.

105 NAC, DIA, RG 10, vol. 3908, file 107,297-1, J.D. McLean, Secretary, Department of Indian Affairs, 31 December 1897.

106 Ibid., Lomas to McLean, 10 January 1898.

107 NAC, DMF, RG 23, file 583, pt. 1, Maitland-Dougall to McNab, 7 March 1898.

108 Ibid., McNab to Deputy Minister, 10 March 1898.

109 Ibid., Prince to McNab, 19 March 1898.

110 Ibid., Dept. of Fisheries to Hewitt Bostook, 19 March 1898.

111 NAC, DMF, RG 23, file 1469, pt. 1, Prince to McNab, 4 February 1898.

112 Ibid., Indian Superintendent Vowell to DIA, 29 March 1898. The accused is identified in the report as Jim Quillshemet, but is likely the same person as Jack Quilshamult. Abner Thorne, pers. comm., 3 January 2000. I refer to them as the same person in the text.

113 Ibid., Edward Musgrave to Minister of Marine and Fisheries, 11 April 1898.

114 Ibid., DIA Secretary to Deputy Minister of Marine and Fisheries, 7 April 1898.

115 Ibid., 12 April 1898.

116 *Victoria Daily Colonist*, 20 April 1898. The justices of the peace were E.M. Skinner, H.O. Welburn, and C. Livingstone.

117 NAC, DMF, RG 23, file 583, pt. 1, W.W. Stumbles report on a meeting of the Victoria Board of Trade Committee to investigate the Cowichan weir fishery, 14 August 1899.

118 *Victoria Daily Colonist*, 28 September and 10 October 1899, letters to the editor from Edward Musgrave.

119 Marshall, *Those Who Fell from the Sky*, 158, argues that the 'Cowichan Petition of 1909' included the first reference to the *Royal Proclamation of 1763* as confirmation of Native title in British Columbia.

120 NAC, DMF, RG 23, file 583, pt. 1, J.D. McLean, DIA Secretary, to J. Hardie, DMF Acting Deputy Minister, 30 July 1900; RG 23, file 1469, pt. 2, J.D. McLean to F. Gourdean, DMF Deputy Minister, 17 April 1902.

121 NAC, DIA, RG 10, vol. 3828, f. 60,926, W.H. Lomas, Indian Agent at Quamichan, to Moffat, Acting Indian Superintendent, Victoria, 23 August 1889. Tina Loo, 'Dan Cranmer's Potlatch: Law as Coercion, Symbol and Rhetoric in British Columbia, 1884–1951,' *Canadian Historical Review* 73 (1992): 125–65, suggests that courts were reluctant to convict Natives for potlatch offences as well.

122 NAC, DMF, RG 23, file 583, pt. 1. A copy of the petition is attached to a letter from the Superintendent General of Indian Affairs to John Costigan, Minister of Marine and Fisheries, 28 January 1896. The list of petitioners

reads: 'John S. Clark, Roderick Reid, Malcom Reid, Jacob Heck, James O. Heck And 280 others.'

123 Parenteau, '"Care, Control and Supervision,"' 21, notes that sympathy for native 'poachers' on the Atlantic coast was 'one of the primary barriers to the eradication of poaching throughout the Atlantic salmon fishery.'

124 Pritchard, *Vancouver Island Letters*, 103, Verney to his father, 1 November 1862.

125 Norcross, *Warm Land*, 20–4. See Williams, *St. Peter's Quamichan*.

126 Jean Barman, *The West Beyond the West: A History of British Columbia* (Toronto: University of Toronto Press, 1991), 140.

127 Harris, *Resettlement*, 155.

128 A 1901 promotional pamphlet, *Cowichan, Vancouver Island ... Fishing, Shooting, Mining, Farming, Lumbering* (Victoria: Colonist Printing and Publishing Co., 1901) emphasized the similarities between 'the Cowichan district and the Old Country.' During his years in the Cowichan Valley in the 1890s my great-grandfather J.C. Harris, read Karl Marx, joined the Fabian socialists, and grew increasingly disenchanted with the genteel pretensions of this transplanted English society on Vancouver Island that he had initially enjoyed. In his reminiscences he wrote: 'Cowichan is hardly the place to be influenced by radical opinions. There are very many highly respectable people there, living on remittances and pensions, who felt that their world had little need of reform, and certainly none of reconstruction and revolution.' In 1896 he left for the rougher edges and the dubious agricultural prospects of the mining boom in the Kootenays. BCA, MS-1094.

129 David Demeritt, 'Visions of Agriculture in British Columbia,' *BC Studies* 108 (1995–6): 32–3.

130 Ibid., 36, 38.

131 See Kathryn Bridge, *Henry & Self: The Private Life of Sarah Crease, 1826–1922* (Victoria: Sono Nis Press, 1996), and *The Crease Family Archives: A Record of Settlement and Service in British Columbia* (Victoria: Provincial Archives of British Columbia, 1982).

132 Eve Darian-Smith, *Bridging Divides: The Channel Tunnel and English Legal Identity in the New Europe* (Berkeley: University of California Press, 1999), 37, connects her analysis of landscape directly with law by suggesting 'the grounding of [English] law in the mythologized rural English landscape.'

133 NAC, DMF, RG 23, file 1469, pt. 1, Captain John T. Walbran to Captain Gaudin, Agent of Marine and Fisheries, Victoria, 5 October 1895.

134 There were two types of seine nets used in Cowichan Bay: drag seines

and purse seines. Drag seines are pulled through the water, collecting all fish that are too large to escape through the mesh. Purse seines are deployed in a circle around a school of fish. The bottom of the net is drawn tight to enclose the fish and the net is pulled in. Fisheries sanctioned this fishery even though fishing for salmon by means other than drift nets was prohibited until amendments to the 1894 Fishery Regulations by Order-in-Council, 2 May 1904, *Canada Gazette*, vol. 37, p. 2207.

135 NAC, DMF, RG 23, file 583, pt. 1, McNab to Deputy Minister of Fisheries, 8 November 1898.

136 Ibid., Father Geolb VanGoethem to W.W. Stumbles, 28 October 1899.

137 Ibid., W.W. Stumbles to Commissioner of Fisheries, 14 August 1899.

138 The petition is signed with an 'X' by a person identified as 'Chief Joe Komiaken, Head chief of the Cowichans.' This is probably Comiaken Chief Joe Kukhalt, who testified at the hearings of the 1902 British Columbia Salmon Commission and the Royal Commission on Indian Affairs for the Province of British Columbia in 1913. See notes 142 and 178. The petition is witnessed by Harry Stuart and Father Geolb VanGoethem, and may well have been drafted by the latter. NAC, DMF, RG 23, file 583, pt. 1, 28 October 1899.

139 *Fisheries Act*, R.S.C. 1886 c.95, s. 14, as amended by 54–5 Vic., c. 43, s. 1.

140 NAC, DMF, RG 23, file 583, pt. 1, Prince to Sword, 27 September 1900.

141 Ibid., John Hardie, Acting Deputy Minister of Marine and Fisheries to Mr Wm. Lumley and others, 2 October 1900.

142 NAC, DMF, RG 23, file 2918, pt. 1, W.R. Robertson, Indian Agent, reporting on a meeting of 40 Cowichan at his office, 29 January 1902. The chiefs are identified in the letter as 'Chief See Heel Tun of Quamichan' and 'Joe Kukulth, Chief Comeakin Band.' These two chiefs testified to The Royal Commission on Indian Affairs for the Province of British Columbia in 1913. See note 178.

143 Ibid., open letter from the Cowichan, transcribed by C.M. Tate, submitted to the British Columbia Salmon Commission, 1902.

144 Ibid., BC Salmon Commission, 1902, 16th Session, Nanaimo, 5 February 1902.

145 NAC, DMF, RG 23, file 583, pt. 1, Charles Durham, Grand Secretary Treasurer of the BC Fishermen's Union, to Gourdeau, Deputy Minister of Marine and Fisheries, 7 April 1902.

146 Order-in-Council, 4 June 1902, *Canada Gazette*, vol. 35, p. 2466.

147 NAC, DMF, RG 23, file 583, pt. 1, Colvin to Sword, 22 March 1902.

148 NAC, DMF, RG 23, file 1469, pt. 2, Detective Sergeant Thos. Palmer to Hayward, 31 March 1902.

149 Ibid., R. Small, MLA, to Senator Templeman, 10 February 1902.

150 NAC, DMF, RG 23, file 1469, pt. 1, Hayward to James H. Sutherland, Minister of Fisheries, 24 April 1902.
151 Ibid., Sword to Prince, 9 May 1902.
152 Ibid., Hayward to Sutherland, Minister of Marine and Fisheries, 14 May 1902.
153 Ibid., Petition sent to Sutherland, June 1902.
154 NAC, DMF, RG 23, file 1469, pt. 2, Galbraith to Senator Templeman, 26 August 1902.
155 Ibid., Notes from Evans's testimony to the commission, 6 August 1902.
156 NAC, DMF, RG 23, file 583, pt. 1, C. Drinkwater, Assistant to the President of the CPR, to Gourdeau, Deputy Minister of Marine and Fisheries, 21 August 1905. J. Michael Thoms, 'Illegal Conservation: Two Case Studies of Conflict between Indigenous and State Natural Resouce Management Paradigms,' MA thesis, Trent University, 1995, discusses the CPR's promotional work on the Nipigon River in Ontario.
157 Figures are contained in a statement from C.B. Sword, NAC, DMF, RG 23, file 1469, pt. 2.
158 Ibid., Robertson to Vowell, 22 May 1905.
159 Ibid., Pedley, Deputy Superintendent General of Indian Affairs, to Gourdeau, Deputy Minister of Marine and Fisheries, 31 May 1905.
160 Ibid., Edward G. Taylor, Inspector of Fisheries, to R.W. Venning, Assistant Commissioner of Fisheries, 19 July 1905.
161 *Rod and Gun and Motor Sports in Canada* 8 (October 1906), 357.
162 Ibid., 8 (May 1907), 1037.
163 Canadian Pacific Archives, X1027, 'Fishing Waters and Game Haunts of Western Canada reached by Canadian Pacific' (1941).
164 T.T. Phelps, *Fishing Dreams* (London: The Batchworth Press, 1949) 216–17. Thanks to Michael Thoms for this citation.
165 Parenteau, '"Care, Control and Supervision,"' 3.
166 Stautes of British Columbia, 1898, c.24.
167 BC Sessional Papers, 1906, 'Provincial Game and Forest Warden's Report, 1905,' D-1.
168 Ibid., extracts from Mr Heald's Report sent to Gourdeau, Deputy Minister of Fisheries, 2 January 1907.
169 *The Daily Colonist*, 9 December 1906.
170 NAC, DMF, RG 23, file 1815, pt. 1, Galbraith to Prince, 31 March 1907.
171 Ibid., 30 June 1907.
172 Ibid., Edward G. Taylor to R.N. Venning, Assistant Commissioner of Fisheries, 24 June 1907.
173 *Cowichan Leader*, 20 July 1907.

174 Ibid., p. 2.

175 BC Sessional Papers, 1908, M24, R.G. Tatlow, Acting Premier, to W. Templeman, Acting Minister of Marine and Fisheries, 29 May 1907.

176 BCA, Department of Fisheries, GR-0435, box 1, file 6, L. Rattray, President Cowichan Anglers Association, to J.H.S. Matson, n.d.

177 Ibid., file 7, Cowichan Conservation Association Secretary to W.H. Hayward, M.P.P., 18 April 1914.

178 NAC, DIA, RG 10, vol. 11024, file AH3, 'Evidence of the Royal Commission on Indian Affairs for the Province of British Columbia.' The chiefs are identified as Charlie Seehaillton, Joe Kukahalt, Charley Selpaymult, George Quiochqult, and Charley Kutsowat. Thanks to Abner Thorne for helping me to identify these individuals. The other Cowichan who testified were identified as Donnet Charlie, Daniel Dick (Clemclemeluts), Babtiste Bod (Comiaken), Johnnie Page (Khenipsen), Thomas Pierre (Comiaken), Charlie Quiquarton, Fred Thorne (Somenos), Modeste Seehaillton (Quamichan), Antoine Sanpatiste, Jimmy Scowaset (Khenipsen), and John Elliott, who also acted as interpreter.

The commission met again on 6 June 1913 at Duncan and heard from Suhiltun, John Elliott, and Thomas Pierre, as well as a woman identified as Annie Kakalatsa, the only Cowichan woman to testify. She testified that a white settler had encroached on one of the upstream reserves and an important fishing station.

179 NAC, DMF, RG 23, vol. 164, file 583, Found to Cunningham, 7 March 1912.

180 Ibid., Cunningham to Found, 11 June 1912.

181 Pacific Regional Federal Records Centre, Burnaby (PRFRC), DMF, RG 23, vol. 2038, file 10-3-31, Taylor to Chief Inspector Cunningham, 22 July 1913.

182 *Cowichan Leader*, 11 March 1914.

183 The letter is reproduced in the transcript of the royal commission conference on Indian fishing rights, 9 April 1914, in the 'Evidence of the Royal Commission on Indian Affairs for the Province of British Columbia' ('Royal Commission Evidence'), vol. 1, p. 414. Archived at UBC Special Collections.

184 Ibid., 413–27. The meeting was held 14 April 1914, in Victoria. Present at the meeting were Commissioners Macdowall, Shaw, and McKenna, Chief Inspector Cunningham, and Inspectors Williams and Taylor from the Dominion Department of Fisheries, Deputy Commissioner McIntyre and Assistant Commissioner Babcock of the Provincial Fisheries, and Inspector Ditchburn and Agent Robertson of Indian Affairs.

185 Ibid., 418.

186 Ibid., 421.

187 Ibid., 433.

188 The Cowichan who testified were indentified as Modeste, son of Schaalten (Suhiltun) the Head Chief of the Cowichan; Comiaken Chief Joe Kokahamult (Kukhalt); Clemclemalutz Chief George Quiochqult (Queoqult); Somenos Chief Charley Quitquaten; Khenipsen Chief Charley Selapymult (Tsulpi'multw); Koksilah Chief Charley Culsowault (Kutsowat); and Quamichan headman Bill Hotalsilock.

189 Royal Commission Evidence, vol. 1, 432.

190 Ibid.

191 NAC, DIA, RG 10, v. 3908, f. 107,297-2, transcript of a meeting of the Royal Commission on Indian Affairs for the Province of British Columbia with Representatives of the Dominion and Provincial Fisheries Officials in Regard to Fishing Privileges of Indians in B.C., Victoria, December 1915, pp. 20–1, 23.

192 Ibid., 37.

193 NAC, DIA, RG 10, vol. 9165, file B-6, 'Fisheries Concessions,' 9 July 1917. The committee members were A. Day, H.F. Prevost, and A.H. Peterson. The full report, approximately 7500 words, was reprinted in the *Cowichan Leader*, 12 July 1917.

194 *The Daily Colonist*, 27 February 1918.

195 NAC, DIA, RG 10, vol. 9165, file B-6, copy of 'Report of Cowichan Bay Licence,' C. McLean Fraser, n.d.

196 *The Daily Colonist* printed a daily synopsis of the evidence presented at the commission. For the Duncan hearings see 4–5 and 7–8 October 1919. Clippings are also contained in NAC, DIA, RG 10, vol. 9165, file B-6.

197 *The Daily Colonist*, 7 October 1919.

198 *Cowichan Leader*, 11 September 1919.

199 Ibid., 8 October 1919. The speaker is identified as Comiaken chief Big Joe, probably the same person as Joe Kukhalt.

200 Ibid., Chief Charlie of Somenos, Johnson See-et-teen, and Chief Edward of Chemainus also testified.

201 *Canada Gazette*, vol. 51, p. 925, *Special Fishery Regulations for the Province of British Columbia*, 9 February 1915, s. 2, as amended, Order-in-Council P.C. 2539, 11 September 1917.

202 Ibid. s. 8(2)(c). Any person buying any fish or portion of any fish caught under such permit [food-fishing permit] shall be guilty of an offence against these regulations.

203 PRFRC, DMF, RG 23, vol. 2038, f.10-3-31, A. Easton to Major J.A. Mother-well, Chief Inspector of Fisheries, 30 January 1924.

204 *Fisheries Act*, R.S.C. 1914, c. 8, as amended by 8–9 George V, s. 3 c. 22.

205 Minor amendments had been made by Order-in-Council, 29 April 1922, *Canada Gazette*, vol. 55.

206 Brigadier General C.D. Gartside Spaight, the president of the Cowichan Fish and Game Preservation Association, wondered 'if the lawyer who defended the Chink and who generally defends in all these prosecutions were to draw up suggested amendments to the Act?' PRFRC, DMF, RG 23, vol. 2038, file 10-3-31, Spaight to Motherwell, 12 March 1924.

207 *Canada Gazette*, vol. 58, p. 3037.

208 Authorized under the *Special Fishery Regulations for the Province of British Columbia*, Order-in-Council, 26 April 1922, P.C. 895, s. 19(12)(b), *Canada Gazette*, vol. 55.

209 PRFRC, DMF, RG 23, v. 2038, f.10-3-31, Motherwell to Spaight, 10 September 1924.

210 PRFRC, DIA, file 974/20-2, quotation contained in a memorandum on the 'History of the Cowichan Fishing Dispute,' H.M. Jones to Deputy Minister, 25 June 1956.

211 PRFRC, DMF, RG 23, v. 2038, f.10-3-31, Motherwell to Found, 1 September 1929. In 1929 Fisheries changed the designation of its highest officers in the province from inspector to supervisor.

212 Ibid., Tait to Motherwell, 3 November 1930.

213 Ibid., 14 November 1930.

214 Ibid., A.H. Lomas to J.A. Motherwell, 5 March 1930.

215 Ibid., 27 September 1838.

216 Ibid., 21 October 1932.

217 Ibid., Tait to Motherwell, 9 March 1933.

218 Ibid., 15 September 1933.

219 Ibid., Memorandum from A. Mackie regarding meeting with Andrew Paul, 1 December 1933.

220 Ibid., Tait to Motherwell, 27 September 1938.

221 Ibid.

222 Ibid., 9 May 1934.

223 Ibid., 21 August 1934.

224 Ibid., Motherwell to Found, 2 October 1935.

225 Ibid., Found to Dr. H.W. McGill, Deputy Supt. Gen. Indian Affairs, 26 June 1936.

226 Ibid., Tait to Motherwell, June 1937. Tait reported that Indian Commissioner for British Columbia McKay, Indian Agent Graham, Rev. Father

Lauzon, Inspector of Fisheries Lloyd, Fisheries Guardian Sherman, and various Cowichan Chiefs and headmen attended the meeting.

227 Ibid., Found to Indian Affairs, 13 August 1937.

228 Ibid., Tait to Motherwell, 1 September 1937.

229 Ibid., Tait to Inspector Lloyd, 16 July 1938.

230 The changing conception of contract, particularly the rise of contract as a binding promise in the nineteenth century, is the focus of Patrick Atiyah's *The Rise and Fall of Freedom of Contract* (Oxford: Clarendon Press, 1979).

231 *Vancouver Sun*, 4, 6, and 7 September 1973.

232 The names of the accused were Joseph Daniel Jack, Harold Lewis Joe, Calvin Patrick Antoine, John Jimmy, Bernard Joe, Gordon Leon Goldsmith, Samuel Johnny Jimmy, Wilburt Joseph Canute, and Charles Rice.

233 *R. v. Jack* (1979), 100 D.L.R. (3d) 193. He would return to this judgment and the priority of Aboriginal food fisheries in *R. v. Sparrow*, [1990] 1 S.C.R. 1075.

234 PRFRC, DIA, file 974/20-2, memorandum on the 'History of the Cowichan Fishing Dispute,' H.M. Jones to Deputy Minister, 25 June 1956.

235 Copies of the 'Cowichan Indian Band By-law, 1956, no. 1' and 'Cowichan Indian Band By-law, 1983, no. 2' are reproduced as appendices A and E respectively in Jennifer Lynn Jones-Desjarlais, 'The Scales of Justice or the Native Claim to the Management of Reserve Fisheries,' LLM thesis, UBC, 1985.

236 *R. v. Jimmy* (1987), 15 B.C.L.R. (2d) 145.

Chapter 4: Law and Colonialism

1 Peter Fitzpatrick, *The Mythology of Modern Law* (London: Routledge, 1992), 107–11.

2 A.V. Dicey, *Introduction to the Study of Law of the Constitution* (London: Macmillan, 1885), 187.

3 In the Australian context, for example, see David Neal, *The Rule of Law in a Penal Colony: Law and Power in New South Wales* (Cambridge: Cambridge University Press, 1991).

4 For an introduction to work on law and violence see Austin Sarat and Thomas R. Kearns, eds., *Law's Violence* (Ann Arbor: University of Michigan Press, 1992).

5 John Austin, *The Province of Jurisprudence Determined* [1832] (London: Weidenfeld & Nicholson, 1955).

6 Roger Cotterell, *The Sociology of Law: An Introduction* (London: Butterworths, 1984).

7 H.W. Arthurs, 'Without the Law': Administrative Justice and Legal Pluralism in Nineteenth-Century England (Toronto: University of Toronto Press, 1985).

8 David Sugarman, '"A Hatred of Disorder": Legal Science, Liberalism and Imperialism,' in Peter Fitzpatrick, ed., Dangerous Supplements (Durham: Duke University Press, 1991), 34–67.

9 W. Wesley Pue, 'Revolution by Legal Means,' in Patrick Glenn, ed., Contemporary Law 1994 Droit contemporain (Montréal: Editions Yvons Blais, 1994), 1–30; Rob McQueen and Pue, eds., 'Misplaced Traditions: The Legal Profession and the British Empire,' Law in Context 16 (1999).

10 Martin Chanock, Law, Custom and Social Order: The Colonial Experience in Malawi and Zambia (Cambridge: Cambridge University Press, 1985), 219.

11 Sally Engle Merry, 'Law and Colonialism,' Law & Society Review 25 (1991): 889–922, provides a useful review of the literature.

12 Ranajit Guha, A Rule of Property for Bengal (Paris: Mouton, 1963).

13 Bernard S. Cohn, Colonialism and Its Forms of Knowledge: The British in India (Princeton: Princeton University Press, 1996), 3.

14 Ibid., 16.

15 See, e.g., Francis G. Snyder, 'Colonialism and Legal Form: The Creation of "Customary Law" in Senegal,' Journal of Legal Pluralism 19 (1981): 49–90, who argues in the African context: 'Produced in particular historical circumstances, the notion of 'customary law' was an ideology of colonial domination. The concept of 'customary law' itself manifested an attempt to reinterpret African legal forms in terms of European legal categories, which formed part of the ideology of those classes most closely associated with the colonial state' (76). See also Sally Falk Moore, Social Facts and Fabrications: 'Customary' Law on Kilimanjaro, 1880–1980 (Cambridge: Cambridge University Press, 1986).

16 June Starr and Jane F. Collier, eds., History and Power in the Study of Law (Ithaca and London: Cornell University Press, 1989), 9.

17 Merry, 'Law and Colonialism,' 890–1.

18 Francis G. Snyder and Douglas Hay, eds., Labour, Law and Crime: An Historical Perspective (London: Tavistock, 1987) combines historical case studies of Western Europe and parts of Africa and Asia to explore the relationship between law, labour, and crime.

19 See, e.g., E.P. Thompson, 'Time, Work-Discipline and Industrial Capitalism,' in Customs in Common: Studies in Traditional Popular Culture (New York: New Press, 1993), 352–403.

20 Douglas Hay, 'Property, Authority and the Criminal Law,' in Hay et al., eds., Albion's Fatal Tree: Crime and Society in Eighteenth-Century England (London: Allen Lane, 1975), 17–64.

21 Hay, 'Property, Authority and the Criminal Law,' 56. J. Langbein, 'Albion's Fatal Flaws,' *Past & Present* 98 (1983): 96–120, disagrees vehemently, suggesting that the criminal law was no more important than the flush toilet. In response to Langbein's criticism, see Linebaugh, '(Marxist) Social History and (Conservative) Legal History: A Reply to Professor Langbein,' *New York University Law Review* 60 (1985): 212–43.

22 E.P. Thompson, *Whigs and Hunters: The Origin of the Black Act*. New York: Pantheon Books, 1975.

23 Thompson, *Customs in Common*, 4–5.

24 Ibid., 9 (emphasis in original).

25 In the colonial context see Terence Ranger, 'The Invention of Tradition in Colonial Africa,' in Eric Hobsbawm and Ranger, eds., *The Invention of Tradition* (Cambridge: Cambridge University Press, 1983), 211–62.

26 Thompson, *Whigs and Hunters*, 264.

27 Neal, *Rule of Law in a Penal Colony*, 194–5. This is not to minimize the differences within England, where the urban poor in the nineteenth century were often described as a different race. See, e.g., Gareth Stedman Jones, *Outcast London: A Study in the Relationship between Classes in Victorian London* (Oxford: Clarendon Press, 1971).

28 Snyder and Hay, 'Comparisons in the Social History of Law: Labour and Crime,' in *Labour, Law and Crime*, 12.

29 Fitzpatrick, *Mythology of Modern Law*, 111.

30 Peter Fitzpatrick, *Law and State in Papua New Guinea* (London: Academic Press, 1980).

31 Ibid., 39.

32 Ibid.

33 Frantz Fanon, *The Wretched of the Earth*, trans. Constance Farrington (New York: Grove Press, 1966), 31.

34 Jeannine Purdy, 'Postcolonialism: The Emperor's New Clothes,' in Eve Darian-Smith and Peter Fitzpatrick, eds., *Laws of the Postcolonial* (Ann Arbor: University of Michigan Press, 1999), 203–29.

35 James C. Scott, *Weapons of the Weak: Everyday Forms of Peasant Resistance* (New Haven: Yale University Press, 1985).

36 James C. Scott, *Domination and the Arts of Resistance: Hidden Transcripts* (New Haven: Yale University Press, 1996). While emphasizing the importance and distinct role of European law in colonial settings, Fitzpatrick would agree with many who suggest the possibility of resistance. See Peter Fitzpatrick, 'Law, Plurality and Underdevelopment,' in David Sugarman, ed., *Legality, Ideology and the State* (London: Academic Press, 1983), 150–82.

37 Ranajit Guha, 'Chandra's Death,' in Guha, ed., *A Subaltern Studies Reader,*

1986–1995 (Minneapolis: University of Minnesota Press, 1997), 34-62. The point has also been made strongly by feminist scholars of empire. See, e.g., Anne McClintock, *Imperial Leather: Race, Gender and Sexuality in the Colonial Contest* (London: Routledge, 1995).

38 In the introduction to the inaugural *Subaltern Studies: Writings on South Asian History and Society*, Vol. 1 (Delhi: Oxford University Press, 1982), Guha reveals the influence of European social historians, particularly E.P. Thompson, *The Making of the English Working Class* (London: V. Gollanz, 1963), who had earlier sought to rewrite the history of the European labouring classes by giving voice to the workers, not just the union leaders.

39 Guha, 'Chandra's Death,' 40.

40 Merry, 'Law and Colonialism,' 891.

41 John Griffiths, 'What Is Legal Pluralism?' *Journal of Legal Pluralism and Unofficial Law* 24 (1986): 1–55, characterizes this as 'weak legal pluralism.'

42 Hamar Foster, 'International Homicide in Early British Columbia,' in Jim Phillips, Tina Loo, and Susan Lewthwaite, eds., *Essays in the History of Canadian Law*, Vol. 5, *Crime and Criminal Justice* (Toronto: Osgoode Society for Canadian Legal History, 1994), 61.

43 Chris Arnett, *The Terror of the Coast: Land Alienation and Colonial War on Vancouver Island and the Gulf Islands, 1849–1863* (Burnaby, BC: Talonbooks, 1999).

44 Barry M. Gough, *Gunboat Frontier: British Maritime Authority and Northwest Coast Indians, 1846–1890* (Vancouver: UBC Press, 1984), 210.

45 Tina Loo, *Making Law, Order, and Authority in British Columbia, 1821–1871* (Toronto: University of Toronto Press, 1994), 3.

46 Ibid., 4.

47 Tina Loo, 'The Road from Bute Inlet: Crime and Colonial Identity in British Columbia,' in Phillips, Loo and Lewthwaite, *Essays in the History of Canadian Law*, Vol. 5, 131.

48 Tina Loo, 'Dan Cranmer's Potlatch: Law as Coercion, Symbol and Rhetoric in British Columbia, 1884–1951,' *Canadian Historical Review* 73 (1992): 133.

49 Ibid., 165. Robin Brownlie and Mary-Ellen Kelm, 'Desperately Seeking Absolution: Native Agency as Colonialist Alibi?' *Canadian Historical Review* 75 (1994): 543–56, argue that Loo overstates Native agency and unduly minimizes the coercive nature of law.

50 Tina Loo, 'Tonto's Due: Law, Culture, and Colonization in British Columbia,' in Hamar Foster and John McLaren, eds., *Essays in the History of Canadian Law*, Vol. 6, *British Columbia and the Yukon* (Toronto: Osgoode Society for Legal History, 1995), pp. 128–70.

51 Douglas Harris, 'The Nlha7kápmx Meeting at Lytton, 1879, and the Rule of Law,' *BC Studies* 108 (1995/6): 5–25.

52 Sally Engle Merry, *Colonizing Hawai'i: The Cultural Power of Law* (Princeton: Princeton University Press, 2000).

53 Russell Smandych and Rick Linden, 'Co-existing Forms of Aboriginal and Private Justice: An Historical Study of the Canadian West,' in Kayleen M. Hazlehurst, ed., *Legal Pluralism and the Colonial Legacy* (Aldershot: Avebury, 1995), 1–38, and Smandych and Gloria Lee, 'Women, Colonization and Resistance: Elements of an Amerindian Autohistorical Approach to the Study of Law and Colonialism,' *Native Studies Review* 10 (1995): 21–46, have made a preliminary attempt to apply the legal-pluralism and law-and-colonialism literature to the coexistence of Aboriginal and Hudson's Bay Company legal forms in eighteenth- and nineteenth-century North America.

54 Sally Engle Merry, 'Legal Pluralism,' *Law & Society Review* 22 (1988): 872 (emphasis added).

55 Merry describes the 'new legal pluralism' as follows: 'The concern is to document other forms of social regulation that draw on the symbols of law, to a greater or lesser extent, but that operate in its shadows, its parking lots, and even down the street in mediation offices. Thus, in contexts in which the dominance of a central legal system is unambiguous, this thread of argument worries about missing what else is going on; the extent to which other forms of regulation outside law constitute law.' Ibid., 874.

56 Bain Attwood, 'Introduction, The Past as Future: Aborigines, Australia and the (Dis)course of History,' in Attwood, ed., *In the Age of Mabo: History, Aborigines and Australia* (St Leonards, NSW: Allen & Unwin, 1996), vii–xxxviii, discusses the silence that enveloped Australia's colonial relationship with Aborigines. See also Ann McGrath, ed., *Contested Ground: Australian Aborigines under the British Crown* (St Leonards, NSW: Allen & Unwin, 1995).

57 Merry, *Colonizing Hawai'i*, 21.

58 Cohn, *Colonialism and Its Forms of Knowledge*, 57.

59 A few important studies include Harold Innis, *The Fur Trade in Canada: An Introduction to Canadian Economic History* (Toronto: University of Toronto Press, 1956); Arthur J. Ray, *Indians in the Fur Trade: Their Role as Trappers, Hunters and Middlemen in the Lands Southwest of Hudson Bay, 1660–1870* (Toronto: Toronto University Press, 1974); Jennifer S.H. Brown, *Strangers in Blood: Fur Trade Company Families in Indian Country* (Vancouver: University of British Columbia Press, 1980); and Sylvie Van Kirk, *Many Tender Ties: Women in Fur-Trade Society in Western Canada, 1630–1870* (Winnipeg: Watson and Dwyer, 1980).

60 Richard White, *The Middle Ground: Indians, Empires and Republics in the*

Great Lakes Region, 1650–1815 (Cambridge: Cambridge University Press, 1991).

61 Hamar Foster, 'Sins against the Great Spirit: The Law, the Hudson's Bay Company, and the MacKenzie's River Murders, 1835–1839,' *Criminal Justice History* 10 (1989): 27.

62 John Phillip Reid, 'Principles of Vengeance: Fur Trappers, Indians, and Retaliation for Homicide in the Transboundary North American West,' *Western Historical Review* 24 (1993): 21–43; 'Restraints of Vengeance: Retaliation-in-Kind and the Use of Indian Law in the Old Oregon Country,' *Oregon Historical Quarterly* 95 (1994): 48–92.

63 Harris, *Resettlement of British Columbia*, 57.

64 Ibid., 63.

65 Jo-Anne Fiske, 'From Customary Law to Oral Traditions: Discursive Formation of Plural Legalisms in Northern British Columbia, 1857–1993,' *BC Studies* 115/116 (1997/8): 267–88.

66 See Patrick Macklem, 'First Nations Self-Government and the Borders of the Canadian Legal Imagination,' *McGill Law Journal* 33 (1991): 382–456.

67 Jeremy Webber, 'Relations of Force and Relations of Justice: The Emergence of Normative Community between Colonists and Aboriginal Peoples,' *Osgoode Hall Law Journal* 33 (1995): 623–60.

68 See Brian Slattery's influential article 'Understanding Aboriginal Rights,' *Canadian Bar Review* 66 (1987): 727.

69 Dianne Newell, *Tangled Webs of History: Indians and the Law in Canada's Pacific Coast Fisheries* (Toronto: University of Toronto Press, 1993).

70 Alicja Muszynski, *Cheap Wage Labour: Race and Gender in the Fisheries of British Columbia* (Montreal and Kingston: McGill-Queen's University Press, 1996).

71 Izaak Walton, *The Complete Angler, 1653–1676*, ed. by Jonquil Bevan (Oxford: Clarendon Press, 1983) provides an excellent academic treatment of this much-published and popular book. See also Jonquil Bevan, *Izaak Walton's The Compleat Angler: The Art of Recreation* (Brighton: Harvester Press, 1988).

72 For an introduction into the literature on the social constructions of nature, see William Cronin, ed., *Uncommon Ground: Rethinking the Human Place in Nature* (New York: W.W. Norton, 1996).

73 See Bill Parenteau, '"Care, Control and Supervision": Native People in the Canadian Atlantic Salmon Fishery,' *Canadian Historical Review* 79 (1998): 1–35.

74 See J. Michael Thoms, '"A Place Called Pennask": Fly-fishing and Colonialism in British Columbia,' *BC Studies* (forthcoming).

75 Ralph Mathews and John Phyne, 'Regulating the Newfoundland Inshore Fishery: Traditional Values versus State Control in the Regulation of a Common Property Resource,' *Journal of Canadian Studies* 23 (1988): 158–76, explore the coexistence of local and state regulation in a non-Native fishery.

76 Peter Usher, 'Aboriginal Property Systems in Land and Resources,' in Garth Cant, John Overton, and Eric Pawson, eds., *Indigenous Land Rights in Commonwealth Countries: Dispossession, Negotiation and Community Action* (Christchurch, NZ: Dept. of Geography, University of Canterbury and the Ngai Tahu Maori Trust Board, 1993), 43.

77 David Feeny, Fikret Berkes, Bonnie J. McCay, and James M. Acheson, 'The Tragedy of the Commons: Twenty-Two Years Later,' *Human Ecology* 18 (1990): 1–19.

78 Michael Kew, 'Salmon Availability, Technology, and Cultural Adaptation in the Fraser River Watershed,' in Brian Hayden, ed., *A Complex Culture of the British Columbia Plateau: Traditional Stl'átl'imx Resource Use* (Vancouver: UBC Press, 1992), 201–6.

79 Wayne Suttles, 'Coping with Abundance: Subsistence on the Northwest Coast,' in *Coast Salish Essays* (Vancouver: Talonbooks, 1987), 45–63.

80 See the discussion in Fikret Berkes, *Sacred Ecology: Traditional Ecological Knowledge and Resource Management* (Philadelphia: Taylor & Francis, 1999), 9–12.

81 Fikret Berkes, 'Traditional Ecological Knowledge in Perspective,' in Julian T. Inglis, ed., *Traditional Ecological Knowledge: Concepts and Cases* (Ottawa: International Program on Traditional Ecological Knowledge and International Development Research Centre, 1993), 3.

82 Fikret Berkes, 'Fishery Resource Use in a Subartic Community,' *Human Ecology* 5 (1977): 291, 306.

83 Fikret Berkes, 'Common-Property Resource Management and Cree Indian Fisheries in Subarctic Canada,' in Bonnie J. McKay and James M. Acheson, eds., *The Question of the Commons: The Culture and Ecology of Communal Resources* (Tuscon: University of Arizona Press, 1987); Feeney et al., 'Tragedy of the Commons'; Berkes, 'Indigenous Knowledge and Resource Management Systems in the Canadian Subarctic,' in Berkes and Carl Folke, eds., *Linking Social and Ecological Systems: Management Practices and Social Mechanisms for Building Resilience* (Cambridge: Cambridge University Press, 1998), 98–128.

84 P.A. Berringer, W. Green, and V. Smith, 'Ehattesaht Traditional Fisheries Systems,' in Barry Sadler and Peter Boothroyd, eds., *A Background Paper on Traditional Ecological Knowledge and Modern Environmental Assessment*

(Vancouver: UBC, Centre for Human Settlements, 1994), 42–3. See also Dianne Newell and Rosemary E. Ommer, eds., *Fishing Places, Fishing People: Traditions and Issues in Canadian Small-Scale Fisheries* (Toronto: University of Toronto Press, 1999).

85 E.P. Thompson, 'The Moral Economy of the English Crowd in the Eighteenth Century,' in *Customs in Common*, 188.

86 Ibid., 187.

87 Thompson, 'The Moral Economy Reviewed,' in *Customs in Common*, 261.

88 Loo, 'Dan Cranmer's Potlatch,' 147–50, notes the sympathy of a local settler population and the reluctance of the courts to convict natives for potlatch offences as factors diminishing the oppressive potential of the potlatch prohibition.

89 *R. v. Cooper*, [1979] 4 C.N.L.R. 81.

90 *R. v. Marshall*, [1999] 3 S.C.R. 456; *R. v. Marshall*, [1999] 3 S.C.R. 533.

91 *R. v. Sparrow*, [1990] 1 S.C.R. 1075.

92 Recently appointed Supreme Court of Canada Justice Binnie noted the court's failure in *Sparrow* to address the commercial fishery and the problems this posed for Native efforts to create a measure of political and economic self-sufficiency. W.I.C. Binnie, 'The Sparrow Doctrine: Beginning of the end or end of the beginning?' 15 *Queen's Law Journal* 15 (1990): 217–53.

93 *R. v. Van der Peet*, [1996] 2 S.C.R. 507.

94 *R. v. Gladstone*, [1996] S.C.R. 723. For a critique of the judgment see Douglas C. Harris, 'Territoriality, Aboriginal Rights and the Heiltsuk Spawn-on-Kelp Fishery,' *University of British Columbia Law Review* 34 (2000): 195–238.

95 See Lamer C.J.'s decision in *Gladstone*.

96 See *R. v. Houvinen*, [1998] B.C.J. 2064 (BC Prov. Ct.) (QL); *R. v. Cummins*, [1998] B.C.J. 125 (BC Prov. Ct.) (QL).

Bibliography

Primary Sources

Archives

Archives Deschâtelets, Ottawa
    Reminiscences of Rev. Father Coccola

British Columbia Archives
    British Columbia Attorney General, GR-0429
    British Columbia Department of Fisheries, GR-0435
    British Columbia Department of Lands, GR-1402
    British Columbia Provincial Secretary, GR-494
    Dawson, George, B/G/47
    Fort Victoria Correspondence, A/C/20/Vi
    Great Britain, Colonial Office Correspondence, GR-1486
    Harris, Joseph Colebrook, MS-1094
    Scottish Record Office, MS-1640
    Gilbert Malcom Sproat Letterbooks
    Sir Matthew Ballie Begbie Bench Books

Canadian Pacific Archives
    Fishing Waters and Game Haunts of Western Canada reached by Canadian
        Pacific

Hudson's Bay Company Archives
    Fort Kilmaurs Journal
    Babine Post Journals

National Archives of Canada
  Department of Indian Affairs, Record Group 10
  Department of Justice, Record Group 13
  Department of Marine and Fisheries, Record Group 23
  Federal Collection of Minutes of Decision, Correspondence and Sketches,·
    Joint Indian Reserve Commission and Indian Reserve Commission [copy
    held by the Department of Indian Affairs, Vancouver regional office]

Pacific Region Federal Records Centre
  Department of Indian Affairs, Record Group 10
  Department of Marine and Fisheries, Record Group 23

University of British Columbia Libraries and Special Collections ·
  A.C. Anderson, 'A History of the Northwest Coast,' 1878
  Commission on the Salmon Fishing Industry in BC, 1902, unpublished
    reports
  Dominion – British Columbia Fisheries Commission, 1905–1907, Evidence
  Department of Marine and Fisheries, Record Group 23
  Evidence of the Royal Commission on Indian Affairs for the Province of
    British Columbia
  Henry Doyle Papers
  Papers of the International Pacific Salmon Fisheries Commission

Printed Reports and Reference Material

British Columbia Fishery Commission Report, 1892 (Wilmot Commission).
    Ottawa: Queen's Printer, 1893.
British Columbia Salmon Commission, 1902.
British Columbia. *Journals of the Legislative Assembly of British Columbia, 1878.*
– Sessional Papers, 1878–1912.
Canada. Department of Indian Affairs Annual Reports, 1876–1910. Canada,
    Sessional Papers.
– Department of Marine and Fisheries Annual Reports, 1873–1910. Canada,
    Sessional Papers.
*Columbia Mission Reports, 1878–1895: Twenty-sixth Report of the Missions of the
    Church of England in the Diocese of British Columbia, For the Year Ending
    December 31st, 1888, and up to May 31st, 1889.* London: Rivingtons, Waterloo
    Place, 1889.
*Dominion–British Columbia Fisheries Commission, 1905–1907: Report and Recom-
    mendations.* Ottawa: Government Printing Bureau, 1908.

Evidence Submitted to the British Columbia Fisheries Commission. Victoria: Times Publishing and Printing Co., 1906.

Great Britain. House of Commons, Parliamentary Papers, 1860, 1863, 1866.

Johnson's Dictionary of the English Language. London: 1882.

Journals of the Colonial Legislatures of the Colonies of Vancouver Island and British Columbia, 1851–1871. Edited by James E. Hendrickson. Victoria: Provincial Archives of British Columbia, 1980.

Letter from the Methodist Missionary Society to the Superintendent–General of Indian Affairs respecting British Columbia Troubles: with affidavits, declarations, etc. Toronto, 1889.

A New English Dictionary. Oxford: Clarendon Press, 1909.

Papers Connected with the Indian Land Question, 1850–1875, 1877. Victoria: Queen's Printer, 1987.

Thirty-First Report of the Columbia Mission, February 1st 1897 to January 31st 1898. London: Sampson Low, Marston & Co., 1898.

Newspapers and Magazines

Cowichan Leader (Duncan)
Cranbrook Courier
Daily British Colonist (Victoria)
The Daily Colonist (Victoria)
The Daily News (New Westminster)
Daily Times (Victoria)
Mainland Guardian (New Westminster)
The Province (Vancouver)
Rod and Gun and Motor Sports in Canada
Skeena District News (Port Essington)
Trade Register
Vancouver Sun
Weekly Standard (Victoria)
The World (Vancouver)

Reported Cases

The Queen v. Robertson, [1882] S.C.R. 5.
R. v. Cooper, [1979] 4 C.N.L.R. 81.
R. v. Cummins, [1998] B.C.J. 125 (BC Prov. Ct.) (QL).
R. v. Gladstone, [1996] 2 S.C.R. 723.
R. v. Houvinen, [1998] B.C.J. 2064 (BC Prov. Ct.) (QL).

R. v. Lewis, [1996] 1 S.C.R. 921.

R. v. Marshall, [1999] 3 S.C.R. 456.

R. v. Marshall, [1999] 3 S.C.R. 533.

R. v. Nikal, [1996] 1 S.C.R. 1013.

R. v. NTC Smokehouse, [1996] 2 S.C.R. 672.

R. v. Sparrow, [1990] 1 S.C.R. 1075.

R. v. Van der Peet, [1996] 2 S.C.R. 507.

R. v. White and Bob (1964), 52 D.L.R. (2d) 481 (S.C.C.), affirming 50 D.L.R. (2d) 613 (B.C.C.A.).

Reference as to the Constitutional Validity of Certain Sections of the Fisheries Act, [1914] A.C. 153, overturning [1928] S.C.R. 457.

Saanichton Marina Ltd. v. Tsawout Indian Band (1987), 18 B.C.L.R. (2d) 217 (B.C.S.C.).

St. Catherine's Milling & Lumber Co. v. The Queen (1888), 14 App. Cas. 46 (J.C.P.C.).

British Columbia Statutory Instruments

Act for the Preservation of Game, British Columbia Archives, Colonial Office Correspondence, 306/1, 20 April 1859.

Preservation of Game Act, R.S.B.C. 1871, c. 12.

Summary Convictions Act, S.B.C. 1889, c. 26.

Fisheries Act, 1901.

Canada Statutory Instruments

Fisheries Act, S.C. 1868, c. 60.

An Act respecting the extension and application of 'The Fisheries Act,' to and in the Provinces of British Columbia, Prince Edward Island and Manitoba, S.C. 1874, c. 28.

Proclamation to extend and apply to British Columbia, S.C. 1874, c. 28, 8 May 1876.

Salmon Fishery Regulations for the Province of British Columbia, Order-in-Council, 30 May 1878.

Fishery Regulation, Order-in-Council, 11 June 1879.

Fisheries Act, R.S.C. 1886, c. 95, as amended by 52 Vic., c. 24; 54–55 Vic. c. 43; 57–58 Vic., c. 51; 61 Vic., c. 39.

Fishery Regulations for the Province of British Columbia, Order-in-Council, 26 November 1888.

Departmental Order to define tidal boundary for salmon net fishing in
   Cowichan River estuary, 28 September 1889.
Consolidated Fishery Regulations for the Province of British Columbia, Order-in-
   Council, 18 July 1889.
Fishery Regulations for the Province of British Columbia, Order-in-Council, 14
   March 1890, as amended by Order-in-Council, 7 November 1890.
Fishery Regulations for the Province of British Columbia, Order-in-Council, 3
   March 1894, as amended by Order-in-Council, 2 May 1904.
Fishery Regulation, Order-in-Council, 4 June 1902.
Fisheries Act, R.S.C. 1906, c. 45.
Fisheries Act, R.S.C. 1914, c. 8, as amended by 8–9 Geo. V, c. 22.
Special Fishery Regulations for the Province of British Columbia, Order-in-Council,
   9 February 1915, as amended by Order-in-Council, 11 September 1917.
Special Fishery Regulations for the Province of British Columbia, Order-in-Council,
   26 April 1922, P.C. 895.
Fisheries Act, R.S.C. 1927, c. 73.

Cowichan Tribes First Nation By-laws

Cowichan Indian Band By-law, 1956, no. 1.
Cowichan Indian Band By-law, 1983, no. 2.

Great Britain Statutory Instruments

The Black Act, 9 Geo. I, c. 22.
Royal Proclamation of 1763
*An Act to enlarge the Powers of Justices in determining Complaints between Masters
   and Servants and between Masters, Apprentices, Artificers and others* (1823), 4
   Geo. IV c. 34.
British North America Act (1867)
Salmon Fishery Act (1861), 24 & 25 Vic., c. 109.

Secondary Sources

Abel, Kerry, and Jean Friesen, eds. *Aboriginal Resource Use in Canada: Historical
   and Legal Aspects*. Winnipeg: University of Manitoba Press, 1991.
Anderson, A.C. 'Notes on the Indian Tribes of British North America, and the
   Northwest Coast.' *The Historical Magazine* 7 (1863).

Arnett, Chris. *The Terror of the Coast: Land Alienation and Colonial War on Vancouver Island and the Gulf Islands, 1849–1863*. Burnaby, BC: Talonbooks, 1999.

Arthurs, H.W. *'Without the Law': Administrative Justice and Legal Pluralism in Nineteenth-Century England*. Toronto: University of Toronto Press, 1985.

Atiyah, Patrick. *The Rise and Fall of Freedom of Contract*. Oxford: Clarendon Press, 1979.

Attwood, Bain, ed. *In the Age of Mabo: History, Aborigines and Australia*. St Leonards, NSW: Allen & Unwin, 1996.

Austin, John. *The Province of Jurisprudence Determined*. London: Weidenfeld & Nicholson, 1955 [1832].

Barman, Jean. *The West beyond the West: A History of British Columbia*. Toronto: University of Toronto Press, 1991.

Barnett, Homer G. 'The Nature of the Potlatch.' *American Anthropologist* 40 (1938): 349–58.

Bell, Leonard M., and Ronald J. Kallman. *The Cowichan-Chemainus River Estuaries: Status of Knowledge to 1975*. West Vancouver: Fisheries and Marine Service, Pacific Environment Institute, Environment Canada, 1976.

Bennett, Marilyn G. *Indian Fishing and Its Cultural Importance in the Fraser River System*. Fisheries Service, Pacific Region, Department of the Environment and Union of British Columbia Indian Chiefs, April 1973.

Berkes, Fikret. 'Fishery Resource Use in a Subartic Community.' *Human Ecology* 5 (1977): 289–307.

– 'Common-Property Resource Management and Cree Indian Fisheries in Subarctic Canada.' In Bonnie J. McKay and James M. Acheson, eds., *The Question of the Commons: The Culture and Ecology of Communal Resources* 66–91. Tuscon: University of Arizona Press, 1987.

– 'Traditional Ecological Knowledge in Perspective.' In Julian T. Inglis, ed., *Traditional Ecological Knowledge: Concepts and Cases*, 1–10. Ottawa: International Program on Traditional Ecological Knowledge and International Development Research Centre, 1993.

– 'Indigenous Knowledge and Resource Management Systems in the Canadian Subarctic.' In F. Berkes and Carl Folke, ed., *Linking Social and Ecological Systems: Management Practices and Social Mechanisms for Building Resilience*, 98–128. Cambridge: Cambridge University Press, 1998.

– *Sacred Ecology: Traditional Ecological Knowledge and Resource Management*. Philadelphia: Taylor & Francis, 1999.

Berringer, Patricia Ann. 'Northwest Coast Traditional Salmon Fisheries: Systems of Resouce Utilization.' MA thesis, University of British Columbia, 1982.

Berringer, P.A., W. Green, and V. Smith, 'Ehattesaht Traditional Fisheries

Systems.' In Barry Sadler and Peter Boothroyd, eds., *Traditional Ecological Knowledge and Modern Environmental Assessment*, 41–50. Vancouver: UBC, Centre for Human Settlement, 1994.

Bevan, Jonquil. *Izaak Walton's The Compleat Angler: The Art of Recreation*. Brighton: The Harvester Press, 1988.

Bierwert, Crisca. *Brushed by Cedar, Living by the River*. Tuscon: University of Arizona Press, 1999.

Binford, Lewis R., *For Theory Building in Archaeology: Essays on Faunal Remains, Aquatic Resources, Spatial Analysis, and Systemic Modeling*. New York: Academic Press, 1977.

Binnie, W.I.C. 'The Sparrow Doctrine: Beginning of the End or end of the Beginning?' *Queen's Law Journal* 15 (1990): 217–53.

Bishop, Margaret W. *And So They Came to Cowichan*. Victoria: Robinson Press, 1975.

Blair, Peggy. 'Solemn Promises and *Solum* Rights: The Saugeen Ojibway Fishing Grounds and *R. v. Jones and Nadjiwon*.' *Ottawa Law Review* 28 (1996–7): 125–43.

– 'Taken for 'Granted': Aboriginal Title and Public Fishing Rights in Upper Canada.' *Ontario History* 92 (2000): 31–55.

Blyth, Gladys Young. *Salmon Canneries: British Columbia North Coast*. Lantzville: Oolichan Books, 1991.

Boas, Franz. *Sixth Report on the North-Western Tribes of Canada*. London: British Association for the Advancement of Science, 1890.

– *Chinook Texts*. Washington: Government Printing Office, 1894.

– *The Indian Tribes of the Lower Fraser River*. London, 1894.

Boas, Franz, ed. *Folk-Tales of Salishan and Sahaptin Tribes*. New York: Kraus Reprint Co., 1969.

Borrows, John. 'With or Without You: First Nations Law (in Canada).' *McGill Law Journal* 41 (1996): 629–65.

Bowsfield, Hartwell, ed. *Fort Victoria Letters: 1846–1852*. Winnipeg: Hudson's Bay Record Society, 1979.

Boxberger, Daniel L. *To Fish in Common: The Ethnohistory of Lummi Indian Salmon Fishing*. Lincoln: University of Nebraska Press, 1989.

Boyd, Robert T. 'Commentary on Early Contact-Era Smallpox in the Pacific Northwest.' *Ethnohistory* 43 (1996): 307–28.

– *The Coming of the Spirit of Pestilence: Introduced Infectious Diseases and Population Decline among Northwest Indians, 1774–1874*. Seattle: University of Washington Press, 1999.

Bridge, Kathryn. *Henry & Self: The Private Life of Sarah Crease, 1826–1922*. Victoria: Sono Nis Press, 1996.

Brown, Jennifer S.H. *Strangers in Blood: Fur Trade Company Families in Indian Country*. Vancouver: University of British Columbia Press, 1980.

Brownlie, Robin, and Mary-Ellen Kelm. 'Desperately Seeking Absolution: Native Agency as Colonialist Alibi?' *Canadian Historical Review* 75 (1994): 543–56.

Cail, Robert E. *Land, Man and the Law: The Disposal of Crown Lands in British Columbia, 1871–1913*. Vancouver: University of British Columbia Press, 1974.

Cannon, Aubrey. 'Conflict and Salmon on the Interior Plateau of British Columbia.' In Brian Hayden, ed., *A Complex Culture of the British Columbia Plateau: Traditional* Stl'atl'imx *Resource Use*, 506–24. Vancouver: UBC Press, 1992.

Cant, Garth, John Overton, and Eric Pawson, eds. *Indigenous Land Rights in Commonwealth Countries: Dispossession, Negotiation and Community Action*. Christchurch, NZ: Department of Geography, University of Canterbury, 1993.

Carrothers, W.A. *The British Columbia Fisheries*. Toronto: University of Toronto Press, 1941.

Chanock, Martin. *Law, Custom and Social Order: The Colonial Experience in Malawi and Zambia*. Cambridge: Cambridge University Press, 1985.

Chitty, Joseph. *A Treatise on the Game Laws and on Fisheries* [1812]. New York: Garland Publishing, 1979.

Christophers, Brett. *Positioning the Missionary*. Vancouver: UBC Press, 1998.

Clastres, Pierre. *Society against the State: The Leader as Servant and the Humane Uses of Power among the Indians of the Americas*. New York: Urizen Books, 1974.

Clayton, Daniel. 'Geographies of the Lower Skeena.' *BC Studies* 94 (1992): 29–58.

– *Islands of Truth: The Imperial Fashioning of Vancouver Island*. Vancouver: UBC Press, 2000.

Codere, Helen. *Fighting with Property: A Study of Kwakiutl Potlatching and Warfare, 1792–1930*. Seattle: University of Washington Press, 1950, 1966.

Cohn, Bernard S. *Colonialism and Its Forms of Knowledge: The British in India*. Princeton: Princeton University Press, 1996.

Cole, Douglas, and Ira Chaikin. *An Iron Hand upon the People: The Law against the Potlatch on the Northwest Coast*. Vancouver: Douglas & McIntyre, Ltd., 1990.

Cotterell, Roger. *The Sociology of Law: An Introduction*. London: Butterworths, 1984.

Coulson, H.J.W., and Urquhart A. Forbes. *The Law Relating to Waters, Sea, Tidal and Inland*. London: Henry Sweet, 1880.

Craig, J.A., and R.L. Hacker. 'The History and Development of the Fisheries of the Columbia River.' *Bulletin of the Bureau of Fisheries* 49 (1940).

Craven, Paul. 'The Law of Master and Servant in Mid-Nineteenth-Century Ontario.' In David Flaherty, ed., *Essays in the History of Canadian Law*. Volume 1, 175–211. Toronto: The Osgoode Society, 1981.

– '"The Modern Spirit of the Law": Blake, Mowat, and the Breaches of Contract Act, 1877.' In G. Blaine Baker and Jim Phillips, eds., *Essays in the History of Canadian Law*. Volume 8. *Essays in Honour of R.C.B. Risk*, 142–70. Toronto: The Osgoode Society, 1999.

Craven, Paul, and Douglas Hay. 'The Criminalization of "Free" Labour: Master and Servant in Comparative Perspective.' *Slavery and Abolition* 15 (1994): 71–101.

Cronin, William, ed. *Uncommon Ground: Rethinking the Human Place in Nature*. New York: W.W. Norton & Co., 1996.

Curtis, Edward S. *The North American Indian*, Vol. 9. New York: Johnson Reprint Corp., 1913.

Darian-Smith, Eve. *Bridging Divides: The Channel Tunnel and English Legal Identity in the New Europe*. Berkeley: University of California Press, 1999.

Darian-Smith, Eve, and Peter Fitzpatrick, eds. *Laws of the Postcolonial*. Ann Arbor: University of Michigan Press, 1999.

Demeritt, David. 'Visions of Agriculture in British Columbia.' *BC Studies* 108 (1995–6): 29–59.

Dicey, A.V. *Introduction to the Study of Law of the Constitution*. London: Macmillan, 1885.

Dorcey, Anthony H.J., ed. *Perspectives on Sustainable Development in Water Management: Towards Agreement in the Fraser River Basin*. Vancouver: Westwater Research Centre, University of British Columbia, 1991.

Drucker, Philip. *The Native Brotherhoods: Modern Intertribal Organizations on the Northwest Coast*. Washington: U.S. Govt. Printing Office, 1958.

– *Cultures of the North Pacific Coast*. San Francisco: Chandler Publishing, 1965.

– 'Rank, Wealth and Kinship in Northwest Coast Society.' In Tom McFeat, ed., *Indians of the North Pacific Coast*, 134–46. Ottawa: Macmillan, 1978.

Drucker, Philip, and Robert F. Heizer. *To Make My Name Good: A Reexamination of the Southern Kwakiutl Potaltch*. Berkeley: University of California Press, 1967.

Duff, Wilson. 'The Fort Victoria Treaties.' *BC Studies* 3 (1969): 3–57.

– *The Indian History of British Columbia*. Volume 1. *The Impact of the White Man*. Victoria: Royal British Columbia Museum, 1969.

- *The Upper Stalo Indians of the Fraser River of B.C.* Anthropology in British Columbia, Memoir no. 1. Victoria, 1952.
Duff, Wilson, ed. *Histories, Territories, and Laws of the Kitwancool.* Anthropology in British Columbia, Memoir no. 4. Victoria: Royal British Columbia Museum, 1959, 1989.
Dworkin, Ronald. *Law's Empire.* Cambridge, Mass.: Harvard University Press, 1986.
Dyck, Jos C. '"And Then We Will Mind the Law": The Enforcement of Federal Fisheries Regulations in British Columbia and the Resistance of Native Fishers, 1894–1916.' MA thesis, Simon Fraser University, 1994.
Everitt, Nicholas. *Shots from a Lawyer's Gun.* London: Everett & Co., 1910.
Fanon, Frantz. *The Wretched of the Earth.* Translated by Constance Farrington. New York: Grove Press, 1966.
Feeney, David, Fikret Berkes, Bonnie J. McCay, and James M. Acheson. 'The Tragedy of the Commons: Twenty-Two Years Later.' *Human Ecology* 18 (1990): 1–19.
Fisher, Robin. *Contact and Conflict: Indian–European Relations in British Columbia, 1774–1890.* Vancouver: UBC Press, 1977, 1992.
Fiske, Jo-Anne. 'From Customary Law to Oral Traditions: Discursive Formation of Plural Legalisms in Northern British Columbia, 1857–1993.' *BC Studies* 115/116 (1997/8): 267–88.
Fiske, Jo-Anne, and Betty Patrick. *C'is dideen khat' When the Plumes Rise: The Way of the Lake Babine Nation.* Vancouver: UBC Press, 2000.
Fitzpatrick, Peter. *Law and State in Papua New Guinea.* London: Academic Press, 1980.
- 'Law, Plurality and Underdevelopment.' In David Sugarman, ed., *Legality, Ideology and the State*, 150–82. London: Academic Press, 1983.
- *The Mythology of Modern Law.* London: Routledge, 1992.
Fitzpatrick, Peter, ed. *Dangerous Supplements: Resistance and Renewal in Jurisprudence.* Durham: Duke University Press, 1991.
Flaherty, David H., ed. *Essays in the History of Canadian Law.* Volume 1. Toronto: The Osgoode Society, 1981.
Forester, Joseph E., and Anne D. Forester. *Fishing: British Columbia's Commercial Fishing History.* Saanichton: Hancock House Publishers, 1975.
Foster, Hamar. 'The Saanichton Bay Marina Case: Imperial Law, Colonial History and Competing Theories of Aboriginal Title.' *UBC Law Review* 23 (1989): 629–50.
- 'Mutiny on the *Beaver*: Law and Authority in the Fur Trade Navy, 1835–1840.' In Dale Gibson and W. Wesley Pue, eds., *Glimpses of Canadian Legal History*, 15–46. Winnipeg: Legal Research Institute, 1991.

- 'Sins against the Great Spirit: The Law, the Hudson's Bay Company, and the MacKenzie's River Murders, 1835–1839.' *Criminal Justice History* 10 (1989): 23–76.
- 'International Homicide in Early British Columbia.' In Jim Phillips, Tina Loo, and Susan Lewthwaite, eds., *Essays in the History of Canadian Law.* Volume 5. *Crime and Criminal Justice,* 64–111. Toronto: Osgoode Society for Canadian Legal History, 1994.
- 'Letting Go the Bone: The Idea of Indian Title in British Columbia, 1849–1927.' In H. Foster and John McLaren, eds., *Essays in the History of Canadian Law.* Volume 6. *British Columbia and the Yukon,* 87–127. Toronto: The Osgoode Society for Canadian Legal History, 1995.
- 'British Columbia: Legal Institutions in the Far West, from Contact to 1871.' *Manitoba Law Journal* 23 (1996): 293–340.
Foucault, Michel. *Power/Knowledge: Selected Interviews and Other Writings 1972–1977.* Ed Colin Gordon. New York: Pantheon, 1980.
- *Discipline and Punish. The Birth of the Prison.* Trans. Alan Sheridan, 1977. New York: Vintage Books, 1995.
Galois, Robert. 'The Indian Rights Association, Native Protest Activity and the "Land Question" in British Columbia, 1903–1916.' *Native Studies Review* 8 (1992): 1–34.
- 'The History of the Upper Skeena Region, 1850 to 1927.' *Native Studies Review* 9 (1993–4): 113–83.
Ghai, Yash, Robin Luckman, and Francis Snyder, eds. *The Political Economy of Law: A Third World Reader.* Delhi: Oxford University Press, 1987.
Gibson, Dale, and W. Wesley Pue, eds. *Glimpses of Canadian Legal History.* Winnipeg: Legal Research Institute, 1991.
Gladstone, Percy. 'Native Indians and the Fishing Industry of British Columbia.' *Canadian Journal of Economics and Political Science* 19 (1953): 20–34.
Glavin, Terry. *Dead Reckoning: Confronting the Crisis in Pacific Fisheries.* Vancouver: Greystone Books and David Suzuki Foundation, 1996.
Glenn, Patrick, ed. *Contemporary Law 1994 Droit contemporain.* Montreal: Éditions Yvons Blais, 1994.
Gordon, Bob. 'Critical Legal Histories.' *Stanford Law Review* 36 (1984): 57–126.
Gough, Barry M. *Gunboat Frontier: British Maritime Authority and Northwest Coast Indians, 1846–1890.* Vancouver: UBC Press, 1984.
Griffiths, John. 'What Is Legal Pluralism?' *Journal of Legal Pluralism and Unofficial Law* 24 (1986): 1–55.
Groot, C., and L. Margolis, eds. *Pacific Salmon Life Histories.* Vancouver: UBC Press, 1991.
Guha, Ranajit. *A Rule of Property for Bengal.* Paris: Mouton, 1963.

– 'Chandra's Death.' In Guha, ed., *A Subaltern Studies Reader, 1986–1995*, 34–62. Minneapolis: University of Minnesota Press, 1997.

Guha, Ranajit, ed. *Subaltern Studies: Writings on South Asian History and Society, Vol. 1*. Delhi: Oxford University Press, 1982.

Hackler, J.C. 'Factors Leading to Social Disorganization among the Carrier Indians at Lake Babine.' MA thesis, San Diego State, 1958.

Hale, Mathew. 'De Juris Maris et Brachiorum Ejusdem.' In F. Hargrave, ed., *A Collection of Tracts Relative to the Law of England*. Volume 1, Part 1 [1787], 1–44. Abington: Professional Books Ltd., 1982.

Hansen, Lise C. 'Treaty Fishing Rights and the Development of Fisheries Legislation in Ontario: A Primer.' *Native Studies Review* 7 (1991): 1–21.

– 'A Rejoinder to Waisberg and Holzkamm.' *Native Studies Review* 8 (1992): 57–60.

Hardin, Garrett. 'The Tragedy of the Commons.' *Science* 162 (1969): 1243–48.

Harring, Sidney L. *White Man's Law: Native People in Nineteenth-Century Canadian Jurisprudence*. Toronto: Osgoode Society for Canadian Legal History, 1999.

Harris, Cole. *The Resettlement of British Columbia: Essays in Colonialism and Geographical Change*. Vancouver: UBC Press, 1997.

– *Making Native Space: Colonialism, Resistance and Reserves in British Columbia*. Forthcoming.

Harris, R.C., ed. *The Historical Atlas of Canada*. Volume 1. Toronto: University of Toronto Press, 1987.

Harris, Douglas C. 'The Nlha7kápmx Meeting at Lytton, 1879, and the Rule of Law.' *BC Studies* 108 (1995/6): 5–25.

– 'Territoriality, Aboriginal Rights and the Heiltsuk Spawn-on-Kelp Fishery.' *UBC Law Review* 34 (2000): 195–238.

– 'Indian Reserves, Aboriginal Fisheries, and Anglo-Canadian Law in British Columbia.' Forthcoming.

Hay, Douglas. 'Master and Servant in England: Using the Law in the Eighteenth and Nineteenth Centuries.' In Willibald Steinmetz, ed., *Private Law and Social Inequality in the Industrial Age*, 227–64.

Hay, Douglas, Peter Linebaugh, John G. Rule, E.P. Thomspon, and Cal Winslow, eds. *Albion's Fatal Tree: Crime and Society in Eighteenth-Century England*. London: Allen Lane, 1975.

Hayden, Brian, ed. *A Complex Culture of the British Columbia Plateau: Traditional Stl'atl'imx Resource Use*. Vancouver: UBC Press, 1992.

Hazlehurst, Kayleen M., ed. *Legal Pluralism and the Colonial Legacy*. Aldershot: Avebury, 1995.

Helm, June, ed. *Handbook of North American Indians*. Volume 6. *Subarctic*. Washington: Smithsonian Institution, 1981.

Hendrickson, James E., ed. *Journals of the Colonial Legislatures of the Colonies of Vancouver Island and British Columbia, 1851–1871*. Victoria: Provincial Archives of British Columbia, 1980.

Hewes, Gordon W. 'Aboriginal Use of Fishery Resources in Northwestern North America.' PhD thesis, University of California, 1947.

– 'Indian Fisheries Productivity in Pre-Contact Times in the Pacific Salmon Area.' *Northwest Anthropological Research Notes* 7 (1973): 133–55.

Higginbottom, Edward N. 'The Changing Geography of Salmon Canning in British Columbia, 1870–1931.' MA thesis, Simon Fraser University, 1988.

Hill-Tout, Charles. 'Report on the Ethnology of the South-Eastern Tribes of Vancouver Island, British Columbia.' *Journal of the Royal Anthropological Institute of Great Britain and Ireland* 37 (1907): 306–74.

Hobsbawm, E.J. *The Age of Empire, 1875–1914*. London: Cardinal, 1987.

Hobsbawm, E.J., and Terance Ranger, eds. *The Invention of Tradition*. Cambridge: Cambridge University Press, 1983.

Hukari, Thomas. *The Cowichan Dictionary of the Hul'qumi'num' Dialect of the Coast Salish People*. Duncan, BC: Cowichan Tribes, 1995.

Hunt, Alan. *Explorations in Law and Society: Toward a Constitutive Theory of Law*. New York: Routledge, 1993.

Hunt, Alan, and Gary Wickham. *Foucault and the Law: Towards a Sociology of Law as Governance*. London: Pluto Press, 1994.

Hurst, J. Willard. *Law and Economic Growth: The Legal History of the Lumber Industry in Wisconsin 1836–1915*. Cambridge, Mass.: Belknap Press, 1964.

Inglis, Julian T. *Traditional Ecological Knowledge: Concepts and Cases*. Ottawa: International Program on Traditional Ecological Knowledge, 1993.

Innis, Harold A. *The Cod Fisheries: The History of an International Economy*. New Haven: Yale University Press, 1940.

– *The Fur Trade in Canada: An Introduction to Canadian Economic History*. Toronto: Toronto University Press, 1956.

Jamieson, Stuart, and Percy Gladstone. 'Unionism in the Fishing Industry of British Columbia.' *Canadian Journal of Economics and Political Science* 11 (1950): 146–71.

Johnstone, Kenneth. *The Acquatic Explorers: A History of the Fisheries Research Board of Canada*. Toronto: University of Toronto Press, 1977.

Jones, Gareth Stedman. *Outcast London: A Study in the Relationship between Classes in Victorian London*. Oxford: Clarendon Press, 1971.

Jones-Desjarlais, Jennifer Lynn. 'The Scales of Justice or the Native Claim to the Management of Reserve Fisheries.' LLM thesis, University of British Columbia, 1985.

Juda, Lawrence. *International Law and Ocean Use Management: The Evolution of Ocean Governance*. London and New York: Routledge, 1996.

Kelm, Mary-Ellen. *Colonizing Bodies: Aboriginal Health and Healing in British Columbia, 1900–1950*. Vancouver: UBC Press, 1998.

Kennedy, Dorothy I.D., and Randy Bouchard, '*Stl'atl'imx* (Fraser River Lillooet) Fishing.' In Brian Hayden, ed., *A Complex Culture of the British Columbia Plateau: Traditional* Stl'atl'imx *Resource Use*, 266–354. Vancouver: UBC Press, 1992.

Kerr, J.B. *Biographical Dictionary of Well-Known British Columbians: With a Historical Sketch*. Vancouver: Kerr & Begg, 1890.

Kew, Michael. 'Notes on Indian Communities on Babine Lake.' Unpublished manuscript located in Special Collections at the University of British Columbia.

– 'Salmon Availability, Technology, and Cultural Adaptation in the Fraser River Watershed.' In Brian Hayden, ed., *A Complex Culture of the British Columbia Plateau: Traditional* Stl'átl'imx *Resource Use*. Vancouver: UBC Press, 1992.

Kew, Michael, and Julian Griggs. 'Native Indians of the Fraser Basin: Towards a Model of Sustainable Resource Use.' In Anthony H.J. Dorcey, ed., *Perspectives on Sustainable Development in Water Management: Towards Agreement in the Fraser River Basin*, 17–47. Vancouver, University of British Columbia, Westwater Research Centre, 1991.

Knight, Rolf. *Indians at Work: An Informal History of Native Indian Labour in British Columbia, 1858–1930*. Vancouver: New Star Books, 1978, 1996.

La Forest, Gerard V. *Water Law in Canada: The Atlantic Provinces*. Ottawa: Information Canada, 1973.

Lane, Barbara. 'A Comparative and Analytic Study of Some Aspects of Northwest Coast Religion.' PhD thesis, University of Washington, 1953.

– 'Federal Recognition of Indian Fishing Rights in British Columbia.' Vancouver: Union of BC Indian Chiefs, April 1978.

Langbein, J. 'Albion's Fatal Flaws.' *Past & Present* 98 (1983): 96–120.

Levy, D.A., and K.J. Hall. *A Review of the Limnology and Sockeye Salmon Ecology of Babine Lake*. Vancouver: University of British Columbia, Westwater Research Centre, 1985.

Linebaugh, P. '(Marxist) Social History and (Conservative) Legal History: A Reply to Professor Langbein.' *New York University Law Review* 60 (1985): 212–43.

Llewellyn, K.N., and E. Adamson Hobel. *The Cheyenne Way: Conflict and Case*

Law in Primitive Jurisprudence. Norman: University of Oklahoma Press, 1941.

Loo, Tina. 'Dan Cranmer's Potlatch: Law as Coercion, Symbol, and Rhetoric in British Columbia, 1884–1951.' *Canadian Historical Review* 73 (1992): 125–65.

– *Making Law, Order, and Authority in British Columbia, 1821–1871*. Toronto: University of Toronto Press, 1994.

– 'The Road from Bute Inlet: Crime and Colonial Identity in British Columbia.' In Jim Phillips, T. Loo, and Susan Lewthwaite, eds., *Essays in the History of Canadian Law*. Volume 5. *Crime and Criminal Justice*, 131–42. Toronto: Osgoode Society for Legal History, 1994.

– 'Tonto's Due: Law, Culture, and Colonization in British Columbia.' In Hamar Foster and John McLaren, eds., *Essays in the History of Canadian Law*. Volume 6. *British Columbia and the Yukon*, 128–70. Toronto: Osgoode Society for Legal History, 1995.

Lutz, John. 'After the Fur Trade: The Aboriginal Labouring Class of British Columbia, 1849–1890.' *Journal of the Canadian Historical Association* (1992): 69–93.

– 'Work, Wages and Welfare in Aboriginal–Non-Aboriginal Relations, British Columbia, 1849–1970.' PhD thesis, University of Victoria, 1994.

Lyons, Cicely. *Salmon: Our Heritage. The Story of a Province and an Industry*. Vancouver: British Columbia Packers Ltd, 1969.

Lytwyn, Victor. 'Ojibway and Ottawa Fisheries around Manitoulin Island: Historical and Geographical Perspectives on Aboriginal and Treaty Fishing Rights.' *Native Studies Review* 6 (1990): 1–30.

Mackie, Richard Somerset. 'Colonial Land, Indian Labour and Company Capital: The Economy of Vancouver Island, 1849–1858.' MA thesis, University of Victoria, 1984.

– *The Wilderness Profound: Victorian Life on the Gulf of Georgia*. Victoria: Sono Nis Press, 1995.

– *Trading beyond the Mountains: The British Fur Trade on the Pacific, 1763–1843*. Vancouver: UBC Press, 1996.

Macklem, Patrick. 'First Nations Self-Government and the Borders of the Canadian Legal Imagination.' *McGill Law Journal* 33 (1991): 382–456.

Malinowski, Bronislaw. *Crime and Custom in a Savage Society*. Paterson, NJ: Littlefield, Adams, 1926.

Marchak, Patricia, Neil Guppy, and John McMullan, eds. *Uncommon Property: The Fishing and Fish-Processing Industries in British Columbia*. Toronto: Methuen, 1987.

Marshall, Daniel P. *Those Who Fell from the Sky: A History of the Cowichan Peoples*. Duncan, BC: Cowichan Tribes, 1999.

Masco, Joseph. '"It Is a Strict Law That Bids Us Dance": Cosmologies, Colonialism, Death and Ritual Authority in the Kwakiutl Potlatch, 1849–1922.' *Journal of Comparative Studies in Society and History* 37 (1995): 41–75.

Mathews, Ralph, and John Phyne. 'Regulating the Newfoundland Inshore Fishery: Traditional Values versus State Control in the Regulation of a Common Property Resource.' *Journal of Canadian Studies* 23 (1988): 158–76.

McCay, Bonnie J., and James M. Acheson, eds. *The Question of the Commons: The Culture and Ecology of Communal Resources.* Tuscon: University of Arizona Press, 1987.

McClintock, Anne. *Imperial Leather: Race, Gender and Sexuality in the Colonial Contest.* London: Routledge, 1995.

McCue, June. 'Treaty-Making from an Indigenous Perspective: A Ned'u'ten–Canadian Treaty Model.' LLM thesis, University of British Columbia, 1998.

McEvoy, Arthur. *The Fisherman's Problem: Ecology and Law in the California Fisheries, 1850–1980.* Cambridge: Cambridge University Press, 1986.

– 'Toward an Interactive Theory of Nature and Culture: Ecology, Production, and Cognition in the California Fishing Industry.' *Environmental Review* 11 (1987): 289–305.

McFeat, Tom, ed. *Indians of the North Pacific Coast.* Ottawa: Macmillan, 1978.

McGrath, Ann, ed. *Contested Ground: Australian Aborigines under the British Crown.* St Leonards, NSW: Allen & Unwin, 1995.

McKervill, Hugh W. *The Salmon People.* Vancouver: Whitecap Books, 1967, 1992.

McQueen, Rob, and W. Wesley Pue. 'Misplaced Traditions: The Legal Profession and the British Empire.' *Law in Context* 16 (1999): 1–16.

Meggs, Geoff. *Salmon: The Decline of the British Columbia Fishery.* Vancouver: Douglas & McIntyre, 1991, 1995.

Meggs, Geoff, and Duncan Stacey. *Cork Lines and Canning Lines: The Glory Years of Fishing on the West Coast.* Vancouver: Douglas & McIntyre, 1992.

Merry, Sally Engle. 'Legal Pluralism.' *Law & Society Review* 22 (1988): 869–96.

– 'Law and Colonialism.' *Law & Society Review* 25 (1991): 889–922.

– *Colonizing Hawai'i: The Cultural Power of Law.* Princeton: Princeton University Press, 2000.

Moore, Sally Falk. *Law as Process: An Anthropological Approach.* London: Routledge & Kegan Paul, 1973.

– *Social Facts and Fabrications: 'Customary' Law on Kilimanjaro, 1880–1980.* Cambridge: Cambridge University Press, 1986.

Moore, Stuart A., and Hubert Stuart Moore. *The History and Law of Fisheries.* London: Stevens and Haynes, 1903.

Morice, A.G. *Fifty Years in Western Canada: The Abridged Memoirs of Father A.G. Morice, O.M.I.* Toronto: Ryerson Press, 1930.

Mulholland, David. *The Will to Power: The Missionary Career of Father Morice.* Vancouver: UBC Press, 1986.

Muszynski, Alicja. *Cheap Wage Labour: Race and Gender in the Fisheries of British Columbia.* Montreal and Kingston: McGill-Queen's University Press, 1996.

Nader, Laura, ed. *Law in Culture and Society.* Berkeley: University of California Press, 1969.

Neal, David. *The Rule of Law in a Penal Colony: Law and Power in New South Wales.* Cambridge: Cambridge University Press, 1991.

Neeson, J.M. *Commoners: Common Right, Enclosure and Social Change in Commonfield England, 1700–1820.* New York: Cambridge University Press, 1993.

Newell, Dianne. 'Dispersal and Concentration: The Slowly Changing Spatial Pattern of the British Columbia Salmon Canning Industry.' *Journal of Historical Geography* 14 (1988): 22–36.

– *Tangled Webs of History: Indians and the Law in Canada's Pacific Coast Fisheries.* Toronto: University of Toronto Press, 1993.

– 'A Dynamic Tradition: Canada's Pacific Coast Commercial Fishery and Aboriginal Rights.' In Garth Cant, John Overton, and Eric Pawson, eds., *Indigenous Land Rights in Commonwealth Countries: Dispossession, Negotiation and Community Action*, 45–55. Christchurch, NZ: Department of Geography, University of Canterbury, 1993.

Newell, Dianne, and Rosemary E. Ommer, eds. *Fishing Places, Fishing People: Traditions and Issues in Canadian Small-Scale Fisheries.* Toronto: University of Toronto Press, 1999.

Nielsen, Larry A. 'The Evolution of Fisheries Management Philosophy.' *Marine Fisheries Review* 38 (1976): 15–23.

Norcross, E. Blanche. *The Warm Land.* Duncan, BC: E.B. Norcross, 1959.

O'Donnell, Brendan. 'Indian and Non-Native Use of the Babine River: An Historical Perspective.' Department of Fisheries and Oceans, Native Affairs Division, Issue 2, Policy and Program Planning, August 1987.

– 'Indian and Non-Native Use of the Cowichan and Koksilah Rivers: An Historical Perspective.' Department of Fisheries and Oceans, Native Affairs Division, Issue 8, Policy and Program Planning, July 1988.

Parenteau, Bill. '"Care, Control and Supervision": Native People in the Canadian Atlantic Salmon Fishery.' *Canadian Historical Review* 79 (1998): 1–35.

Phelps, T.T. *Fishing Dreams.* London: The Batchworth Press, 1949.

Phillips, Jim, Tina Loo, and Susan Lewthwaite, eds. *Essays in the History of Canadian Law.* Volume 5. *Crime and Criminal Justice.* Toronto: The Osgoode Society for Canadian Legal History, 1994.

Pritchard, Allan, ed. *Vancouver Island Letters of Edmund Hope Verney, 1862–1865.* Vancouver: UBC Press, 1996.

Provincial Archives of British Columbia. *The Crease Family Archives: A Record of Settlement and Service in British Columbia.* Victoria: Provincial Archives of British Columbia, 1982.

Pue, W. Wesley. 'Revolution by Legal Means.' In Patrick Glenn, ed., *Contemporary Law 1994 Droit contemporain*, 1–30. Montreal: Éditions Yvons Blais, 1994.

– 'Locating Hurst.' *Law and History Review* 18 (2000): 187–95.

Purdy, Jeannine. 'Postcolonialism: The Emperor's New Clothes.' In Eve-Darian Smith and Peter Fitzpatrick, eds., *Laws of the Postcolonial*, 203–29. Ann Arbor: University of Michigan Press, 1999.

Ralston, Henry Keith. 'Patterns of Trade and Investment on the Pacific Coast, 1867–1892: The Case of the British Columbia Salmon Canning Industry.' *BC Studies* 1 (1968–9): 37–45.

– 'John Sullivan Deas: A Black Entrepeneur in British Columbia Salmon Canning.' *BC Studies* 32 (1976–7): 64–78.

Ranger, Terence. 'The Invention of Tradition in Colonial Africa.' In Eric Hobsbawm and T. Ranger, eds., *The Invention of Tradition*, 211–62. Cambridge: Cambridge University Press, 1983.

Ray, Arthur J. *Indians in the Fur Trade: Their Role as Trappers, Hunters and Middlemen in the Lands Southwest of Hudson Bay, 1660–1870.* Toronto: Toronto University Press, 1974.

– 'Fur Trade History and the Gitksan-Wet'suwet'en Comprehensive Claim: Men of Property and the Exercise of Title.' In Kerry Abel and Jean Friesen, eds., *Aboriginal Resource Use in Canada: Historical and Legal Aspects*, 301–15. Winnipeg: University of Manitoba Press, 1991.

Raz, Joseph. *The Authority of Law: Essays on Law and Morality.* Oxford: Clarendon Press, 1979.

Reid, John Phillip. 'Principles of Vengeance: Fur Trappers, Indians, and Retaliation for Homicide in the Transboundary North American West.' *Western Historical Review* 24 (1993): 21–43.

– 'Restraints of Vengeance: Retaliation-in-Kind and the Use of Indian Law in the Old Oregon Country.' *Oregon Historical Quarterly* 95 (1994): 48–92.

Reynolds, Henry. *The Law of the Land.* Ringwood: Penguin Books Australia Ltd, 1987.

Richardson, Allan. 'Control of Productive Resources on the Northwest Coast of North America.' In Nancy M. Williams and Eugene S. Hunn, eds., *Resource Managers: North American and Australian Hunter-Gatherers*, 93–112. Washington: American Association for the Advancement of Science, 1982.

Rohner, Ronald P., ed. *The Ethnography of Franz Boas: Letters and Diaries of Franz Boas Written on the Northwest Coast from 1886 to 1931*. Chicago: University of Chicago Press, 1969.

Romanoff, Steven. 'Fraser Lillooet Salmon Fishing.' In Brian Hayden, ed., *A Complex Culture of the British Columbia Plateau: Traditional* Stl'atl'imx *Resource Use*, 470–505. Vancouver: UBC Press, 1992.

Rozen, David L. 'The Ethnozoology of the Cowichan Indian People of British Columbia. Volume 1. Fish, Beach Foods, and Marine Mammals.' Unpublished, 1978. Archived at the Xwi7xwa Library, First Nations House of Learning, University of British Columbia.

Said, Edward W. *Orientalism*. New York: Vintage Books, 1978.

– *Culture and Imperialism*. New York: Vintage Books, 1993.

Sarat, Austin, and Thomas R. Kearns, eds. *Law's Violence*. Ann Arbor: University of Michigan Press, 1992.

Saville, John, ed. *Democracy and Labour Movement: Essays in Honour of Donna Torr*. London: Lawrence & Wishart, 1954.

Saywell, John F.T. *Kaatza: The Chronicles of Cowichan Lake*. Sidney: Cowichan Lake District Centennial Committee, 1967.

Schalk, Randall F. 'The Structure of an Anadromous Fish Resource.' In Lewis R. Binford, ed., *For Theory Building in Archaeology: Essays on Faunal Remains, Aquatic Resources, Spatial Analysis, and Systemic Modeling*, 207–49. New York: Academic Press, 1977.

– 'Estimating Salmon and Steelhead Usage in the Columbia Basin Before 1850: The Anthropological Perspective,' *Northwest Environmental Journal* 2 (1986): 1–29.

Scholefield, E.O.S. *British Columbia from the Earliest Times to the Present*. Vancouver: S.J. Clarke Publishing, 1914.

Scott, James C. *Weapons of the Weak: Everyday Forms of Peasant Resistance*. New Haven: Yale University Press, 1985.

– *Domination and the Arts of Resistance: Hidden Transcripts*. New Haven: Yale University Press, 1996.

Shephard, M.P., and A.W. Argue. 'The Commercial Harvest of Salmon in British Columbia, 1820–1877.' *Canadian Technical Report of Fisheries and Aquatic Sciences* 1690 (1989).

Simon, Daphne. 'Master and Servant.' In John Saville, ed., *Democracy and Labour Movement: Essays in Honour of Donna Torr*, 160–200. London: Lawrence & Wishart, 1954.

Slattery, Brian. 'Understanding Aboriginal Rights.' *Canadian Bar Review* 66 (1987): 727.

Smandych, Russell, and Rick Linden. 'Co-existing Forms of Aboriginal and

Private Justice: An Historical Study of the Canadian West.' In Kayleen M. Hazlehurst, ed., *Legal Pluralism and the Colonial Legacy*. Aldershot: Avebury, 1995.

Smandych, Russell, and Gloria Lee. 'Women, Colonization and Resistance: Elements of an Amerindian Autohistorical Approach to the Study of Law and Colonialism.' *Native Studies Review* 10 (1995): 21–46.

Smith, Donald B. 'Aboriginal Rights in 1885: A Study of the *St. Catherine's Milling* or Indian Title Case.' In R.C. Macleod, ed., *Swords and Ploughshares: War and Agriculture in Western Canada*. Edmonton: University of Alberta Press, 1993.

Snyder, Francis G. 'Colonialism and Legal Form: The Creation of "Customary Law" in Senegal.' *Journal of Legal Pluralism* 19 (1981): 49–90.

Snyder, Francis G., and Douglas Hay, eds. *Labour, Law, and Crime: An Historical Perspective*. London: Tavistock Publications, 1987.

Sparrow, Leona Marie. 'Work Histories of a Coast Salish Couple.' MA thesis, University of British Columbia, 1976.

Spradley, James P. *Guests Never Leave Hungry: The Autobiography of James Sewid, A Kwakiutl Indian*. New Haven: Yale University Press, 1969.

Sproat, Gilbert Malcolm. *The Nootka: Scenes and Studies of Savage Life* [1868]. Edited and annotated by Charles Lillard. Victoria: Sono Nis Press, 1987.

Stacey, Duncan. 'Technological Change in the Fraser River Canning Industry.' MA thesis, University of British Columbia, 1970.

– *Sockeye and Tinplate: Technological Change in the Fraser River Canning Industry*. Victoria: BC Provincial Museum Heritage Record no. 15, 1982.

Starr, June, and Jane F. Collier, eds. *History and Power in the Study of Law: New Directions in Legal Anthropology*. Ithaca: Cornell University Press, 1989.

Stewart, Hilary. *Indian Fishing: Early Methods on the Northwest Coast*. Vancouver: J.J. Douglas Ltd, 1977.

Sugarman, David, ed. *Legality, Ideology and the State*. London: Academic Press, 1983.

– '"A Hatred of Disorder": Legal Science, Liberalism and Imperialism.' In Peter Fitzpatrick, ed., *Dangerous Supplements*, 34–67. Durham: Duke University Press, 1991.

Sumner, William Graham. *Folkways: A Study of the Sociological Importance of Usages, Manners, Customs, Mores, and Morals*. Boston: Ginn and Co., 1906.

Suttles, Wayne. *Coast Salish Essays*. Vancouver: Talonbooks, 1987.

Suttles, Wayne, ed. *Handbook of North American Indians*. Volume 7. *Northwest Coast*. Washington: Smithsonian Insitution, 1990.

Taylor, Joseph E., III. *Making Salmon: An Environmental History of the Northwest Fisheries Crisis*. Seattle: University of Washington Press, 1999.

Teit, James. *Traditions of the Thompson River Indians of British Columbia* [1898]. New York: Kraus Reprint Co., 1969.

Tennant, Paul. *Aboriginal People and Politics: The Indian Land Question in British Columbia, 1849–1989*. Vancouver: UBC Press, 1990.

Thompson, E.P. *The Making of the English Working Class*. London: V. Gollanz, 1963.

– *Whigs and Hunters: The Origin of the Black Act*. New York: Pantheon Books, 1975.

– *The Poverty of Theory and Other Essays*. London: Merlin Press, 1978.

– *Customs in Common: Studies in Traditional Popular Culture*. New York: New Press, 1993.

Thoms, J. Michael. 'Illegal Conservation: Two Case Studies of Conflict between Indigenous and State Natural Resource Management Paradigms.' MA thesis, Trent University, 1995.

– '"A Place Called Pennask": Fly-fishing and Colonialism in British Columbia.' *BC Studies*, forthcoming.

– PhD thesis, Dept. of History, UBC, in progress.

Tobey, Margaret L. 'Carrier.' In June Helm, ed., *Handbook of North American Indians*. Volume 6. *Subarctic*, 413–32. Washington: Smithsonian Institution, 1981.

Tough, Frank. *'As Their Natural Resources Fail': Native Peoples and the Economic History of Northern Manitoba, 1870–1930*. Vancouver: UBC Press, 1996.

Tyhurst, Robert. 'Traditional and Comptemporary Land and Resource Use by Ts'kw'ayláxw.' In Brian Hayden, ed., *A Complex Culture of the British Columbia Plateau: Traditional* Stl'atl'imx *Resource Use*, 355–404. Vancouver: UBC Press, 1992.

Usher, Peter. 'Aboriginal Property Systems in Land and Resources.' In Garth Cant, John Overton, and Eric Pawson, eds., *Indigenous Land Rights in Commonwealth Countries: Dispossession, Negotiation and Community Action*, 38–44. Christchurch, NZ: Department of Geography, University of Canterbury and the Ngai Tahu Maori Trust Board, 1993.

Van Kirk, Sylvia. *Many Tender Ties: Women in Fur-Trade Society in Western Canada, 1630–1870*. Winnipeg: Watson and Dwyer, 1980.

Van West, John J. 'Ojibway Fisheries, Commercial Fisheries Development and Fisheries Administration, 1873–1915: An Examination of Conflicting Interest and the Collapse of the Sturgeon Fisheries of the Lake of the Woods.' *Native Studies Review* 6 (1990): 31–65.

Waisberg, Leo G., and Tim E. Holzkamm. 'The Ojibway Understanding of Fishing Rights under Treaty 3: A Comment on Lise C. Hansen, "Treaty Fishing Rights and the Development of Fisheries Legislation in Ontario: A Primer."' *Native Studies Review* 8 (1992): 47–55.

Walters, Mark D. 'Aboriginal Rights, *Magna Carta* and Exclusive Rights to Fisheries in the Waters of Upper Canada.' *Queen's Law Journal* 23 (1988): 301–68.

Walton, Izaak. *The Complete Angler.* Ed. Jonquil Bevan. Oxford: Clarendon Press, 1983.

Ware, Reuben M. *Five Issues, Five Battlegrounds: An Introduction to the History of Indian Fishing in British Columbia, 1850–1930.* Chilliwack: Coqualeetza Education Training Centre, 1983.

Waterman, T.T., and A.L. Kroeber. 'The Kepel Fish Dam.' In *American Archaeology and Ethnology.* Volume 35. *1934–1943,* 49–80. New York: Kraus Reprint Corp., 1965.

Webber, Jeremy. 'Relations of Force and Relations of Justice: The Emergence of Normative Community between Colonists and Aboriginal Peoples.' *Osgoode Hall Law Journal* 33 (1995): 623–60.

White, Richard. *The Middle Ground: Indians, Empires, and Republics in the Great Lakes Region, 1650–1815.* Cambridge: Cambridge University Press, 1991.

– *The Organic Machine: The Remaking of the Columbia River.* New York: Hill & Wang, 1995.

Whitehead, Margaret. *They Call Me Father: Memoirs of Father Nicolas Coccola.* Vancouver: UBC Press, 1988.

Wickwire, Wendy C. 'To See Ourselves as the Other's Other: Nlaka'pamux Contact Narratives.' *Canadian Historical Review* 75 (1994): 1–20.

Williams, David Ricardo. *One Hundred Years at St. Peter's Quamichan.* Duncan, BC: Duncan Print-Craft, 1977.

– *Trapline Outlaw: Simon Peter Gunanoot.* Victoria: Sono Nis Press, 1982.

Williams, Nancy M., and Eugene S. Hunn, eds. *Resource Managers: North American and Australian Hunter-Gatherers.* Washington: American Association for the Advancement of Science, 1982.

Wright, Roland. 'The Public Right of Fishing, Government Fishing Policy, and Indian Fishing Rights in Upper Canada.' *Ontario History* 86 (1994): 337–62.

Illustration Credits

Figure 1.1 (73) Cowichan Valley Museum, no. 992.10.9.1

Figure 2.1 (81) Eric Leinberger, cartographer

Figure 2.2 (82) National Archives of Canada, Dept. of Indian Affairs, RG 10, vol. 3672, file 901/20-2, pt. 1. Redrawn by Eric Leinberger, cartographer.

Figure 2.3 (85) Archives Deschâtelets, Ottawa

Figure 2.4 (86) Finlayson map: British Columbia Archives, A/C/20/Vi3F, Ft. Victoria Correspondence Outward, R. Finlayson to P. O'Reilly, 29 May 1871. O'Reilly map: Federal Collection of Minutes of Decision, Correspondence & Sketches, vol. 13, P. O'Reilly (Indian Reserve Commissioner), May 1889 to October 1894, file 29858, vol. 7 [Indian Land Registry no. B-64648] [copy held by DIA Vancouver Regional Office]. Redrawn by Eric Leinberger, cartographer.

Figure 2.5 (88) Skinner map: Canada Lands Survey Records British Columbia 15, Natural Resources Canada, Legal Surveys Division, Vancouver. Redrawn by Eric Leinberger, cartographer. Helegesen map drawn by Eric Leinberger, cartographer.

Figure 2.6 (93) British Columbia Archives, A-04171, Hannah and Richard Maynard, photographers

Figure 2.7 (94) Archives of the United Church of Canada, Toronto, no. 93.049P/2779N

Figure 2.8 (97) British Columbia Archives, A-05314

Figure 2.9 (104) British Columbia Archives, G-03743, F.C. Swannell, photographer

Figure 2.10 (108) National Archives of Canada, Dept. of Marine and Fisheries, RG 23, file 583, pt. 1

Figure 2.11 (124) British Columbia Archives, F-07916, F.C. Swannell

Figure 3.1 (130) Eric Leinberger, cartographer

Figure 3.2 (132) National Archives of Canada, C-65097, F. Dally, photographer

Figure 3.3 (132) National Archives of Canada, C-10334, F. Dally, photographer

Figure 3.4 (134) British Columbia Archives, B-03532

Figure 3.5 (157) *Thirty-First Report of the Columbia Mission, February 1st 1897 to January 31st 1898*, 2. London: Sampson Low, Marston & Co., 1898

Figure 3.6 (159) *Columbia Mission Reports, 1878-1895: Twenty-sixth Report of the Missions of the Church of England in the Diocese of British Columbia, For the Year Ending December 31st, 1888, and up to May 31st, 1889*, 15. London: Rivingtons, Waterloo Place, 1889

Figure 3.7 (160) British Columbia Archives, PDP-03157, Josephine Crease, painter

Figure 3.8 (164) British Columbia Archives, A-09730

Figure 3.9 (169) British Columbia Archives, H-07047

Figure 3.10 (184) *Vancouver Sun*, 1973, Steve Bosch, photographer

Index

British Columbia Fishery Commission (1892), 74–6
British Empire, 53, 92, 156–8 fig. 3.5
Brodeur, L.P., 55, 84, 91, 113–16, 118–19, 121
Browne, John, 50–2
Bulkley Valley, 98, 123, 213
Burrard Inlet, 55, 69
Bute Inlet, 37, 69, 90, 197

California, 18, 23
Canada, United Provinces of, 40
Canada West. See Ontario
Canadian Pacific Railway, 163–6, 205
canners, salmon, 17, 42–3, 48, 54, 60, 79, 104, 117, 125, 160–1, 204, 207
cannery workers, 16–18, 53, 77, 95, 116–18, 203–5
canning industry: fishing in Cowichan Bay, 159–61, 166–7, 172–3; Fraser River, 9, 14–16, 39, 41–2, 53–5, 56–8, 60, 64, 141, 144–5, 160, 205; introduced to BC, 9, 39, 202–3; Nass River, 9–10, 48, 61–3, 65, 67; Skeena River, 9–10, 61–3, 79, 92–5 figs. 2.6 and 2.7, 103, 105, 109, 114–15, 116, 121–2, 125–6, 205
Cannon, Aubrey, 21
Capital City Packing & Canning Company, 166–7
capitalism, 193–4, 200
Caplin, Charlie, 74–5
Carrier, 80, 83. See also Lake Babine, social organization
cartography, 5
Cathcart, George, 173
Catholics, 153, 171, 182, 251 n. 52, 253 n. 87. See also Oblates
Chanock, Martin, 188–9

Charlie, Harrison River, 52, 54
Chemainus, 131, 174
Chilcotin, 37, 197
Chinese, 53, 175, 203
Chinook (American Indians), 21–2
Chinook language, 51, 53, 141
chinook salmon (*O. tshawytscha*), 8, 20, 128, 131, 133, 177–8, 180, 211
Chitty, Joseph, 29
chum salmon (*O. keta*), 8, 128, 133, 161, 166–7, 173, 176–80, 211
class, 11, 135, 192–3
Clemclemeluts, 129, 130 fig. 3.1, 138, 168, 177
Coast Salish, 18–20, 129, 135, 210. See also Cowichan, social organization
Coccola, Rev. Nicholas, 84, 85 fig 2.3, 91, 102, 103, 106, 111–14, 118, 121–2
cod, 9
Cohn, Bernard, 189–90
coho salmon (*O. kisutch*), 8, 128, 133, 160–1, 173, 177
colonialism, 3–5, 11, 13, 128, 183; administrative, 186, 198–9; settler, 186, 188, 198–9; violence of, 187, 194. See also law and colonialism
Colonial Office, 137, 200
colonization, 18, 186
Columbia River, 18, 21, 22, 39, 47, 209
Colvin, R., 73, 162–3
Comiaken, 129, 120 fig. 3.1, 138, 161, 168, 174, 177
Commission on the Salmon Fishing Industry in BC (1902), 161
common law, 9, 19, 187, 199; of fisheries 15, 17, 27–33, 38, 225 n. 56; received into BC, 27–8. See also public right to fish